Mississippi Liberal

Mississippi Liberal

A Biography of Frank E. Smith

Dennis J. Mitchell

University Press of Mississippi
for the Mississippi Historical Society
Jackson

www.upress.state.ms.us

Copyright © 2001 by the Mississippi Historical Society
Published by the University Press of Mississippi for
the Mississippi Historical Society through a generous grant from
the Phil Hardin Foundation.

Photographs courtesy of Mrs. Frank E. Smith

09 08 07 06 05 04 03 02 01   4 3 2 1

∞

Library of Congress Cataloging-in-Publication Data
Mitchell, Dennis J.
Mississippi liberal: a biography of Frank E. Smith/Dennis J. Mitchell.
p.   cm.
Includes bibliographical references and index.
ISBN 1-57806-343-4 (cloth: alk. paper)
1. Smith, Frank Ellis, 1918– . 2. Legislators—United States—Biography.
3. United States. Congress. House—Biography. 4. Legislators—
Mississippi—Biography. 5. Mississippi—Politics and government—
1951– . 6. Liberalism—Mississippi—History—20th century.
7. Liberalism—United States—History—20th century. 8. Afro-
Americans—Civil rights—Mississippi—History—20th century.
9. Civil rights movements—Mississippi—History—20th century. I. Title.
E748.S656 M57   2001
328.73'092—dc21
[B]
00-047728

British Library Cataloging-in-Publication Data available

For Mona, Bonnie, David, Julie, Sara, and Zack

CONTENTS

FOREWORD

He grew up amid the soulful legends and harsh realities of the Yazoo-Mississippi Delta country. Inured to tragedy and hardship early in his life as a consequence of the senseless murder of his deputy sheriff-father by a crazed gunman and the subsequent efforts of his widowed mother to rear her family in the bleak years of the Great Depression, Frank Smith understood what it was like to struggle for survival even as he resolved to sail against the wind.

Maybe it was because he never had it easy himself that he was able to identify with so many of his Delta neighbors, black and white, who lived lives of deprivation and despair. Because he had been an underdog, he chose to serve those others who were underdogs. Such a choice is never easy. It was particularly difficult in the Delta of the 1940s, 1950s, and 1960s.

Returning to Mississippi after combat duty in Europe during World War II, Frank Smith found a Deep South in massive transition. The old social and economic structures that had been unassailable bulwarks of the Delta's rigidly segregated plantation society were beginning to be challenged. President Harry Truman in the fall of 1947 issued his historic call for an end to racial discrimination. The Strom Thurmond-led forces of the Dixiecrats vowed never to surrender.

It was in this atmosphere that the young veteran, whose life experiences had sent him a different, more realistic and compassionate message, began his quixotic political journey. From the Mississippi Senate, to which he was elected in 1948, he took on much of the old Delta establishment to win a seat in Congress two years later. By 1954, after the *Brown v. Board of Education* decision, the fat was really in the fire, and the reasonable voices of politicians like Smith were getting drowned out in the cacophony of rage that was thundering across the Delta cotton fields.

It would have been easy for a lesser man than Frank Smith to join the frenzy that was being stirred by the Citizens' Council organized that summer in his hometown of Greenwood. Without bombast, however, he continued to look for answers based on a respect for law and a commitment to justice. He deeply believed that the Constitution meant what it said about equality under the law.

As the growing tensions of the fifties flamed into the fiery confrontations of the sixties, Smith found the political terrain increasingly difficult and more menacing. Nevertheless, he plunged into the presidential campaign of 1960 to support his longtime congressional friend and colleague, John Kennedy, in a battle against the states' rights forces of Ross Barnett. The ultimate payoff came two years later, when Smith saw his old adversaries, led by the Citizens' Council, redistrict him out of the congressional seat that he had held for twelve tumultuous but productive years.

There was still plenty of fire and intellectual energy left in him, though, and he would devote the next twenty-five years to the pursuit of the same dreams that had marked his earlier journey. He would have a decade on the board of the Tennessee Valley Authority, another race for Congress, brief periods in journalism and academia, and, finally, four years as my invaluable colleague and counselor in charge of creative ideas during my term as governor of Mississippi.

When the history of this fascinating and turbulent period is finally written, what undoubtedly will stand out is how few truly visionary and courageous southern political leaders were willing to lay their careers on the line in defense of the ideas that marked their lives.

This uncommon man who spoke for and served the common people is one public figure of those times whose contributions to civility, decency, honor, and justice will emerge as increasingly significant with the passing of the years.

For some of us who shared the public arena with him during this era, he will always remain a source of inspiration and motivation and the personification of courage and fidelity to duty that sustained us in some of the darkest hours.

For all of us, his contributions—whether we have been aware of them or not—have helped make our state and country infinitely better. That is why this moving account of the life and career of an exceptional leader represents such a meaningful addition to our understanding of who we are and where we have come from. Perhaps, most important, it will serve to remind us of our continuing duty to defend our democratic institutions against bias and bigotry and to underscore how much is still left to do if we are to attain the kind of fair and just society that Frank Smith devoted his life to achieving.

William F. Winter

PREFACE

I first met Frank Ellis Smith as a character in a book — his autobiography, *Congressman from Mississippi.* What interested me about Smith was his defiance of the segregationists. I wondered how a congressman from Mississippi in the 1950s could not be a segregationist.

I grew up in George Wallace's Alabama during the 1950s and 1960s. The first images I saw, when we got our television in 1957, were of the soldiers of the 101st Airborne Division escorting black children past screaming whites into the Little Rock high school. I was raised a racist, as were most southern whites, but the civil rights movement destroyed my view of history, society, and personal relationships, which had been born of the Civil War, Reconstruction, and a century of life as a defeated "nation." My first ideas about the past owed their origins to the United Daughters of the Confederacy and the history textbooks they approved for my classrooms, but I was also a patron of the public library, where I read other accounts of the Civil War and Reconstruction. The seeds of doubt planted by Bruce Catton and other historians made me doubt the UDC-approved version of southern history.

Black people were a distant and unimportant part of my early world, despite the fact that my family lived only a block from a black area of town. I never mingled with blacks. Occasionally on Sunday afternoons black children, dressed in their best clothes, would venture to my street, but we stared at one another and never spoke. One old black woman lived at the end of the alley near my home, and she came to symbolize black society for me. Isolated among white homes, "Crazy Mary," as the whites called her, kept a vicious dog chained to the front porch of her gray, weathered, tin-roofed house. We believed she would brandish a pistol at intruders, and we stayed away. The white family who lived next door bought her groceries and delivered them to her. When I was nine or ten years old, the city committed her to an insane asylum and took her land for an electrical substation. Years later basketball players from the still-segregated high schools met for a game on the dirt court we had made on the site of her house next to the substation. Both races played an incredibly courteous, restrained game, testing strange waters cautiously. I remember wondering what "Crazy Mary" would have thought.

College, sociology classes, and the victory of the civil rights movement finished the destruction of my southern view of history and society. By the late 1960s it was not acceptable to embrace integration in Alabama, but neither was it punished in my hometown. I was one of only two white Florence State University students to attend the first memorial service for Martin Luther King, Jr., but no one ever mentioned my attendance to me—not even family and friends. Since they did not know how to react to my behavior, they just ignored it. In the 1960s, the old segregated world had spun out of control, and even southerners were coming to accept the inevitability of change. I went to Ole Miss in 1971 to study British history. Immersed in graduate studies, I ignored the Nixon years of benign neglect, but returned to the real world when my having a Ph.D. at first failed to lead to university employment. As a substitute for a college post, I became the assistant director of the Mississippi Humanities Council, which enabled me to travel widely in the state and to meet a variety of people from all sides of Mississippi's tortured struggle towards integration. Frank Smith came to an MHC environmental issues program at the Holiday Inn in Jackson, and that is where I met him in person for the first time. He impressed me as gray, rumpled, and fat. While he waited for his children to pick him up in front of the hotel, we chatted briefly about the day's program, and I mused on the dramatic story he must have to tell.

Mississippi is a fascinating, extraordinarily complex place, and it drew me into its mystery. I read a great deal about the state during those years, and in 1980 Jackson State University offered me an opportunity to become a college professor. While struggling to establish myself as an academic, I encountered Smith once more when I visited Governor William Winter's office. Smith invited me to lunch in the Sillers Building cafeteria, and, in the elevator going back to his office, I asked if anyone were writing his biography. When he said no, I volunteered.

For the next two years, I visited him and taped oral history interviews, a process that allowed Smith to get to know and trust me. He admitted that he had lied to me earlier, saying his papers were no longer extant. He did in fact have many of his congressional papers at his home, and he offered to loan them to me. My pickup overflowed the snowy winter day that I claimed a temporary home for them in the JSU library. I spent the next several years reading through Smith's lifetime correspondence.

As a teacher of world history, I was unable to focus solely on the biography. I spent a summer in New York studying British political culture. I ran teacher seminars on Mississippi culture. I took Fulbright travel-study tours of Africa and India. I spent two summers learning to speak Shona and visited Zimbabwe. I studied Asian culture at the East-West Center in Hawaii. Through it all, however, I continued to work on this biography, and, after Smith left the governor's office, he and I developed the habit of dining each Tuesday at the historic Mayflower Cafe in Jackson.

Smith enjoyed seeing the various political figures who frequent the restaurant, but my favorite memory of lunch at the Mayflower is the one we shared with the writer Margaret Walker Alexander. I had persuaded Margaret Walker to teach literature for a week at a summer seminar on Mississippi culture being held for high school teachers. I was going through a divorce that summer and she undertook the role of friend and confidant to me. When I told her about the biography, she became interested and agreed to join Frank and me at our weekly lunch. My ex-wife had my car, and I was driving a recently purchased Volkswagen bug. (I expect we made an interesting party emerging from that gold VW on Capitol Street.) After a delightful lunch, we dropped Smith at Choctaw Books, and Margaret Walker turned to me and confessed, "I wondered when you came to Jackson State what you had to offer. I think now that I see." I hope she was right—that I do have something to offer.

Be warned. Smith and I became good friends. The positive upshot for this book is that he told me more in unguarded moments than I would have learned from all the papers or formal interviews. The negative upshot is that I may be biased because of my relationship with him. I have made every effort to tell the truth, but I began this book because I admired a man who could escape racism and try to lead other white southerners to accept integration. Having lived my early life steeped in southern myths and racism and having escaped its embrace later along with the rest of the nation, I was fascinated by a man who did it alone and provided a role model for younger southerners like me.

ACKNOWLEDGMENTS

Jackson State University supported my research and the writing of this book with both a grant that allowed me to travel to the Kennedy Library and with a semester's sabbatical. The JSU library provided a temporary home for the Smith Papers and a research room for several years. Interlibrary loan services at JSU were superb. The late Sammy Cranford located and made available important papers from the Walter Sillers collection before they had been catalogued and sorted.

Many historians read portions of the manuscript and made suggestions as the manuscript went through revisions. Charles Eagles read an early version and Tony Badger a much later one. Ray Skates provided detailed editing and useful ideas for this last version. None of them is to blame for any errors that may remain.

Chrissy Wilson did some fine editing and worked with Helen and Fred Smith to select the photographs.

William Winter encouraged me through the years of research. The Phil Hardin Foundation provided financial support for the series and for this book.

Mississippi Liberal

CHAPTER ONE

Birth and Death
in the Delta

Leflore County deputy sheriff Frank Smith had lunch with his wife
and two sons and then played with his baby daughter on the side
porch of his home near the Yazoo River in Greenwood. He had
routine duty that July afternoon in 1926—to deliver a jury summons
in Money, a nearby Delta village. As he drove north, the deputy saw a
black man carrying a suitcase alongside the gravel road. Despite the unusual look of the man's straightened hair, Smith stopped and offered him
a ride, as he did all men walking the county's roads. He was not particularly suspicious, but, because the man was a stranger, Smith checked a
stack of cards he kept on the front seat. The cards listed escaped Parchman prisoners for whom the state paid a fifty-dollar reward. There was
no card fitting this man's description, but any unknown black was suspect; therefore they talked with the reserve dictated by Mississippi's system of segregation. The passenger, Sylvester Mackey, riding in the back-
seat as was also required by custom, said he had left his job near Yazoo
City and was going to visit his grandmother at Phillip.

After a few questions, Deputy Smith grew wary and, without stopping, ordered Mackey to open his suitcase. To his surprise, it contained
Mackey's baseball uniform and pistol cartridges. As soon as the deputy
saw the cartridges, he asked, "Where is the gun?" Mackey feared jail or
worse because he knew that black men with guns could not pass unchallenged through the Mississippi Delta. Smith had not drawn his gun,
which was wedged between the car seat and the front door, but Mackey
drew and fired, striking him in the side. After the first shot, Mackey's
gun jammed, and Smith opened the car door and fell out, crawling toward the side of the road. Mackey ran to the front door, grabbed Smith's

pistol from the car, and, standing over him, fired again, striking him in the left side of his back.

As Mackey fired the last shot, a black couple, Mitchell Jackson and his wife, rounded a curve and witnessed the assault. Frightened by their approaching automobile, Mackey ran into the field alongside the road. The couple stopped, put Smith into their car, and took him to the Greenwood hospital.[1]

Mackey asked for water at a house three hundred yards down the road and went into the woods, heading toward the railroad tracks. That afternoon, as a large group of men and bloodhounds tracked Mackey across the cotton fields, the Greenwood *Commonwealth* commented that "[if] the negro is located, he will likely be killed."[2]

A group led by the Greenwood police chief found Mackey in a tenant house that evening. Milling around the house, the men considered burning it—none was eager to face the desperate, armed man. finally, the Greenwood assistant police chief volunteered to go in alone. Opening the door, he saw a room bare except for a bed. The policeman knew Mackey had to be underneath. When he dived for it, two shots from Mackey's pistol left powder burns on his face. In retreat, the policeman blasted under the bed with his shotgun. After the exchange, Mackey surrendered to the police chief, who quickly got him into a car and sped toward Greenwood, but a large crowd of men stopped them on the Money road.[3]

No doubt they intended to lynch Mackey. The practice in the Delta at that time was to burn blacks for serious crimes such as Mackey's. The usual method was to place logs around the accused man and douse him with gasoline before setting him afire. Coroners' juries, in order to observe legal niceties, found that these deaths were due to "causes unknown."[4]

The sheriff, who had been visiting his wounded deputy in the hospital, arrived just as the crowd was about to lynch Mackey. Smith, who had recently been part of an unsuccessful attempt to prevent a lynching in a neighboring county, had asked the sheriff to bring Mackey in and to see that the law took its proper course. Told of the wounded man's plea, the crowd reluctantly released Mackey. The evening newspaper editorialized that, although people had a moral right to take the law into their own hands, in this instance it was best to let the law proceed.

The community was not entirely convinced that they should honor Smith's pleas to follow the judicial process. The sheriff moved Mackey to Clarksdale in a neighboring county where he would be safer. When Smith died from his wounds, the governor sent National Guard troops to Clarksdale to prevent a lynching. The *Commonwealth* assured the public that Mackey could not escape death in the courts, but a few days later it inflamed the dangerous situation by commenting that there had been a series of shootings of white people by "negroes" in Mississippi and Alabama. The paper warned that blacks were "pushing the limit of endurance" and predicted a "terrible reckoning."[5]

Passions subsided quickly, and no extra guards were required in the courthouse for the trial a week later. The community had obviously decided to let the legal system handle Mackey. People gathered in the impressive, gray stone courthouse to watch a special grand jury indict Mackey amid "bursts of laughter" from the large crowd. The newspaper, sounding apologetic about the necessity for a trial, explained that defense counsel had been appointed by the court and had to serve even though they found it distasteful to defend Mackey. At the perfunctory trial, Mitchell Jackson provided an eyewitness account of the shooting. The next day the jury found Mackey guilty, and the judge sentenced him to hang. The *Commonwealth* reporter expressed the community's hatred of Mackey, describing him as expressionless, with a face of "brutish vacuity" and an "animalistic type of intelligence." According to Mississippi law, Mackey had to wait a month to die.

Reportedly, he broke down and cried only once after he returned to his cell. Refusing a minister, he remained expressionless and quiet until the day of his death. Although noon was the customary hour for hanging in Mississippi, Mackey was taken to the county farm outside Greenwood before sunrise on August 27. Despite the cool morning, Mackey sat on a porch near the gallows sweating but displaying no other sign of emotion. He walked steadily to the gallows, which was screened by burlap cotton wrapping to comply with the legal requirement that hangings be private. "Only thirty deputies" and Smith's relatives were allowed inside the screen. At the last moment, Mackey asked a black minister, who was present at the hanging, to pray and to conduct his funeral later. With that arranged, Mackey faced the rising sun, and accepted the hood; the sheriff hit the lever to spring the trap. Mackey took twelve minutes to die on the rope.[6]

Frank Ellis Smith, Deputy Smith's oldest son, spent a lifetime trying to understand why his father died and what to do about it. He could have hated Mackey for taking his father's life, or he could have expanded and generalized his hatred to include all black people. Many would have. Many did. When he came to understand Mississippi's social system and the fact that white people had created it, he could have hated the system and/or the people who made it, but he did not hate. Instead, he tried to understand the root of the problem by studying history and sociology. When he freed himself from his society's racist mindset, he blamed racism. Once years later when he was expounding on his theories of racial equality, Smith's gentle mother reminded him that it was a black man who had killed his father. Smith never forgot that fact, but he decided that both his father and Mackey were victims of the society that had brought them together on the Money road.

Without the violent, personal stimulus of his father's death, Smith might never have completed the mental process that freed him from his racist culture. The incident robbed him of his father and set him on a course leading to the rejection of the social/racial mindset that had led to it. He remembered vividly that his father asked the community to abide by the legal process. He came to believe that it was the racist customs and system of segregation that prompted Sylvester Mackey to shoot Frank Smith on the Money road that July day and that if it had been an integrated society, one in which a white man and a black man did not automatically confront each other as faceless enemies, his father would not have died.[7]

Smith's intellectual journey was long and lonely because he was born into the most southern place on earth—the Mississippi Delta, located in the state most committed to segregation. During the time of Smith's childhood, the favorite word used to describe Mississippi was feudal. "It was rural, agricultural, isolated. It had its ruling nobles, its lords of the plantation manor—and its peasants, its vassals." Caste and class dominated every person's life. "The highest virtues were honor and duty, loyalty and obedience.... [I]t was an unusual (not to say foolhardy) person who showed a flagrant disregard for the assigned boundaries and conventions."[8]

As William Faulkner said, the past lived vibrantly. Mississippi whites had retaken control of the state during Reconstruction, making saints of Confederate leaders. They celebrated the "Lost Cause," with Jefferson Davis's and Robert E. Lee's birthdays as state holidays. They named Davis's retirement home on the Gulf Coast a shrine. A stone Confederate soldier guarded every county courthouse to remind the black majority that whites ruled.

6

Theodore G. Bilbo, who adopted the title "Man of the People," was governor when Smith was born. Bilbo championed the "rednecks" and their hill country. He and James K. Vardaman had broken the hold of the Delta planters over state government at the turn of the century. Their populist "revolt of the rednecks" had laid bare the class antagonisms of the white minority in Mississippi and energized political life. Since Reconstruction, politics had consisted of the local bosses caucusing to decide who would take each position in the party, so that the whites voting Democratic in the general election had no choice of candidate. Mississippi had never been a democracy. The black majority had been powerless except for a brief period during Reconstruction. Repressing the black population created a government based on fraud, force, and conspiracy, but the adoption of the "whites only" primary had unleashed a populist force that allowed poor whites to vote for their champions against the planters. Redneck victories proved ephemeral. During Smith's boyhood, the planters regained control of the state through their power in the legislature. They isolated Bilbo, and slowly strangled the newborn possibility of "whites only democracy."[9]

The planters who controlled the Delta magnified the characteristics of Mississippi and the South. During World War I, the Delta remained a frontier for ruthless men clearing the swampy wilderness of cypress, oak, sweet gum, and cane to plant cotton in the dark, rich earth. Planters owned the land and financed the clearing, planting, and harvesting. They sold the crops grown by black sharecroppers and kept the profits. It was a frontier of white capitalists exploiting a politically and economically helpless black caste, having more in common with Kenya or Rhodesia than with the rest of America.

One of its native writers, David Cohn, described the physical Delta as "a violent earth. Its flat black fields cry out for fruition.... Heat stands upon the Delta during the long days and nights; it pours as from a giant furnace an unending stream of white dazzling light upon the earth; it stings the flesh...."[10] Mississippi's Delta stretches from Memphis in the north to Vicksburg in the south. On the west the Mississippi River divides it from Arkansas and Louisiana. Its eastern border is the Yazoo River, which snakes along a row of hills peopled by poor white farmers who had worn out the land growing cotton as their cash crop. A hill dweller dropping from the bluff into the Delta realizes at once that he has entered an unfamiliar country. A hill person never feels comfortable in the Delta because the land is flat and the horizon too distant. There is no protective landscape, because the natural vegetation has been stripped away to reveal the rich black topsoil deposited several feet deep by centuries of flooding.

Before the Civil War, frontiersmen usually bypassed the Delta, because they considered it a hopeless swamp. The first scattered settlers were sons of planters from the East who brought slaves to clear the forest and plant cotton. Malaria and mosquitoes kept the planters' families away in the beginning, and, while a few built plantation houses on the river bends, the rich earth never became a land of elegant "antebellum" homes. The rare substantial house fell into the untamed rivers, and the planters never attempted to emulate the elegance of Natchez or Virginia in the harsh Delta environment. Planters were isolated, dependent on riverboats to bring in supplies and take out cotton. The few roads became bottomless mud when it rained. The Civil War, which came fast on the heels of the first settlement, put an end to slavery, but the demise of the old plantation system did not stop the exploitation of the new frontier.[11]

When the Civil War ended, some planters turned directly to black hired labor. Others assumed that freed slaves would not continue to work as they had in plantation gangs and experimented with Chinese coolies. The colonial world was using Chinese labor to replace African slaves, and Mississippi Delta planters joined the trend. They imported Chinese laborers on long-term contracts and set them to work clearing and planting, but the Chinese could not be kept in perpetual servitude. The experiment with coolie labor failed when the Chinese fled the fields to open small grocery stores and shops. Just before Smith's birth, new Chinese immigrants joined their relatives in Mississippi to escape revolution at home, and boosted the Asian Delta population.[12]

The ethnic landscape diversified further near the end of the 1800s when the railroads came through the eastern Delta, opening more land in the Yazoo basin to settlement. In response to the opportunity created by the railroads, planters imported Italian agricultural laborers in an effort to break their reliance on black labor, but, because the Italians were white, the oppressive caste-like social rules that had been applied to blacks did not work. The Italians proved too difficult for the planters to control because they tried to market their own cotton. They grew vegetable gardens and protested the high prices in plantation stores. They also had a champion in the Italian government, which investigated their complaints.

Finally, the planters abandoned labor experiments and turned completely to black labor, holding their workers in a sort of peonage. Because blacks had been effectively stripped of their citizenship, they could be exploited with impunity. After the boll weevil hit the Natchez district in 1907, planters actively recruited black sharecroppers to complete the clearing and planting of the Delta. In the sharecropping system, planters furnished their "partners" with seed, tools, housing, medical care, and loans in return for a set portion of the crop made by the farmer and his family. Most sharecroppers never caught up with their debts, much less turned a profit, so they frequently descended into a peonage close to slavery. Planters regularly forbade tenants to leave plantations before settling debts at the company stores, and state laws enforced planter control. Because of this system, planters assumed they could treat blacks like slaves. In one outrageous instance in the 1940s, a white farmer imprisoned a black woman with a chain around her neck, an incident that came to light because the Tallahatchie County sheriff felt compelled to release her.[13]

Sharecropping started because it seemed, at first, to promise a better life to poor, landless blacks, who preferred it to the gang methods used with slave labor. Seeking a better life on the rich soil, blacks poured into the Delta until they outnumbered the combined whites and Chinese by overwhelming majorities. To ensure control of the people and the land, Delta whites exploited their privileged caste. The southern caste system involved a complex set of social customs and taboos common to the entire region. Blacks were required to address all whites with titles of respect such as Mr., Mrs., or Captain and were never to use a white person's first name. Conversely, custom dictated that whites should address blacks only by their first names and never grant them titles of respect. Rarely, an educated black might be called "professor" if he demonstrated the proper attitude and deference toward whites, and an older black favorite might be called "aunt" or "uncle." But that was the limit.

Blacks could not enter or even knock at the front door of a white home; they had to wait until all whites were served in a store before a white clerk would fill their orders. Hundreds of such indignities and intentional insults constantly reinforced the economic subjugation of blacks to the white minority. In the Delta, the massive black population magnified these practices and the planters' control. In much of the South the white majority ruled a restive black minority, but in the Delta blacks were a large majority, a situation that altered the segregation system.[14]

The Delta was notorious for not always practicing segregation regarding sexual relationships between white men and black women. White men could and did take advantage of their power over blacks to misuse black women, both as mistresses and in houses of prostitution. Interracial marriage was, however, forbidden, and even a sexual advance by a black man toward a white woman would be an excuse for lynching.[15]

Mississippi consistently led the nation in lynching. The Delta aristocracy liked to blame excesses on "rednecks," but they, too, relied on violence as their ultimate weapon to enforce the economic and social system. A leading Delta aristocrat, LeRoy Percy, fought the Ku Klux Klan in Greenville and personally threatened to kill the Klan leader if his family were harmed; but, in part, he did it to protect his labor supply. Percy knew much about black history and respected blacks more than he did poor whites, yet he approved the actions of a white overseer who killed a black tenant to restore "order" on one of his plantations. The aristocracy despised the lower class for its lack of taste and its methods, but they shared the goal of maintaining the system of segregation. They simply preferred using the state as their agent. For example, during the flood of 1927, Percy and the other planters used the National Guard to keep blacks from leaving the Delta. Yet everyone knew "lynch law" provided the ultimate tool for suppression of blacks. Between 1882 and 1927, 517 blacks were lynched in Mississippi. Usually they were shot or hanged, but in special circumstances they were burned alive or burned and then dragged behind wagons or automobiles. Lynching was not questioned because it had become the "ritualized expression of the values of the united white communities."[16]

Just as non-Mississippians feared the state for its reputation, Mississippi's non-Deltans, black and white, feared the Delta for its violence. Sensitive to their minority status, Delta whites quickly enforced caste rules to protect themselves, but they accepted blacks' crimes against one another as normal. Their disregard for black crime and violence encouraged lawlessness. Even if black-on-black crimes came to official attention, most blacks had a white protector to whom they could appeal. White employers or "friends," understanding almost nothing of the black community, interceded for their retainers regardless of their guilt or innocence and usually obtained an offender's release. On the other hand, crimes against whites frequently meant quick and violent death outside the judicial system for blacks who committed any breach of segregation etiquette, much less a serious crime against a member of the white caste.

In some respects, blacks were allowed more freedom in the Delta than in the hills, but the price was an air of violence, which oppressed everyone.[17]

Seeking to maintain a rigid caste system, the most thoughtful and articulate of the Delta planters, William Alexander Percy, disliked any influx of white hill people, who blurred the clear caste lines with their poverty and ignorance. He called the white immigrants "an alien breed of Anglo-Saxon." He complained, "We had changed our country attractively for them. Malaria had been stamped out; electric fans and ice had lessened the terror of our intolerable summer heat; we had good roads and drainage and schools...."[18] He feared that the Delta would be overwhelmed by "rednecks and peckerwoods" who would "control government" and "fix culture." Although many of the planter families might have originated in the hills, they agreed that society needed to be divided clearly into the "superior" white group and the "inferior" poor black segment.

Even Percy perceived among the poor whites, whom he despised, a subgroup he admired. "Forming a small intermediate white class were the managers and slave-drivers and bosses, men of some ability and force, mostly illiterate. These in time become plantation-owners, often buying up and operating successfully the places lost by their former employers. Here is an ironic and American and encouraging phenomenon. Their children are being what is known as well educated. They will be the aristocrats of tomorrow; they make excellent professional Southerners now."[19]

He was describing Frank Smith's family. Having migrated from the adjoining hills, the Smith family lived on the edge of the Delta for generations. They settled in Carroll County during the 1830s and built a substantial farm in an isolated area near the Delta. Yeoman rather than planters, the first generations looked down on the Delta as a dangerous swamp. Bears and wolves roamed out of the swampy wilderness up to their doors. They usually ventured only fifteen miles into the Delta to haul "provisions" by oxcart from Sidon landing on the Yazoo River. Into the late 1800s, they undertook the trip infrequently because it required two days' hard labor.[20]

Smith's ancestors owned few slaves and produced no romantic Civil War heroes. The most famous family story involved Smith's great-grandfather Douglas Smith, who owned a small farm called Bright Corner in Carroll County. Douglas left his family and ventured into the Delta to work as an overseer while a slave couple ran his farm. Once, when he returned, his slaves told him that a neighboring planter's cattle had roamed across Bright Corner unchecked during his absence. A few days later, Douglas was sitting on a fence at his farm when the offending planter rode past. Douglas challenged the planter, demanding that he keep his cattle confined to his own property. The planter argued, beat Douglas with a cane, and rode away. The instrument used for the beating indicated the planter's contempt for Douglas as an inferior not deserving a gentleman's treatment. Within days, Douglas was waiting on the road with a shotgun and killed the man. He left for the Arkansas frontier, fearing that the planter's family might take revenge, but returned when tempers had cooled. He was never indicted because the community judged the killing as justifiable homicide. He lived out his life in Carroll County as a respected member of the community.[21]

Far from the county seat and any town life, the Smiths farmed the hills on into the twentieth century. Douglas's son—Smith's grandfather—accumulated little wealth, but saw to it that his children received some high school education at a time when most Mississippians did not complete elementary school. Just before World War I, Smith's father, Frank, spent one year at French Camp Academy, a private boarding high school. As young men, Smith's father and his brother Ocie continued a family tradition by seeking temporary employment in the Delta. They entered the Delta first at Cruger, a village at the foot of the hills on the edge of the Delta, to operate a general store. When the store went broke, they moved a few miles north, still hugging the line of hills, to Sidon, where another brother, Harry, farmed and did contract work on Leflore County roads. Frank Smith clerked in a store and sought an opportunity to buy a farm.[22]

Shaded by oaks, nestled between the "hill" of the railroad tracks on the east and the line of trees along the Yazoo River on the west, Sidon sheltered its inhabitants from the flat monotony of the cleared Delta fields. Enjoying a boom encouraged by the fortunes made in cotton during World War I, the little village prospered briefly and attracted many hill folk. Sidon had two churches, a steam gristmill, a bank, two public cotton gins, and general stores. It had been founded as a river landing and later became a stop on the Mississippi Valley Railroad. The population in 1900 had been only 148, but the Delta's prosperity attracted enough migrants so that Sidon had more than doubled its population by 1920. Sadie Ellis, Smith's mother, was among the immigrants from adjoining Holmes County. After finishing high school at Kosciusko, she attended a summer training program at the University of Mississippi to qualify as a teacher and moved to Sidon to begin her career. After teaching briefly, she married Frank Smith and bore her first son, Frank Ellis Smith, the following year, 1918.[23]

Smith's father took a job as a deputy sheriff for Leflore County and, with the promise of a steady income, made the initial payment on a two-hundred-acre "place." Sidon was a hill enclave, and hill people called farms "places" and themselves "farmers," not planters. As a small child, Smith played while watching his father work. Smith remembered driving the mules to grind sorghum and riding into town on top of a wagon loaded with cotton for the gin. He ate squirrels shot by his father during his official travels about the county and fish from his father's trotline in the Yazoo. Times were not easy for the struggling father and mother, but Smith recalled the love and comfort of the family, which grew with the birth of a brother, Fred, and later a sister, Sadie. Adding to the young family's financial difficulties, a flue fire destroyed their house when Smith was five. They lost all of their possessions except his mother's piano.

Smith started school in Sidon from a rented home on the bank of the Yazoo. The family's fortunes improved when Frank Senior was promoted to chief deputy sheriff. The promotion required a move to the county seat, Greenwood, and made it likely that Frank would soon be elected sheriff. Being sheriff would have made his fortune, because the sheriff also served as tax collector, a fee-paid official who collected a large salary. (State law limited the office to one term because it was too powerful to leave in one man's hands for long.) In the 1920s in a rich county such as Leflore, the sheriff could invest in land and probably insure his family's prosperity with the profits of one term in office. The older Smith could have become a planter and the younger a planter's son; perhaps his life would have developed in a more typical Delta pattern.[24] Instead, at an early age Smith became a rebel who rejected his society's racism and thus its whole structure of values.

Smith owed his rebellion to a mix of personal experiences and the analysis of southern society provided by outside observers. His ideas probably began to develop following the shock of his father's death, which drove him to introspection. He retreated into a world of ideas where books, magazines, and distant intellectuals were his favorite companions. Looking back, he believed that his origins in the middle ground between the planters and the rednecks were also a key factor. If his family had joined the planters, he would have felt the need to defend segregation because his family's economic existence and social position would have depended on it. If he had been a redneck, he would have lacked the education and family support needed to explore ideas. Hortense Powdermaker, a sociologist who studied the Delta only a few miles from Smith's home, found a young man similar to Smith in the town she examined in the 1930s. What made her young liberal different from his peers, she thought, was his rejection of the myth of southern history. She identified no aristocrats living in the community, but believed that, aside from this one young man, all the other middle-class whites took on the burden of the defeated Confederate aristocracy. This man stood out because he recognized that he was descended from small farmers. Because he rejected the myth of southern history, her young man refused to accept his assigned role in society as his peers did. Smith, too, escaped the powerful myth of southern history. That was the essential first step in escaping the southern segregationist mindset.[25]

Understanding his class status and the truth about the past, Smith dreamed the American frontiersman's dream of democracy and equality rather than the planter's dream of plantation and exploitation. Smith's people were ordinary Americans living in an extraordinary place and time. They lived in a racist society and participated in its customs, yet remained decent, honest people who carried on their lives ignoring the injustice and oppression they practiced and the violent oppression at the base of their society. The amazing fact about Smith's life is that he did think deeply about race and accepted racial equality as a desirable goal decades before his neighbors and his family did. His family, friends, and neighbors did not spend their lives pondering the nature of society. Smith's people were frontiersmen, not a group noted for reflection, soul searching, or intellectualism. Smith's ancestors had been slave owners on a small scale before the Civil War and had lived according to the South's social and caste rules without questioning them.

Smith could not explain fully how or why he came to differ from his family in his basic values. His family taught him its Christian religion and its democratic values, but he did not know why he began to understand what the rest of the family failed to perceive. He tried, even while abandoning their basic view of the world, to see his family at its best and to believe that what they taught him led to his radically different ideas.[26] He was sensitive and intelligent, selecting from his own culture the frontiersman's thread of democracy, from Christianity the essence of the brotherhood of man, and from intellectuals whose works he read a host of liberal social, political, and historical ideas. At the same time he rejected the frontier's materialism and willful ignorance of higher culture. He refused to accept religious fundamentalism and some liberals' arrogant dismissal of the "common man's" ignorance.

Smith grew up in Greenwood, which lies ten miles north of Sidon and is spread along the same river. His home was in north Greenwood, the fashionable area of the city, separated from the business district and the black sections by the river. The heart of north Greenwood is "the boulevard," a row of small mansions built during the prosperous days of World War I when planters left their farms to line the north road leading out of the city with imitation English and Spanish houses. In 1923, the Smiths rented a small house three blocks east of the boulevard among the more modest homes spreading away from the main street.[27]

With a population of about ten thousand, Greenwood was a metropolis compared to Sidon. Greenwood existed for cotton. It supplied planters. It bought, ginned, stored, and sold cotton. The seasons of planting and harvesting dominated this city, where men risked their fortunes on the weather and the international marketplace. There was no permanent aristocracy, only a precariously wealthy upper class. Greenwood contained Gritney and Ram-Cat Alley, where booze and sex were readily available. It earned a reputation as a tough town for blacks. One black woman who had lived "all over" the Delta labeled it the meanest town in existence. The population also included Chinese and Italians, who were treated differently from Anglo-Saxon whites and from blacks. With one of the world's largest cotton markets, Greenwood could take on the air of a bigger city. When crops were good, planters demanded and got the best in clothes, automobiles, and travel. Merchants went to New York for the latest fashions, and smart businessmen sometimes increased prices, counting on snob appeal to sell their wares.[28]

When he was still new to north Greenwood, Frank remembered, he visited a schoolmate's big house, played too late, and walked the dark miles back to his home in tears at being so alone in such a large frightening world. Luckily his first elementary school was within easy walking distance of home, and he felt protected and safe there. But he did so well that his second-grade teacher advised his family to allow him to skip half a grade. With the promotion, he was taken out of north Greenwood and sent to Jefferson Davis, a school across the Yazoo River. The change, again, placed Smith in a wider world—one where most of his classmates had failed at least one grade, where the boys were bigger, and where some of the girls were already sexually active. He had grown up in small-town Sidon and protected north Greenwood. Smith knew nothing of life in south Greenwood and had never made friends outside north Greenwood and Sidon. The bright little boy felt shy and out of place in his new school and uncomfortable with his new classmates.[29]

One of his most vivid memories is of selling a tin pencil holder to a "foreign"-looking classmate so that he could buy milk at recess. Since his family was still struggling financially, he normally did not have the dime required for milk, but that day he wanted it badly enough to sell the tin container that his father had given him from the sheriff's office. After he had enjoyed his milk, he balked at parting with the tin, and the boy embarrassed him by complaining to the teacher.[30]

Despite his contacts with the city, Smith lived on its edge. Congressman Will Whittington's plantation began at the end of his street, and woods lined the nearby Yazoo River so that he had the advantages of country spaces in the city. Smith roamed the Whittington "pasture" with his brother and the children of a black tenant who had a house near them. In the summer, little Frank played in the Yazoo bottom hunting for crawdads. In the fall he picked possum grapes.[31]

Smith was not athletic. When he and his younger brother, Fred, had the normal brotherly fights, Smith lost. His disillusionment with physical abuse began as a youngster when he and two friends set up a Coke stand under an oak tree down the street from his house. Bullies took it over, and one of his friends deserted him to join the bullies. Incapable of mounting a physical defense, he felt victimized; from an early age, Smith was unaggressive and bookish.

When he was eight, Smith's world shattered. He remembered his mother telling him that his father had been shot in the arm; he also recalled the neighbors taking care of his six-month-old sister and some cousins charging into their house seeking his father's guns to use in hunting the assailant. He could remember nothing of the funeral, the trial of the murderer, or the memorial service the community held to eulogize his father. It took him a lifetime to come to grips with the events of that summer.[32]

Although he would eventually come to condemn his community's racism, Smith understood that his society was not simply violent and racist. He knew that it was also a kind and caring community, one that looked after him and his family. Even at eight, suffering from the shock of his father's death, Smith was aware of the fund-raising campaign carried on by the *Commonwealth* to provide for his family. Throughout the trial and the time of the hanging, the newspaper ran donation appeals for the murdered deputy's family, then published the names of donors and the amounts they gave. The campaign raised several thousand dollars. Sadie Smith used the money to buy a house one block east of their rented one at the end of Claiborne Street facing the wooded bank of the Yazoo. That house, provided through the generosity of the community, would become Smith's home for many years.

After Frank Smith's death, Sadie Smith, who had no college degree or marketable qualifications, had to support her children. She used the funds from her husband's small insurance policy to take a business school secretarial course, and she got a job in the sheriff's office. As an "office deputy," she primarily collected taxes. She never forgot, nor let her family forget, that their livelihood came from the community.[33]

After the wrenching disruption caused by his father's death, Smith's life settled into a new routine, with his mother working and his grandmother joining the household. A black cook prepared the family meals. Smith's family, which he considered poor compared to their white neighbors, still employed black maids or cooks at little cost just as most middle-class whites did. Smith's mother returned home for lunch each day and often took young Sadie to the courthouse with her in the afternoon. All three children grew up in and around the courthouse, observing at close hand the trials and elections. Thus Smith was raised as an intimate member of the community close to its political functioning and conscious of his debt to it.[34]

His younger brother, Fred, fit more easily into Delta life because he loved the fields and physical, outdoor work. Fred labored on his uncles' farms and spent his life hunting and tramping the woods. Their uncle Harry tried to assist his dead brother's children as much as possible, but, without his father to urge him to the outdoors, Smith began to spend more and more of his time with books.

He enjoyed weekends, because they were often spent visiting in Sidon. His happiest childhood memories seemed to be connected to the old home where, counting the Smiths and Ellises, he was related to half the town. There he played baseball with the other children. Entertainment options were limited: often Smith and his cousin Gordon made a game of choosing north or south, and competed by counting the number of cars passing through Sidon in their direction. In the shade of oaks, dozens of relatives ate huge meals and gossiped between trips to church functions. Men and children ate first and then women. Fried chicken and vegetables were followed by watermelon or homemade ice cream. Iced tea glasses were emptied after the meal and used for the ice cream. In the heat of the Delta summer, the Smiths and Ellises savored cool treats.[35]

At eleven, Smith gained a degree of financial independence when a family friend gave up a paper route and passed it on to him. In the summer, Smith rode back to the Leflore County Courthouse with his mother when she returned to work from lunch. He then spent two hours reading, either in the public library or on the shady side of the Confederate monument in front of the courthouse. Both the shaded marble of the monument and the library basement offered cool refuges from the stifling Delta heat. At three o'clock when the paper was ready for delivery, Smith put down his book, walked to the newspaper office, picked up his load of papers, and crossed the Yazoo to deliver the *Commonwealth* to the planters' houses along the boulevard. At the end of the row, he left a paper in a tree for his only black customer, who lived farther north than he walked. When school was in session, he walked the few blocks from Jefferson Davis school to the newspaper office, delivered his papers, and walked home. He never bought a bicycle to ease this task because he spent most of his income on books and magazines. While he delivered, he dreamed of writing or editing a newspaper.[36]

CHAPTER TWO

An Intellectual Journey

S mith's introspection, his weight, his lack of interest in physical activity, and his absorption in reading marked him as an outsider in Greenwood. It was his exposure to a larger world in books and journals that caused Smith to question racism. The life of the mind mattered most to him. In his society, the deepest racial prejudice was the norm, yet he was able to accept racial equality. As a young man, Smith sympathized with the torments described by Thomas Wolfe, another boy who became an intellectual in nonintellectual surroundings. Smith's comment on Wolfe's *Look Homeward, Angel* was "In some ways youth can be a fearsome and awful experience."[1] Smith felt his "otherness." His mental journeys, in which he ranged far from the Delta, were both exciting and "fearsome" because his ideas endangered ties to home and family. He wanted to be accepted. He cared for his family, but he became convinced at a relatively young age that they were acting immorally by participating in segregation. Isolated intellectualism, enabling Smith to see his culture differently and to escape mentally from it, was not a unique accomplishment, but it was a formidable task in the Mississippi Delta of the 1930s.

Those living in the Delta detested intellectuals because they knew such people opposed segregation. David Cohn described the Delta's reaction to ideas: "The Delta does not go far afield in its reading. It has an instinctive Anglo-Saxon dislike of ideas. It reads the local newspapers which report what everybody already knows...." Deltans read only "best seller" books, he said. Blacks were isolated by their ignorance, Cohn thought, and whites by their lack of curiosity. The Delta cut itself off from the outside world, he alleged, unless some event threatened to lower the price of cotton, because Deltans were completely materialistic. "Disturbing ideas," he said, "crawl like flies around the screen of the Delta."[2]

Cohn's invisible screen against outside influences was very real. Cohn and Smith lived in an exploitative society dependent on the continuation of a peonage system from which white Deltans excluded foreign "cultures" because they threatened to expose the true nature of segregation, sharecropping, and lynching. Cohn said, "Culture is distrusted. One who bears it or seeks it is regarded as being unfit for the stern struggle of life."[3] "Culture" was an activity, he wrote, left to white women so they would have something to do in the afternoons.

Mildred Spurrier Topp, daughter of Greenwood's leading photographer, agreed with Cohn's analysis in her depiction of the city. In two farcical, autobiographical books, she captures Greenwood's energy, prejudices, and humor. In her account, Greenwood's leading "aristocratic" family lived in "Stratford on the Yazoo," and the mother of that family led the United Daughters of the Confederacy, which in turn dominated the "cultural" life of Greenwood.

Topp depicts culture arriving in Greenwood when a Jewish merchant on his annual buying visit to New York purchased a painting of a man kneeling in what appears to be prayer before an indistinct background. After the merchant donated the painting to the Baptist church, the minister called a meeting of the congregation to determine the subject of the painting and what to do with it. The meeting erupted into frenzied debate when a garrulous, retired teacher suggested that it was U. S. Grant. That would have been impossible to accept, so the congregation voted that the man was Stonewall Jackson, and the matter was decided. Later in Topp's novel, the "aristocracy" adopted a phony artist and former lightning-rod salesman, who had won the heart of a rich widow, as their arbiter of art, literature, and music. According to Topp, no real intellectual life existed in Greenwood.[4]

Yet Greenwood's relative affluence provided it with a public library superior to those in most Mississippi towns. During Smith's childhood the library was staffed by Sanders Smith, a poet and a thinker as well as a librarian, who later left Mississippi because his ideas made him uncomfortable in his native state. Perhaps he was partially responsible for stocking the shelves with the "subversive" literature that began Smith's intellectual odyssey. Smith educated himself by reading his way through the public library's books and consuming the *Nation* and the *New Republic* faithfully. He spent his paper route salary, $1.50 per week, on books and magazines. He read everything, but especially liked biographies and history. Scouring Greenwood beyond the library for more to read, he used a book rental service at a drugstore. He belonged to the Book-of-the-Month Club and the Literary Guild. The *New Republic* guided his tastes in books, movies, people, and ideas. His exploration of the world of ideas is the real story of Smith's childhood, because it was his reading and the ideas he found in his intellectual odyssey that shaped his development.[5]

When he was fifteen, Smith found *Brown Americans,* by Edwin R. Embree, in his school library. A history of black Americans distributed to schools throughout the South by the Rosenwald Fund to counter prevalent American prejudices, the book opened with the information that Africans had a host of advanced cultures from which slaves were torn when they were shipped to the New World. It praised the stamina and intelligence of "Negroes" who adapted to the strange environment and survived harsh, hostile conditions in America. Embree stressed that "brown Americans" did very well when given an opportunity. "With the freedom and opportunities of northern cities, Negroes have grown to the full stature of American life even faster than many of the immigrant groups from Europe," he said.[6]

Embree's purpose was to demolish the historical, social, and economic myths supporting segregation, and he successfully influenced Smith, whose understanding of history changed dramatically. Seeing the historic myths destroyed proved to be the most important step for Smith. Embree provided Smith with white heroes such as John Fee, the son of a Kentucky slave owner, who became an abolitionist. Embree described Fee's conversion in terms likely to appeal to those whites raised in a segregated society. "He had been brought up amid slavery. His own father and most of the men to whom he looked up with respect were slave owners. It had been natural for him to accept the system but he was sensitive and conscientious. After many discussions and a great deal of lonely thinking, he made up his mind that holding fellow human beings in slavery was contrary to the teaching of Jesus. Yet he dreaded the results of this conviction and did not abandon his native society easily."[7] As a sensitive young man questioning segregation in Greenwood, Smith identified with Fee. He rejected the history of slavery and racism. Embree's book emancipated Smith.

Although Smith encountered professional, educated black people in Embree's book, the first intelligent black man the young Mississippian got to know well was James Weldon Johnson. He did not "meet" Johnson in person but through the pages of Johnson's autobiography, *Along This Way*. The book gave Smith the opportunity to know a black man and to understand segregation from the black man's point of view. In the 1940s, Smith wrote that Johnson's autobiography provided "an idea of how a Negro of culture and sensibilities feels...."[8] This indirect experience was the only opportunity open to him in his culture. Smith lived in a society with a black majority, but he could never know his black neighbors in the same way that he came to know Johnson, because segregation would not allow it. He had to settle for a vicarious experience. But such experiences were the norm for Smith, who preferred books to the people around him.

Johnson depicts his life and encounters with segregation in a manner imbued with humor and almost with detachment. His story of once being asked to leave a first-class "white" railcar captured the insanity of the system of segregation for Smith. According to Johnson's account, he responded to the conductor's request that he leave the white car by inspecting the "colored" car, where he found a white sheriff and a crazy white prisoner. He insisted that they had to move to the white car if he went to the colored one. The conductor agreed, and, immediately after the transfer, the prisoner thrust his chained arms through the window, cutting himself. He then began to swear horribly. Witnessing the scene with satisfaction, Johnson left the white car with a smile.[9] There could be no more devastating critique of the segregation system than this witty account by an accomplished, smiling observer. Longing to be a writer, Smith admired Johnson's style and wit and could never again accept the indignities imposed on blacks as justified.

Johnson's careers in teaching, newspaper work, music, the foreign service, and the NAACP impressed the young Smith, who had never traveled but who dreamed of being a newspaperman. Johnson gave Smith insight into the world of black people and made it clear that segregation was based on the false assumption of black inferiority. Johnson concluded his autobiography with the prediction that blacks would be absorbed into the American population.[10] Smith's decision to agree was an intellectual leap away from his home.

Segregation was rigidly enforced in Greenwood. No one dared openly to question the social and political system built on it. Certainly Smith came into contact with black people—the maids who worked for the family and the children of the sharecropper near his home—but all those contacts were governed by segregation practices. Smith never defied the conventions of his society in his personal contacts with black people, and he never developed an authentically personal relationship with a black person. The divide between black and white was too vast to be challenged by a child. But there were some gray areas in his society, which a perceptive observer might have noticed and which might have engendered doubt about the differences between black and white. For example, caste-like rules separated Greenwood's sizable Italian population from the rest of white society; while Italians were not allowed the same social status as other whites, they were undeniably white, a fact that entitled them to the full privileges of that status in dealings with blacks. Italians were not separated from the larger white society in all Delta communities, but they were in Greenwood. The Chinese confused the system even more. They were not allowed to attend white schools and sometimes could not get a haircut "even in an Italian barbershop." In Greenwood, Ray Joe, a prominent Chinese businessman, tried to send his son to the white school instead of the black one and was rebuffed, but the county paid for a private tutor for his son. Whites tutored him and accepted him in the Boy Scouts but not in the white public school.[11] Smith knew of these anomalies in his town but could not remember or explain how they influenced him. He admitted he could have absorbed them. In later years he took pride in the support he received from both communities and in the service he rendered to the Delta Chinese as their congressman.

As Smith remembered it, Greenwood furnished no heroes or role models and no teachers capable of shaping his thinking toward racial equality. He pointed to his mother's basic human decency and to his father's courage in asking from his deathbed that his black killer not be lynched. He credited the religion he learned in Sunday school with teaching him that all human beings are equal, while admitting that he found most people did not practice the ideals they mouthed and that he was disillusioned by most traditional churches. Hearing his Sunday school teacher advocate the lynching of a black prisoner shocked him. But many others, who continued to believe in racism, recognized these disparities. Smith was persuaded to change his mind because his sense of being an outsider in his society sent him looking for comfort and perhaps a means of confirming his sense of superiority over those who despised the books and ideas that he valued so highly.

In 1943 in a letter written to a fellow "intellectual," Tom Sancton, Smith speculated that the lack of a dominating male influence could have provided the freedom to develop differently. At a young age, Sancton had also lost his father in a violent accident. Searching for a reason to explain how they both rejected racism growing up in the South, they settled on the loss of their fathers as one explanation.[12]

For a combination of reasons, Smith rejected his society's value system and needed to replace it. He did that between the ages of eight and fifteen as he explored his world of books, borrowing ideas and gradually accepting new values. He seemed largely oblivious to his immediate surroundings and could recall little influence coming from his school and family experiences. Two authors provided Smith a worldview and a sense of purpose for his life. Lincoln Steffens, the muckraker, wrote an account of an open, honest life that Smith admired and emulated. Steffens's *Autobiography* demonstrated, Smith said, "how certain articulate people have developed into liberal thinkers, recounting the various influences that have shaped their way of thinking."[13]

The fatherless Smith admired the freedom enjoyed by the young Steffens; he had grown up on horseback in California with an understanding father who encouraged him to develop an independent mind. Smith seemed to follow Steffens's example in studying only what interested him in college and by refusing to worry over grades. He shared Steffens's doubts about accepting traditional, established religion. Most important for Smith, Steffens presented a worldview that recognized the complexity of human beings and society. Although he was a crusading journalist, Steffens saw good and bad in all people. The bosses and banking barons Steffens described were not evil, nor were the reformers saints. He refused to present the world in simplistic terms.[14] This complexity and the search for a clear understanding of a far-from-perfect world must have been particularly important to Smith, because all of the people he knew were racist. He knew that they were wrong but that they were not evil. He knew that they were good people capable of sacrifice and nobility—and that he loved them.

Steffens lived fully through wars, revolutions, and crusades; he approved of most efforts for change but concluded his autobiography with a prediction—that the Russian Revolution and the American evolution would end in the same "meeting place." Not regretting his efforts at reform, he ended his autobiography with this line: "And as for the world in general, all that was or is or ever will be wrong with that is my—or our—thinking about it."[15] He refused to endorse communism or any one of the revolutions with which he sympathized; instead he called for understanding the world better through a revolution of the mind. Smith took Steffens's message to heart because he had already committed his mind to a revolution in his world, the Mississippi Delta. Smith made his commitment to the most difficult type of revolution, a changing of Mississippi minds and hearts. He based his decision on a firm understanding of the complexity of the place and the people. Even as a teenager, Smith did not call for destruction of the rotten system but for a constructive commitment to revolution in the hearts of the racists. Having adopted this mission as an adolescent, Smith remained remarkably consistent in his commitment to that goal throughout his life.

He got help in deciding his specific mission and methods from Vincent Sheean's *Personal History*. As Smith yearned to leave the Delta and explore the world in preparation for becoming a writer, he discovered a man who had lived his dream. Sheean's wanderings as a journalist took him to Paris, Africa, China, Russia, and Palestine. He wrote about revolutions, revolts, and wars against imperialism, and he encountered an infinite variety of white racist behavior. A black American who had deserted from the French foreign legion in order to join Muslims fighting for independence saved Sheean's life in Africa. In China, Sheean met "Mr. Chen," a half-black and half-Chinese native of Trinidad who fought for the revolution because he hated whites for all of their crimes against the colored peoples of the world. Sheean had access to the colonial world of the British clubs and bars but found himself progressively unable to share the colonial rulers' company or their racism. Sheean saw a pattern in white racism and in the worldwide revolutions against imperialism that Smith must have recognized in the Mississippi Delta.

Despite his sympathies, Sheean could never become a revolutionary. He fell in love with an American communist in China and followed her to Moscow. When she died, he held an imaginary conversation with his dead communist friend and used their dialogue to make sense of his part in the revolution which, he thought, had to come.[16] In his imagination, she said to him that "the immediate job is to get rid of the present arrangement and contrive a more satisfactory one without these nation-race-religion tags to help the functioning of capital and empire." Sheean protested that he was not and could not be a revolutionary, to which she replied, "You do not have to be." Everyone was not born to act, she said, advising him to make his contribution in his own way. She would have fought, she said, but that was not his way. "Your work, if you ever do any that amounts to a damn, will have to be some kind of writing, I suppose; I don't know much about that, but it might be a good idea to try to learn how to write . . . [and] . . . to see things as straight as you can and put them into words that don't falsify them. That's programme enough for one life, and if you can ever do it, you'll have acquired the relationship you want between the one life you've got and the many of which it's a part."[17] Through Sheean, Smith formed connections to the wider colonial world that resembled the Delta and found a mission in life: he would learn to write and use that writing to change his world.

His desire to change the world and to lead the romantic life of a foreign reporter is not unusual but is significant because it shaped his life. He remained consistently dedicated to the ideas absorbed from these books. As a young man, he would advise his fiancée to read them; as a TVA director, he would recall their impact on him.

Smith had begun to write long before he read Sheean, but, after reading *Personal History*, he had a goal. He wanted to become a newsman and to bring about change through his writing. He had written his first newspaper piece at the age of six for the children's page of the Memphis *Commercial Appeal*, and his father carried a copy about in his wallet to demonstrate his older son's talents. Later, Smith wrote for and edited boyhood magazines printed by companies collecting fees from young writers who paid to see their work in print. Of course, the circulation was limited to fellow enthusiasts, but it gave Smith experience.[18]

In high school, he got his first regular column in the *Bulldog Broadcast*, which was published as a page of the *Commonwealth* once each week. "Frankly Speaking" gave the shy young man a forum in which to castigate those who irritated him. He chastised the girls for being silly gossips and for failing to study seriously, and he tried the old journalist's trick of starting a fight to create interest. Picking on the sophomore class for being noisy and immature, he condemned them for not reading "worthwhile books" and once for the "senseless race hatred and contempt that pervades 90 per cent of them." He considered himself a serious intellectual and used his column to tell Greenwood he was different. Fellow students were not his only targets. He also advised a young history teacher who took up current events in her history club to use his favorite magazines, the *New Republic* and the *Nation*, in addition to her more conservative news magazines. Smith cared about history and current events and wanted to spread his views on both. It disturbed him to see students misinformed. Later, when the same history teacher got some of her facts wrong in class, Smith confronted her before the class, and she dismissed him for impertinence.[19]

Another incident on the day his teacher dismissed him illustrated Smith's vanity about his intellectualism. His uncle, the sheriff, came to get him to testify against a potential juror in a sensational murder case. The prospective juror had told Smith that he would vote to acquit if chosen for the case. Smith had told the prosecutor, who was his neighbor, and the prosecutor called Smith as a witness to disqualify the man. After the sheriff located Smith, who was not in his history class, Smith went to the courthouse with his *New Republic* in hand, hoping that the national reporters covering the trial would notice the magazine and be impressed by his budding intellectualism.[20]

In his senior year of high school, Smith was a liberal and a pacifist who believed among other things that American intervention in the First World War had been a mistake brought about by the monied and munitions interests. He inclined toward socialism. Smith was conscious of being poor — of always owing a big bill at the grocery store — but he knew he was not really poor compared to the black population or the white sharecroppers. The poor of both races lived in shotgun shacks, and had no sheets or pillowcases for their beds or even basic clothing such as underwear and socks. As the New Deal programs multiplied, he noticed that hunger was being wiped out in Sidon for the first time in his memory. Highly conscious of class differences, he embraced governmental action to aid the poor, identifying with them and despising the planters.[21]

Society's materialism offended Smith. When wealthy cousins from Texas visited the Smiths, they clashed with him. His young sister, Sadie, accepted a ride in their chauffeur-driven limousine to buy an ice cream, but Smith refused. Unimpressed by Smith's intellectual pretensions, they sent him a book from Texas on how to get rich quick. He thought that they were implying that he should busy himself with making money for his family rather than dabbling with books. He was furious, perhaps because he felt some guilt over his pursuit of intellectual matters at a time when his family did need money. Recognizing how precarious his family's financial situation was, Smith feared he could slip into the poverty surrounding him. He saw that neither the planters nor the middle class displayed any sympathy for the poor. Near Sidon, a government resettlement project brought in poor whites, but the town rejected them. Elsewhere in Leflore County, poor whites were denied employment by planters who advocated starving them out to be rid of them. Asked to employ

27

whites as cotton pickers, one planter responded, "I won't have any G—
damned white croppers on my place.... All I want are niggers who will
do what I tell them to."[22] Smith's reading and sensitivity led him to reject such attitudes, to embrace racial equality, to sympathize with the
poor, and to favor governmental intervention in the economy as the
best means of assisting the poor of both races.

Despite financial hardships, Smith's mother encouraged his intellectual ambitions and made an effort to improve the family's financial position by running for circuit clerk of Leflore County. She had been a
popular administrator at the sheriff's office, serving under her brother-
in-law and every other man elected since her husband's murder. She
ran hard but lost to an older, male opponent. Normally, Sadie Smith
was a reserved woman who held in her feelings and said little about her
troubles, but on election night she lay on the living room floor and cried.
Smith remembered it as the most bitter political loss of his life, overshadowing all of his later disappointments. He hurt for her, but her loss also
meant that he would not be able to go to a college out of state as they
had planned. They had hoped that, if she won, he would be able to leave
the South for some university where he would find fellow intellectuals
who shared his ideas.[23]

Through journals and books, Smith had read his way out of the Delta.
He practiced writing in the pages of the school paper, and dreamed of
leaving the state to attend some distant college such as Harvard or Yale
where he might find kindred liberal minds. In Greenwood, he dared
tell only his family and some of his young friends who, with the reck-
lessness of youth, were willing to tolerate the idea of improving the lot
of the "Negro" in theoretical conversations. But even his family did not
fully support his ideas.[24] It was his intellectualism — and his search to
understand fully the circumstances of his father's death — that set Smith
apart. He chose to become a lonely rebel in an environment hostile to
intellectuals.[25]

CHAPTER THREE

Moorhead

Sunflower Junior College in Moorhead grew out of a state agricultural high school. Many of Mississippi's agricultural high schools had been transformed into junior colleges to save them from closure when towns and counties began to build their own high schools. When Smith arrived, Moorhead, as it was known to students, had three hundred fifty students enrolled in the junior college and two hundred in the high school. The library housed two thousand books, and the president was a product of Iuka Normal School and Mississippi College. Smith later wrote an article about him called "Life with Papa," depicting the president as a tyrant with a clown's sense of the comic but no sense of humor. The school paid faculty members one hundred twenty-five dollars per month for teaching five classes and chaperoning students. Most faculty held only bachelor's degrees, and, if they expected a raise, they were advised to spend their summers working toward master's degrees. Some faculty members lived in the dorms; each sat at the head of a table in the dining room. The administration assigned students to seating in the dining room and marched them to church on Sunday. Dating was supervised, but the students kissed and snuggled in the church's dark corners. To encourage "intellectual" pursuits, rules mandated that all students belong to either the Wilson or Lee "literary society," so that they were organized for debates and academic competitions. The curriculum required six hours each in English, history, a foreign language, and math or chemistry. Students who cut class were quarantined in the infirmary if they were sick, or, if their absences were unexcused, they worked clearing "new ground" for the school farm. Work other than that performed as punishment on the farm or in the cooperative dining hall cut college costs to ten dollars per month. "Christian organizations" were stressed, and the only outside lecturer invited to campus during Smith's first year spoke about Robert E. Lee. Moorhead fell far short of Smith's dream of a place where he could share his liberal views with other intellectuals, but it was all that his mother could afford.[1]

He rebelled against the "establishment" with youthful zeal and paid a price. For example, he grew a long nail on his little finger for no reason other than to illustrate his "difference." The boys in the dorm held him down and cut it off to show him what they thought of his gesture. Smith did not sulk over his chastisement, but the attack multiplied his determination to be different. He entered into the spirited life of the dorm, serving as lookout for a dice game in his room that began one Saturday when the boy who delivered the *Clarion-Ledger* offered to "go double or nothing" for the paper bill. The game ran all day and involved a number of students before it ended. One of the big losers wrote to a friend in Greenwood. The friend's father, who was a Presbyterian minister, saw the letter and reported the incident to the school president. A minor scandal ensued, and the president threatened to expel Smith. Smith's mother supported him, and the president allowed him to stay in school.[2]

Smith spent a good deal of time reading in the Moorhead library, where he met Willie Ruth Townshend, who worked there as a National Youth Administration student assistant. Smith brought her Pearl Buck's *The Good Earth* to read, and they quickly became friends, despite the fact that she was a pretty young extrovert and he a shy intellectual. They discovered a common interest in editing *Sunflower Petals,* the school newspaper. She was a friend of David Holloman, whom Smith had met in the dorm. She encouraged their friendship, and, for the next several years, they were a threesome, attending parties and dances and running *Petals.*[3] Smith remained shy, but their friendship helped him to move more easily in social gatherings.

A sophomore held the position of editor in chief of the newspaper during their first year, but Smith became associate editor in chief, while Willie Ruth was assistant editor and Holloman business manager. Smith wrote his own column titled "Higher-Down on the Lower-Ups," named after Fred Sullens's column in the *Jackson Daily News,* "The Low Down on the Higher Ups." Sullens was the combative, colorful editor of the *Jackson Daily News* whom Smith admired for his style and ability to outrage his readers. Cribbing much of his material from the *New Republic,* Smith condemned the antiunion activities of "southern businessmen" and accused President Roosevelt of turning to the right. Following the lead of liberal writers at the time, he endorsed the investigation of munitions manufacturers who were accused of influencing United States foreign policy in order to increase their profits. Among the disconnected news items and statements of opinion making up his column, one sentence stood out as definitely his own: "It is surprising that there is so much race prejudice existing in Southern Colleges when one reflects that college teachers are supposed to have more than ordinary intelligence." Racism proved to be his theme for the fall. The second issue of *Petals* contained an unsigned editorial condemning lynching and calling for justice and fair treatment for blacks. In the next, Smith signed an editorial characterizing the race prejudice of his fellow students as "sickening" and asking them, "Do you believe that you are better than somebody because the color of your skin is different from theirs? Can you be a Christian and practice un-Christian racial discrimination? Do you believe in liberty and justice for all?"[4]

Smith's editorial appeared on the day before Thanksgiving 1934, a holiday that Moorhead students were required to spend at school. The administration decreed that students wear their best clothes for chicken and dressing in the dining hall and then forced their participation in physical contests to celebrate the holiday. Even the unathletic, such as Smith, had to perform. When he failed to do the required chin-ups, he was condemned to run the "hot line." The hot line consisted of the male students standing in two rows to hit the runner as he passed between them. The big football players, who led the hot line, removed their belts with relish for Smith's run and punished him for his opinions. Willie Ruth understood that Smith was being beaten for standing for "things that they did not appreciate or understand." She sympathized with her new friend and thought the members of the hot line cowards by comparison.[5]

Uncowed, Smith continued to use the paper to espouse his ideas. He spent hours clearing the swampy canebreaks in the "new ground" that winter as punishment for his gambling escapade. While the work kept him from his reading, it made him more of a "regular fellow." Apparently he was not unpopular with the majority of students; he was, after all, elected to the student council. For her misdeeds Willie Ruth was put to work in the kitchen, which Smith enjoyed, because a former Townshend family cook allowed Willie Ruth to pilfer pickles and extra desserts for Smith.[6]

Despite the rough, frontier atmosphere, Smith tried hard to be a serious intellectual at Moorhead. In the paper, he called Huey Long an "American Hitler" for censoring a student newspaper at Louisiana State University. He appealed for a "united liberal party," suggested a student movement against the ROTC and for Negro rights, criticized fellow students for pursuit of the "unimportant" and for being "a-twitter over the latest chattering movie." He lambasted schoolteachers who defended the United States's entry into the First World War, and, referring to his own instructor (sister to John Stennis), he asked, "Do you want hundreds of thousands of our best citizens to be killed to give capitalism its fee?"[7]

His seriousness did not prove all consuming. Smith's student work-study National Youth Administration job was to report the school's sports news for the Jackson *Clarion-Ledger* and the Memphis *Commercial Appeal*. His employment made him a spectator at every school event with a bit of power to shape the news. The football coach appreciated Smith's work, and Smith enjoyed reporting sports; but he felt that the school president was cheating him because the newspapers paid far more than the NYA stipend that he received and he believed that the president pocketed the difference. He despised the president for his weak education, his prudish rules of conduct, and his dictatorial manner.

Smith and his friends antagonized the president to the point that he decided to eliminate them from the student council. Smith had been elected as a freshman, and, under the old system, he and his friends would have remained on the council in their second year. But the president decided that the tradition of holding over members of the student council who had been elected as freshmen would end and that members such as Smith, who would be put off the council after one year, could not run again. To extract a measure of revenge, Smith and his friends put up a slate of "outsiders" and "disreputable" students, who won the next election. Smith and the president were constantly at odds. Once Moorhead's president picked up Smith hitchhiking back from Greenwood, where he had gone without permission for an exhibition baseball game. The president's only comment was "twenty-five hours in the new ground."

Smith enjoyed baiting and ridiculing authority figures, and he had a keen sense of humor. During a YMCA-staged "radio broadcast," Smith sat in a chair with his feet propped up and gave exercise instructions as if he were a gymnast.[8]

He refused to study what did not interest him, such as French and math. As a result, he spent the summer of 1935 attending school to make up classes. In the fall, he returned as editor of *Petals,* exhibiting in its pages an interest in pacifism and the dichotomy between Christian beliefs and actions. He called on pacifists to keep the United States out of the war developing in Europe. When Hitler occupied the Rhineland, Smith said Hitler should be allowed to keep it. Urging Christians and educators to show backbone and to work for the improvement of human beings, he endorsed the work of Sherwood Eddy, a local "Christian socialist." Eddy had organized Mississippi tenant farmers into a socialist cooperative providing education and health care facilities, prompting Smith to write, "The co-operative farm is the only real solution to the tenant problem...."

Smith called "organized religion" a "vested interest of capitalism" and accused ministers of being investors in "reactionary industrial enterprises." In politics, Smith called for a third party composed of "radicals and progressives" who believed in the "abolition of industrial capitalism" to hold back "incipient fascism." He was a radical in his surroundings, but he was not the only Mississippi student holding liberal, pacifist views. In Jackson, some Millsaps College students took a pledge not to fight if war came. At Moorhead, a mock student legislative session voted 242 to 66 for an old-age pension for every citizen who was over sixty and unemployed.[9]

Nevertheless, Smith got the reputation of being a "communist" for his views on race. As he and Willie Ruth walked across campus, people would sometimes come up behind them and call them "nigger loving commies."[10] Willie Ruth never told Smith, or anyone else, that she suffered a more traumatic experience as a result of the opinions expressed in the school paper. In the early spring as she stood outside the dorm waiting for a friend to take her to a nearby home to ride horses, three boys stopped their car to say that her friend could not come and that he had asked them to take her. Instead of going to the horse stable, the boys took her to the Sunflower County farm. In back of some of the buildings an iron kettle stood boiling. A group of men gathered around the kettle were passing a bottle of whiskey and holding their dogs. One of the boys hustled her to the pot, put in a stick, and lifted out a human hand, telling her to shake hands with her "brother" whom she "worried over so much." She went into shock. The pot contained the body of a black man who had been slain by a pursuing posse as he tried to escape after a theft. She believed that the men were feeding the meat off the man's bones to the dogs. She dared not tell anyone for fear that her family would find out about the incident and be provoked to violent revenge on the boys and men who had abused her.[11]

Though Smith did not know of his friend's experience, he had heard enough horror stories to understand the violent nature of his society's racism. As a result, he never ventured beyond intellectual attacks on segregation, nor did he get involved in social-political experiments such as Sherwood Eddy's cooperative. He wanted to be a writer or a newspaper editor, not a martyr. In May 1936, as he prepared to graduate from Sunflower Junior College, Smith wrote to Fred Sullens, editor of the *Jackson Daily News*, asking for a job. He told Sullens hopefully that he been writing sports columns for two years at school. Sullens replied bluntly, advising Smith to take a full college course and a year of journalism school, because without it "you cannot hope to be anything more than a hack writer." Whatever you do, he said, do not write sports. Sportswriters are a dollar a day and "few of them are worth a damn."[12] Dozens of other applications for employment and requests for scholarships produced similar results.

Having no money for any further education, Smith faced the difficult task of finding employment in depression-era Greenwood. His family's political connections got him summer work measuring cotton fields for farmers participating in the New Deal's Agricultural Adjustment Act to document their adherence to acreage restrictions. Then he worked as what he called a "flunky" in Greenwood's only factory—one that manufactured electronic testing equipment. A blueprint machine replaced him, and he did not succeed as an assembly line worker. He tried to secure employment at several gas stations, but the owners employed young men whose families brought in a great deal of trade. His could not. In desperation, Smith went to work at his typewriter trying to establish himself as a freelance writer. Never an easy task, from Greenwood in 1937 it seemed almost impossible. He remembers his start as a "rough" year because his relatives criticized him for "living on" his widowed mother. He withstood the family pressure to find other work because he enjoyed the intellectual effort far more than physical labor and because he would not abandon his dreams.[13]

He tried to write fantasies such as a romantic novel about a newspaperman in a midwestern city run by a tough political boss. He wrote historical fiction and gothic southern short stories. Those did not sell. What he called hack writing for newspapers and magazines paid a few dollars for each piece. He wrote large sections of the *Clarion-Ledger's* hundredth anniversary issue, sports stories, and articles about bow fishing. And occasionally he made a big strike. What he called the proudest day of his life came when a check for one hundred dollars arrived from *Coronet* magazine for a human-interest history piece on the Civil War entitled "The Polite War." Because he stayed at home to write he had been given the job of preparing lunch, and that day he placed the check under his mother's plate so that she would find it when she sat down to the table. That sale justified his decision to make his living by writing, but there were few such checks. Most of the time he only eked out an income, but his luck improved when he won a promotional "bank night" drawing at the movies. Most of the three hundred dollars went to settle the family grocery bill, but his mother later bought a car, which Smith borrowed.[14]

His most interesting pieces were opinion articles on the South. In *Common Sense*, Smith discussed the prospects for a progressive third party. Discovering, he thought, widespread discontent in the continued election of populists, he contended, "It [political discontent] can and should be organized into a new political party expressing the desire of the majority of the people for a fairer distribution of the wealth of the rich lands and industries of the region." Huey Long's following, he said, proved the point, but he recognized the danger of fascism among the same voters. Citing the success of demagogues such as Bilbo, he worried that white populists were potentially more fascist than progressive. Knowing that economic development provided the only hope for lasting progress, Smith urged a program to end tenant farming and passage of laws to protect workers. "Leaders who realize that only in a political party outside the domain of monopolistic capitalism will it be possible to gain for Americans security and plenty will have to take the pioneering steps." He anointed Maury Maverick, an appropriately named Texas populist, as the best bet for leadership and turned to the question of the "Negro vote." Recognizing that truly enfranchising blacks would mean losing southern whites' votes, Smith urged delay. Given that most blacks lacked the education necessary to be informed voters, he said, it would be "useless to try to give the Negro the ballot" until blacks' economic and educational needs had been addressed. Liberals would destroy themselves by trying to enfranchise blacks too soon because most "whites [are] too backward to use their voting power intelligently."[15] In *Plain Talk*, he described the South as an American colony and urged federal efforts to reverse that status, mentioning national aid to southern universities and the multiplication of the Tennessee Valley Authority model across the region as possibilities.[16]

In another article, he assessed Mississippi "as the very heart of agricultural feudalism... [and] the state where industrial Fascism is gaining its firmest foothold." Not impressed with the Balance Agriculture with Industry program drawing low-wage jobs to the state, Smith noted that labor strikes and race problems could lead working-class whites and blacks to recognize their need for unity. Standing in the way, he thought, was the absence of good newspapers. He called Fred Sullens the "combination of the undesirable features of H. L. Mencken and William Randolph Hearst." Lamenting the political situation, he said the state "has not had a progressive, or even efficient, state administration within the past fifty years." Pat Harrison, the powerful U.S. senator, he dismissed as a "shrewder-than-average politician with no social vision."[17] Smith believed a Mississippi progressive party was possible, if a man with "natural ability as a leader" would undertake to build an organization.

His writing income provided the means for an active social life. He escorted Willie Ruth, who was attending Delta State College, to parties organized by the Delta's young adults in abandoned stores closed by the depression. While she danced in the front, he gambled in the backroom with other young men. He ventured to surrounding towns with Holloman for visits with other young ladies. When *Reader's Digest* picked up his *Coronet* article, Smith spent the money he had earned to buy Willie Ruth an expensive bottle of perfume. He found freelancing a pleasurable existence. He was not making much money, but no one was in the thirties. He had avoided manual labor, and he was the professional writer he had dreamed of becoming.[18]

A lynching story drew Smith to Oxford. Dale Mullen, the son of the *Oxford Eagle's* editor, and Lawrence Hutton, son of the lawyer who had defended the lynched man, invited Smith to come and help them write the story. Having read his account of a murder in *True Detective*, they considered Smith an established writer and hoped that he would be able to sell the story. It seemed a good one. An Oxford mob had lynched Ellwood Higgenbotham in 1935 near the university because the members of the mob feared that the jury, then deliberating, might fail to convict Higgenbotham of murder for killing a planter in a gunfight. Mullen told Smith that Hutton knew all of the details about the incident. The court records were available, and they would split half the proceeds with him. Mullen offered to supply Smith bed, food, and a typewriter. *Ken,* a downscale version of *Esquire,* expressed an interest in the idea, and Smith began to visit Oxford, researching the article. Mullen and Smith developed a strong friendship. The three young men dreamed of selling their article and moving to New York to escape the wrath of the lynchers and to establish themselves as writers.[19]

Mullen, Smith said later, was the first "intellectual" he had met. Mullen described Smith as the "shyest person" he had ever known. Mullen, an aspiring author whose articles had been rejected by the *New Republic* and *Southern Review,* introduced Smith to a wide circle of friends in Oxford and Memphis.[20] He said of one man he wanted Smith to meet, "He insists on being a Southerner and an Agrarian, but I nonetheless think him the healthiest and sanest intellectual I know."[21] And, he promised to introduce Smith to a "girl" who "dotes on intellectuals." The two men enjoyed being young, bright, and adventurous. In one invitation to Smith, Mullen wrote, "For Christ's sake don't plan on spending any money in Memphis: a couple of dollars is all you need." Smith did meet a "girl" in Memphis and they became "practically engaged," but she was not an intellectual and did not fully share Smith's views on the South. Because she could not accept integration, Smith resisted commitment to her.[22]

Dreams of changing the South dominated Smith's life. During his free-lance writing period, Lillian Smith's *North Georgia Review* provided the main source of his education about the South and race. Lillian Smith ran a girls' school to make her living and published the *Review* to influence southern attitudes about race and politics. She later became infamous in the South by writing a novel on the theme of interracial love. Leading historians, sociologists, and writers contributed to her *Review,* as did Frank Smith. His association with the *Review* began with an article rejected by coeditor Paula Snelling, who added that "we are charmed to find another person who is unequivocally liberal in viewpoint...."[23] Lillian Smith and Snelling visited him in Greenwood in 1939, and he escorted them around the Delta for a day, visiting cooperative experiments and sharing ideas on the South's future.[24]

After three years of freelancing, Smith began to doubt that he was going to change the South quickly. When he made an effort to start his own magazine in the summer of 1939, he planned it as a money-making venture. It would be called *Delta,* and would cater to the moneyed people of Mississippi and Memphis. It would have been a combination of *Town & Country*, the *Saturday Evening Post*, and the *New Yorker*. Certainly, it could not have crusaded for much change and still sold to planters. Funds never materialized, and Smith abandoned the planned magazine. The big Oxford article on the lynching failed to sell because *Ken*'s lawyers were too concerned about potential libel suits. Smith grew tired of "not getting anywhere" and grew restless. He tried to find an assignment as a war correspondent, and, when that failed, he decided to go back to school. His recent visits to Oxford no doubt prompted a desire to settle near his new friend, Mullen. Fred Smith made it possible for his brother to enter college by joining the navy and earmarking a portion of his pay for Smith's education.[25]

He had no high expectations for the University of Mississippi, but it was all he could afford. The state did not offer the opportunity for the liberal education Smith desired. A knowledgeable critic during this period described Mississippi's institutions of higher learning as dead from the shoulders up and incapable of providing the atmosphere for the cultivation or even an exchange of ideas. Smith thought that junior colleges, for all their limitations, were better institutions than the state's universities. Based on what she knew of the University of Mississippi, Lillian Smith worried in a letter to Smith that his good mind would be spoiled: "[D]on't let anybody there make you change your ideas. That is[,] cling to your own independent way of using your own eyes and ears.... I suspect you are correct when you say that there is little to disturb the complacency of the believers in the status quo in the course you are attending.... I am very interested in you and your future and don't want to see you get under the influence of any one who would cause you to become a middle-of-the roader or one who would make the road of compromise look too necessary."[26]

History was his choice for a course of study, and Ole Miss had a three-man history department. Bell Wiley would become a noted Civil War historian, and James Silver would become famous for supporting integration at Ole Miss and writing a book about it. During his first year at the university, Smith worked for Wiley as a graduate assistant, and the second year he taught "business school history" to football players and others taking the course to raise their averages. Smith failed too many of them and had to allow them to take a makeup exam in order to pass half the class. Smith was not especially impressed with his courses. He did well enough, winning first place in Joe Matthews's class, where Matthews held a contest and posted rankings. Smith, who dated his break with segregation from his encounter with Embree's revision of black history, was far ahead of his professors as a liberal. He found barely adequate intellectual stimulation in Oxford, but his views were not notably altered there. He had already abandoned the southern historical myths, and his historical training simply filled in some details. Silver said that he learned from Smith on the "race issue."

Smith had drifted away from the pacifism of his teenage years as Hitler became an obvious threat to world order and made the nature of fascism clear. Smith tempered his young radicalism as he attempted to find employment or other means of livelihood over the years. In order to have a private room, he joined a fraternity and became its president, but he took little interest in campus politics. He considered teaching and seemed to be on his way to graduate school to become a Civil War historian when the Second World War broke out.[27]

In 1941 Smith was twenty-three. His youthful radicalism and burning desire to change the world had been blunted, and he was headed toward an academic life where he thought he would be more an observer than a participant in events. Yet he was still promoting a cooperative farm at Cruger by inviting its leaders to the university to speak. He had matured out of his shyness and had become a man of strong, independent opinions. He disliked swearing and refused all his life to do it. He had no quarrel with drinking but never developed any fondness for alcohol. He loved Cokes, playing cards, eating, and reading all day in bed. Smith desired what he considered the easy, intellectual life and seemed set to pursue it as a college professor. But the war intervened.[28]

CHAPTER FOUR

Private Smith Goes to War

Jim Silver once said that he did not expect much of Frank Smith until he proved himself in the army. Willie Ruth agreed that military service made Smith's career. Those two people appreciated Smith's intellect, but even they required proof of his "manliness" before they fully recognized his potential. Others—his family, acquaintances in Greenwood, and school friends who were less impressed by intellectual powers—needed even more proof. Mississippi's frontier culture demanded masculine, physical attainments from Smith before it would make him a leader. Silver, whose war experiences were limited to a tour in the Pacific with the Red Cross, pursued sports, hard drinking, and women as substitutes to prove his manliness. Willie Ruth, who claimed "to put Smith first," married a handsome football player rather than Smith. In school, in the army, and later in politics, Smith suffered from society's preference for the slim, the athletic, and the physically adventurous. He lacked those attributes, but he possessed intellect, vision, and determination. The war provided Smith the opportunity to venture out of Mississippi, to prove his manliness by a test accepted by his culture, and to return with a war record enabling him to enter into politics.[1]

Smith and his friend Dale Mullen drove to Grenada to enlist in the navy soon after Pearl Harbor. Both men failed the physical. Smith had a perforated ear drum and weighed too much, but the army doctors were less selective when the draft called. Mullen and Smith went to war with some reservations and lingering doubts. Mullen wrote to Smith, "I am sure that the U.S. is on the right side of this war [but] not sure enough to want to go killing people. [N]othing that the Japs or the Nazis can do will convince me that I personally could improve the situation by killing some of them. But nonetheless one has to go to this war.... I prefer not to fight with a gun—fighting with a gun, however, is better than not fighting at all."[2] They had shared enough of the pacifism generated by World War I and doubts born of "intellectualism" to distrust the patriotic call to arms.

Smith's mother drove him to the Greenwood draft board on February 9, 1942. The country had gone on daylight-saving time that morning. It was pitch black and raining as a group of thirteen young men assembled. The board made Smith acting corporal, and he led the group to Camp Shelby for ten days of processing. Smith was miserable. He missed his creature comforts, and he hated army life. He went to Fort Bragg in North Carolina for boot camp, where his first lieutenant proved to be an incompetent leader disliked by all the men. Smith applied for admission to officer candidate school in order to escape enlisted life.[3] From home his mother encouraged his ambitions. "You have got it in you and I know you can make good. Uncle Harry is mighty glad. He says you will stand a chance of getting something when you get through whipping the japs."[4] Finally Smith had done something of which his family and society could approve.

Waiting to hear from officer candidate school, Smith entered artillery school at Fort Bragg. There he began to study the mathematics that he had refused to learn at Moorhead. The despised math proved easy for him compared to the physical challenge of boot camp. The first formation assembled at 6:30. After breakfast they ran half a mile and then did half an hour of exercises.

Probably because of his college degree, the army decided to make Smith an officer. Transferred to Fort Sill, Oklahoma, Smith continued to have problems keeping up with the training pace because all officer candidates had to "double time," or run at all times. Smith, who could not run well or for very long, feared that he would "wash out" because of his physical abilities, but he determinedly struggled through the exercises. His biggest problem was "staying awake in class" through days that concluded with a "study period" at 10:00 in the evening. Worst of all, he complained, "We have to keep neat and shiny all the time, something else that doesn't agree with me."[5] Halfway through the course an officer reassured him that he was doing well, and he gained the confidence to finish strong. Still, petty regulations annoyed Smith, and he vowed to request overseas duty as soon as he received his commission, so as to escape the spit-and-polish rules that were relaxed in combat.[6]

To Smith one of the most exciting aspects of OCS was the integration of blacks in the ranks. He told Willie Ruth that "we have bi-racial education here. There are 2 Negroes in my section of the class and only the fact that neither happens to be named Smith keeps me from being in the same tent with them." He reported that he usually ate with "one of them" because height put them close in formation. Both black candidates were from northern cities and relatively well educated. Smith thought that few southern blacks would get into officer candidate school because of their limited educational opportunities, but he supported the integration as a good first step.[7]

After mastering the math necessary to aim and hit a target, Smith found firing a 105 mm howitzer just another intellectual challenge. He had a talent for solving the problems and dropping the shells on target. The army commissioned him and sent him back to Camp Shelby, Mississippi, to help form a new artillery battalion with noncommissioned officers from a New England National Guard unit, draftees, and a mixture of officers ranging from a regular army lieutenant colonel to Smith and other "ninety day wonders." For a few days there were no enlisted men and little to do, which Smith thought "nice after the torture of Fort Sill."[8]

When the men arrived, Smith oversaw the training of telephone operators, linemen, and fire direction personnel. They wore wool uniforms in the Mississippi summer but toiled relentlessly, Smith thought. He managed, with some effort, to keep up with his men running in formation and to retain the breath to order them to halt. The 243rd Field Artillery Battalion was activated in August 1942 and reviewed by President Roosevelt, who happened to be on a political tour of the South at the time.[9]

Smith began to enjoy army life. He visited New Orleans for the first time and marveled at the sight of the French Quarter filled with wartime crowds and then the sobering sight of the same streets in the morning. When the battalion was sent to Florida, he visited tourist parks to pull alligator tails and stopped at roadside stands to drink all of the orange juice he could hold for ten cents. He rode a dive bomber along the coast and watched soldiers pick up girls at Miami hotels. On another trip, he slept in the lobby of the best hotel in Fort Worth. He played poker all night and missed breakfast finishing the last hand in the morning.[10]

In the midst of his army life, news from home signaled the end of the family as he had known it. His eighteen-year-old sister, Sadie, married an air force machinist from Illinois and moved to Florida. His brother, Fred Cecil, who had joined the navy before the war to escape the Delta, had gone to war in the Pacific aboard the *Juneau* and died in the battle of Guadalcanal. Smith fully appreciated his brother's "unselfish" support despite the fact that they were opposites in most things, and he grieved his loss. He told Willie Ruth, "It will take the rest of my life to get used to his not being around." But he said that he intended to spend his life "trying to see what I can do to make sure that all of these sacrifices will not have been in vain."[11]

After his unit completed its training in Mississippi and Florida, it was stationed in South Carolina. There he met an Alabama girl, Helen McPhaul, who had joined the war effort making maps. They quickly fell in love despite an awkward beginning on a blind date. His best army buddy, Bud Harrison, dated Helen's friend. They spent weekends commuting to see the ladies after being transferred again to Fort Bragg. Smith had to borrow a car, scrounge gasoline, and miss sleep in order to spend weekends in South Carolina. Both couples later married.

Not until February 1944 did the army assign Smith's unit their weapons for the European invasion. They received eight-inch guns taken from the navy and mounted on field artillery carriages. The guns were the biggest in the army and had to be towed by tractors and put into position by cranes. They would fire twenty miles, but were inaccurate at best. The men of the 243rd boarded the *Queen Elizabeth* at Hoboken, New Jersey, without bands or cheering crowds. The men, loaded with gear, struggled to keep up with WACs, who were not required to carry their bags on board. Then they strained to see the Statue of Liberty over all the shoulders in front of them.[12]

After an unescorted but uneventful crossing, they camped near the Welsh border, where they awaited orders for the invasion of Europe. Smith, who had never traveled before he joined the army, looked upon the period as his European tour, finishing off his education. He explored British pubs and country homes, bought a bicycle to see more of the countryside, and quickly abandoned English beer for cider. He celebrated July 4, 1944, at Purple Sycamores, a fine country home on a hill with a view "that you read about." At the Sycamores, the soldier guests and their English host picked strawberries and drank scotch until that gave out and then switched to gin and orange juice. He spent the next Saturday in the Horse and Jockey with two female telephone operators up from London and a young woman whom he had met at the Purple Sycamores. "My principal occupation through the evening was drinking three pints of cider and singing, or trying to sing, the songs one of the London girls played on the piano." A dance at the recreation hall capped the evening. Smith visited Stratford-upon-Avon. Inspired by the experiences, he even tried football, resulting in injury and a stay in the infirmary. Travel excited him. "This," he said, "is the first real trip I've ever taken."[13]

D-Day was in June, but the heavy guns of the 243rd did not land in France until August 1944. The 243rd fought an unusual direct fire operation against fortifications at Saint-Malo and then moved toward the front line as the army advanced through Laval, Le Mans, Chartres, Paris, and Villecy. During the Germans' winter counterattack, they spent the Battle of the Bulge in the Saar-Moselle pocket.

Captain Smith fought the war from the fire direction center of his unit. Smith's army school performance in the United States had earned him quick promotions. His title was assistant S3 or assistant to the operations officer. In the fire direction center, Smith received information from forward spotters in light planes and on the ground. Then men called "computers" used the map coordinates to calculate the positioning of the guns. After each shot hit, spotters called corrections into the fire direction center, and Smith made new calculations that he relayed to the gunners. He lived through battles with a telephone attached to one ear, directing the eight-inch guns and then recalculating the position for firing. He wrote to Helen, "I like to shoot artillery this way, having to strain every nerve, with everything in an uproar. It gives a chair-borne soldier like me the closest thing to the thrill of combat that I have yet found...."[14]

Generally, fighting filled less of a soldier's life than looking after his own basic human needs. One of the unit diarists wrote of the artillery's experience, "Seldom does the excitement of war penetrate deep enough to erase from their minds the sense of their own discomforts...." Smith agreed, telling Helen, "War can be miserable, getting soaked, wet and chilled, going to bed in the mud and rain and getting up before dawn in the same rain." Smith managed the basic problems of human existence better than most soldiers. His first "shower" in France required carrying water an eighth of a mile from a well and pouring it out of his helmet over his head. Just as he lathered up, a French woman and her daughter walked past. He flushed with embarrassment, but they pretended not to see him, and so he continued. Smith saw little of the French because he worked and slept in the fire direction center, which he usually located in some type of permanent structure, ranging from barns to châteaux. His job spared him sleeping in tents and on rare occasions provided a tub and hot water.[15]

Food, he told Helen, was discussed among soldiers more than sex. He complained that there was never enough to eat, but he made himself as comfortable as possible during a war. A unit diarist reported, "[T]he Epicurean Ass't S-3 is known to have amassed the largest larder of delectable foods we have seen. . . . Spilling out of christmas [*sic*] boxes, piled high in heaps around his bed, lining the window sill and bulging from his pockets are all shapes, sizes and varieties of spam, cheese, creamed honey, jams, jellies, cookies, crackers, candies, bolonies, nuts, cakes, dates, and chocolate bars." What set off this observation about Smith was the arrival of a Coke in a package from home. The diarist described Smith stumbling through the confusion and litter of the fire direction center one morning, standing in front of the fire, and opening the bottle. "In the silence of the room, hissed a sibiliant [*sic*] whisper: 'He's got a real, honest-to-God, coca-cola.' "[16] Smith reported somewhat later scrounging the tastiest morsel since leaving home when he procured a "sandwich made of bacon and pineapple, flavored with Durkee's." No longer required to keep neat and shiny in battle, Smith knew that he made a rumpled sight of a soldier: "My pockets are always filled with all sorts of odds and ends, sugar cubes, lemon powder, bouillon powder, salt, K ration crackers, etc. . . ."[17]

Smith had scrounged a lounge chair for his comfort in the fire direction center. It was a gift from a grateful French innkeeper whose laundry room had once served as the fire direction center. Having noticed Smith's fondness for the chair, she presented it to him as a parting gift. For the rest of the war it went into the unit's trailer for each move and allowed Smith to recline during the days and nights he spent on duty in the fire direction center. When the unit was in action, Smith could not leave the center even to eat.[18]

Smith did his job well and was awarded the Certificate of Merit. His commander recommended that he be given a Bronze Star, but higher command denied the request. "I think he [the general] did exactly right, for I have certainly not risked my neck any way as much as 90% of the infantrymen in the army."[19] He admired infantrymen and assured Helen that he was safe compared to most of them. "My only contact with the enemy is dodging snipers and a few occasional bombs. . . ."[20] Later the army accepted his commander's recommendation, and Smith got the Bronze Star. Smith did not lack courage. Once a young man in his unit, who reminded Smith of his dead brother, got lost while out placing road markers. Smith volunteered to search for him in a night of rain, sleet, and gale-force winds. He poked around buildings and explored unmarked roads in unsecured territory without finding the man, who appeared dry and unharmed the following morning.[21]

Smith longed for more action than he saw in the fire direction center. Writing to Helen with one hand and holding a telephone to his ear with the other, Smith reported blowing up two guns that had been giving his unit problems but agonized that he had simply relied on information from the forward spotter: "I wish I could get out to the front to do some of that. Back here in FDC I don't get much more than a vicarious excitement. I'm not interested in looking for trouble, but I would like to see little more chance at forward observation. I think I'm a good shot."[22] His colonel kept him in the FDC, but he did get out once to the forward position: "Capt. Smith, anxious to fire as observer at least one mission against the enemy before the war was over, asked to go to the OP today.... It was a quiet day interrupted only by the sight of a U.S. tank firing on a pillbox across the Saar. To see better, Smith lead [sic] the OP party...down to the rivers [sic] edge to watch the battle across the stream. They soon discovered their box seat was much to[o] close to the show, when a machine gun fire streaked over their heads. While the others crouched in a hollow, Lewandowski laid [sic] across the seat of his jeep, turned it around, using his hands to work the controls, and the party leaped on and raced for safety. No hits, no runs and one error: going there in the first place."[23] Smith was more suited to direct the firing from Madame Beals's chair.

The artillery, which was normally miles behind the front lines, felt closest to the war after a breakthrough. One of the unit diarists wrote, "We move every other day; villages are still smoking when we pass through; the roads are jammed like [a] 5th ave. traffic snarl with tanks, trucks and guns moving up, while the wrecked equipment of yesterday's fighting are heaped along the sides and here and there we pass a little huddle of bodies flung in the ungainly attitudes of death. Reassuringly, most of the dead we have seen on this move have been Krauts.... [I]t is still possible to see the terrible results of artillery fire around us."[24]

Despite seeing the piles of bodies and watching soldiers who wandered back from the front with their arms blown off, Smith never lost his intel-

lectual distance from the war. Though close enough to hear and to see
the war, he still found time to read and to carry on a massive correspondence. On the eve of the invasion, he received the following periodi-
cals in the mail: *Time,* the *New Republic, Common Sense, Reader's Digest,
Field Artillery Journal,* the Sunday Memphis *Commercial Appeal,* and the
Greenwood Commonwealth. He complained that it was "hard to get hold
of the exact books" that he wanted while fighting the war, but he continued to read a prodigious number, ranging from popular novels to a
book on the Sermon on the Mount.[25]

One of his primary occupations was the long-distance education of
Helen McPhaul. He told Willie Ruth that he had had to suppress a strong
desire to get married before he left the United States because "certain
other factors make it seem not the best idea to do so. The big question
mark is what might be called intellectual incompatibility—not that I'm
any more intelligent but we just don't think the same things about things
southern—It doesn't matter much now, but it might after the war when
I get mixed up with what I intend to do in Mississippi."[26] He had dated
other women and considered them as partners, but none of them agreed
with him on the "race issue." He could not believe they would live with
his social and political ideas. Helen, he felt, just made him think that
she "likes everything" without truly meaning it. He wanted her to believe in racial equality before they married.[27]

Smith's romance with Helen continued by mail, but centered on the
theme of intellectual compatibility, especially concerning racial attitudes.
On the ship to Britain, Smith wrote, "I want you to get along with all
my friends as well as my ideas, with which a good many of my friends
do not agree. When you start to think about things, remember that a
lot of my ideas and convictions are going to get me into a lot of relative
trouble someday—trouble that may not be very pleasant to people
who care about me and still don't argue [agree?] very much with my
ideas. You should have been more particular with whom you fell in
love.... There are a lot of other boys who are nice and who don't have
vagaries like mine...."[28]

He apologized for teaching in his letters, but he offered Helen a correspondence course. He advised her to read reviews of all the latest books
and to read those that had shaped his thinking. He gave first place to
Steffens's autobiography, Sheean's *Personal History,* and Embree's *Brown
Americans.* "I would like to suggest to you," he said, "to read books that

show how certain articulate people have developed into liberal thinkers...." On the South, he recommended Wilbur Cash's *Mind of the South*, Clarence Cason's *90 Degrees in the Shade*, and Jonathan Daniels's *A Southerner Discovers the South*. Perhaps to continue his theme of warning about potential difficulties, Smith remarked that both Cash and Cason had killed themselves after writing their books, but he quickly reassured her: "I wouldn't say there was anything significant to their suicides...." Smith encouraged Helen to subscribe to the *New Republic*, and he wrote Lillian Smith to secure back issues of the *South Today* for her.[29]

On race, Smith offered this advice: "It is not a negro problem, it is a white problem. And we've got to think of it that way. It's not just a question of being sympathetic, although that helps, it is teaching ourselves to think completely without prejudice. I think we can...." Smith had no sympathy for racists, calling them fascists. "The racial haters at homes [*sic*] are fascists at heart, whether they know it or not. The tragic fact is that they do not know it."[30] He believed that changing the South would take a long time and did not advocate any radical action. Commenting on Helen's observations about segregated streetcars in Washington, Smith wrote, "I know there is no hope of ending Jim Crowism on southern buses and streetcars in the near future, but there ought to be requirements that buses have two entrances."[31] Partitioning the vehicles would allow whites and blacks each to enter separate portions without confronting one another directly. In other words, in 1945 he had no hope of ending the system, but he wanted to make it more humane.

Smith was a gradualist committed to working toward changing minds. He said of a lynching making news at the time, "To try to turn people away from that kind of thinking is what I want to do, and it's not going to be a very popular thing to do on the scene."[32] When Helen moved to Washington, Smith offered her this advice about dealing with blacks in the capital: "I think you will get adjusted to negroes without any trouble. I don't want you to go out of your way to find any situation, but face them as they come and try to see how much of the things we have been brought up to see only with prejudice are really nothing at all. What we've got to do is to rid ourselves of prejudice and also any self-righteousness about having lost those prejudices."[33] That was a tall order for a southern white in the 1940s, but Smith was satisfied with Helen's efforts. By January 1945, he felt that he and Helen had reached compatibility, and he told Willie Ruth he intended to ask Helen to marry him when he returned. "I think I fell in love when I found that her heart was in the right place on the issues that confront the South."[34]

Smith's dedication to changing southern minds shaped everything in his life, affecting even his choice of a wife. He told Willie Ruth that getting one person to think with a "humanitarian mind" would help, but that they could not hope to "completely change" the South. Smith felt his efforts were a moral crusade full of danger, one requiring changes in people's hearts and minds before their behavior would be affected. His and Willie Ruth's efforts at Moorhead made them feel exceptionally close. Willie Ruth worried that Smith's marriage would alter their relationship and suggested that Smith not tell Helen of their special friendship until after the wedding. "[O]r don't you remember what a hard time I had marrying myself off but refusing to give you up. I always considered you first."[35] Perhaps she overdramatized the relationship, but the bond of fellowship among those southerners who rejected racism was certainly real. To Smith and his few cohorts, it seemed to be a secret society.

Although Smith's idealism about the South extended to national politics and caused him to favor left-leaning candidates as a rule, he moved to the right in the political spectrum, becoming by the end of the war a confirmed New Deal liberal. In his teenage years, Smith had been highly critical of Roosevelt, calling him reactionary and right-wing, but as a result of his military experience, Smith lined up behind Roosevelt. During the war, Smith wrote an outline for a book he entitled "Democrats at War," in which he described the democracy "practiced and thought among the men who are fighting and preparing to fight."[36] He grew to believe that Roosevelt led a crusade against fascism and that Roosevelt represented the best hope for mankind, in contrast to Stalin, who embodied communism, and Churchill, who stood for colonialism.

Despite his growing admiration for Roosevelt, Smith still had some misgivings about the New Deal. He worried that Roosevelt lacked enough commitment to the postwar internationalism that Smith thought would be needed to insure the continuation of the crusade for a better world. He supported Henry Wallace for vice president and then for the cabinet because he admired Wallace's internationalism. Smith worried that Roosevelt, who worked with southern conservatives in Congress, would play into their hands and lose the developing "Negro" vote in northern cities. He hoped that somehow there could be an end to the solid South dominated by conservative Democrats so that a progressive party could emerge. Smith wanted an aggressive liberalism committed to a better world. He said, "I have seen the war take too much not to know that to fight against it [fascism, racism, and isolationism] from now on is one of the tasks that fate has given me. Men were not meant to be wasted like this, and they just can't be again...."[37] He welcomed the Labour Party victory in Great Britain as a step in the right direction.[38]

He feared an American retreat into isolationism or a holy crusade against the Soviet Union. He eschewed militarism. "[S]ervice in the army ought to convince anybody of the perils and fallacies and the complete injustice of dictatorship in any form." He wanted postwar preparedness, "but I don't want it to bring about any revival or growth of any type of what we call militarism."[39] Remembering his brother's death and his personal sense of loss, he wrote, "I've tried not to think about it much since then, for that is the only way to keep a normal mind....I can't bring myself to be a good enough soldier to hate either the Germans or the Japs. I believe that all the war criminals in both nations should be exterminated, but as a matter of justice not hatred."[40]

Smith's army experience reinforced his democratic ideas. Serving as unit censor for the 243rd, he read the men's mail to ensure they gave away no military secrets. Commenting on the experience, he said, "I'm learning more about my fellow human beings. For people as a whole, the more you know of them, the more you like them."[41] Mentioning that his orderly was not "very good" at waiting on him, he continued, "[B]ut I don't blame anybody for that and don't expect anything."[42] He liked the individuals in the army but had difficulty with the organization or, for that matter, with any depersonalized institution. He wrote, "It is not that I don't believe in the institutions wholeheartedly, it is just that I believe in keeping anything from growing pompous by well-placed humor, either subtle or ribald, whichever happens to fit best."[43] The church was the institution from which he expected the least, because he found organized religion devoid of the spirit he thought the world needed. "The essence of Christianity," he said, "is the Beatitudes, and it is too bad that so many Christians don't have much idea of what they mean."[44] But he did have faith in democracy and in the possibility that people could be led to understand the world as he did and to govern themselves well. "When I actually do get away from it [war] and become a civilian I think that I have an even more important job to work on . . . doing more than my share of seeing that this doesn't happen again, and trying to help make one of the results of this war be a better civilization for everybody to live in. That sounds very idealistic and over-dramatic, but it is exactly what I want, and I believe that it can happen if enough people work for it."[45]

When the war ended in Europe, Smith volunteered for the Pacific. Instead, his unit transferred to military police duties in Germany. He hated the work, which consisted of guarding prison pens and rounding up stray German soldiers. He chaffed at how "little men use that power to emphasize their meanness." He feared that he would "explode" before he got out and would have preferred combat in Asia.[46]

He did enjoy sightseeing. Sent to Paris to train as the education officer for his battalion, he sampled the nightclubs. He visited the Brenner Pass and saw Berchtesgaden, Hitler's "eagle's nest." He ran into General Patton at Valhalla, and Patton ordered him to remove some unsightly gas cans along the road. He obtained leave in London, dated a "Georgia girl," and limped from sight to sight in too-small shoes. He was there for the famous theater season at the end of the war. He saw John Gielgud's *Hamlet* and Vivien Leigh's *The Skin of Our Teeth* and got stranded in Luxembourg for nine days. He gloated to Helen, "I know far more about London and Paris from personal experience than I know about New York. The Army is making a cosmopolite out of this country boy."[47]

Still, his dream was to go back to Mississippi and start a "liberal" newspaper to begin the education of his people. Through his writing, he had made contact with a kindred soul who wrote for the *New Republic* and had some hopes of gaining support from "northern liberals." More realistically, he determined to take advantage of the GI bill for further education at Columbia or in Washington while he tried to develop a career as a writer. But writing he saw as a means of supporting his dream paper. He told Helen that "the main thing will be just to assure myself of a livable income from another source (writing) while I am getting the paper started. It all can be done, and will be." He knew what he wanted to do, but he had no resources to start a newspaper. He feared that his "craving for creature comforts" would distract him from his planned efforts at change in Mississippi. He warned Helen, "Don't ever let me think about sacrificing my convictions for security, no matter what the temptation. . . ."[48]

Smith returned, personally notified his previous girlfriends of his intentions, and proposed to Helen. She had moved to Washington, and so, after their marriage in Alabama, they settled briefly in the nation's capital. He entered American University and sent some of his articles and stories out for review, but word soon arrived of a job on a new "liberal" newspaper in his hometown.

CHAPTER FIVE

Newspapers and Politics

In his history of southern liberals, *Speak Now Against the Day*, John Egerton uses the analogy of a stoplight to describe the South at the end of the war. Liberals saw the green light. Organizations such as the Southern Regional Council in Atlanta expected economic growth and hoped it would lead to a racial settlement. The ruling oligarchy saw a red light and thought it time for a U-turn. They feared race mixing and an end to their segregated world. Perhaps 80 percent of southern whites sat staring at a yellow light—confused, fearful, waiting. Between 1945 and 1950 the green-light liberals and the red-light reactionaries struggled for control of the light's switch, but it was an uneven match. The hard, powerful elite ruled from the courthouse to the nation's Capitol as if by divine right.[1]

Mississippi had changed during the war. Two hundred and fifty thousand Mississippians had served in the armed forces. Many, like Frank Smith, traveled to Europe, while others went to Asia. Around the world they saw different societies that were not divided into Mississippi's simple white-over-black. Black Mississippians fought, too, and many came back unwilling to accept segregation. Thousands of troops from throughout the United States trained in Mississippi, and many trainees married "natives." So through travel, marriage, and widened contacts, Mississippi's "magnolia curtain" began to lift.[2]

Would Mississippi abandon segregation? The war had sown confusion about segregation's rules—eating, for example. Smith went to Camp Shelby to be processed out of the army. Intending to travel to Louisiana for a visit with Willie Ruth, he offered transport to any of the other men in the room. Two former officers, one white and one black, accepted. Leaving Shelby in the late afternoon, they soon grew hungry and agreed to stop for a meal in a small town. Only then did they realize their predicament. Smith and his white passenger went into the restaurant and asked if the black man could eat with them. The owner said no, but he could eat in the kitchen. They relayed the decision to him, but he refused and would not allow them to bring food out. Most embarrassed individuals readjusted to segregation quietly, surrendering to social pressures. Smith did so in this instance. But in some cases the question of interracial dining sparked near riots. In Jackson, a white officer passing through on his way to Shelby ordered three meals in a downtown grill and had two black soldiers join him. The manager tried to persuade them to leave, and the officer threatened federal prosecution. Word of the confrontation spread quickly, and a crowd gathered outside the grill to see a white man eating with two blacks. The police took all three soldiers into custody for their own safety and turned them over to military authorities, who escorted them back to their train. The crowd observed the events and did not disperse for several hours.[3]

There are scattered stories of white Mississippians rejecting the old segregationist rules. Lt. Van T. Barfoot from Carthage was one who did. Because he had won the Medal of Honor, the Silver Star, and the Bronze Star, Senators Bilbo and Eastland went to a function honoring Barfoot in Washington. Not suspecting Barfoot's racial views, Bilbo asked him if he had had much trouble with "nigras" in Europe. Barfoot said no. He believed blacks fought as well as whites. "I've changed my ideas a lot about colored people, since I got into this war, and so have a lot of other boys from the South." He told Bilbo that he had dinner with a black captain during his trip to Washington. "I've fought with colored men — why shouldn't I eat with them?"[4] Confronted by a such a hero, Bilbo and Eastland could only fume in silence.

Small, tantalizing items in the newspapers attested to the rising winds of change. In Moselle, two sets of brothers, both white, on the morning of primary day argued over allowing blacks to vote. In the afternoon they met again at a service station where the Gerald brothers shot the Phillip brothers, killing one of them. Violent confrontations between whites over black rights represented a change in Mississippi, but many stories stayed the same. Papers reported, as they had often done in the past, that a posse of whites pursued a black man through the countryside. What made this page-one news was that this black was armed with a "high powered army rifle." Black Mississippians had begun to fight in a variety of ways for their rights. Black teachers in Jackson sued for pay equal to that of white teachers. Three blacks were allowed to serve on a jury in south Mississippi. In Greenwood, black veterans organized their first Mississippi chapter of the Veterans of Foreign Wars. Across the state black veterans led a movement to register to vote. These disjointed signs of change pointed toward an impending showdown between the segregationists and blacks demanding their civil rights.[5]

Mississippi political leaders saw the red light and U-turned long before reaching the intersection. During the war, Eastland had anticipated trouble and tried to block absentee voting for soldiers. He also delivered an infamous diatribe on the floor of the Senate against black soldiers. John E. Rankin, representing the eastern Mississippi hills, railed in the House of Representatives against Jews, "niggers," and "kikes." As chairman of a veterans' affairs committee, he held up the GI bill of rights for some time because he feared the education and unemployment provisions would benefit black veterans as well as whites. In 1946, Delta planters "held their noses" and voted for Bilbo, who waged a relentlessly racist campaign for reelection. He abandoned his populism, and they accepted him as a protector of segregation. Governor Fielding Wright went on a statewide radio hookup to warn blacks that, if they were so "deluded" as to believe they could eat in white restaurants, attend white schools, and achieve social equality, they should leave the state for their own good. He did not spell out the consequences, but they were obvious.[6]

While lynching had gone underground, force remained the ultimate white weapon with which to maintain segregation. By the 1940s the white community rarely felt secure enough to conduct public lynchings. In the past, lynchings sometimes had been announced in newspaper notices so that the white public could attend, but white southerners had grown insecure about their right to execute blacks. There were "only" six lynchings in the South during 1946, but there were twenty-four "unlawful" deaths and many near-lynchings such as the one described in Jackson. Southerners still reserved the "right" to maintain segregation by force, but they knew restraint was advisable. From Washington as a freelance writer, Smith tried to publish an article entitled "Killed While Resisting Arrest," exposing a new technique in which the police simply murdered blacks in private executions, but no one bought his article. Bilbo, never one to temper his speeches or miss an opportunity to inflame passions to win votes, used the specter of black voters in his 1946 election campaign and advised whites to visit blacks the night before the election to make sure they did not vote. In Mississippi and throughout the South, violent resistance to integration was widespread and seemed to have the support of the overwhelming majority of the white population.[7]

Smith was one of a small minority of white Mississippians who wished to see black Mississippians achieve their political and social rights as American citizens. His ideas classed him in the fringe with communists, according to Egerton, who found most southern liberals willing to concede segregation if pressed, but few made a positive decision for integration.[8]

Smith knew the odds he faced, but he itched to fulfill his boyhood dream of owning and editing a Mississippi publication to work toward "liberal" reform. In 1945, he wrote to a partner who had helped in his aborted 1939 scheme to establish a Delta magazine, but neither of them had the money needed to found a newspaper. He contacted Hodding Carter, who published the *Delta Democrat Times* in Greenville, to ask about starting a state weekly.[9]

Carter was doing what Smith had dreamed about. He had returned from the war and regained control of his indebted paper, using it to launch attacks against Bilbo and his brand of violent racism. Bilbo made Carter the primary opponent in his reelection campaign. Carter won national recognition and eventually a Pulitzer Prize. He gathered a host of smart young reporters to work for him and was at the center of one of the most exciting papers in the South at a time when newspapers were the exciting place to be. Television had not yet displaced them, and the future looked bright. Mississippi liberals agreed that Mississippi had to have a liberal press to educate the public if change were ever to be possible.[10]

Carter declined to take up Smith's idea for a state paper but told Smith that one of his partners, Jimmy Alsop, intended to establish a paper in Greenwood and that Alsop would offer Smith a position as "desk man." Carter thought this would fit Smith's plans to "freelance" and get him established in journalism. A brief stay in Washington as a GI bill student and unsuccessful freelance writer had convinced Smith that Mississippi would provide better opportunities. Alsop offered employment, and Smith jumped at the job in order to return home.[11]

Smith had known Alsop slightly before the war. At a Delta dance in 1939, Alsop had suggested that they go to Europe to cover the war. Alsop had worked for the *Greenwood Commonwealth* and for newspapers in the Southwest. He had been with Carter during the war, and his family had invested in Carter's Greenville newspaper, where Alsop became associate editor. Alsop soon chafed at being number two in Greenville and announced his intention to establish a "liberal" paper in Greenwood. He told the *Commercial Appeal* that "the people behind the new publication feel that with the progressive attitude in this area comes a need for a liberal newspaper...."[12] Carter agreed to allow Alsop to print his paper on the *Democrat*'s presses at night in order to bring out a morning edition for Greenwood. Alsop moved back to Greenwood and hired Smith to oversee the production of the *Morning Star* in Greenville. Smith arrived in June 1946 to learn the system at the *Democrat*. He and Helen rented a garage apartment and, because he had no car, he rode a public bus to work at five each afternoon. When he was lucky, the Jeep driver who picked up the papers for the trip to Greenwood gave him a ride home at three or four the next morning.[13]

Starting a new paper proved to be a test of skill and endurance. Alsop must have learned it was a mistake to announce the founding of a "liberal" paper. On the front page of the first *Morning Star,* Alsop explained that, contrary to rumor, the *Star* would not be a Greenwood edition of Carter's *Democrat,* which at the time was widely believed to be the most liberal paper in the state. Although it would use some of Carter's editorials, it would, he said, be a local paper and "well rounded" rather than political. Alsop announced that Smith would be "city editor." "[H]e will be in charge of desk work and production at the Greenville end until he can move back to Greenwood when a printing plant is established here."[14]

Initially all went well between Smith and Alsop. Smith wrote a daily column and editorials in addition to setting up the paper from wire reports. In an early note Alsop praised one of Smith's editorials, saying, "That was one of the finest eddys I've ever read...." Alsop promoted Smith to "Mng. Editor" at $225 a month and told Smith that everyone in Greenwood thought he was a "genius." "I agree that you've set everyone on their ear over here with layouts, the sensible heads and your news judgment."[15] But the *Democrat*'s machines broke down. The foreman of the print crew drank and argued constantly with Smith. The papers arrived too late to mail to rural subscribers. In one week the *Star* missed the mailing deadline four days out of six. Smith complained about the lack of news coverage in Greenwood, to which Alsop replied defensively that he had gotten married, had to borrow fifty thousand dollars, and spent all of his time managing, not reporting. To make matters worse, he added, the *Commonwealth,* an established evening daily, remained the "in paper" with the "political cliques." Alsop urged Smith to cut fifteen minutes in each stage of production, to get the paper out on time, and to pamper the mechanical staff. Alsop then undermined Smith's authority with the printing staff. "But one thing I have had to repeat and repeat to the foreman and explain to the operators every time I go over is that you are inexperienced and that a lot of the lags that cause them to sit around waiting for copy is due to lack of coordination and lack of understanding."[16]

When Smith complained about his pay and the long hours, Alsop responded that Smith was not a high-priced desk man. "You are an intelligent boy with no experience who looks as though he could become a good man." He concluded, "If it [the job] is really interfering with your free lance writing and you are looking for a highly paid job with little work or responsibility, we just don't have it."[17]

Apparently the two men smoothed over that row. Just after Frank and Helen Smith's second wedding anniversary, Alsop wrote an article entitled "Star Dust," congratulating them and offering a tribute to their hard work. He explained that Helen had taken over as proofreader to eliminate the many mistakes of the first reader and that the Smiths had spent their anniversary until 2 A.M. putting out the *Star.* He concluded with glowing praise for Smith's ability as editor.[18]

Working the desk, Smith rarely got to be a reporter, but occasionally, by sacrificing sleep, he did. Because of his interest in foreign affairs, he arranged to cover Undersecretary of State Dean Acheson when he spoke to the Delta Council. In that speech, Acheson made the first public announcement of the Marshall Plan to rebuild Europe. Smith correctly called it a major foreign policy statement when other reporters missed the significance of Acheson's remarks. In addition to insight, Smith had a good eye for detail. For example, covering the opening in Rolling Fork of Fielding Wright's gubernatorial campaign, Smith not only got the political news but also provided some flavor of Mississippi campaign style, detailing the pounds of potato salad and the number of Cokes consumed at the rally. Most of Smith's writing consisted of a column called "About Mississippi," dedicated to topics ranging from political biographies of candidates to commentary on newsworthy issues and recycled history pieces from his unsold collection.[19]

Alsop and Smith produced a newspaper that was liberal for the Mississippi Delta in the 1940s. For example, they carried front-page coverage of the arrest of six white men who beat a black man to death for stealing a saddle and followed the article with an editorial from the *Democrat* approving the prosecution of the murderers. In international affairs, they endorsed the United Nations and called for more U.N. powers to keep world peace. On the state level, Smith condemned prohibition and the ridiculous "black market" tax that the state imposed on bootleg alcohol. Mississippi was "dry" but taxed liquor shipped from neighboring states for sale by bootleggers. Smith called for the repeal of prohibition and for a system of state stores to sell liquor. On racial issues, Smith wrote coyly. For example, he asked for increased state funding for black colleges but employed segregationist logic: "Our state has been fortunate enough to escape Federal court litigation over negro education, and none will develop if wise administration continues."[20]

The paper struggled to keep Mississippians in the American mainstream. Writing on foreign affairs, Smith, for example, encouraged Mississippians not to fall prey to isolationism. Commenting on state politics, the paper urged Mississippians not to withdraw from America's progress toward recognizing the rights of blacks. For example, when the U.S. Senate refused to seat Mississippi's demagogic Bilbo because of the threats he made against black voters in his campaign and the national press condemned the state as benighted, Smith refused to become defensive or chauvinistic. Many Mississippi editors reacted by striking back at Bilbo's critics. Smith admitted the country's criticism of Mississippi, but, he said, "there is also no reason to get the idea that the whole world is against us." He urged his readers to develop the state and not to waste time and energy being "mad at the rest of the world."[21] Smith and Alsop used the paper to promote internationalism abroad and mainstream Americanism at home.

Yet despite their original common commitment to a liberal paper, Smith's differences with Alsop flared up again in the spring of 1947 when Smith felt that Alsop undermined their principles in reporting a labor dispute. While telephone workers were conducting a national strike, Alsop wrote that "the little people of the country have had enough of John L. Lewis type dictatorship and monopoly."[22] Calling on President Truman to intervene, Alsop reported that pickets in Greenwood disliked being ordered by union bosses in Atlanta to strike. He said that this strike demonstrated the damage done by nationwide collective bargaining and concluded his editorial with calls for legislative controls on labor. Smith, who supported unions, was furious and wrote privately to Alsop that people of the South were not "naturally destined to make less money [than the national work force]." He said that he had come to work for the *Star* "[b]ecause I thought I was working for something that would help in the long run to put over some progressive ideas for Mississippi." Alsop's item had caused him to think, he said, that "[i]f it [the *Star*] is going to be like that in the future, I don't want to help build it up."[23]

The paper was making progress. In June, Alsop reported that the original estimate had been that it would take a hundred and fifty thousand dollars and four years to reach a circulation of three thousand, but with less than a hundred thousand dollars in one year the paper already had four thousand readers. Alsop announced the end of a "nightmare" year in which, he said, the paper had battled "slander, gossip, and resentment." With the opening of the Greenwood printing plant, he wrote, "Frank Smith no longer will have to plan composition of the entire paper."[24] When the new printing plant opened, Smith returned to Greenwood and plunged into politics.

As a young man in a hurry, Smith naturally gravitated to politics. His father had been tipped to run for sheriff before his death; Smith's uncle served as sheriff. Smith practically grew up in the courthouse where his mother worked. He had not been able to fulfill his ambitions to write while establishing the newspaper, and he was impatient to get ahead. His first target, Leflore County's seat in the Mississippi Senate, was not a highly prized political plum. Leflore had a "swap" arrangement with Tallahatchie County so that they alternated sending a senator to the legislature at each election. This arrangement required each senator to serve only one term before conceding the seat to the other county in the next election. Smith's job at the paper left little time for campaigning, and he could afford to buy only one advertisement in the newspaper. But he had dozens of relatives in the county, and his mother had become an institution in county government, serving in the sheriff's office and the circuit clerk's office ever since his father's death. He did not lack for contacts and family support. When the polls closed on primary election day, Smith went "home" to Sidon to await the results. Smith won, along with a cousin who won the far more important post of county supervisor that night, and they celebrated their victories in the little hometown among relatives. Smith defeated two other candidates, Dr. S. E. Osborne and John R. Roberts, without a runoff, by a 388-vote margin.[25] Smith thus became senator-elect in August 1947, because in Mississippi's one-party system no Republican would challenge him in the general election.

With Smith and Alsop working in the same building, their stormy relationship worsened. Smith supported the ambitions of the Leflore County sheriff to be highway commissioner during the primary election. Alsop, who was campaigning against the sheriff in the newspaper, could not accept what he considered Smith's defiance, and Smith began to resent what he considered Alsop's lack of political insight. Alsop probably saw Smith's political ambitions as a sellout to the county establishment. In a letter to Smith, Alsop had earlier described the Leflore political "clique" as "slightly mouldy"— "the group stirs a faint feeling that I've seen them in a novel or a picture about an old regime."[26] Shortly after his election to the senate, Smith was late with a column, and the printer refused to hold the editorial page for Smith's article. In a rage Smith gave Alsop the choice of firing the printer or accepting his own resignation. Alsop chose to keep the printer and stated in a front-page note that Smith had resigned to pursue his political career.[27]

In fact, Smith was unemployed. He had "resigned" from the *Star* and would not take his seat in the legislature until the 1948 session. He appealed again to Hodding Carter for work, and Carter recommended him to the editors of the Rivers of America series as the writer of a volume on the Yazoo River. Smith was given a contract, and he began to outline the book while he looked for a job.[28]

When Bilbo died, in 1947, the special election to fill his senate seat was scheduled for the general election. That November race was to provide Smith with employment and a start in statewide politics. John Stennis, a judge in the circuit court, was being groomed by Mississippi State College alumni as their candidate for governor, and was running early as a long-shot candidate for the senate. He opposed two congressmen and a former governor. Stennis had first hired Erle Johnston, who had been publicity director in Governor Fielding Wright's 1947 primary race, to be his publicity man. But Johnston was working to develop his county newspaper, and Stennis became dissatisfied with him. One of Stennis's Greenwood supporters recommended Smith for the job; Smith took it readily. Moving to the Stennis headquarters suite at the King Edward Hotel in Jackson, Smith devoted himself day and night to the campaign. He became office manager as well as publicity man. Working in a long sample room of the suite that usually held the wares of traveling salesmen, Smith supervised six to seven typists, answered letters, wrote ads, talked to whoever drifted in day and night, and produced news releases. He created sixty releases from one three-page speech written by Stennis. On Sundays, Smith participated in meetings of "Governor Wright's brain trust," whose members gathered to offer Stennis advice. Smith slept in the bedroom of the campaign suite, never resting from politics throughout the contest.[29]

Smith had been attracted to Stennis when he covered one of Stennis's speeches for the *Star*. Stennis had supported the United Nations, which was unusual for a Mississippi politician. Most Mississippi leaders condemned foreign aid and international organizations. Stennis's standard speech contained a paragraph endorsing federal aid to education, which again was unusual in a state already concerned over attempts to integrate schools. Stennis styled himself as a conservative and a states' rights man, but he asked for a fair deal for labor, and said nothing about race. He said that when he had asked his father what to say on race, "He said 'nothing'—and that is what I am doing."[30] Percy Greene, editor of the state's black newspaper, supported Stennis privately because Stennis appeared to be the most moderate of the candidates. When Truman's Civil Rights Commission released a report requiring Stennis to make a statement, Stennis said, "Our customs and our traditions may be assailed, but we can stand firm on our rights to make our own decisions about such matters."[31] In the climate of the times, Stennis's quiet was helpful. This proved to be the last election in which most southern politicians could use Stennis's tactic. The developing civil rights movement and Truman's actions toward integration soon made it impossible to avoid taking an openly segregationist position.

Stennis's opponents tried to use his moderation against him. Congressman William Colmer secretly spread the word that Stennis was tainted with communism. Congressman Will Whittington from the Delta condemned Stennis for his silence on the Taft-Hartley law, which was the hottest labor issue in the country. Rumors spread that Henry Wallace, the former vice president, had endorsed Stennis and that Drew Pearson, the national columnist, supported him. Mostly, Stennis spoke in generalities, promised to promote agriculture, and used his Mississippi State College support to create a statewide network. Smith did not succeed in getting Stennis wide coverage in the Jackson papers, which all supported better-known candidates, but the *Commercial Appeal, Delta Democrat Times,* and others were receptive. The *Democrat* carried Stennis releases first in their coverage of the election, while the *Commercial Appeal* used them in second place, with Colmer first. Stennis, because he offended fewer people with his talk of agricultural support, got the largest number of votes in a special election that required no runoff.[32]

Stennis took his campaign manager, Bob Morrow, to Washington as his chief assistant, and Smith was invited in second place as "secretary." Smith was disappointed by the offer but went with no intention of remaining in the role of assistant. He made his ambitions clear by refusing Stennis's requests that he resign his seat in the state senate. Smith had his eye on the Delta's congressional district. Smith called himself Stennis's "legislative assistant" to lend more dignity to his position and to bolster his credentials for the race he intended to make when the Delta's Will Whittington decided to retire from Congress.[33]

After six weeks in Washington with Stennis, Smith returned to Jackson for the 1948 session of the Mississippi legislature, where he needed to build a record in order to run for Congress. Walter Sillers, speaker of the Mississippi House of Representatives, dominated the legislature. Sillers, a lawyer and planter from the Delta, had served in the house of representatives since the 1920s. He seriously believed that Harry Truman was either a communist or else dangerously influenced by communists. Sillers naturally opposed any "liberal" or progressive legislation. Oscar Wolfe, a Sillers man, was one of the most influential members of the state senate, where he did Sillers's bidding while waiting to replace Whittington in Congress. Fielding Wright, the governor, opened the political year with an inaugural address challenging the national Democratic party to abandon civil rights legislation or face an open revolt dedicated to "preserving the Southern way of life."[34]

Mississippi did not join the rest of the South in recognizing the hopelessness of the Dixiecrats. Eastland and Wright tried to "outnigger" one another in mouthing their resistance to integration. Against the entrenched, segregationist, conservative establishment, "thirty or forty" new legislators hoped to make some changes. Almost a dozen were still students at Ole Miss, supported by their GI bill income, and nearly all of them were veterans who had returned from the war hoping that their sacrifices could be translated into a better state and world. Smith knew most of them and considered them idealists moderated by the realities of the Mississippi political situation. Smith, who listed his occupation as "writer" and his mother's address in Greenwood as his home, was one of the group. But he played the game according to the political rules he had learned from childhood. For example, when a candidate ran against Wolfe for senate leadership, Smith quickly promised his support to Wolfe, who was his Delta neighbor. In a one-party state where the normal give-and-take of a two-party system did not exist and politics excluded the majority of the people, neighbors were expected to support one another because they were united in excluding blacks from the process. Major political differences are not aired openly in such a system. In Mississippi's one-party politics, all political decisions were personal. Having spent his childhood in the Leflore County Courthouse, Smith understood this system perfectly, so he avoided personalized attacks while playing a wily game. Twenty senators promised to support Wolfe. Twenty promised to support his challenger, and nine had promised to support both men. Partially to save embarrassment, a compromise emerged by which Wolfe retained leadership but agreed to resign in favor of his challenger before the end of the term. Because Wolfe intended to run for Whittington's congressional seat, he would not be able to continue in the senate post, and so the compromise suited everyone.[35]

Smith signed on as cosponsor of a host of popular bills. Knowing the Delta's support for terminating prohibition, he concentrated his time on alcohol bills; understanding the need to attract veterans' votes, he took an interest in their affairs. He served on five committees, including those likely to interest his district, such as the agricultural and levees committees. He chaired only one — military affairs. He successfully secured the passage of two laws in 1948. One reorganized an office of veterans' affairs more to the liking of the VFW, and the second funded a historical commission to erect historical markers in the state.[36]

The seemingly innocuous historical commission bill demonstrated the problems of legislating in Mississippi's one-party system, showing how racial or ideological conflicts infected apparently innocent attempts to reform. Smith wrote the original historical markers bill to have the history department chairmen at the three largest white schools constitute a commission to decide on the merits of applications for markers. Mrs. Sillers, who headed the Daughters of the American Revolution, heard that the professors were about to be given control of the new commission and protested to her husband; the speaker then had Smith's bill amended in the house to make representatives of the DAR and the United Daughters of the Confederacy members of the commission instead. Smith got half of what he wanted only because the house of representatives' secretary accidentally typed both sets of commissioners into the revised bill. Smith privately gloated that as a result such "reds" as Jim Silver got control of the historical markers commission.[37]

It was not an important issue, but it illustrates the strength of feeling about history. Control of the past concerned segregationists, who knew well that to protect their "way of life" they had to keep close guard over memories of "the war" and Reconstruction. Their version of southern history was central to the segregationist mindset. Smith understood and in his small way attempted to bring about change.

Obviously, the establishment felt threatened by even the most minor changes that might weaken their grip. The "reform" group of young legislators chose as their first cause Sunday movies. Mississippi blue laws made it illegal to open theaters on Sunday. A house of representatives group adopted and persuaded the legislature to enact a law to give local communities the option of having movies and sports events open on Sunday. Smith made the news with a similar assault on the establishment by proposing to legalize the sale of alcohol, with state stores authorized to handle all liquor. He offered a backup bill that was short of ending prohibition but would have legalized personal possession of liquor. When the bills came to a final vote, Smith condemned the "Unholy Alliance" of preachers and bootleggers who combined against the proposal. He said in senate debate, "[I]t is time for the people of Mississippi to demand an end to this unholy league which conspires to defeat law enforcement in our state."[38] He and his cosponsor, Fred Jones, cast their measures in segregationist rhetoric, asking how Mississippians could justify their fight for states' rights if counties were denied local option on liquor. Smith's fight for legalized liquor was meant to be "progressive," but Sillers supported it, too, and the bills were popular in the Delta, where prohibition was openly ignored. But with the hill vote and prohibition forces united against them, he and Jones failed to end prohibition, and it endured into the 1960s.[39]

The only truly progressive piece of legislation to pass in 1948 was a workmen's compensation act. Mississippi was the only state to lack such a law by 1948. The "liberal" house group helped to pass a bill bringing Mississippi labor laws up to national standards. They then arranged to have Smith handle the bill in senate debate. A house sponsor, who described the fight for the bill as the "hardest battle" of his life, sat in Smith's place in the senate, while Smith conducted the bill through debate. He remembered being at the point of "fisticuffs" with Governor Wright while persuading him to sign the act. Significant though it was, the workmen's compensation law was a crumb to the progressives, who were silenced by the uproar created by the states' rights movement in the legislature.[40]

Governor Wright opened the campaign to preserve segregation, and the legislature maintained a hysterical level of excitement over attacks on the "southern way of life." For example, news of an Oklahoma court case in which the law school was ordered to admit a black applicant prompted one of the progressives in the house to introduce a bill to require Mississippi schools to teach both the Mississippi Constitution, which supported segregation, and the United States Constitution, which the Supreme Court seemed to be using to further integration, to all students. Instead, after a heated debate, the house passed a resolution congratulating Oklahoma for its resistance to integration.[41]

Jim Eastland, senior Mississippi U.S. senator, pushed political hysteria to a higher level by returning from Washington to address a joint session of the legislature. Condemning the Truman administration and warning against "Mongrels" among them, he vowed to stand with Wright to defend southern institutions. Quoting John C. Calhoun, he talked of throwing the presidential election into the U.S. House of Representatives, where southern strength would force the election of a president committed to maintaining segregation. A few days later the excited legislature passed a resolution calling on Congress to pass a law to deal with anyone complaining of discrimination by establishing a new agency empowered to remove from the state "such persons, their household goods, including their dogs, their chickens, and all personal belongings."[42]

The Truman administration's tentative moves to assure equality for black Americans fed the ever-growing hysteria in Mississippi that cowed Smith along with other dissidents into silence. Smith intended to return to Stennis's employ and thus had to be extremely careful in his public pronouncements. Because Stennis was quiet on the segregation issue and moderate compared to other Mississippi leaders, his reelection was far from assured. Given his relationship with Stennis and his own ambitions, Smith knew that the most he could do under the circumstances was say nothing and hope that the storm would pass.

While Eastland addressed the legislature, Stennis quietly promised to fight in the Senate Rules Committee to keep the poll tax. But then Stennis seemed to vacillate. In February, he came to Governor Wright's states' rights rally in Jackson. As a voice of moderation, he urged rally participants in the national Democratic party to remain in and to keep the fight for segregation. Wright's plan to withdraw and form a third party, he said, could be considered if the fight were lost in the Democratic party. But then he asked whites to use their "influence over blacks" to head off any integration or voting rights movement.

Fred Sullens, editor of the *Jackson Daily News,* ignored Stennis's quibble over the intended Dixiecrat withdrawal from the Democratic party and said that five thousand faces were "set" with hard determination at the rally with "not even a slight difference of opinion." Sullens declared that there were "no limits" to which the South would not go to protect itself from its unspecified enemies who threatened its "way of life." Smith stayed away from the rally. His only open protest was to refuse to buy and wear a "States' Rights" button when most of the legislators adopted it as the universal symbol of support for Wright's program to protect segregation. It had been clear from the summer of 1947 that southern politicians would not lead the region toward any progressive solution to its problems. They preferred "feudalism." Seeking a liberal wing in the Mississippi Democratic party in 1947, a political science researcher found one acknowledged liberal working as a state bureaucrat in Jackson. He patiently explained to the investigator that there were no supporters for a liberal wing of the party. There were no businessmen willing to bankroll a liberal, no patronage, and no establishment of any sort willing to support a liberal. He felt his bosses liked to keep him in his office so as to watch him closely in case he thought of embarking on any liberal crusade. He said the best he could do was to try to slip a progressive idea or two into the governor's speeches he was sometimes asked to write.[43]

When the legislature adjourned, Smith returned to Stennis's office in Washington hopeful, despite the Dixiecrat revolt, that nationally the political situation could be salvaged. He learned his way around Capitol Hill while trying to intervene in Mississippi politics. Smith did constituent service for the senator and on his own tried to promote Mississippi support for President Harry Truman. When the Mississippi Democratic party leadership deserted Truman because of his support for civil rights, Smith prodded his former professor Jim Silver and his old friend Philip Mullen, son of the editor of the *Oxford Eagle,* to create a slate of Truman electors for the 1948 presidential race. In July, Mullen wrote that unless George McLean, editor of the Tupelo paper, or Dennis Murphree, a former governor, could be persuaded to take part it would be best to pass on the project. "I'm not kidding myself that a great many of the 'ordinary' people are in favor of the whole thing. There is no way you can rationalize with them after Nigger has been yelled. Too, there is bound to be a wave of sympathy for the delegation, Mississippi standing against a hostile and misunderstanding world."[44]

All the leaders passed, and Smith refused to be a Truman elector, but Silver got law students to work for a Truman slate and Mullen went along. Their efforts had no effect. From his place in the press gallery, Smith watched the Mississippi delegation walk out of the Democratic convention in Philadelphia, and afterward all the leading Mississippi Democrats abandoned the national party for the Dixiecrats. Truman's victory in November did nothing for his idealistic supporters in Mississippi. By December, Mullen wrote that he and his father were going to "wind up" the "laughing stock" of Mississippi politics if the Democratic party did not provide at least patronage rewards for them and others who were loyal to the national party. He reported that during the half-time at the University of Mississippi "Law Day football game" some students had staged a "scene" in which Mullen went begging to President Truman and got a quarter. He concluded, "The ridicule is getting tiresome." He warned Smith, "I'm writing you all of this because if you hadn't punched me along, and encouraged me, I never would have got mixed up in the thing."[45] He threatened to give Smith credit in a report to the national Democratic party.

Although Mullen received nothing for his support of Truman, he did not follow through on his threat because he knew it would destroy Smith's career. Truman won the presidency, and Smith, Mullen, and Silver still nursed some hope for Stennis as a moderating influence on the Mississippi party. Through Smith, Mullen tried to enlist Stennis's support within the Mississippi party against Eastland's men. After Stennis visited the University of Mississippi to make a speech to a student group, Silver commented, "I do hope that he'll move a bit to the left, but I realize that he has to go slowly in a state such as Miss."[46] Smith must have fueled their hopes. He reported to Hodding Carter that Truman would introduce civil rights legislation in Congress late in the session and asserted that a constitutional amendment against the poll tax was "sure" to pass Congress. But the segregationist forces ruled in Mississippi. Wright and Sillers remained adamant Dixiecrats, while most southern leaders quietly and quickly abandoned the party after Truman's victory. In Congress, Speaker Sam Rayburn refused to punish the Dixiecrats and allowed them to keep their powerful committee chairmanships. Smith lamented the decision, but he felt that Eastland was increasingly unpopular among Mississippi politicians and tried to reassure his friends that the situation was not hopeless.[47]

Smith's old friend and first intellectual companion, Dale Mullen, wrote Smith a good-bye as he moved out of Mississippi to work toward a Ph.D. and to begin, he said, an "unambitious" life as a professor. "I will vote for you, but I can not hope for you. [T]here is no hope. If the bomb doesn't get you, erosion will. Aside from that, fighting for the right is probably a pretty good way of life too, maybe as good as professoring. Phil [Mullen] has got to a point where he can no longer be cynical, as he once tried. He must fight for the right; it is more important to him than eating. And I'd be mighty proud to see you in Congress."[48] Silver received a Fulbright grant and went to England in order to have a look at the Labour Party's new socialism. He felt British socialism had gotten a bad press, and so he arranged to write a series of articles on the subject for Carter to publish in the *Democrat*.[49]

Blacks in Mississippi drew the line more and more clearly for white politicians. In March 1949, Governor Wright spoke to a black teachers' meeting in Jackson trying to justify his support for segregation, and, as the audience grew more hostile, the governor began to ramble, claiming he never used the word "nigger." A teacher from a small private college responded that blacks wanted immediate access to opportunities and told Wright, "If you hate me because I am dirty, I'll clean myself; if you hate me because I'm ignorant, I'll educate myself. But if you hate me because I'm black, I can only leave you to the God that made me." Such confrontations made the segregationists more resolute to resist and to cut off Mississippi from national trends.[50]

During the summer of 1949, the liberals' gloom about Mississippi infected Smith, too. He grew discouraged with Stennis and told Mullen that he wished he could work for Lister Hill or Estes Kefauver instead of Stennis. Hill and Kefauver were liberal senators from Alabama and Tennessee. In August 1949, Smith wrote to congratulate Carter on an article he had written about poor whites in the South, concluding, "Perhaps it will cause a few people to understand why the Southern liberal or any Southerner of progressive stripe must primarily concern himself with trying to improve the economic position of his people." But Smith concluded that despite his best efforts for liberal reform his own "usefulness in Washington" had reached the point of "diminishing returns" and he would be "retiring" without "any plans."[51]

Despite his growing pessimism over the prospects for liberalism in the state, Smith continued to shuttle between Washington and Jackson to build a record so that he could make a run at a seat in Congress. In the fall, Smith attended the 1949 special session of the state legislature called by Wright to appropriate highway funds. Smith made news as one of three senate members "on the fence" regarding a gas tax to support the roads project. He intended to support it, but he wanted to milk the publicity that being "undecided" would earn him, and he hoped that not committing immediately would provide some political leverage. Wolfe acted as a "ringleader" to defeat the tax, which Sillers and legislative leaders did not want for a variety of reasons. They hated new taxes, and they did not wish to see Governor Wright grow any stronger. Smith worked for an amendment to require a "standard county unit system" as a means of making county government more efficient. Smith's purpose was to end the county supervisors' control of separate road building fiefdoms in the counties and to introduce savings by centralizing county operations. Neither Smith's plan nor the tax passed, and the special session ended in failure.[52]

When the regular legislative session convened in January 1950, Smith left Stennis's office staff permanently to finish out his senate term and then to run for Congress. With Smith gone, Stennis moved his office staff to the right by replacing Smith with Governor Wright's son. The *Jackson Daily News* noted that this appointment assured Stennis's unity with Wright. Perhaps Smith had too much hope for Stennis. Stennis never wavered in his support of segregation; in a letter to Carter, Stennis revealed strong racist sentiments. When Carter requested Stennis's support for Hawaiian statehood, Stennis responded, "I just can not favor taking any state in the Union that is largely Asiatic."[53] Smith's reputation against such racism was no secret among those who knew him in Washington. A Washington gossip columnist called Smith "an outstanding Southern liberal" and praised him for giving up his seventy-five-hundred-dollar salary in Washington to return to the Mississippi legislature for fifteen hundred dollars.[54]

Though Smith probably hoped that Mississippians would not hear from Washington of his liberalism, he did set out to make a name for himself as a reformer in the 1950 legislature. He began by researching the Mississippi law code and finding two dozen outdated laws to repeal. The laws ranged from Confederate pensions and laws against fishing on Sunday to one that required streetcars to heat their vestibules. Most were unimportant. Smith's goal was to make headlines and keep his name before the voters, but he ran into problems even with these "reforms." For example, when he attempted to end required stop signs at rail crossings, he discovered that railroad companies needed those signs to prevent lawsuits over injuries and damages suffered in accidents. Wolfe, who chaired the transportation committee, killed Smith's bill to repeal that law. The race for the Delta congressional seat generated rumors in the legislature, but Smith was not mentioned as a candidate in the early stages.[55]

He kept busy sponsoring technical and housekeeping bills suggested by National Guard leaders, introducing a measure to provide free car tags to National Guard members, and even a bill "prohibiting abandonment or running at large of house cats." He continued his fight to end prohibition, and, as a corollary to that, he secured the passage of a useful bill to provide for the commitment of alcoholics to hospitals. Basing his bill on a Yale University-produced model, Smith worked with health care professionals to help establish a law to provide treatment for alcoholics.[56]

To supplement his income and to get his name before the voters while serving in the legislature, Smith began to write a syndicated column entitled "About Mississippi." In his columns, he discussed major issues being debated in the legislature and other matters of public note. For example, in his first article, he argued against proposals to amend the U.S. Constitution to limit the tax powers of the federal government. Always favoring an active government, he pointed out that Mississippi received $1,650,000 from the federal government for every $1 million paid in federal taxes. Regarding a proposal to limit the state budget, he pleaded with opponents to consider the services being provided by the funds and argued against diminishing the state's capacity to carry out such services. Clearly, he did not disguise his liberalism in fiscal affairs.[57]

Sometimes Smith's attitudes shocked his colleagues. For example, during a debate over prohibition, his senate seatmate at their double desk in the chamber, Decatur Butler, provoked a widely reported, heated exchange. Replying to Smith's argument for a bill to allow cities in dry counties to legalize beer, Butler asserted that a vote for Smith's bill would violate his own ethics. Smith replied angrily, "What do you mean by that?" Butler retorted, "Are you a Christian?" Given Smith's less-than-fundamentalist beliefs, it was a dangerous question, but Smith responded, "If you want to get down to brass tacks, I think I am. But I don't tell the world if you don't agree with me you're not a Christian." Few Mississippi senators would have uttered such a vaguely worded expression of their faith in Christianity. Smith's ideals and his temper could lead him into trouble.[58]

Since he intended to run for Congress, he was lucky that the establishment—Sillers, Wolfe, and other legislative leaders—paid little attention to him at that point. At the opening of the 1950 session, the *Commercial Appeal* legislative correspondent had carefully listed the aspirants in the legislature for various political offices but failed to mention Smith. Only Wolfe was noted as seeking the Delta congressional seat. At the opening of the legislative session, Sillers had easily survived a minor revolt by the "liberal" group in the house of representatives and seemed all-powerful in Mississippi. He threw his support behind Wolfe to replace Whittington in Washington.[59] The politicians would have probably echoed Alsop's assessment of Smith in 1950 as a "boy" who might become a good man if he were patient and paid his dues. Smith would not wait and gambled his fate and fortune on a run for Congress, defying the establishment and the long odds against him. Given the views Smith had expressed in print during his junior college and freelance writing days, it was a brave or foolhardy decision.

CHAPTER SIX

Election to Congress

The Delta district would never have elected a known liberal to Congress. Its black majority counties gave Truman his lowest Mississippi returns in 1948. Planters and businessmen operated a closed political system in which they gathered to select a candidate who was then elected in the Democratic primary election by a small voting public. Usually no more than forty people turned out for a county caucus, and twenty of those came because a politician had herded them to the meeting to support him. Seventy percent of the population was black and disfranchised. Only a few hundred of the thousands of black Deltans could vote. When black veterans traveled the state to urge their fellow veterans to take advantage of a law exempting them from poll taxes, no one went to the Delta because it appeared too tough to risk traveling there. Poll taxes, as well as the requirement that voters present poll tax receipts for the past two years when voting, also discouraged poor whites. Discrimination against blacks and stringent voting rules made the Delta congressional electorate one of the smallest in the nation. Politics did not engage white Deltans as it did "rednecks" in the hills, where politics was a major source of entertainment. In the Delta, the lower classes had juke joints and liquor to distract them. The upper classes were more concerned with making money. Few planters could be persuaded to accept offices paying small returns compared to the fortunes available to them. They selected the ablest men who would accept political jobs and prided themselves on running low-cost, efficient government. When Smith ran for Congress, Deltans were running the state, as well as their fiefs in the Delta, according to their conservative social and economic ideas, as they had throughout much of Mississippi history.[1]

In 1950, Smith challenged the planters on their home turf. Speaker Sillers of Rosedale, who represented the planter tradition, was the most powerful man in Mississippi. He had followed a family tradition of entering politics and had served since the 1920s in the legislature. Working within the undemocratic political system, he had maneuvered his control over the legislature to the point of absolutism. Mississippi's Catholic bishop once remarked that Sillers was responsible only to God and himself. All speakers were potentially powerful. Mississippi's governors were forbidden to succeed themselves and thus could neither build a strong political base nor compete effectively with the legislature. Sillers could control legislation from his office in the house of representatives. He had extensive land holdings in the Delta and, of course, connections throughout the power structure. He wanted Wolfe elected to succeed Will Whittington, and he usually got what he wanted.

Whittington had migrated to the Delta as a teacher and made himself into a planter as well as a congressman through hard work. He acted somewhat independently of the states' rights Mississippi Democrats and remained in good standing with the national party. For example, while the national party cut other Mississippi congressmen out of the patronage system, he alone continued to exercise his prerogative to appoint postmasters. Whittington came from Greenwood, and there were charges from other towns that because of him most federal funds went to Leflore County. Sillers and other Delta leaders felt that the time had come for other parts of the Delta to have a turn in Congress. Sillers probably desired to have a congressman obligated to him in Washington, and certainly he wanted one who would be unquestionably loyal to the states' rights movement.

Smith was ill suited for Sillers's purposes. His youthful liberalism could not have been a secret in the small world of Delta whites. Moreover, he represented the hill immigrants who William Alexander Percy had predicted would destroy the "aristocratic" control of the Delta. Smith had attended junior college with the children of those immigrants during the depression, and his classmates from Moorhead provided the nucleus of his support. Smith remembered only one "boy" from his Moorhead class who did not support him, and he understood why. The man had gone on from Moorhead to Ole Miss and married a neighbor of Wolfe's, so he could not support Smith for family reasons. All of the other junior college classmates did. Even if they remembered Smith's racial views, the ties binding the white "caste" together were so strong that it never occurred to Smith's former classmates that he might be any danger to segregation.

In Smith's view his Moorhead classmates represented the Delta's lower middle class and shared a sense of unity that separated them from the planters. Although he realized that they did not understand themselves in those terms, he campaigned with them in mind. Willie Ruth Cowan, married to a geologist and living in Jackson in 1950, believed that Smith especially appealed to their "class" of people because he had entered the army as a private and worked his way through the ranks when most college graduates went directly to officer candidate school. Smith's family worked as farmers and held county offices, but none of them had achieved planter status. He could count on "middle-class" support at home, but had no ties to the planters. Nor could Smith count on help from the legal community. According to Carter, not one Greenville lawyer supported Smith in his campaign. Smith remembered two whom Carter overlooked, but the only lawyer to support him actively was an outsider who took no part in the legal "club." Smith did not belong to, or even visit, the Greenwood country club. His supporters were members of the VFW, which served as a sort of poor man's country club in the Delta. Yet all Delta whites automatically received membership in the white caste by virtue of their skin color, and the divisions among them melted away when faced with questions of race. Because they always faced this question, class antagonisms could never be openly discussed or used in political contests. Debates had to be conducted in what amounted to a secret code understood only by the white caste, concealing all divisions from the black population and any outsiders. The divisive election that put Smith in Congress in some respects resembled a Delta family feud.[2]

Smith understood the white Delta code well and was careful not to introduce any "foreign" elements. Carter, an immigrant from Louisiana, offered to support Smith, but Smith asked him to delay any endorsement until the end of the second primary. Bilbo had based his last political race on attacking Carter, whom he had labeled as a liberal or worse, and Smith had no desire to be harnessed with Carter in the public mind. Trumanite Phil Mullen sent Smith two hundred dollars, which Smith accepted, but in his thank-you note, he wrote, "Phil, please don't let anyone know you gave it to me."[3] In jest, Jim Silver offered his services as a "pinko liberal" stump speaker. Smith refused, of course.[4] He ran as the son of Sadie Smith and of a father martyred in the perpetual southern race war, as a clever product of the Greenwood public schools, as a graduate of depression-era Moorhead (Sunflower Junior College), and as a veteran who had worked his way through the ranks. He did not have to tell voters most of these things, because in the small world of the Delta everyone knew his life story by word of mouth.

The Delta district included eleven counties. Three counties held a big percentage of the white population and thus the voters. Greenville, with 23,000, was the largest city and the center of Washington County. Greenwood, the second-largest city and center of Leflore County, had about 16,500 whites. Bolivar County (19,868), with a relatively large population of small white farmers, constituted the third population center. Its major city was Cleveland. "Courthouse rings," or informal "parties" of officeholders, existed in six of the eleven counties, but only two were strong enough to help anyone. The Delta Council, a "super" chamber of commerce representing the planters' interests, backed Wolfe, but had no truly effective means of delivering the votes of the lower-middle-class whites who made up the majority of voters. Its political powers were limited. The sheriffs and county supervisors were the most powerful elected officials, but they had little influence in congressional races.[5]

Whittington, who had reached retirement age, announced his intention not to seek reelection in 1950, and Wolfe declared immediately. Smith uttered some platitudes to the effect that Whittington should reconsider his retirement but then declared his candidacy also. He quickly made the rounds of the prominent citizens in Greenwood, knowing that he had to generate local support to have any chance of winning. There was some local sentiment for supporting Whittington's son, who was serving in the Mississippi House of Representatives, but it never developed into a serious movement. Smith spent long weekends during the legislative session in the Delta talking to whoever would listen. Using his junior college network, he was introduced throughout the Delta. Forrest Cooper, an Indianola lawyer, was making the same rounds, but he withdrew in May, "opening up" Sunflower and Humphreys counties for Smith. Lomax Lamb, a Yale-educated lawyer Smith's age, entered the race. But coming from Marks in Quitman County, he lacked the strong local base that Smith had in Leflore County and Wolfe had in Bolivar.[6]

Smith gathered fifty "boosters" at the Greenwood Leflore Hotel to listen to his platform and to map a campaign strategy. He outlined his views in three neat paragraphs. First, he said he would look after the economic interests of his district, focusing on flood control and agriculture, the most important issues. Second, he promised to fight the "regimentation" of government, the necessary code word meaning that he would fight to prevent federal action against segregation. Third, he argued that he would assist congressional efforts to insure that the United States provided the necessary "world leadership" to combat communism. He passionately believed in the first and third goals. He knew the second was required of him if he wished to represent the Delta. Not a few Mississippi politicians despised what they had to say to get elected. Senator Pat Harrison told Turner Catledge, a fellow Mississippian who became the editor of the *New York Times,* that he could be a statesman for five years, but, during the sixth, he returned home to "sling the shit."[7]

Means Johnston, prominent lawyer, neighbor, and family friend, agreed to be Smith's figurehead campaign manager. That is, he allowed the use of his name without promising to actually work in the campaign. Greenwood's wealthiest citizen, Rowell Billups, a local oil and gas man, offered little money but some free advice. He told Smith to go back to the legislature and introduce a bill to increase gasoline taxes so that the gas and oil lobbyists would buy him off. Grudgingly, Billups gave Smith three hundred dollars because he disliked Wolfe for accusing him of corruption in connection with his gas business. Billups stipulated that Smith had to spend all of the money in Bolivar County, Wolfe's home, because Billups's real interest lay not in seeing Smith elected but in seeing Wolfe embarrassed. Billups had supported Smith's opponent in the 1947 legislature race and obviously had no interest in his winning higher office in 1950. Such were the personal politics of the Delta. In a one-party system where suppression of blacks remained the overriding but unquestioned issue, politics revolved around personal and territorial loyalties. Issues mattered relatively little. Smith knew the best campaign plan was to meet as many voters as possible and ask them for their vote.[8]

With the legislature in session until April, Smith spent long weekends in the Delta doing what he had advised Willie Ruth to do for him. "Talk to everybody you know and tell them whatever appears to be pleasing to their ears."[9] The white Deltans were a small, close-knit society, and Smith's boyhood liberalism was a problem. He warned Willie Ruth, "Quite a rumor campaign has been started against me already. . . ." But he chose to interpret the campaign in a positive light. "I think that is a very [good] indication of the strength developed."[10] Issues might arise, but Smith knew to ignore those and to concentrate on his personal appeal as a homegrown candidate.

He ignored Lamb because he knew there was little difference between them. When they entered the race, their letters appealing to one another for support passed in the mail. Because his family had more money, Lamb had escaped the Delta, as Smith had wished he could, to study at Yale and in Europe. He, too, was a veteran. Smith would admit later that all he had against Lamb was that he was in the race. Smith relied on Leflore County "patriotism" and his impeccable credentials as a local man to eliminate Lamb.[11]

Smith targeted small white farmers throughout the district, walking the furrows of their fields to shake hands as they plowed. There were no large gatherings to address. He spoke to Rotary clubs when he could get an invitation. Mostly he drove from village to village, stopping to chat in stores or in streets where men lounged. He visited lawyers' offices and wrote news releases stating what he would have said if he had had an audience. The *Commercial Appeal* correspondent assured him that it did not matter whether he really made a speech or not. An experienced newspaperman, Smith knew how to produce good copy that could be easily used. As a result he received good, steady coverage. Such crossroads villages as Darling and Coxburg provided datelines for speeches that he would have made if an audience could have been gathered. In the first primary he spoke thirty-six times on radio stations across the Delta. He spent Billups's donation on radio announcements and speeches, made from a Cleveland radio station owned by one of Wolfe's local enemies, convincing Wolfe of a major conspiracy against him.[12]

Lamb, too, carried on a door-to-door effort. Starting in the south end of the district, he tried to meet and persuade every voter in person. One day he reported meeting a man three times in different locations, only to knock on his door that evening. He laughed and asked how many of him there were in the county. He hired no campaign workers and had only his law office secretary to help him.[13]

Wolfe received the support of the establishment. Sillers helped him to draft his campaign platform. Members of the legislature and lawyers outside Leflore County flocked to support him. Newspaper accounts described him as a "brilliant" member of the legislature, but he was more aloof than either Lamb or Smith. Almost always in coat and tie and wearing a boutonniere, he seemed to be counting on the power of the establishment to put him in office—a reasonable expectation under the circumstances.[14]

In organization and resources Smith's campaign fell between the bare-bones Lamb approach and the well-heeled Wolfe effort. In the first primary, which ended on August 22, Smith spent four thousand dollars. He hired six workers—two young women and four men. He spent just over a thousand dollars advertising on radio and in newspapers. The *Democrat* printed materials for him as a contribution. Helen worked full-time for him. Willie Ruth worked part-time out of Jackson. His mother canvassed for weeks door-to-door in Delta towns such as Indianola and Leland. She had remarried L. C. Spencer, a Carroll County planter, a union that provided important new family allies. Smith's new stepbrother, L. C. Spencer, Jr., manager of the electrical cooperative in Greenwood, became an important and influential supporter. In Coahoma County, Smith's cousin, J. W. Smith, who was circuit clerk, headed off a rumor that Stennis had fired Smith from his staff. To dispel the rumor, J. W. Smith obtained a letter from Stennis stating that Smith had left Stennis's office by his own choice. Stennis refused to play any wider role in the race for fear it would hurt his own chances of reelection in 1952. No other political leader helped Smith except the Leflore County supervisors, who endorsed him out of local patriotism.[15]

The Delta district included some of the most conservative elected officials in Mississippi. Jim Eastland and Walter Sillers were Smith's neighbors. Fielding Wright lived in the southern end of the district. Smith could not tell the voters what he believed and be elected. To gain political power, he lied. Civil rights and communism were themes of his press releases. He condemned both, of course, and sometimes he combined them. "It will be sound common sense for the Congress to demand that the Truman civil rights program be discarded in the interest of national unity. We can not be divided in the face of our insidious and powerful enemy."[16] He denounced Truman regularly and went out of his way to oppose "creeping socialism"—meaning the expanding role of the federal government. Socialism, he said, worked only in "anthills and beehives." When the Korean War began during the campaign, he naturally shifted more attention to foreign affairs. He supported U.S. intervention and urged greater mobilization to fight communism. Almost nothing in his public remarks separated him from his opponents. He called for cutting domestic spending in order to pay for the war and generally said what he knew his audience wanted to hear.[17]

He did oppose communist aggression and he did hope the United States would play a role in keeping world peace, but he made no references to the United Nations, an organization he had always privately supported. He had abandoned his youthful flirtation with socialist ideas long before the race, but he privately supported labor unions and government initiative in the economy, neither of which he dared approve as a candidate. Secretly he favored Truman's civil rights policies, but he railed against them in order to get elected. He rationalized his lies by thinking he could work within the system to change it. Smith made the most noise about the "age issue." He argued that the district needed to send a young man to build seniority in Congress. Wolfe was sixty. Smith was thirty-two. Lamb was thirty-three, but Smith ignored him.

Smith and Wolfe exchanged barbs on the age issue through the press but avoided the debates that Lamb called for until the end of the contest, when all three appeared at a forum in Greenville. A careful listener might have detected some small ideological differences among the three candidates as they made statements and answered questions from the audience. Wolfe lauded his own experience and claimed roots as a small farmer. He listed the offices he had held and harped on states' rights and fighting communism at home as well as abroad. Lamb talked of voting his conscience, of working his way around the world as a young man, and of coming to know the "peoples of the earth." Smith spoke of his loss of a brother in the war and his sense of commitment to public service generated by his war experience. He described himself as "forward looking" because he had campaigned for Senator Stennis and, unlike Wolfe, vowed to cooperate with the national Democratic party in seeking committee appointments.

Lamb and Smith came across, despite their rigid adherence to segregationist dogma, as more liberal young men shaped by the same experiences. Smith planted better questions in the audience and came away sounding like an expert on relations with Spain and the Fair Labor Standards Act of 1938. While neither Wolfe nor Lamb knew enough to have positions on either issue, Smith demonstrated that the Fair Labor Standards Act was a dangerous threat to cotton producers and outlined lengthy, specific changes needed in the law. Thus in the last public appearance of the campaign, Smith got to play the expert in the largest population center.[18]

Smith and Lamb shook the foundation of the Delta establishment in the first primary. All three candidates took their home bases with large majorities, but together Smith and Lamb out-polled Wolfe in several counties. Of the two young veterans, Smith had the largest base in

Leflore County and did well in adjoining Holmes County, which includes hill and Delta territory. Smith and Wolfe seesawed back and forth in the lead with only a handful of votes separating them in the end. Lamb conceded defeat and opted to endorse neither Smith nor Wolfe in the second primary as both scrambled to pick up his voters. Sillers advised Lamb to support Wolfe because Wolfe would probably serve only a few years, while Smith could be in Congress for more than thirty years, if he were elected. Sillers urged Lamb to practice law and bide his time to replace Wolfe.[19]

Perhaps Lamb did tilt to Wolfe, because Wolfe opened the second primary campaign from Lamb's stronghold, the Quitman County Courthouse. In an effort to unite the Delta against Smith's base, Wolfe complained of the poor grace displayed by Leflore County in monopolizing the congressional seat. "Certainly the people of the other ten counties don't feel it is a solemn obligation to make Greenwood the permanent congressional capitol of the district." He also added a "populist" appeal, promising to support legislation to increase aid for the "aged needy."

Declaring that the result of the first primary demonstrated the popular opposition to "cliques" and "rings," Smith came out fighting. He challenged Wolfe to a series of debates and accused him of cowardice for refusing. Claiming that Wolfe knew that he was incapable of debating and would be a poor spokesman against the "fluent" enemies of the South in Congress, Smith claimed to be the candidate capable of protecting the South. Smith continued to stress the age theme, saying that Congress was no place to retire aging politicians.[20]

For the second primary, Wolfe hired Erle Johnston to be his campaign advisor. Johnston, a newspaperman, had been the publicity man in Governor Wright's successful campaign. Probably because of Johnston's research and media advice, Wolfe began to try to make Smith look foolish. Wolfe, for example, accused Smith of introducing a bill to have policemen kill house cats and distributed a cartoon of Smith shooting cats with a pistol. With the Korean War in progress, Smith shifted attention to war experience, saying in one speech, "I think your representative in Congress should be a man who has smelled gunpowder...." In a press release Smith claimed to have been decorated by General Patton for action at the Battle of the Bulge. He had received a Bronze Star, but this was dramatizing his war experience to the maximum. He then pointed out that Wolfe "avoided any form of service" in the First World War. In another speech, Smith taunted Wolfe for refusing to debate, remarking that it would have provided Wolfe "a fine opportunity to hurl his personal castigations at me. But apparently he feels my physical presence would restrain him to more discretion." Descending to the same tactic of personal insult, the slim Wolfe commented on Smith's substantial waistline. Smith responded, "I plead guilty to being fat, but I would point out that I was just as fat when I was going through some of the hardest fighting in Europe. I am going to make this weight felt in Washington."[21]

Early in September, Sillers publicly entered the fray. Speaking to a large assembly of Wolfe supporters in the courthouse at Cleveland, Sillers warned that "minority groups," meaning civil rights lobbyists, were too strong in government and that a young man was more likely to yield to their efforts than Wolfe was. In other words, using all the code words, Sillers accused Smith of being soft on integration. Wolfe followed up Sillers's attack, charging Smith with an attempt to integrate the Mississippi National Guard with a military discipline bill that he had introduced in the senate. Smith pointed out that Wolfe had voted for the bill, which was never intended to be a means of integrating the guard. A National Guard major general came to Smith's defense with a statement saying that the guard leadership had asked Smith to introduce the bill as a part of a package of work approved by the guard and that there had been no intention of integrating. Smith tried to connect Wolfe to black voters by noting that the residents of Mound Bayou, an all-black town in the Delta, had voted seventy-one to four for Wolfe in the first primary.[22]

Having failed in his effort to play the race card, Wolfe turned to charges of corruption. Wolfe appeared in Greenwood to accuse Smith of receiving money from a group of gasoline dealers, whom Wolfe had exposed for running a racket to steal gasoline taxes. It was true that Smith had received money from one member of the group, and, as the donor insisted, had spent all the money in Bolivar County where it did him relatively little good. But hearing all of Smith's radio advertisements in his hometown convinced Wolfe that a much bigger plot existed against him. Smith retorted that this was a lie and fired an equally ridiculous shot at Wolfe, alleging that Wolfe had big labor connections through his brother-in-law, who represented railway unions in Jackson.[23]

The campaign degenerated into a dirty, hard-fought battle, with both sides using rumor and innuendo as well as public charges. Rumor had it that Stennis was secretly backing Smith. Wolfe waved a letter from Stennis eschewing any part in the contest. Rumor had it that Smith was not "safe" on race. In the last days of the primary both candidates broadcast constantly from the radio stations throughout the area. Smith used car caravans, driving from Greenwood to Greenville and stopping in towns along the route to advertise his campaign. On the day before the election, Hodding Carter published a glowing endorsement of Smith. Depicting Smith as a war hero who was needed in the current emergency in Korea and praising him as a man of the "everyday people," Carter reminded readers of how Smith's father had died. Carter recalled Smith's role in Stennis's victory over the same Delta forces seeking to elect Wolfe. Later that night, Sillers went on a Delta-wide radio hookup, preceding Wolfe's final appeal to the voters. Overshadowing his candidate's remarks, Sillers condemned Hodding Carter as "unfit to live in white society" and called for the election of Wolfe as the hope for saving the southern way of life, implying strongly that Smith was a dangerous liberal.[24]

Carter did not assuage the planter's paranoia when he addressed the new Negro Voters League in Greenville that night. Enlightened Greenville — unlike other Mississippi towns — had some black voters. Sillers, horrified, heard that "several hundred" blacks had attended the meeting. He noted in a letter to a supporter that Carter went to speak to the blacks shortly after writing an editorial for Smith, and said that, while he did not know what Carter told the black voters, "If we judge by his writings and past utterances, I don't know that it would be a hard guess to make."[25] Carter did not openly endorse Smith to the black voters, but he made his choice clear and felt that Smith had earned blacks' votes by his moderation on the race issue. Smith, he said, did not go "out of his way to bring in a spurious racial issue, or to call up the old, dead ghosts, or to denounce anyone whom the Negroes knew to be their friend."[26] In other words, using the necessary code words Carter tried to communicate what he knew but could not say about Smith.

Smith predicted victory by two thousand votes, and he came close to that figure, winning majorities in all but four counties. Most of the Lamb vote went to Smith. In Washington County, the leading planter-businessman, LeRoy Percy, an intelligent and progressive planter, switched from Lamb to Smith and helped to carry Greenville. Smith's hard work and veteran's appeal paid dividends. Relatives scattered throughout the district helped. His mother's support quieted any fears of liberalism, and Smith further buried those apprehensions with his promises to fight for the poll tax and against antilynching legislation, for states' rights and against socialized medicine.[27]

Despite Smith's professed conservatism, practiced observers who knew the code could easily tell the difference between him and Wolfe. Carter hailed Smith's election as "the arrival of the twentieth century in Delta politics." Carter knew Smith and no doubt was far more aware of his ideas than he would tell the public. He gloated over the defeat of the "professionals" and the "legal eagles" by Smith's band of "amateurs." He called Smith "unassuming, fat, and ordinary looking: but having a mind and a spirit and a backbone which make him a part of the American picture and the American hope. . . ." By comparison Carter had called Wolfe a throwback to another era. Carter berated Sillers for calling him a "pink Negro-lover" and reveled in the victory of a man he believed represented American ideals rather than the "feudal" planter system in the Delta.[28]

Smith used a campaign contribution intended to reduce his campaign debt and took Helen to New Orleans to celebrate their victory. He had no income, and the actual election would not be until November. He would not take his seat in Congress until January. He told a reporter friend that he intended to work on his long-delayed history of the Yazoo River, but he did not; he dived into the political rounds immediately. He met with the head of the Mississippi Farm Bureau in Jackson. He traveled to Washington to find an apartment and to begin lobbying for committee assignments needed to become an effective representative. Stennis put him on his payroll for one month, easing the transition to Washington. Unaware of Smith's earlier lobbying, Stennis endorsed Smith to Boswell Stevens at the Mississippi Farm Bureau. Assuring Stevens that his letter was not solicited by Smith, he wrote, "[I]n my opinion [Smith is] an able and outstanding young man, who has great depth of character as well as splendid training and a deep sincere desire to serve the best interests of the people. . . ." Stennis went on to assure Boswell that he could deal with Smith. "At the time he left here, he was one of the best informed men on Governmental affairs on Capitol Hill. . . ."[29]

Edgar Poe, correspondent for the New Orleans *Times-Picayune*, who had known Smith from his earlier stay in Washington, commented on Smith's liberal racial attitudes. "For years he has advocated better educational and economic opportunities for the [black] race."[30] Smith knew he had to suppress his ideas on race and keep them from those who had not known him before his election to Congress. He would have liked to abandon some of his conservative facade in Washington. For example, he wanted to furnish his office with Harry Truman's autographed portrait, but his conservative assistant convinced him that visiting Mississippians would report him as a traitor if he did.[31]

Ironically, one of the most racist, conservative districts in America had elected a closet liberal and a secret integrationist to represent it in Congress. Given the power of incumbency in Mississippi's one-party system, Smith could have looked forward to thirty years or more in the House of Representatives. However, the Delta had lost population as blacks migrated to the North escaping peonage, and the last census had cost Mississippi a seat in the House of Representatives. Depending on the redistricting actions of the state legislature controlled by Sillers, Smith could have been relegated quickly to one term. The *Commonwealth* had observed in August that the "politicos" were watching the race against Wolfe as a test of their hold on the Delta electorate.[32] The next question was, would they allow Smith to keep his seat or would they remove him by redistricting him into an impossible race with a strong opponent?

CHAPTER SEVEN

Congressman Smith

ongressman Smith believed that he could help his country and
his state by promoting liberal ideas in the House. Young and relatively inexperienced but shrewd and idealistic, he hoped, despite the compromises he had made regarding segregation, that he could
be an effective congressman. He thought of himself as a liberal and believed in a liberalism born of the depression, the New Deal, and his war
experiences. His ambition would require him to overcome tremendous
odds.

First, there was the simple fact that a freshman congressman has little
power to do much of anything. Congress had not changed much since
Woodrow Wilson observed in his classic study that the rules of the House
of Representatives had been framed "for the deliberate purpose of making usefulness unattainable by individual members."[1] The seniority system placed value on experience and rewarded longevity. A new member
had to do his homework on the complicated, detailed legislation coming before his committee so that he could contribute in the "mark-up"
sessions, in which the members write laws. Nothing lost a member more
respect and standing among his peers than bombastic speeches for the
public followed by lack of knowledge in committee work.[2] Learning the
quiet discipline required of congressmen is difficult for any young, aggressive politician. It must have been doubly so for Smith, who was convinced of the righteousness of his secret cause.

Second, Smith was in the wrong place at the wrong time to be a liberal.
Liberalism was on the wane. Truman's health care reforms had gone
down to defeat, and his plans to duplicate the Tennessee Valley Authority in other river valleys had fared no better. The country was at war in
Korea, and the red scare threatened to smear any outspoken liberal as

86

a communist. Richard Nixon won a Senate seat in 1950 by screaming "commie" at his Democratic opponent. Joseph McCarthy lied his way onto the national political stage, bullying the entire political establishment into fearful silence. Facing the change accelerated by the Second World War, the public suffered from irrational fears. In local churches across the South, anticommunist ministers frightened congregations with the crudest stories and propaganda, making government employees sound evil simply by association. Some Americans suspected that fluoride in their drinking water was a communist plot to destroy them. In Mississippi the state senate demanded a probe of "pinko college professors." Oddly, most southern governors' races in 1950 went to moderates, but the defeat of liberals in Senate races in North Carolina and Florida pointed toward the rise of reaction. The next year in Mississippi, Hugh White defeated Paul B. Johnson, Jr., by portraying him as a Truman civil rights liberal.[3]

The House of Representatives in 1950 belonged to the conservative southern Democrats who controlled committee chairmanships. The leader of the southern conservative forces was Howard W. Smith. Judge Smith, as he was known, chaired the Rules Committee as a southern gentleman of the old school, distrustful of government and determined to protect the "southern way of life." If a bill inimical to white southern interests made its way through a committee chaired by one of the northern Democrats, Judge Smith could take care of it. Every bill had to pass through the Rules Committee in order to reach the floor for a vote. Judge Smith would simply refuse to report a bill. He would assign it rules such as unlimited amendments that made its passage impossible. In some cases, he simply went back to Virginia to inspect his farms, and the committee could not meet to act on legislation.[4]

Many southern conservatives had rallied to the Dixiecrats in 1948, deserting Truman because of his civil rights program. There had been some sentiment for stripping the Dixiecrats of their seniority, but Speaker Sam Rayburn had declined to punish any of them, allowing the southern conservatives to retain their control of the House of Representatives. Thus, the House of Representatives lacked any Democratic party discipline. Judge Smith and the other southern conservatives cooperated freely with the Republican minority to dominate the House. A liberal southerner had few friends in Congress.[5]

Third, having been elected from Mississippi, Congressman Frank Smith joined one of the most conservative and powerful delegations in the

House. In 1951, the Mississippi delegation opposed Truman more consistently than that of any other state, with only Smith voting for the president more than half of the time. The dean of the Mississippi House delegation was William (Bill) Colmer, who represented the Gulf Coast. He worked alongside Judge Smith as the chief lieutenant on Rules. Colmer disliked Frank Smith for ideological reasons and "gave him the knife" whenever possible.

Jamie Whitten, from north Mississippi, served on the Appropriations Committee and chaired the Agriculture Subcommittee of Appropriations, which meant that he eventually became the "permanent secretary of agriculture" and the second most powerful member of the delegation. Whitten and Smith had belonged to the same fraternity at the University of Mississippi, and, aside from the prospect of being thrown into a district together, got on well. The most striking public difference between them was in foreign affairs; Whitten was an isolationist and Smith an internationalist.

The other members were less powerful. John Rankin, an old populist, embarrassed the delegation with his crude racism. He was always spoiling for a fight, and most tried to avoid him, but John Bell Williams associated himself with Rankin when he first arrived in Congress. Williams served on a minor committee, Interstate and Foreign Commerce, which was of limited value to the state. He and Smith had little contact. Tom Abernethy, Smith's neighbor in the district to the east, served on the Agriculture Committee, which might have been more important but for Whitten's role on Appropriations. Abernethy had turned cynical and hard. He and Smith were friendly in a personal way, but in Congress Abernethy was another who opposed Smith whenever possible because of his racial views.

Arthur Winstead, who served on Armed Services, had no close relations with Smith. They differed on almost all political issues, especially about race. Winstead disliked Smith's liberalism, no doubt feeling about Smith as he did about Carl Elliot of Alabama. He told Elliot, "These do-gooders like you—you all go all over the country and the countryside stirring up trouble for the rest of us and making nothing but trouble for yourself. I spend as much time as I can back home sitting on the coupling poles of the wagons of my constituents. I know what they want and I get it for them."[6] In Smith's opinion, his colleagues were uninterested in anything not affecting Mississippi, and he found it a chore to get along with them. For the first two years they all jockeyed for position in the upcoming redistricting by the legislature, and under those conditions it was difficult for them to begin as friends.[7]

Fourth, Smith faced the possibility of being redistricted into one of his senior colleagues' districts. Mississippi had lost about five thousand people between the 1940 and the 1950 census. The decline reduced the state's number of representatives from six to five. Smith was the newest member in the Mississippi delegation and thus might have expected to be eliminated.[8]

Smith's political future depended on Walter Sillers. As speaker, Sillers controlled the Mississippi House of Representatives where the congressional district lines would be redrawn. Sillers had made it plain throughout the primary campaigns that he neither liked nor trusted Smith. Smith thought he could count on Sillers's desire to keep the Delta intact as a distinct district undiluted by many hill folk. But Smith had a great deal to worry him. Sillers knew Smith to be a closet liberal. He hated Smith's friends such as Hodding Carter, and no one could predict what Sillers would do. Nevertheless, Sillers recognized the value of a congressman's services and offered Smith the opportunity to begin a friendly relationship by writing to extend his best wishes despite "election differences."[9]

Smith jumped at the invitation and worked to convince Sillers that he was valuable to the district. Smith understood that every congressman has two constituencies—the people who elect him and his fellow congressmen whose votes he needs in the House—but in this case Sillers loomed so large that he was really a third constituency.

Smith set out to prove his worth to his district's voters by being an effective ombudsman. With his fellow congressmen, he tried to be helpful showing new members the ropes, sending congratulatory and condolence letters, and doing his committee homework carefully. He also voted for funding local development projects that were of no interest to him or his district, assuming other members would remember when he needed a vote. Finally, to demonstrate his worth to Sillers, who was a Dixiecrat and segregationist, Smith had to prove his wholehearted support for segregation.

Smith knew that a congressman's value and power depended upon the committee positions he held. Committee assignments had been reduced in 1946 in a major reform of Congress, limiting the number of standing committees and discouraging the appointment of special committees, a measure that limited the number of places available. Because flood control meant life to the Delta, Smith set out, well before he was seated in Congress, to win a place on the Public Works Committee. Public Works was important and highly desired because of the construction legislation it oversaw and the possibilities of bringing home the bacon to a district. The Agriculture Committee would have been the other natural choice, but Whitten and Abernethy had taken that area already. Smith's predecessor, Whittington, had chaired the Public Works Committee, and it was a tradition for the Delta to hold a seat to look after its special interest in flood control. There should have been no opposition to Smith's appointment, but redistricting politics intervened.

Fearing Smith as a future opponent, Whitten tried to block Smith's appointment to Public Works. When Smith asked his predecessor, Whittington, how to proceed, Whittington advised him to ignore Whitten and to write to everyone as if he had never heard of Whitten's protests. Whittington said history and tradition would prevail for Smith, if he took his stand as a good member of the Democratic party. Whittington prided himself on maintaining good relations with the national Democratic party, and he told Smith, "I am the only member of the Mississippi delegation whose recommendations for appointments within his district are accepted by the Democratic administration."[10]

Smith was pleased with the advice to be a good Democrat. He lobbied as such for the position and seemed assured of it until John Bell Williams, his congressional neighbor to the south, tried to take it. Williams, too, was concerned about redistricting and wanted to prevent Smith from building any power base. Smith feared provoking a fight within the congressional delegation, so he took a back route to defeat Williams. Smith wrote his stepbrother, Louie Spencer, suggesting that someone in the Rural Electrification Association should approach John Rankin, an old New Dealer who backed the Tennessee Valley Authority, about supporting Smith for Public Works. Smith suggested that Rankin be informed that he was friendly both to the TVA and to the REA. Spencer had the call placed by a friend in the electrical cooperative group. Williams dropped out of the running for the post, and Smith told Spencer, "After our fellow congressman got out of the picture, there wasn't too much trouble...."[11] Through effective lobbying and political maneuvering, Smith secured his first goal, the proper committee assignment. He was the only freshman appointed to the Public Works Committee that year.

Stennis helped with Smith's transition by restoring him to his payroll for a month and providing an office. Whittington held a lunch for Smith in the House cafeteria and invited him to sit in on the last sessions of the Public Works Committee that Whittington chaired. This support helped Smith get his career off to a good start.[12]

His first six months in Congress were unusually well documented by a political scientist who chose to study Smith as an example of how a congressman worked. Smith had the good fortune to be assigned an office on the top floor of the New Office Building. His suite consisted of two rooms, low ceilinged and functional. The outer room contained five desks in the center, with file cabinets and steel bookshelves lining the walls. Decoration consisted of a post office map of the third district and a "garish" Mississippi tourist map. Smith's small private office had a substantial desk, three leather chairs, a sofa, a desk, and a small typewriter table abutting his desk. His only wall decoration was an Army Corps of Engineers map of flood control projects planned and completed in the Delta. All furnishings were government issue.[13]

The Congress provided twenty thousand dollars for staff. Smith hired David Williams, a young lawyer from Holmes County, as an assistant, three young women from Mississippi as stenographers, and a "field man" in the district. His office was frugal. Since there were no funds to buy file folders, files were kept in large mailing envelopes that were provided by Congress.[14]

Using this staff, Smith sought to deliver the best possible service to all who asked for it, because, with a relatively small literate population in his district, those who requested help would be the same people who paid their poll taxes and voted. Smith was a steady worker who quickly developed habits. He arrived at the office at nine each morning, opened the mail, assigned the routine tasks to Williams, and then answered more important letters himself. At first the mail load was light, averaging around twenty letters per day. Smith insisted that all letters be answered the day they arrived and required that the office be manned all day on Saturdays, because, he said, people in the Delta worked six days a week. He drank a Coke at ten o'clock and at one had lunch with buttermilk in the House cafeteria. He ate with whomever he found there in an effort to meet more people and at first spent a good deal of time in the cloakroom of the House getting to know his colleagues. Early in 1951, Smith was working on a Federal Housing Authority problem affecting

Sillers's sharecroppers. Many such tasks followed, so that, by the fall of 1951, Sillers wrote, "This is about the promptest actions I ever got ou[t] of any legislator."[15]

The word spread that Smith got things done, and the requests multiplied over time. An assistant's letter demonstrates the flavor of the services Smith's office rendered in what was described as a not particularly heavy week's mail. The office sent three petitions on behalf of Delta post offices to the Memphis headquarters and transmitted a list of bidders on a new post office building to the town's chamber of commerce. They got the immigration service to extend the departure date for a constituent's relative. The staff refereed a family fight between a VA hospital patient's wife, who did not want him home, and his mother and father, who did. The office got another veteran admitted to the hospital. Smith had to fend off a constituent's interest in a television station, a project that clashed with the interests of the local chamber of commerce. He was asked to recommend a man to be manager of the Sunflower River Wildlife Management Project. Another correspondent requested material that he could use to introduce Senator Stennis, who was giving a speech in Mississippi. Smith's office failed to have a constituent's air force commission restored, but they got another veteran returned to active duty. They saw to the establishment of a bank on the Greenville AFB. Smith's assistant concluded the litany of service work with this report: "Those absolutely unintelligible letters from [B] that you sent to me were sufficiently deciphered for us to get him a reversal of the denial of his social security benefits. The LeFlore Hunting & Fishing lads got their road approval. [A] few of our Chinese constituents have their visas. Greenwood did not get the Navy band this year. I sidestepped a race issue letter... promising it would be on your desk when you return. ... We've had the usual assortment of passports, visas, assurance forms, allotments, and hardships."[16] Smith seemed to solicit ombudsman work. After a visit with Hodding Carter in Washington, he wrote to ask if Carter wanted information about raising catfish in his private lake. Carter responded, "Ever since you have been elected to office, the catfish in my lake have been dying. Would you please advise me if I should take this up with the electorate or you should take it up with the Dept. of Ag. (free fish division) to tell me why catfish die in artificial lakes after dark horses are sent to Congress."[17] In response Smith talked to a catfish expert in Washington, told Carter to test his water, and wrote to the Mississippi Game and Fish Commission on Carter's behalf.[18]

This work was not only dull but was often frustrating. When Smith called the Bureau of the Budget to ask for speedy consideration of funding for flood control projects in his district, the staff brushed him aside. When he undertook to get the head of defense mobilization as the keynote speaker for the Delta Council annual meeting, he failed. The second choice, a senator, turned him down, and he had to settle for a Republican midwestern governor. Then at the spring meeting, after all his work, Smith was assigned to introduce the second speaker instead of the governor.[19]

Thanks to Whittington, most of the flood control work in the Delta had been authorized and was either complete or under construction. Smith needed to watch and fight for continued funding, but his main role at first was to be a friend to the Army Corps of Engineers, the organization that developed and built the dams, levees, and reservoirs. The corps needed friends, because it had come under fire. Truman had proposed to place the corps under the control of the Interior Department. The chairman of the House Appropriations Committee attacked the corps, and a senator had launched a crusade against it for being a "pork barrel" agency. A highly critical scholarly study published in 1950 accused the corps of lacking professional standards and catering to Congress. Smith did verbal battle with one and all on behalf of the corps. His support for the St. Lawrence Seaway, even in defiance of Sillers, moved him quickly up the seniority ladder on the committee, because other members who opposed the seaway were removed by the House leadership. By the summer of 1951, a reporter guessed that Smith's calls to the corps merited more respect. The engineer in charge of the Vicksburg district developed the habit of visiting Smith in his Greenwood office between sessions to discuss what needed to be done in Congress the next year.[20]

Fall 1951 found Smith touring water projects in North Dakota and then traveling from Memphis to New Orleans on a corps boat to attend the Mississippi Valley Flood Control Association meeting. He had been appointed to a public works subcommittee to look into flood control and navigation projects authorized but not funded by Congress. When Truman's budget provided "only" $47 million for Mississippi River projects, Smith denounced the figure as half of what was needed. He exaggerated, because there were several projects benefiting his district on the list, and, despite the departure of the long-serving Whittington, the federal funds continued to roll into the Delta.[21]

The second must-do for a Delta congressman was supporting agriculture, and despite the fact that he had no committee assignment or experience in agriculture, Smith read *Progressive Farmer* regularly and spoke out actively. During the first year, he promoted a new Delta crop—rice. Introduced to the Delta in 1947 by a Cleveland-area farmer, rice growing had spread to over one and a half million acres in several states by 1950. Mississippi had fallen behind neighboring states in developing it, but the use of new methods of drying, combine harvesting, and chemical insect control seemed about to launch rice as a major Delta crop. Sillers, who owned some "buckshot" land unsuitable for cotton and other traditional Delta crops, saw rice as an opportunity and requested Smith's support in his first letter to his new congressman. Even as Smith prepared to take his new seat in the House, he called for the lifting of rice planting quotas, which threatened to inhibit rice planting in Mississippi. He attracted some press coverage, and his maiden speech in Congress was a plea to support the American rice industry so that it could feed Asian populations in danger of falling to the communists. Smith won praise for these efforts in the Delta press and in Drew Pearson's nationally syndicated column. Senator Eastland arranged to raise the rice quotas, and Smith had his name linked to the victory. Rice acreage increased tenfold between 1950 and 1953.[22]

In Smith's second major House speech, he defended subsidies paid to farmers. *Fortune* had attacked government waste in subsidizing farmers, and Smith leaped to their defense. He rejected the word "subsidy" as applied to farm price supports and cleverly responded that the Luce publications received subsidies in the form of low mail rates. He defended the parity payments to farmers as a "minimum wage" and claimed that inflation had robbed farmers of half the amount they should receive to keep their living standard at 1914 levels. He ignored the large payments going to planters who made fortunes from government subsidies because they were his most important constituents.[23]

Despite the fact that agriculture held no personal interest for him, Smith acted as a good advocate for farmers' interests. He defended the soil conservation program in a letter to the editor of the *New York Times* and remembered the type of farmers who mattered most in his district—the planters. For them Smith worked to ensure that they could import Mexican labor. He looked into the federal law requiring the payment of minimum wages at some cotton gins. He became a leader in a movement urging farmers to stockpile cotton in order to force up the price. One hundred congressmen signed a statement endorsing the idea and published it in the *Wall Street Journal*. When H. L. Mitchell, president of the farm labor union, criticized his campaign, Smith accused Mitchell of operating the union for his personal benefit. This outburst, probably calculated to earn the gratitude of Delta planters, was far from the thinking of the idealistic college student who admired cooperative experiments as the only means for sharecroppers to escape their peonage.[24]

So the young congressman compromised his ideals in order to win political power, but his shifts on farm policy were small compared to the change required on race. Given Sillers's suspicion of his racial beliefs, Smith could not afford to simply ignore the issue and expect to have Sillers protect his district in the upcoming redistricting battle. As a rule Smith tried to maintain a helpful silence on race and not contribute to the problem as demagogues such as Bilbo had; but to win over Sillers, Smith had to declare himself. In his early newsletters, Smith toed the states' rights, racist line. For example, he approved the conviction of Willie Magee for rape. Magee, a black man, probably had an affair with a white woman but was accused of rape as a result. The Mississippi Supreme Court threw out two of Magee's convictions, and Magee's case became world famous. Leftist groups made it a cause célèbre, eliciting protests on behalf of Magee from world luminaries such as Jean-Paul Sartre and Albert Einstein. Despite the public outcry and the weak case against him, Magee died for his "crime" on May 7, 1951, in the Laurel courthouse to the cheers of seven hundred whites gathered on the lawn. Smith could have been silent as he often was on such issues, but he needed the mantle of southern racism to appease Sillers. In some instances, he simply turned what he believed completely around and stated the opposite. On integration of the army he wrote in one newsletter, "The armed services should never become an instrument to modify the established customs of any group of citizens." He called integration a dangerous experiment that would weaken the armed forces. Just a few years earlier he had written but could not sell an article praising the experiments with integration during the war and touted them as a major success that strengthened the army. Smith accused the Communist Party of using the Civil Rights Congress to stir up strife and rioting. The CRC was a high-profile organization that had intervened on behalf of Willie Magee. Supported by the entertainer Paul Robeson and other famous black leaders, it did have communist support. When Sillers wrote to Smith comparing the Civil Rights Congress's operations to a rattlesnake crawling about in a child's nursery, Smith quickly agreed that the congress should be made illegal and indicated that such a law was being prepared.[25]

To the public, and especially to Sillers, Smith depicted himself as the protector of segregation and the southern way of life. Appearing on an NBC Saturday morning talk show, he extolled that way of life. When the White House inserted a clause in the agriculture bill requiring nondiscrimination clauses in contracts, Smith "called this matter to the attention of other Southern congressmen" and demanded that it be deleted or the bill might be killed. When a friend of Sillers wrote asking Smith's views on states' rights, Smith produced a long letter stating the classic case for the states' rights movement, complete with historical precedents. To be sure Sillers got the message, Smith sent him a copy.[26]

When he thought it was possible, Smith was more moderate. For example, an important supporter in the district reported that an outraged woman had stopped him in the post office to complain that her son was forced to live in army barracks with "colored" troops. He asked Smith to try to do something about integration in the army or at least to condemn the situation in a newsletter. Smith replied bluntly that nothing could be done. When his lawyer cousin wrote suggesting changes in the legal system to keep judges "safe" on race issues, Smith brushed his arguments aside. When Forrest Cooper, who had almost run against Smith, prosecuted white police officers for beating black men in Sunflower County, Smith congratulated him. To reinforce such prosecutions Smith said they were needed to convince the nation that "we are capable of handling our own problems." Even with his staff, Smith practiced discretion in what he revealed about his real beliefs. His assistant, David Williams, had no idea that Smith harbored a secret belief in racial equality, while his more liberal-minded secretary learned the truth early and knew that he hid the fact from Williams. Keeping the secret was a necessary part of Mississippi politics.[27]

Smith tried to do what he thought was possible. He turned down offered office space in a Greenwood hotel because he knew blacks were not allowed to walk in the front door. Custom did not allow Smith to address his black constituents as Mr. and Mrs., and post office workers would have reported it if he had, but he tried to treat his black constituents with respect. After much experimentation in the office, he adopted a neutral "Dear Friend." Relations with the Delta Chinese were less fraught with danger for him, and he became a favorite with Chinese seeking assistance with visas.[28]

His maneuvering must have taken a toll. In January 1951, he told Carter, "I've been alternately impressed and dejected by some of the situations I find here. I am impressed by the sincerity of people from all sides in regard [to] our present situation, and dejected by so many others who can only see the political angles in the matter. The worst offenders are probably my colleagues from Mississippi. I'm getting along with all of them, but sometimes it is a chore."[29] They were, he said, negative about anything not affecting Mississippi.

As a well read liberal with war experience, Smith was more interested in foreign policy than in cotton, and he wanted to make a difference if he could. He had not forgotten his pledge to justify his brother's sacrifice for a better world, and he hoped to use the Delta's historical commitment to free trade to play a role in supporting strong American involvement in international affairs. As Stennis's assistant in 1948, Smith had delighted in preparing reading lists for the senator on foreign and military affairs. In his first six months, Smith introduced thirteen bills and resolutions. Six dealt with foreign affairs and the armed forces. He adopted the repeal of the Buy American Act as his special target. The act required the federal government to buy more expensive American goods — electrical generators, for example — when less expensive foreign products were available. Smith offered repeal of the act as a cost-saving measure for the taxpayer and as a way to boost trade with our allies. Quickly, he joined a half-dozen other southern congressmen, such as Hale Boggs, William Fulbright, and John Sparkman, who defied the growing isolationist sentiment of their region and supported American world leadership. But even in foreign affairs, Smith did not feel free of the Sillers factor. When Eastland introduced a resolution to withdraw the United States from the United Nations if China were accepted as a member, Smith supported a similar resolution in the House.[30]

Smith was a cold warrior, criticizing even Truman, whom he usually supported, for not moving far enough to mobilize the country to fight communism in Korea. Smith consistently voted for foreign aid, the United Nations, and a strong defense. His first display of temper in the House came during debate on a bill to establish universal military training. An isolationist trying to limit Truman's power in foreign affairs prompted Smith to ask him if he would have stayed out of World War II and allowed Germany and Japan to win. As the man tried to evade the question, Smith pursued him relentlessly in debate until others in the House joined the verbal chase.[31]

When Truman fired General Douglas MacArthur, Smith supported the president. Smith's assistant rushed to the office when he heard the news of Truman's action. Knowing what Smith would do, he hoped to convince his boss not to endorse Truman's action because he believed it would hurt Smith badly in Mississippi. Smith's field representative reported that he could find no one in the Delta who agreed with Smith's position and finally just kept quiet about the issue to protect himself. Smith had received seventy-five letters demanding Truman's impeachment, and he knew there were no votes in his support for the president. But, he said, "There are some things . . . where a man's conscience has to have more weight than political expediency."[32] He explained to a Delta supporter that he believed the United States had to avoid a full-scale war with China that could only strengthen the Soviet Union.[33]

Smith believed that he was helping his country and the world by providing intelligent leadership and that compromising on the race issue ultimately contributed to the greater national good. He felt that leaving politics to those people in the Delta who believed in racism would lower the level of the Delta's representation. He believed those who were racist continued to hold racist beliefs out of ignorance and lack of an adequate education. Therefore, he also made it his mission to support education. He promoted student foreign exchange programs in his district. He praised the National Science Foundation and voted for it. He supported the National Defense Education Act, which his colleagues opposed because it increased federal influence in education. Having faith in himself and his liberal ideas, he wanted to make a better world, but he had to work around the violent prejudices of his people to have an opportunity. He became adept at working around. He twisted his vote to support Truman on the MacArthur firing into a states' rights position, telling a constituent, "If the Constitution is going to save the South, we certainly must abide by it today [by supporting the president]."[34]

Back in the district during 1951, the political talk centered on redistricting, the governor's race, and a possible challenger to Smith in the next election. Smith desired no role in the governor's race. He told his cousin, Gordon Smith, "My present idea is to generally stand off."[35] He gave his allies complete freedom to work for the man of their choice.

Phil Mullen tried to enlist him against Paul Johnson, Jr., Senator East-land's candidate, but Smith refused to be drawn into the fight.[36]

Smith looked strictly after his own interests. His assistant was from a conservative political family. He employed Woodley Carr as his field representative. Carr served as the veterans' affairs representative for the Sunflower County Board of Supervisors. In those years after the Second World War, the county took an interest in seeing that veterans received all of their benefits, and no doubt Carr's job helping "vets" to obtain their "government checks" put him in a position to help Smith. Carr fit Smith's needs, because he blended into the local political scene and because he was shrewd enough to see all sides of an issue. For example, Carr commented unfavorably on nationally reported police brutality against black prisoners in Indianola. He called police "whippings" too common and said that the majority of people deplored it: "[M]y reaction is the deed was stupid and cruel on the part of the law enforcement officers who set themselves up as judge and jury."[37] He felt the policemen should and would be punished. In addition to observations on the local situation, Carr provided Smith with news on wedding anniversaries, graduations, and deaths so that Smith could send the proper letters to his constituents. Smith attended assiduously to those tasks with an eye toward reelection.[38]

Traditionally, congressmen had little patronage except post office appointments, which some political insiders considered essential for the building of district support. Smith felt he could not exercise the traditional patronage at first because the other members of the Mississippi delegation had been stripped of their appointment rights after they supported the Dixiecrats. To reward Truman supporters during the 1948 campaign, the patronage had been given to a group of Truman loyalists. They abused the appointment power by selling the offices. Whittington had been the only member of the Mississippi House of Representatives delegation to retain normal patronage powers as a reward for his service to the national Democratic party. Smith could have taken Whittington's patronage, but, not having Whittington's seniority and prestige, he feared being identified as a Trumanite.

Despite the dangers, some of Smith's supporters urged him to take the appointments. A campaign worker from Cleveland, Curtis Saxton, recalled Smith explaining that he would take the patronage only if Sillers approved, because Sillers distrusted him on the states' rights "question."

But Saxton argued that Smith should assert himself by seizing the opportunity. He told Smith that he was strong enough "to go it on [his] own."[39]

Smith did not agree and consulted Sillers, who advised, "[I]t may be wise to weigh well the attitude of your colleagues before making [a] final decision."[40] Smith understood Sillers's threat and refused to accept post office patronage for the "time being."

Smith complied with Saxton's suggestion that he use other patronage possibilities. For example, he asked his stepbrother to influence the disposition of Rural Electrification Association (REA) gasoline business to Smith supporters. By the spring of 1951, Smith had even started "to take an interest" in post office appointments despite the dangers. Having begun, Smith tried to use as much patronage as possible. For example, he attempted to influence appointments such as legal staff positions in the Office of Price Administration. He lost the post office patronage to Sillers in 1952 because Sillers supported Eisenhower for president, and the Republicans rewarded him with the patronage.[41]

Smith's only interference in local elections was to support a young teacher, Clarence Pierce, for Carroll County's seat in the legislature. Smith needed Pierce because Smith considered Leflore County's member, who would have been his natural advocate, inadequate for the task of presenting his case in the legislature. He wanted a diehard advocate with strong connections in the senate committed to his cause. Smith had known Pierce from his days in the Mississippi Senate when Pierce was chief page. Smith knew that he could count on Pierce and, although Pierce was young, Smith believed that he would be effective. Carroll County was outside Smith's congressional district at this point, and he had to be careful that the scheme did not backfire on him. He could have been accused of meddling where he did not belong. Congressional courtesy required members to respect one another's districts, and so Smith was violating one of the unwritten political rules in supporting Pierce. But redistricting upset the status quo and called many "rules" into question. Smith was not assured of support on redistricting within his district. LeRoy Percy, a planter who supported Smith, reported, in February 1951, that the Delta would be split in the redrawing of the district lines. Wolfe was trying to add Bolivar County to Whitten's district to exact some revenge on Smith. Whitten, who told Smith he had no desire to be dumped into a race with him, reported to Smith the names of Deltans scheming to join his district. At the same time that he tried to make Smith believe he was cooperating with him, Whitten promoted the idea of merging his and Smith's districts among their colleagues in the House. At the center of the political storm, Sillers kept quiet and made no commitment to Smith.[42]

Whitten and Smith agreed that they did not wish to be pitted against one another and hoped to place two other members into a race. Smith wrote Spencer, "Jamie has told me several times about contacts people have made with him from our district, but I think it is very obvious that he doesn't want to be put in with me." However, Smith added, "I may turn out to be the best alternative." He described an element of cooperation between them—"we are all looking for a way out."[43] Whitten, Smith's fraternity brother, invited him to join a regular poker game among the delegation's members. By the spring of 1951, Smith was playing each Monday night with four Mississippi congressmen: Whitten, Williams, Colmer, and Winstead. Governor Wright and Fred Sullens, editor of the *Jackson Daily News,* joined the group when visiting Washington. Smith did not remember discussing redistricting at the games, but being in the group probably helped him not to be odd man out when the legislature redivided the districts.[44]

Smith's plan was to take his stand on the "democratic principle" that population distribution among the congressional districts should be equal, ignoring the fact that the majority in his district was not allowed to vote. Because the Delta was the second-largest district in population, he argued, it should be saved essentially as it was and some other districts redivided. He wanted to get legislators on the record favoring this "principle" before the election. None of that would help much without Sillers's approval. Smith sent Sillers the census data, and Sillers promised Smith a lunch at Sillers's Rosedale plantation in "November or December" to discuss redistricting. Smith never got that lunch, and Sillers did not assure Smith of his support.[45]

Lamb was threatening to run again, and Smith's friends worried that the legislature would fail to redraw the lines, forcing a statewide race for all members of the House of Representatives. The plan for a statewide runoff was a sure way to eliminate Smith; he would lose because he had few voters in his district—the majority of the population in the Delta was black and not allowed to vote. All the other members would have larger numbers of voters, presumably loyal, to support them. Smith could carry all of the whites in his district and still easily be eliminated by the other congressmen if their voters remained mostly loyal.[46]

None of the "social set," the "rabid gentry," or the "ultraconservatives" of the Delta liked Smith. They were considering sacrificing the Delta district to be rid of him. The matter was unsettled when the legislature met in 1952, and Sillers was not pleased to have William Winter running against him for speaker. Winter had been elected to the Mississippi House of Representatives in 1948 — one of those young veterans eager to change Mississippi. Silver had promoted a relationship between Smith and Winter, but Smith stayed well away from Winter's candidacy. Still, Sillers knew they were in the same camp ideologically, and he disliked even the hint of opposition. To neutralize the appearance of a serious challenge to his reelection, he made a deal with J. P. Coleman. Coleman, the attorney general, had been friendly to the young reformers and might have benefited from their revolt, but Coleman deserted Winter. In return, Sillers supported Coleman's legislative program for the session. Thus Sillers retained unchallenged control over the legislature and redistricting.[47]

Smith had helped to elect Pierce, the young senator from Carroll County; Pierce then had arranged to sit on the committee handling redistricting. With his stepbrother's assistance Smith promoted support in south Mississippi among the REAs and got financial assistance for lobbying from the Mississippi Power and Light lobbyist. MP&L, no friend of public power projects, wanted Rankin eliminated because of his support for the Tennessee Valley Authority, which dated back to the 1930s. Of course, Smith supported TVA, too, but he did not remind MP&L of that, because he needed their money. Despite Smith's cooperation with Whitten in Washington, Pierce warned from Jackson that "Jamie" was not Smith's friend. He urged Smith to have Stennis "touch up" J. P. Coleman, and urged Smith to go directly to Sillers, who refused to declare his intentions. The politics were fierce. Pierce warned Smith to write him at the Walthall Hotel in Jackson because all of the post office people in Vaiden were loyal to Tom Abernethy, the congressman for Pierce's district, and could not be trusted.[48]

Not until March 10 did Sillers write Smith about redistricting. Then he wrote only a postscript on a letter about agricultural policy: "A group of Delta Folk are meeting with the House Census and Apportionment Committee tomorrow (Tuesday) night to urge that the Third District be not disturbed. I think we have a good chance on that score."[49] Pierce reported from the meeting that Sillers argued that the Delta should remain unchanged for three reasons: "(1) flood control, (2) negroes,

(3) drainage and etc." Geography and population remained the same regardless of who was in Congress, Sillers said. Obviously, Smith's campaign to assure Sillers he could be trusted had worked. Sillers must have decided that Smith's effectiveness as an advocate for flood control and other government programs outweighed his potential as a threat to segregation.[50]

Carr, Smith's Delta field agent, did not feel that Sillers's declaration completely settled the question of redistricting the Delta. He warned that the Delta people were leaving everything to Sillers, and Sillers had enemies in south Mississippi. He warned further that Abernethy's and Rankin's backers would cut a deal on anything with anyone. J. P. Coleman was going all out for Abernethy. Carr felt that Pierce had lost his effectiveness as Smith's representative toward the end of the fight because he was too closely identified with Smith's campaign. Whittington, with a Delta Council committee, went down to lobby for Smith and came back worried about an effort on the part of "Coahoma County lawyers" to put Coahoma, Quitman, and Tunica counties into Whitten's district. Smith wrote to his cousin in Clarksdale asking him to combat the move.[51]

In the end Rankin and Abernethy, the two nonpoker players, were condemned to battle one another. Smith told his cousin he had been too "tied up" with redistricting to write before April. "We really had a struggle. . . . I think that the help that Louie Spencer got us from South Mississippi from the R.E.A. people was perhaps a decisive factor."[52] Carr agreed that south Mississippians had made the difference to Smith, but not knowing the role of the REAs, he attributed south Mississippi's support to a trade-off on a gas tax law. That tax had hurt the Delta's interests while helping the populous coast; therefore, Carr theorized that the coast representatives had tried to make amends by supporting the Delta's fight to save Smith's district.[53]

Safe from being redistricted into battle with an opponent, Smith settled into Congress for the long stay that the South usually accorded its representatives in Washington. Wolfe remained convinced that Billups, not Smith, had beaten him, and still wanted to go to Washington, but he found little support. The Greenville "gentry" who had refused to work for Smith in the redistricting fight now rushed to claim credit for his victory. Lamb looked for encouragement and found none. Hodding Carter reported Lamb's disappointing search to Smith in early May. Just over a week later Smith told his cousin in Clarksdale that Lamb had been to Sillers, who informed Lamb that he would support Smith; not until June 9 did Sillers write to Smith to let him know he had convinced Lamb not to run again.[54]

Smith could have relaxed and settled into the lethargy that was allowed and even encouraged by the closed, one-party system in Mississippi, but he did not. A presidential election loomed, and, now that he was safe from redistricting, Smith began to act independently of Sillers and other Dixiecrats in support of the national Democratic party. He knew Sillers would disapprove. In May, Sillers wrote of his hopes to throw the election into the House of Representatives in 1952. Clearly, he indicated a desire to continue the states' rights movement he had helped to lead in 1948.[55]

From the Delta, Smith's field agent sent pessimistic reports. The Democratic county caucus meeting in Indianola elected him as a delegate to the state convention, but he said he would not be an active member because "[i]t was a burning hot States Rights group. . . . I guess I'm just not a very good states righter, but follow the practice of doing as the Romans when in their midst." He saw the "States Rights group" destroying an opportunity to build a two-party system and "hastening the day for the negro [sic] bloc vote in our state." In a truly perceptive evaluation, he hoped the people could "grow into it [acceptance of black voting rights]," but he feared progress would come only through "strife." He worried about the future and concluded, "I do deplore the fact that our generation has to be the one to bear so much of the burden."[56]

Smith saw the dangers and determined to work to keep Mississippi in the national Democratic party in 1952. Attempting to reclaim the states' rights section, he contacted Sillers and Wright to ask for their help. Sillers replied that he would be willing to remain in the party if the platform were "softened" on civil rights and if Richard Russell, a Georgia senator, were nominated for president. He concluded by asking if a slate of former "states righters" would be seated at the national convention in Chicago. Sillers was not blind to the advantages of using the federal government for his interests. The letter outlining the plan to throw the presidential election into the House of Representatives ended with several postscripts asking Smith for information about agricultural policies affecting his business interests. He bluntly told Smith the best way to avoid a fight for his seat in Congress was to get $6–8 million for Mississippi levee work to protect Rosedale from flooding. Deciding to stay in the party, Sillers got the Delta's county caucuses together before the district meeting and "fixed it" for Smith to be named

a delegate to Chicago. The fix was necessary because the other Mississippi representatives, frightened by the lingering Dixiecrat movement,
were not seeking election as delegates. Carr warned Smith after his election as a delegate, "Do be careful at the Chicago convention." While he
professed the utmost respect for Smith's judgment, the field agent urged
Smith to beware of the "loudest talkers," who would try to hurt him and
who would be glad to "misquote" him to do so. He concluded, "My main
reason for making the foregoing statements is that a number of rabid
gentry have never recovered from the fact that they could not name
the man of their choice to congress, and while they may pretend to
be your friends if they ever have the chance they will knife you in the
back."[57]

Carr reported that the state convention was "under control." Five Tru-
manites or "loyal Democrats" from the 1948 campaign caucused in Sunflower County, but "certainly no self respecting Democrat would be seen
publicly with any of them." So there was no serious challenge mounted
at the state level against the states' righters returning to the Democratic
party. Carr's assessment was that people were generally dissatisfied with
"what is going on" in the Democratic party; he felt that the majority might
go for "Ike."[58]

Smith feared the strong Republican sentiment, too, and set out to
reunite the Democrats with their southern wing at the convention. During the opening ceremonies, Smith arranged to have a Mississippi Medal
of Honor winner speak to the convention and escorted him to the platform for a speech. Behind the scenes, he joined with Lister Hill and John
Sparkman, moderate Alabama senators, to urge the "northern" delegates in the most important convention test case to seat Virginia without the requirement of a party loyalty oath. Smith played a prominent
role, appearing on television at the convention and in *Newsweek*. It was
exciting. A resolution was offered to require a loyalty oath, and Stennis
called a caucus of the Mississippi delegation on the convention floor,
but when they could not hear one another speak, they adjourned to a
caucus room behind the platform. In the mad struggle to push their
way to the room, Smith's delegate badge was ripped off. With Mississippi
in line, Smith lobbied northern delegations, especially the congressmen
whom he knew. *Newsweek* reported Smith was "partly responsible" for
Illinois's changing its vote on Virginia. He rushed over at a key point
and shouted that if the Illinois delegates wanted Adlai Stevenson nominated, they had better support Virginia or face a southern walkout. The

Morning Star depicted him as hustling among delegations in Chicago to work out the compromises necessary to restore the South to the party. Not everyone appreciated his role. An alternate delegate returned to write in his Collins newspaper of "political quislings" and called the deal the biggest double cross in history. Mississippi, he said, had crawled into bed with Truman. Smith bragged to Jim Silver, "We had the Mississippi delegation ready to vote for him [Stevenson] if at any time, it had been necessary to put him over."[59] He told Willie Ruth he "had as much as anyone" to do with the key decision to seat Virginia. He felt that the fight in Chicago and the continuing battles in the presidential election in the South were "a great opportunity for the moderate and liberal elements in the South to make a very important step forward." He believed the Chicago convention had prevented the creation of martyrs among the states' righters and at the same time stopped the "radical element" from expelling the South from the Democratic party.[60]

The Mississippi Democratic party seemed lined up behind the national party, but many Mississippians contemplated the previously unthinkable—voting Republican. Smith declared he would go to the state convention in August to head off an attempt to put Dwight Eisenhower on the Democratic ticket in Mississippi. The effort died and he did not have to go, but Sillers headed a Democrats for Eisenhower organization. In his district, Smith scheduled luncheon speeches to report on the Chicago convention and tried to dampen the growing enthusiasm for Eisenhower. He worked openly for Stennis in the 1952 primary, sending a hundred letters to leaders in the Delta. Stennis thanked Smith and promised his support for "anything in which you are interested." In the fall, Smith traveled the Delta stumping for Stevenson, while the other congressmen hid out in Washington to avoid the divisions in the party at home. Smith was the only Mississippi House member to work actively for Stevenson in 1952. He did so because he believed in Stevenson, an intellectual and the type of candidate Smith supported with enthusiasm. When Stevenson won Mississippi but lost the national election, Smith and his young secretary heard the news in the Greenwood office and cried together.[61]

Smith's most vivid memory of the 1952 presidential campaign in Mississippi was of speaking to a racially mixed audience in Greenville's Washington County Courthouse. Smith and Whittington addressed the group, along with a representative from the governor's office. Nothing unusual happened. It was simply the first time in Smith's memory that blacks and whites had gathered together to hear a political speech without being segregated into separate groups. Stevenson carried Mississippi that fall, and Carr assured Smith that supporting the national ticket would not hurt him in "future years."[62]

Smith had accomplished impressive political feats. He won the 1950 primary over Wolfe against the planter establishment in the Delta. He then convinced the leader of that establishment, Sillers, to support him in redistricting and to help eliminate his opponents for reelection. He helped to return the states' rights Mississippi Democrats to the national party and to win the state for the liberal Stevenson. Some of his friends were amazed by his political acrobatics. Silver hoped Smith did not believe the "stuff" written in his newsletters to woo Sillers. Phil Mullens asked Smith, "How in the world can you so well justify your actions of political expediency and then bitterly criticize those contrary actions of political expediency in others."[63] A more common reaction came from a wartime friend who recognized Smith on television at the Democratic convention pleading with "young Roosevelt" to vote to seat Virginia: "I feel that in spite of your early 'progressive' leanings that our nation is in safe hands."[64] In other words, he was willing to believe that Smith had either not meant what he had said when he was young, or that he had seen the error of his ways.

Smith had fought his way into politics and acquired a position from which he felt he could play a leadership role. It was a dangerous and potentially disastrous role because he wanted eventually to lead white southerners to accept black equality. Most white southerners did not want to be led in that direction, and, if his constituents had discovered his secret agenda, they would have dismissed Smith in short order. His secret complicated his political life and engendered deep emotional feelings among supporters and opponents in Mississippi. Liberals appreciated his daring and intelligent representation. For example, Carter promised to do everything possible to convince the Delta that Smith was essential. In the University of Mississippi history department where Smith was well known, Silver and a young professor of Italian descent, George Carbone, enjoyed the conspiracy of keeping the secret liberal in Congress. Carbone promised that "we'll keep you in Washington if it kills us and if I have to organize every wop in the Delta."[65] On the other hand, the department's staunch segregationist worked constantly to eliminate Smith from Congress.[66] The "rabid gentry" would have enjoyed knifing Smith in the back. But he had played the system successfully—

the system Silver would later label the "closed society." The tortured, unwritten rules of the white-ruled conspiracy that passed for a political system in Mississippi did not allow outright confrontation. As long as Smith played the political game by the rules that he had learned so well growing up in Greenwood, he could maintain his tenuous balancing act and try to lead his people down pathways they had no intention of taking. Most amazing of all was the fact that Smith was an intellectual in the political game. He was incapable of the backslapping, good-old-boy politics often practiced in Mississippi. His young secretary, who had grown up among people who practiced the traditional art, reported that she found it painful to watch Smith try it. Smith, she said, fit none of the Mississippi stereotypes.[67]

CHAPTER EIGHT

National Democrat

After redistricting, Smith knew he would be safe for a decade. Incumbency was so strong in Mississippi that Smith no longer feared Sillers. Their correspondence dropped off precipitously and all but ended in 1953. Smith's newsletters dropped racial themes. Free of immediate threat, Smith set out to acquire more power in the House of Representatives. To the few observers who looked closely, it became evident that Smith's heart lay with the national party and far from the conservatism and racism demanded by the majority of voters in Mississippi. At the national level, the Republicans had control of the House and the presidency. Sillers had forged an alliance with the national Republicans and retained control of the Mississippi House of Representatives, so chances of liberal reform and access to power on Smith's part seemed slim.

The selection of office staff provided the first sign of Smith's new independence. When David Williams, Smith's first assistant, wanted to return home to build a law practice, Smith hired as a replacement a newspaper reporter who had worked for Hodding Carter. Robert Tims had Delta connections through Greenwood's novelist Mildred Topp, but he had grown up on the Gulf Coast and had served in the air force, where he acquired a belief in racial equality. Carter brought Smith and Tims together because he knew they shared some of the same social and political ideas, but despite their shared liberalism the association did not work out. Tims did not like being an assistant and stayed only a year before moving on to an advertising firm in New Jersey. Smith went outside the state for his next assistant—Audrey Matthews. A former aide to Stennis, Clyde Matthews, introduced them. Audrey and Clyde Matthews lived as husband and wife at the time, although he was still married to another woman in Mississippi. Audrey Matthews proved to be an able assistant who had no ties or sympathies with Mississippi. Smith trusted her to handle constituent services and office chores, freeing him to undertake other work. She supported his political ideas with efficient contacts to the bureaucracy, clever editing, and humor when needed. Matthews understood the hill, knew how the system worked, and proved to be a strong, outspoken woman.[1]

His distancing himself from Mississippi's racism and hiring an outsider to be his assistant did not mean that Smith had abandoned his state. In his office, for example, Smith set up a system that he maintained throughout his tenure for employing young people from Mississippi seeking an education. He placed them in his patronage jobs as elevator operators and House postal employees, keeping them employed as long as they went to school and made good grades. He examined their grade reports; if their grades fell or they dropped out, Smith sent them home. In some cases he allowed correspondence courses for those who fell behind, but he took education seriously and required his charges to do the same. Since his teenage years, Smith had believed that Mississippi's racism was based on ignorance and lack of education. His handling of the tiny patronage at his disposal was an effort to educate a few.[2]

Office workers came and went, as did the college student patronage workers. His secretaries were hired from the district, but most were young and attractive and did not stay long. After he had spent a few years in Washington, his office served as a clearinghouse for information among those who had married and gone back to Mississippi or out to the rest of the world. Young men, usually lawyers, came to work brief stints as "researchers." Smith offered them an opportunity to claim some Washington experience and in return he got inexpensive help, but Smith did not acquire another professional-level staff person until 1957.[3]

Lack of staff limited the work Smith could undertake, but, in addition to his committee and district requirements, he always managed to carry on at least one major crusade for the betterment of the republic. He first chose to challenge the Buy American Act. This act required various government departments to buy American goods as along as they did not cost over 25 percent more than foreign alternatives. He told Silver, "I have been taking an active interest in trade legislation, because this seems to be a field where somebody needed to do something, and because there also appears to be a chance for me to do some important work without fear of political repercussions at home."[4] The nineteenth-century liberal concept of free trade as a means of fostering peace among nations appealed to Smith, who also remembered the high tariffs as a cause of the Great Depression and the breakdown of world trade. Because cotton had always prompted many Mississippians to favor free trade, Smith felt he could sell this "liberal" policy at home. Campaigning in 1952, Smith had called for "less foreign aid and more foreign trade." His assistant, David Williams, reported that Abernethy congratulated Smith on the ploy, commenting that "this would sufficiently confuse the public and help to cover your voting record."[5]

In the House, Smith spoke in favor of free trade and debated tariff proponents. Trying to cast his crusade in Cold War rhetoric, he argued that the least expensive defense option for the United States would prove to be strengthening our allies' economies by providing them markets to build up their industry. Buying from our allies would create prosperity for them while supplying ourselves with low-priced goods. He endorsed an open trading system with the free world that would enhance U.S. security and save money on armaments. He cited Japan as an example of an ally that we had to develop through wise trade policies. Challenged by an isolationist who claimed it would be cheaper to give no foreign aid and protect our markets with tariffs, Smith reminded the House that the highest tariffs in U.S. history had coincided with bread lines and unemployment for this country. The *Congressional Digest* quoted Smith's remarks and indicated Smith's speeches were being recognized as the standard for free traders on the Hill.[6]

In addition to his crusade against the Buy American Act, Smith worked for reciprocal trade agreements, customs simplification, and support for overseas investment. He complained that Eisenhower could not be persuaded to read anything on trade and was dominated by tariff-minded Republican advisers. From Smith's district, Carr, his field man, told Smith that he was getting "wonderful press" on the Buy American crusade, probably in part because Carter's *Delta Democrat Times* endorsed Smith's efforts loudly and often.[7]

The next year Smith led a House debate to defeat a Republican effort inserting a Buy American (tariff increase) clause into the funding bill for the Interior Department. The *Washington Post* editorialized that Smith had saved Eisenhower from his own party and that Eisenhower owed Smith a debt.[8]

Not satisfied with stopping new Buy American or tariff increase laws, Smith worked to repeal the original act. The president had appointed a commission to study its repeal but had not acted on the commission's findings. Smith tried to needle the president by introducing a bill framed around the recommendations made by the president's own commission. Later, Smith nudged the president again by urging the secretary of defense to consider buying Japanese equipment for a dam in Oregon. In December 1954, President Eisenhower issued an executive order in effect repealing the Buy American law. He reduced the price percentage between foreign and American goods allowed under the act from 25 percent to 6 percent. The *Washington Post* noted Smith had fought alone for repeal and gave him the credit for Eisenhower's action.[9]

Smith dropped his attempt to rescind the act altogether but continued to speak for free trade. He enjoyed the lonely crusade. He complained to a friend at home of being ignored and misunderstood. Mississippi needed free trade to sell cotton to the world, he said, but, in his opinion, the whole Mississippi congressional delegation "went down the line" on the protectionist side. He wanted more recognition from people at home, but he enjoyed being called a "cloud rider" by a fellow congressman in a free trade debate. He gloried in being the lonely intellectual and liked to be a wit. When a free trade opponent in House debate accused him of failing to understand "practical matters of trade" because he was an author and intellectual, Smith asked the speaker to yield. He pointed out to the House that his book *The Yazoo River,* published by Rinehart, could be purchased at any bookstore for four dollars. He got a roar of laughter from the House.[10]

The Yazoo River was published in 1953. Smith found the time to finish the book during a full schedule, saying, "Well, I've done it [writing] in spare time at night. It hasn't involved any great organized effort. The kind of research I've done for writing is just something I carry on at all times. I read a great deal, and I'm able to retain a lot of that without any kind of formal note-taking."[11] His editor called *Yazoo* the best history in the American River Series and said that it was also the "best treatment of the contemporary Deep South I have yet encountered."[12] The *Christian Science Monitor* commented, "Mr. Smith has a literate mind for a man engaged in such practical matters as getting elected every two years. He writes with a clarity and a balanced restraint. . . . Would there were more like Representative Smith in Washington — in both Houses." The *Chicago Tribune* noted that "the author is something of a rarity, a politician who can write."[13]

As the result of his success with *Yazoo,* the *Virginia Quarterly* invited Smith to write an article describing the South's current state and to predict its likely development. He provided a balanced account, accentuating the positive. Noting, for example, that blacks had been gaining more financially than whites since the war, he predicted progress toward a "peaceful and orderly" relationship between the races and hoped segregation barriers would fall by consent. His writing reinforced his growing reputation as an intelligent, "moderate" spokesman for the South, which was the role he sought. He began another work on the history of frontier democracy in the Old South, but politics would overwhelm his ambitions as a writer. It never came into print.[14]

Family responsibilities increased for Smith in 1953 when, a week before Christmas, he and Helen adopted twin infants, Kathy and Fred, from the Washington Home for Foundlings. The babies provided instant family joy and responsibility. Smith's pleasure was muted only by extensive oral surgery at about the same time. The family spent that Christmas in Washington and did not return to Mississippi until the next summer, when the twins were beginning to walk.[15]

Smith remained close to his mother despite the distance and separation, writing letters to share the pleasure he still got from his participation in political life. He attended his first lunch at the White House in 1953 and provided his mother with a full account as soon as he returned to his office. Seating, he explained, was by seniority, so he was far from President Eisenhower, but since the president mostly talked about golf and fishing, it was not much of a loss to be at the other end of the table. The lunch served by six waiters was impressive, consisting of an unidentifiable soup, sherry roast beef, potato soufflé, brussels sprouts, cream cheese, an avocado and grapefruit salad after the main course, and pumpkin pie for dessert. A tour was given after lunch, and Smith described in detail a jeweled sword presented to the president by the king of Saudi Arabia and the bomb shelter under the White House.[16]

The capital was a pleasure to Smith, not the parties and social scene, but life on the Hill and his use of the Library of Congress, which supplied him with books. As always, he read voraciously, but he also took time for baseball. He enjoyed taking Mississippi visitors or one of the staff to see the Senators play. He began to play golf regularly and continued to play poker with the other members of the Mississippi delegation. He had paid off his campaign debts from the 1950 election out of his congressional salary, and he had no other campaign expenses because he did not have a contested election every two years. In Mississippi's one-party system, his reelection was automatic. Smith just tried not to remind voters there was an election. For the first time since he had married, he had achieved some financial as well as political security.[17]

Smith believed the government could do much good, and he joined many other Democrats in supporting Eisenhower. He always tried to be positive — to support rather than to oppose. In 1953, Smith voted with the Republican president 57 percent of the time, and two years later, he increased that figure to 72 percent. The South as a whole and Mississippi in particular gave the president far less support. Smith also distinguished himself from his Mississippi colleagues by voting with the American Federation of Labor more than half the time in 1954. His colleagues cast only a third of their votes for labor. Hubert Humphrey, the liberal civil rights advocate from Minnesota, admired Smith's interest in open government and asked Smith to introduce a freedom of information act in the House. Smith's votes and reputation did not go unnoticed by politicians back in the district, and many of his votes were unpopular at home. But his record helped Smith in the House, and he advanced in Congress when the Democrats retook control of the House in the middle of Eisenhower's first term.[18]

By 1955, Smith was leading a revolt against the Appropriations Committee because it had cut flood control funds. Securing a promise from the House leadership not to oppose his challenge, Smith marshaled Democratic and Republican allies. Calling together fifty congressmen, Smith assigned five amendments to different speakers. Each amendment was designed to restore the cuts. Smith acted as whip, never speaking himself. His amendments carried, overturning the Appropriations Committee recommendations for the first time in twenty-seven years. Smith's management elicited widespread praise. Otto Passman of Louisiana said that no member "ever served any more effectively, unselfishly, and untiringly [than Smith]" or been more willing to help "colleagues and constituents, thinking of the end result...." Whitten, even though he was on Appropriations, was so moved that he wrote Smith a letter of praise and congratulation. Covering the vote, the *Clarion-Ledger* observed that Smith had been shrewd in allowing others to "carry the banner," because nothing else so won a politician's heart as being asked to lead.[19]

By 1954, it had become obvious that Smith's initial rapid rise in seniority on the Public Works Committee had ended. Clifford Davis, a long-serving member from Memphis, chaired the flood control subcommittee and seemed likely to do so indefinitely. Smith's other subcommittee, roads, was chaired by John Blatnik of Minnesota, who likewise seemed entrenched. Public Works chairman Charles Buckley, a machine politician from New York, seemed immovable as well. Seeing promotions blocked on Works, Smith began to look for other ways to advance. His best friend in Congress, Bob Jones of Alabama, advised Smith to seek appointment to the Atomic Energy Committee, which they both saw as a "coming committee" with the probable increase in the use of nuclear energy. Despite several requests, the appointment was never made.[20]

Public Works was considered a "semiexclusive" assignment because of its power and influence. That designation meant Smith was barred from serving on any other committees of much rank. The exclusive committees were Appropriations and Ways and Means. In 1955, Smith was offered a spot on Ways and Means but turned it down because of the importance of flood control to his district. Instead in 1955 he asked to be assigned to the House Administration Committee as a means of being appointed to the joint Senate and House committee responsible for the Library of Congress. This fulfilled a personal wish to be associated with the literary side of Washington — to be invited to lunch with poets, for example. It held no political advantage. As the price for his appointment Smith had to serve on the accounts subcommittee of the Administration Committee. Examining other members' expenses was no way to win friends, but Wayne Hayes had turned the "little" committee into a power base by controlling members' parking spaces and offices. Once, when Smith was in London and wanted entrance to a royal event and the American embassy could not get the tickets, he called Hayes, who produced them in short order.[21]

Preparation, attendance, and attention to detail made Smith a strong committee member, but he had a temper. Smith cared intensely about his work, and he sometimes reacted to criticism or to what he considered gross ignorance with angry "sputtering." In one confrontation, a member who had been a star athlete at Princeton questioned whether Smith was being sincere with an amendment or simply trying to kill the bill under consideration. Smith responded, "If you want to call me a liar why don't you do so and I'll knock you down." Peace was restored when the fellow assured Smith he did not doubt his sincerity. Smith's outbursts were honest and did not make permanent enemies.[22]

After 1955, Smith increasingly was asked to present committee reports to the House for passage. This role is a mark of respect because most representatives do not have the time to prepare for votes and often do not even know what they are voting on. They rely on the committee system and their trusted colleagues when they vote. Smith spoke less often in these years, but it was always to present legislation for passage. Although he did not chair a committee or subcommittee, he was often asked to handle legislation from his committees and subcommittees — roads, flood control, and administration. Seniority is everything in the House, and Smith had attained enough of it by 1959 to be trusted by Rayburn to chair a committee of the whole House during the consideration of a billion-dollar military construction bill. Smith apologized to a supporter in Greenwood for breaking off a telephone conversation to attend to his duties, saying, "[This] is the most important assignment I've yet had along these lines from the Speaker...."[23]

The most important recognition of his leadership in the House was probably in the override of Eisenhower's veto of funding for flood control and other public works in 1959. Eisenhower had vetoed 145 bills between 1953 and 1959, and all had been upheld. Congress had been beaten to the "point of humiliation." Eisenhower claimed to stand for fiscal responsibility, and his bureau of the budget imposed cost-benefit analysis on harbor, canal, and flood control projects. Over and over, the Congress passed and the president vetoed funding for public works projects. Between 1957 and the override in 1959, Smith became the Democratic point man in attacking the president. In 1958, in the House, he responded point by point to the twenty-nine presidential objections in a veto message. In the press, Smith accused the president of trying to dot the i's and cross the t's for Congress, reducing it to a rubber stamp. It was serious business, but Smith and his friend Bob Jones tried to inject some humor by offering an amendment to a foreign aid bill, requiring projects built abroad with U.S. funds to meet the same budget bureau standards as domestic projects. Tongue in cheek, Smith alleged his amendment would eliminate waste.[24]

Smith believed that what the president called pork barrel spending was the only way for the nation's poor districts to share equitably in the country's booming economy, but his district stood to benefit from the bill, so this was no altruistic fight. Greenville would get major funding for a harbor and an industrial park created when the sludge from dredging the harbor was used to fill in lowlands along the Mississippi River. Smith's fights in the various committees for the controversial, expensive project earned this comment from the *Delta Democrat Times*: "[T]he outsiders can get very little done for their district because the rest of Congress won't cooperate. This Frank Smith became an insider as quick as anybody I ever watched. He is very effective on the Hill."[25]

The next year when the president vetoed the Democrats' projects once again, Smith chaired an ad hoc group of twenty-eight House members to override. Threatening to offer an amendment if Appropriations refused to challenge the president, the ad hoc group got the override bill out of committee, and, in a dramatic confrontation with Rayburn as he presided over the House, four of the group persuaded the Speaker to allow the vote. Few speeches were made because everyone knew the issue and the bill. When the override vote was announced, the House erupted in noisy celebration, and wits spoke of a rare alliance between the northern and southern wings of the Democratic party.[26]

At the same time Smith advocated spending for flood control, canals, and harbors, he opposed the president's efforts to create the interstate highway system. Membership on the roads subcommittee of Public Works landed Smith in the middle of the battle to build the interstate highway system and, because of his district's interests, he had to oppose it. This was a fight Smith did not relish because it placed him in opposition to a building program clearly needed by much of the nation. Representing a state that would not benefit much from the interstate system and possibly would be hurt when federal funding for secondary roads dried up, Smith opposed the interstate highways until forced to participate in negotiations producing the present system. Of course, Smith was not alone in representing these interests. Congress held back the development of interstate highways so long that the more populous states began to build toll roads. Then the inadequacy of highways during the Korean War made it a national defense issue and forced Congress to do something. After "exhaustive" hearings, the House roads subcommittee advised reliance on toll roads in 1953.

Out of patience with Congress, Eisenhower took the initiative by appointing a special commission that recommended an interstate system financed by bonds, which would have left Congress without control of the funding. Smith followed the lead of Senator Albert Gore of Tennessee in condemning the president's plan as a banker's bill. Gore was the chairman of the Senate Roads Committee that passed a bill expanding the traditional federal aid program to build the interstate system.

In the House subcommittee, Smith played a key role in developing a compromise plan combining elements of the president's and Gore's proposal. He presented the plan to the House on behalf of the committee as one that was fair to both the "poorer," more sparsely populated states and the big, wealthy states, but it failed to pass. In 1955, when a colleague claimed all forty-eight governors had endorsed a new plan, Smith protested that Mississippi's governor had not and the Speaker retorted that Smith had opposed interstate funding from the beginning. Smith made his point time and again: interstate highways should not be allowed to deprive secondary roads of funding. His position was that Mississippi would be hurt; therefore he would not approve the plan that injured his state. Foes of the president's plan designated Smith to draft an alternative plan. His bill called for direct congressional appropriations and increased funding for secondary roads as the price for building the interstate highways. Deep into negotiations and drafting in 1955, Smith had to refuse a trip to the NATO Parliamentary Conference in order to finish work on the bill. He took his case to the press with letters to the *New York Times* and other major papers.[27]

The president gave in to the Democrats, and the House roads subcommittee worked closely with Ways and Means while the two corresponding Senate committees did the same. The resulting compromise created the Highway Trust Fund, gave labor the wage rate formula they had demanded, provided funding through a single project model similar to flood control funding, and gave more money to the populous states. Smith was soon making the most of the result in his district, encouraging Clarksdale to lobby for an interstate route through the Delta and announcing that millions were available to his state for only a 10 percent match.[28]

After construction had been under way for a few years, the Public Works chairman appointed Smith to a special investigating committee to ferret out the fraud involved in building interstate highways. Republicans charged partisanship, but the committee carried out a fair inspection. They found corruption, but recommended little legislation because most corruption resulted from shortcomings in the state road building departments receiving the funds for the massive project.[29]

In his committee work, Smith proved to be a typical congressman. He looked after the interests of his district and tried to advance through the committee system. He proved effective by doing the hard close work required and by learning to work well with his colleagues. If he had been content with his committee work and the usual support of his district's interests, Smith could have had a much longer congressional career.

CHAPTER NINE

Cloud Riding

Smith entitled a chapter of his autobiography "Cloud Riding" because a member of the House of Representatives accused him of being an impractical idealist. Not happy doing the expected, he loved the accusation. His best friend in Congress, Bob Jones, said that Smith was not content to be a "local representative." Smith always wanted to be involved in national and international affairs and to be out in front of his constituents. Not motivated by immediate concerns about reelection for a decade, Smith took the long view with remarkable independence.

This is well illustrated by his most notable legislative accomplishment, which resulted from a personal crusade to label the textiles sold to consumers in the United States. He began the effort as a means of promoting cotton and ended it as a consumer advocate. From his district, Smith was under frequent pressure to protect the sale of cotton now that synthetics such as nylon and rayon were on the market. Having become widely available during the war, those products cut into the demand for cotton as producers switched to the cheaper synthetic materials and created the wash-and-wear revolution in 1952. Walter Sillers suggested that Smith sponsor an excise tax on synthetics; instead, Smith decided to advocate the labeling of clothes so that buyers would know if they were purchasing cotton, synthetics, or a blend of the two. Before Smith's act became law, neither manufacturers nor retailers were required to tell the buyer the content of most materials. Smith argued that if consumers were given enough information they would choose cotton as the superior product. His efforts to pass the measure illustrate the trials and tribulations faced by any congressman trying to legislate.[1]

His detailed and constant work proved his persistence. Modeling his bill on the wool labeling act and a long-pending bill advocated by Lister Hill in the Senate, Smith introduced his first textile labeling bill in 1955. It did not get far. No lobbying group supported it, and so Smith began to pressure the Cotton Council and the American Farm Bureau Federation to push the bill. By fall he had their support, and, during the remainder of 1955, Smith built a coalition for his bill. He received moral encouragement from a retired executive in the wool industry who had been responsible for the passage of the wool labeling act. The Florida retiree argued that the wool act provided consumers protection from unscrupulous manufacturers who used low-quality fibers instead of better-quality wool. Since the wool act, he told Smith, consumers had switched to better quality cloth.[2]

In January 1956, at the urging of Senator Hill, Smith met with the leader of the southern garment manufacturers. In their meeting, Smith sold the manufacturer by pointing out that the bill would require that the country of origin be identified along with the content of the materials. The executive wrote back that he appreciated "discussing the Japanese import threat and the cotton labeling bill...."[3] Hill congratulated Smith for a job well done. To sell his labeling bill, the free-trade Smith had exploited a semiprotectionist sentiment in the garment industry. Smith probably did not like to emphasize that aspect of the bill. In his comment to Hill on the meeting, he remembered convincing the executive that the bill would require no additional labels because the information could be printed on existing labels at little cost. In the spring Smith added the textile workers' union to his support network.[4]

Congressional leadership referred his labeling bill to a subcommittee of interstate and foreign commerce. Hearings began in the spring but had to be delayed in order to line up the southern garment manufacturers. Their leadership required extra time to turn around members who had opposed the bill. The committee was prepared to call up the bill by the end of the session, but Smith delayed again because he learned that the ranking Republican on the committee and two or three other members would oppose it. Division in committee would have doomed hopes for passage.[5]

During the recess, the chairman of the subcommittee left Congress and was replaced by a southerner. While the public relations staffs of the lobby groups distributed articles and radio ads, Smith persuaded

the departing subcommittee chairman to convene a hearing in New York
so that he could meet with lobby groups representing important manufacturers. The chairman convened the New York meeting and immediately departed. Smith and a staff member then conducted the hearings.
Smith learned, among other things, that the automobile industry opposed his bill because it would require labels on seat covers. In those
days of yearly style changes, manufacturers counted on frayed seat covers to prompt consumers to purchase new cars, and they did not wish
to be forced to install better, longer-lasting seat covers. Smith quietly
dropped automobile manufacturers from coverage under the bill. Myr-
iad questions arose. Sewing thread, for example, was excluded because
only 1 percent was not cotton, and the spools were too small to carry a
label. Smith persuaded DuPont of the advantages offered to their "superior" products by label identification.[6]

As industry support grew, Smith worked with the Federal Trade Commission, the agency that would have the responsibility of enforcing the
legislation. The FTC supplied Smith with examples of children injured
by mislabeled clothes. Smith made some headlines with accounts of
"torch sweaters"—rayon sweaters sold as cashmere—that caught fire
and burned the women wearing them. Smith became convinced of the
importance of textile labeling for consumer protection and touted the
bill on those grounds to members of the Interstate Commerce Committee. The committee cleared Smith's bill but threatened its passage
by offering a rival bill to repeal the wool labeling act and subsume it in
the new one. Smith opposed this plan because it would upset the support
network he had built for his bill and because the wool act had proven
to be effective as it was.[7]

Smith persuaded his Mississippi colleague Bill Colmer of the Rules
Committee to move the adoption of the bill during a committee of the
whole session at the end of the 1957 term. After a short debate, the rival
bills were ignored, and Smith's bill passed unanimously. The *Commercial Appeal* congratulated Smith and forecast victory in the Senate the
next year with sponsorship by Stennis and Hill.[8]

Not counting on them to do the work in the Senate, Smith organized
writing campaigns to convince the chairman of the Senate committee
to hold hearings. The only serious opposition to the act in the Senate
at the committee stage came from the Commerce Department, which
suggested an all-encompassing act to deal with all materials. The senators ignored their suggestions. Smith testified before the Senate com-

mittee and then sat with the senators to answer questions and rebut other witnesses.[9]

As passage seemed more certain, retail merchants and some of their associations began to protest to the Senate. Smith grew quite testy with some Mississippi merchants. He wrote the president of the Mississippi association that their national organization had supported his bill and that the developing opposition "gives rise to serious questions... of double dealing...."[10]

Smith wrote senators to counter the retailers' complaints, and the committee reported the bill. When it looked as if the Senate would adjourn before it reached a vote, Smith called Al Gore, Sr., whom he knew from their work on their respective roads subcommittees. Although campaigning for reelection in Tennessee, Gore used his influence with Lyndon B. Johnson, majority leader of the Senate, to schedule a vote before adjournment. Gore presided over the Senate debate, and Smith was invited to sit in the Senate to advise proponents of the bill during debate. Barry Goldwater, whose family owned department stores, led the opposition, but he appeared so ill informed in the debate that his arguments were easily dismissed, and the bill passed.[11]

As the Federal Trade Commission prepared to draft the rules that were left unspecified in the act, Smith testified before the FTC and urged the regulators to keep consumer interests foremost in mind while drawing up regulations. The law became effective in March 1960. Smith was pleased with the results, even though it earned him few political points at home. Manufacturers wrote to tell him that the act had eliminated fraud and would protect consumers. Consumer surveys reported that two-thirds of those polled were pleased with the labels; however, *Consumer Reports* sneered at the law as an "industry creation" and advocated "performance standards." Performance standards, or washing instructions, were not added until 1971, but Smith's act has proved to be a great success for consumers and cotton growers.[12]

Smith reported that he and his assistant worked almost full-time on the labeling project for two years, and it summarizes Smith's strength as a legislator. He worked hard to master the details, seeking out all the powerful interests, and he compromised when necessary. Knowing the automobile industry could block his bill, he did not insist on consumer protection extending to long-lasting car seat covers. He violated his free trade principles, at least verbally, to appeal to the garment manufacturers' protectionist sentiments. He skillfully exploited all his contacts in

Congress to work the system. In the end he cleverly combined the cotton interests of his district with national consumer protection. Smith loved the game of politics and making it work for the common good. He believed the system could be made to yield gradual, positive change.

He was never a one-issue congressman. Even in the thick of his efforts at domestic legislation, Smith did not abandon his interest in military and foreign affairs. He went to Nevada to observe a demonstration of a nuclear artillery shell. He turned his back to the explosion for protection and then went to inspect the damage. (Obviously the dangers of nuclear radiation were not as well understood in the early 1950s.) As a former artillery officer, he was impressed and advocated arming our forces with the tactical weapon as quickly as possible.[13]

Smith acquiesced in Eisenhower's negotiations ending the Korean War. He complained privately that if Truman and Secretary of State Dean Acheson had done the same thing they would have been charged with treason. But he agreed with the president that the American people did not want to pay the cost of the war and that stopping it was the only way to reduce taxes and balance the budget. Despite the end of the war, Smith remained a cold warrior. Always most concerned with Europe, he joined with thirty other congressmen to urge the president to tighten the union with NATO countries. The president's Middle East policy disturbed Smith. He wanted to support the colonial powers when they captured the Suez Canal. He could not understand why Eisenhower forced them to withdraw. Smith construed Nasser and the Algerian rebels fighting the French as threats to United States interests. Like most of the Congress and the country, he did not understand the anticolonial sentiments sweeping Africa and Asia and confused anticolonialism with communism. Eventually, he came to support the president's Middle East efforts and most of the administration's foreign policy. By the end of Eisenhower's term, presidential aides were thanking Smith for his votes.[14]

Smith served as a volunteer to guard against the isolationists in the House. He believed isolationists ranked with racists as ignorant dangers to national security. To cite one example, some American soldiers were tried in foreign courts for crimes they committed while stationed abroad. A strong band of southern Democrats introduced legislation to exempt American troops from trials in foreign courts. Smith opposed them, arguing in House debate that, to vote for the bill, Americans would have to be willing to grant the same immunity to foreign soldiers committing crimes while training here. The Republican leadership supported

Smith and killed the bill. Part of Smith's self-declared role was to combat ignorance, especially southern ignorance of the world, and he was consistent in seeking out opportunities. Smith spoke out in favor of a strong international U.S. policy and for the United Nations, even in Mississippi where such views were rarely heard in the 1950s.[15]

Smith maintained a lively interest in seeing the world. To continue his education, he did at least one congressional junket each year. In his first year, he and Helen inspected the Panama Canal Zone. Because of his membership on the roads subcommittee and his good standing with the House leadership, he attended international "roads conferences" all over the world. In 1955, he went to an international roads conference in Rome and, following the conference, received "counterpart" funds (foreign currency held by the United States and available to government officials) and a car so that he could "study cotton problems" in Europe. He retraced the path of his unit during World War II while also talking to a few cotton manufacturers along the way. He regularly attended the NATO Parliamentary Conference in Europe, sometimes with Helen, and once he took his assistant along as a secretary. She wrote that she was overwhelmed by the treatment given to congressmen abroad. They were waved through customs and greeted with limousines by embassy personnel. They ate in exclusive restaurants and attended the *folies*. Smith escorted her to a reception hosted by the French national assembly where they were announced as "Congressman Matthews and Mrs. Smith." On other trips Smith visited aircraft carriers and saw the Berlin Wall.[16]

His trips were also a diversion from the race issue. Because he was a secret integrationist, Smith preferred anything to "doing his duty" on civil rights legislation in Congress, but he represented a district requiring him to oppose integration. He was lying to stay in office; the best that can be said was that he tried to do it with some dignity. He regularly called on the attorney general to revoke the tax-exempt status of the NAACP. He occasionally resorted to racist observations such as an article in his newsletter praising segregated southern schools as demonstrably superior to the integrated Washington, D.C., schools. Struggling with a moral dilemma, believing in racial equality, knowing how it had shaped his early life, and desiring above all to lead southern whites to accept it, Smith suffered for his duplicity. He knew whites would not follow him in accepting racial equality and believed that the best he could do was to mitigate the excesses of racism and nourish the better nature of his people.

In his House speeches Smith never mentioned "Negroes." His position during this period is comprehensible only by comparing him to his Mississippi colleagues who spoke at length about "Negroes" and how there was "no problem" with "Negroes" in Mississippi. For example, Whitten, certainly far from the worst racist in the Mississippi delegation, once tried to explain to nonsoutherners why segregation was necessary in the South and not in the North. The North, he told the House, was segregated by living areas, and so "integration" was not a problem. He said that he saw more "Negroes" in a day in his "little town" than he saw in a whole session of Congress. There was a good deal of truth in his observations, but he followed this comment with a defense of the Mississippi officials who handled the Emmett Till case, in which the murderers of a black teenager were found innocent in a trial that outraged the nation.

Smith never commented on the case. By contrast, he opposed an early civil rights bill on constitutional grounds. He argued that the bill put forward by the attorney general to protect civil rights workers would deprive white citizens of their rights. The bill, designed to protect blacks from the type of intimidation widespread in Mississippi, would have allowed the attorney general to prosecute whites defending segregation who were "about to violate the law." Smith claimed that such prior restraint would deny the civil rights of those restrained (the white segregationists). Smith considered his ploy a clever bit of maneuvering. He testified against the bill in committee along those lines and voted against it, but he certainly never opposed civil rights with the same fervor he devoted to textile labeling or flood control. He went through the motions of opposing civil rights legislation because it was necessary for his political survival.[17]

When he first came to Congress, Smith thought that he could simply remain quiet, not contribute to the problem, and do good for everyone in his district, but as the civil rights movement challenged segregation, the white people of Smith's district became obsessed with race. It was a gradual escalation in the early 1950s. Whereas Smith could avoid the issue at first, by the mid-fifties it had become virtually the only topic of any conversation in Mississippi. Governor Hugh L. White, who had run on racist rhetoric, toned down his speeches and spoke to black audiences with more respect than Governor Wright had, which made interracial dialogue more civil. But in the 1952 presidential election white voters in black majority counties voted for Eisenhower and generally moved to the right as a result of their fears of the civil rights movement. Mechanization of agriculture and use of chemicals during the 1950s allowed planters to dispense with black sharecroppers. Black labor, which had been indispensable, became superfluous. Migration shifted the black population to cities in the North and to Delta towns. This lessened the influence and significance of white leaders such as Percy, who had always acted out of self-interest and concern to mitigate the worst impact of racism on the black population. As the agricultural system disintegrated and destroyed what was left of planter paternalism, the black population became a threat and an unwanted problem to whites. Growing fear fed on the nature of Mississippi society. Walker Percy once observed that there was no public space in Mississippi. Whites felt that public places such as restaurants, bus stations, and schools were an extension of the home. Because of their historic bond as a ruling minority, whites saw themselves as members of an extended family—not unlike the feeling one experiences today among whites in southern Africa. Integration to white Mississippians in the Delta did not mean sharing public space. It meant an invasion of their homes and the breakup of their family. There was enormous pressure for whites to conform—to wear the same style of tie, to attend Ole Miss football games, to go to church. Thinking about segregation was discouraged; perhaps they knew it was indefensible.[18]

One of Smith's constituents was Byron De La Beckwith, later convicted of the murder of the Mississippi NAACP field secretary Medgar Evers. Beckwith pestered Smith throughout his congressional career, dropping into Smith's Greenwood office with letters about race addressed to the president. After a few years, the letters became so abusive that Smith refused to transmit them to the White House. The state's incessant race war in which blacks and whites killed one another went on as it always had. For example, Smith's former assistant, David Williams, wrote to describe the recent killing of a white deputy sheriff by a black man as premeditated murder. To play down the nature of the crime, it was reported in the press as resisting arrest, but in fact the black man killed the deputy in revenge for murders the deputy had committed over the years. The deputy was well known to have killed several blacks, including one whom he dragged to death behind his car.[19]

Despite the endless stream of violence that Smith knew about personally from his father's death, he believed there was hope for peaceful change in his state, and he actively sought to keep Mississippians from withdrawing within the state's borders. For example, the head of the Mississippi Board of Health, Felix Underwood, contacted Smith to complain that growing hostility to the federal government on the part of state officials was leading to funding cuts for his department. Smith tried to reassure him about the cuts but indicated that he, too, was disturbed by the trend of forgetting that "we are part of the government and that it has responsibilities to us."[20] Smith advised Underwood to take the line that the federal "invasion of states' rights" resulted from the state's not fulfilling its responsibilities and urged him to maintain active cooperation with the federal government.

Another of Smith's tactics designed to counteract the growing racial animosity was to encourage "moderates" on the race issue to speak out. For example, he wrote to J. O. Emmerich to congratulate Emmerich on a special edition of his *Enterprise-Journal* dedicated to the "Negro's progress" in Pike County. Playing the role of segregationist, which he thought necessary with anyone he did not know well, Smith said, "This type of productive work . . . with the colored citizens . . . is the finest type of rebuttal that we can offer to those who seek to dictate the conduct of our affairs from outside."[21]

The conspiratorial tone of Smith's relationship with liberal or moderate Mississippians was demonstrated in his correspondence with editor Hodding Carter. Intending to visit Smith one fall when he returned to the Delta, Carter addressed Smith in a letter as "Dear Subversive." He wrote, "I will rendezvous with you in some out of sight place so that neither your disciples nor mine will find out."[22] Their tone was joking and made light of a serious fact. They were engaged in a conspiracy not to tell the voters of the district what they both knew about Smith's convictions. When Carter published an autobiography, *Where Main Street Meets the River,* and said more than was safe about his support for Smith in the 1950 election, Smith congratulated Carter for having written the "best introduction" to the small-town South, but joked half seriously, "I am ready to denounce at a moment's notice your version of the 1950 election."[23] The two men knew they were engaging in a counterconspiracy. They considered the Mississippi political system a conspiracy to exclude blacks from voting and had no qualms about their own actions. It was the nature of the place.

In the early fifties Smith was busy with his work in Congress and ignored the early signs of change. In 1953 his field representative, Woodley Carr, warned Smith that the NAACP had opened several chapters in the Delta. The organization was promoting voter registration among blacks, who were paying their poll taxes in large numbers. "This, in my opinion, is the shadow foretelling of coming events." Regarding future elections, Carr said, "Any Delta race is going to have to take them into consideration as they hold the balance of power."[24] Smith, of course, saw any overt sympathy to the growing black vote as political suicide. The Mississippi Democratic party was opposed to blacks voting, and the national party did nothing to support blacks. The party leader, Adlai Stevenson, held a 1953 conference with southern Democrats in Lake Village, Arkansas. Smith attended with some hope for progress on the subject but got little useful guidance from Stevenson.[25]

Despite the obvious signs that massive resistance was growing and in the absence of any national leadership, Smith continued his own balancing act as a "loyal southerner," national Democrat, and sly critic. He continued to believe in and to work for long-term progress. He spoke to the United Daughters of the Confederacy in 1953 on the anniversary of Jefferson Davis's birth, but he chose to talk about Davis's contributions to the United States Congress before the "War Between the States." Having depicted Davis as a loyal American, Smith concluded his talk with the observation that the South's loss of the war was best for everyone and that the UDC members could be proud of their grandfathers' high ideals without wishing they had won the war.[26] Using the "history" segregationists found so important to their worldview, Smith made a conscious effort to stop the drift toward another secession over the civil rights movement and to bolster his plea for continued Mississippi membership in national life. In retrospect, it might seem naive on Smith's part, but he had always believed that ending segregation would be an extremely long process requiring a revolution in the minds of white southerners.

In 1953 Professor Silver drew Smith into the reorganization of the moribund Mississippi Historical Society for the purpose of teaching Mississippians the truth about the past. As a part of their liberal conspiracy, Smith and Silver wanted to wean Mississippians away from the moonlight and magnolia version of history that reinforced racism and political conservatism. Meeting in the fall of 1952 at the War Memorial Building in Jackson, a committee, after some maneuvering, elected Silver as temporary chairman to preside at the first annual meeting of the revived society. In order to see that individuals sharing their "progressive" historical views dominated the organization, Silver made Smith chair of the nominations committee, and Smith enlisted Hodding Carter and Clarence Pierce to ensure his control. Silver commented, "You, of course, can do what you damned please ... now that you have the nominating committee stacked."[27] They tried to persuade William Winter, Silver's student and a political reformer, to become the president after Silver's term ended, but Winter refused, and a "traditionalist" was nominated. At the first annual meeting, Smith's slate of nominees got elected when the "UDC-DAR crowd," who fought the slate on the floor, got carried away and nominated too many "gentlewomen," squandering their votes. One of Smith's nominees, an old friend from Greenwood, reported, "There were half a dozen nominated from the floor for Director, so I figured that I was eliminated as I knew so few, but they were all professors or lady genealogists. After voting ... five or six came by and told me they had voted for me as they did not want the society run by professors."[28]

The first meeting of the society reflected the "liberal" view of the past. The program featured C. Vann Woodward and a paper on William Johnson, "Free Negro Citizen of Ante-Bellum Mississippi." This was not fare palatable to the "confederates" who still insisted on using the term "war between the states" instead of civil war and deifying Jefferson Davis. A complicated struggle for control of the society ensued between the "progressives" and the "confederates," with Smith as an interested observer in Washington.[29]

Smith's efforts to ease Mississipians gently into another way of thinking by altering their historical memories and educating them slammed into the massive wall of resistance created by the *Brown* decision in 1954. His field man reported that the district had gone from being conservative to being reactionary overnight. Fred Sullens, editor of the *Jackson Daily News*, summed up Mississippi opinion in a front page editorial: "This is a fight for white supremacy.... [T]here will be no room for neutrals or non-combatants.... [I]f you are a member of the Caucasian race ... You Are For Us Or Against Us."[30] Eastland had signaled the methods to be used against "moderates" during his reelection race by holding a Senate internal security subcommittee hearing in New Orleans, where he used professional witnesses to accuse southern liberals such as Virginia Durr of being communists. On December 1, Eastland, supported by Governor White and Congressman Williams, addressed two thousand Citizens' Council members in Jackson. Three weeks later Mississippi voters passed (by a two-to-one majority) a constitutional amendment to give the legislature power to abolish the public schools. Risking their political lives, Smith and Stennis asked Mississippians not to abolish the schools and urged the state to "meet the problem calmly." Smith's stance earned him a favorable headline in the *New York Times,* where he explained that the Delta had no Klan and that he hoped for the maintenance of good race relations.[31]

"Moderate," the *Times* called him. The description he prized as a sign of intelligence would soon became a synonym for traitor. Smith deluded himself by believing that gentle persuasion and sly education could change his people's minds about race. Less than thirty miles from Smith's base in Greenwood, the Indianola Citizens' Council organized the town's civic and business leaders. A circuit court judge, a plantation manager, and a Harvard-educated lawyer provided the leadership for a movement that would eventually control the state. Across the South, political, social, and economic leaders would give rise to massive resistance. By March 1956, the rising tide of hysteria had given birth to the Southern Manifesto; southern members of Congress had to sign on or be stigmatized as traitors. Smith signed without hesitation because to resist meant instant political death.[32]

Segregationists began to ferret out those suspected of sympathizing with integration in order to rid the state of them. In 1955 Holmes County residents rallied to chase a doctor, David Minter, and a farm manager, A. E. Cox, out of Mississippi because the two men operated a cooperative farm designed to help poor whites and blacks. The men were accused of being communists and of encouraging whites and blacks to swim together. This was the same socialist, experimental farm Smith had volunteered to help in 1941 when he was leaving Ole Miss. He had invited the farm leaders to speak at the university and then corresponded with them. Knowing of his past interest in the project, Cox and Minter contacted Smith for help. He got the clerk of the House Un-American Activities Committee to supply a letter attesting to the fact that the committee had nothing in its files to connect the men to the Communist party. But they left the county under strong community pressure, and Smith said nothing.[33]

The growing hysteria touched everything. Silver, who was not a religious person, reported to Smith in 1954, "Got the program for the Mississippi Historical Society today. Some son of a bitch put me down for an invocation."[34] Silver got Carter elected president of the MHS in 1955 over groans and protests from the confederates, but soon lost control to the confederates and genealogists and their allies in the universities. Smith watched the struggle from Washington. He understood, when Silver and the "liberals" lost control of the organization, that it was yet another sign of Mississippi's exit from national life.[35]

As Mississippians withdrew behind their magnolia curtain, Smith grew more estranged from his district. He became afraid to talk, even with those who had been close friends. Eventually, he began to spend time only with those whom he could trust. By the mid 1950s he could never avoid the subject of race in Mississippi conversations. Greenwood was home, and it was the heart of resistance. Judge Tom P. Brady, a founding member of the Citizens' Council, made his famous "Black Monday" speech there. He later published the speech as a pamphlet that became the "Bible" for segregationists opposing the *Brown* decision. Most of Greenwood's leading citizens belonged to the Citizens' Council, and Beckwith began to pester the whole community with pamphlets and monologues at various organizational functions. At the beginning of his tenure, Smith had tried to stay in touch with his constituents by scheduling town meetings in courthouses. Few citizens turned out, and, after experimenting with radio, Smith came to rely almost exclusively on newsletters that were picked up by district newspapers and turned into articles and editorials. Although the newsletters helped promote Smith, they did not keep him in touch with his district. The longer Smith remained in office, the less contact he had with his constituents. In 1954, he appreciated the isolation.[36]

Reports surfaced in 1953 of some opposition stimulated by John Bell Williams against Smith as a "liberal." It did not amount to much. Most of the political interest at that point centered on the Senate election. Rumors had spread that Eastland would retire, and most of the representatives, excepting Smith, had been preparing to run for the Senate. Smith assisted Whitten in precampaign activities, but Eastland kept them out of the race when he announced for reelection. He had one moderate opponent, Lieutenant Governor Carroll Gartin. The fact that Eastland had a challenger helped Smith, because Eastland would not allow a contested race for Smith's seat. A divisive primary in the Delta might split the vote he wanted to keep solid for himself. So in a strange political maneuver, Eastland, the neo-Bourbon leader of the resistance forces, helped the leading Mississippi moderate to ward off a challenge.[37]

Smith made his usual rounds of the civic clubs that fall, urging "litigation" as the only method to combat integration and asking his audiences to avoid "rash incidents." Using these moderate words took guts in 1954. Smith's old friend Philip Mullen reported that the Klan was organizing in Canton where he was editing a newspaper. Commenting on the general trend toward intolerance, he said, "It's pretty hard to take — so I'll just have to quit making speeches; even my pleas for racial and religious tolerance, before the Rotary Clubs, will soon be suspect if not already so."[38] Mullen soon left Canton because of the growing air of fear and intolerance.

Smith would survive eight more years in Congress and continue his efforts to save Mississippi from the hard-line segregationists and states' righters who came to dominate the state. He had supporters throughout the state who appreciated the role he played — they would eventually call themselves the Mississippi "underground." William Winter expressed the views of a small but sometimes well-placed minority when he wrote Smith, "[W]e have a deep sense of pride that you represent our state in the intelligent and statesmanlike manner in which you do."[39] Encouraged by such people, Smith did not surrender to the upsweep of segregationist passion.

Although Smith would not openly campaign for a candidate in the 1955 governor's race, he forged an alliance with J. P. Coleman as early as 1954. During the summer primary, Smith got a complaint from Coleman's opponent, Paul Johnson, Jr., that Smith had entered the race for Coleman, to which Smith responded that his field man, Carr, was employed by the Johnson campaign. He did not deny supporting Coleman, which he did because Coleman appeared to be the more "moderate" choice. Smith still hoped, despite the growing signs of withdrawal, that Mississippi could be saved from violence so that it could evolve toward integration.[40]

A violent act near his old home shattered his hopes. After the primary in August 1955, Roy Bryant and J. W. Milam murdered a black teenager, Emmett Till, for making a pass at Bryant's wife as she clerked in the family store at Money. They beat Till and then shot him before pushing his body, weighted with a heavy metal cotton gin fan, into the Tallahatchie River. Smith was in Genoa and got his first information about the Till murder by deciphering the headlines in an Italian newspaper. He wanted to be no closer to the story and made no comment, though the trial captured the national headlines for months. The two men confessed to a *Look* reporter — after a jury had found them not guilty. Till had been visiting from Chicago when he was murdered, and his funeral, as well as his murderers' trial, received national and international press coverage. Till became a martyr to the violent segregation atmosphere dominating Mississippi. White Mississippians felt singled out, persecuted, and abused by the world press. Mentally they cut themselves off from the rest of the nation after the Till murder, making up their minds that it was them and us and that "they" did not understand "us."[41]

Seeking to survive in the increasingly hostile climate, Smith made more of a "segregation record" for himself in 1955. He got more news coverage for his bill requiring the secretary of the treasury to regulate tax exempt organizations, i.e., civil rights organizations, and to revoke their tax exempt status if they misbehaved. He also endorsed a bill to make district federal judges' decisions final, outlawing appeals to the Supreme Court. But Smith refused to abdicate what he considered his responsibility to try to quiet the raging passions. He conducted his usual fall tour in Mississippi, asking civic club members to shun violence and to allow Congress and the courts to handle the integration problem, and he did not hesitate to endorse Stevenson for president. All the other members of the Mississippi congressional delegation quibbled or opposed Stevenson. Colmer told a reporter that he could think of twenty-five other Americans he would prefer to see nominated. Smith answered, "I supported Stevenson in the last election and will do so again."[42]

In January 1956, just after J. P. Coleman's inauguration as governor, Smith wrote his congratulations and a statement of support. "I am confident that your voice will be heard above the hysteria and that our State will have the calm and forceful leadership that is needed so much in the next few years."[43] Smith encouraged Coleman to utilize the services of his cousin Gordon Smith, an ex-FBI agent, who had just been elected to the state senate from Leflore County and seemed ready to cooperate with Coleman to dampen the hard-line segregationists' efforts to control the state. Coleman has been "praised" as the slickest segregationist of all, but at the time he certainly was "moderate" compared to Eastland and the Citizens' Council leadership. Eastland tried to develop "interposition," the idea that states could assert their sovereignty to void federal law, to stop integration. He founded an organization to promote the idea nationally and convinced the Citizens' Council to support it. Reacting to Eastland's interposition ploy, Coleman turned to Silver and Smith for help with historical research to counter it. Smith ordered most

Frank Smith, father of Frank Ellis Smith, with daughter Sadie in 1926, the year he was murdered

Smith and brother Fred Cecil Smith

Frank Ellis Smith, student photo, Moorhead Junior College

Basic training, Fort Bragg, North Carolina, 1942 (Smith, center)

Catching a nap at one of the fire direction centers (France, 1944), where Smith was on duty day and night

Smith and wife Helen McPhaul Smith in Greenwood, shortly after their marriage in 1945

Smith and Helen in front of Brentano's, a favorite bookstore of Smith's, Washington, D.C., 1946

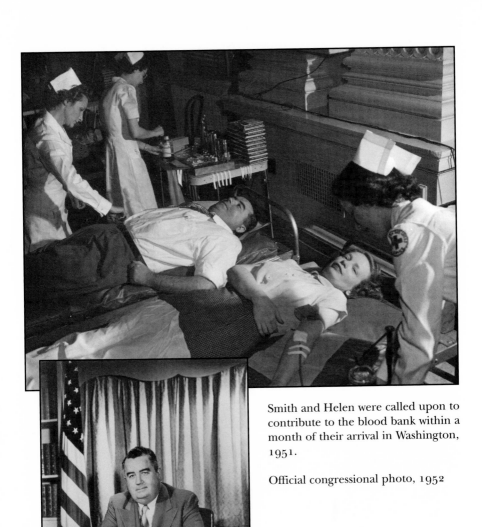

Smith and Helen were called upon to contribute to the blood bank within a month of their arrival in Washington, 1951.

Official congressional photo, 1952

The President and Mrs. Truman

At Home

on Monday afternoon

May 12, 1952

at five o'clock

Invitation to the White House, 1952

Mississippi congressional delegation: Congressman Arthur Winstead, Congressman Tom Abernathy, Congressman Jamie Whitten, Smith, and unidentified women

Smith with adopted twins Fred and Kathy, 1954

Smith (right rear) at NATO annual conference, 1955 (first row, l-r, Senator William Fulbright, Congressman Wayne Hayes, and Senator Lyndon Johnson)

Mississippi congressional delegation with Governor J. P. Coleman (l-r front: Congressman Bill Colmer, Coleman, Attorney General Joe Patterson; rear: Congressman John Bell Williams, Congressman Arthur Winstead, Smith, Congressman Tom Abernathy

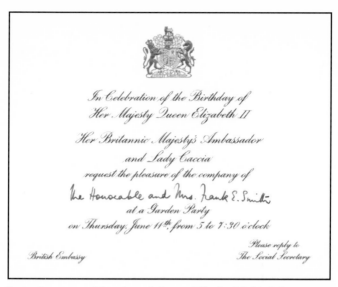

In Celebration of the Birthday of
Her Majesty Queen Elizabeth II

Her Britannic Majesty's Ambassador
and Lady Caccia
request the pleasure of the company of

the Honorable and Mrs. Frank E. Smith
at a Garden Party
on Thursday, June 11th, from 5 to 7:30 o'clock

Please reply to
British Embassy   The Social Secretary

Invitation to a celebration of Queen Elizabeth's birthday.
Smith and Helen attended the party, but the queen was not
present.

Publicity shot in Smith's TVA office for the publication of *Congressman from
Mississippi,* 1964

Directors of TVA: Smith, Aubrey Wagner, A. R. Jones

Visit of President John F. Kennedy to TVA, Muscle Shoals, Alabama,
May 1963 (l-r, TVA director Aubrey Wagner, Kennedy, Smith,
Governor George Wallace)

Governor George Wallace, Smith, President John F. Kennedy at Muscle Shoals, 1963

Commercial Appeal coverage of President Kennedy's Muscle Shoals visit

Response from Robert Kennedy to Smith's condolences on the death of President Kennedy. Script reads, "And he was a Frank Smith man."

Smith with President and Mrs. Sukarno of Indonesia in Loudon, Tennessee, c. 1968

Smith (right) with Governor William F. Winter and Charlotte Capers, director, Public Information, Mississippi Department of Archives and History, on
the publication of the *Inaugural Papers of William F. Winter*, 1980, to which
Smith contributed

Campaign photo, 1972

Campaign photo, 1972

Smith at Mississippi Historical Society meeting in 1986 when he was president, with biographer Dennis Mitchell and wife Janet S. St. Lawrence

Smith at Choctaw Books on Manship Street, Jackson

Smith with son Fred at Choctaw Books at North Street location, Jackson

of the research from the Library of Congress, and Coleman used it to combat Eastland.[44]

Despite the absurdity of Eastland's ideas about interposition, Coleman's job was not easy. The governor of Mississippi had relatively little power compared to the legislature, which was controlled by hard-line segregationists. Winter reported from the house of representatives, "There was pretty rank discrimination in the committee assignments accorded our supporters, and I don't know how much bitterness will result therefrom."[45] Sillers still controlled the house of representatives, and, while he was probably too intelligent to believe interposition would work, he had no intention of allowing the moderates to inch toward integration unopposed. The legislature passed a resolution endorsing Eastland's solution, and Governor Coleman signed it, even though he believed it to be "poppycock."[46]

At the local level, massive resistance gained strength. In Yazoo City fifty-three blacks petitioned to integrate the schools, but within three months economic pressure caused all but six to remove their names from the document. In Belzoni, the Reverend George Washington Lee led four hundred blacks to register to vote between 1953 and 1954. Under pressure, three hundred removed their names from the rolls, and Lee was shot to death. Statewide the number of black voters fell from twenty-two thousand in 1952 to twelve thousand in 1955.[47]

In 1956 the hard-line segregationists began to threaten Smith in his district. In February, an anonymous note was sent to district newspapers attacking Smith's congressional assistant, Audrey Matthews: "You should know your Congressman has as his Secretary—listed in the Congressional Directory—a 'gal of reputation'—not too good either—not a Mississippian, never saw Mississippi, has no vote in the state and brags about it. Are the voters of District 3 going to tolerate such?"[48] The newspapers did not print the "news." But Robert Patterson, one of the founders of the Citizens' Council, began to explore the possibility of running against Smith. That threat was stopped, but two other serious candidates began to investigate their possibilities.[49]

Smith's field man, Carr, must have felt that the boss needed some better contact with the reality of the district, because he sent some long letters earnestly trying to explain the situation as he understood it. He called the Delta a "hot spot" of segregationist activism. The Citizens' Councils were potent, he thought, and would eventually take political power. Newspapers added to tensions with inflammatory reporting, he said. There were planned economic pressures being exerted against individuals, and he seemed to imply that more of this type of conflict could be expected because it was succeeding. The white population was developing an "inferiority complex," he noted, because "[w]e cannot believe that we are now or have ever been guilty of anything wrong in our relations with the negro." He concluded, "[T]hose who talk moderation have their usefulness destroyed in short order."[50] In the spring Carr praised Smith's efforts with the tax exempt organizations bill aimed at civil rights groups and urged him to "play that note on the piano as our people have to be assured and reassured because we are like children in that we fear the unknown."[51] He advised Smith not to take part in the national Democratic convention because no candidate selected there would be acceptable to the Delta. Smith rejected the argument, saying, "I cannot agree with the idea. It is like giving up the fight before we ever get to it."[52] The Delta district caucuses did not elect Smith as a delegate, because, as Smith told a correspondent, the "people who controlled" the caucuses opposed him and knew he favored Stevenson. He had to be added, as a delegate at large, at the state level where Governor Coleman had more influence. The Citizens' Council was pushing for a meeting after the national convention to assess the convention's performance and for an endorsement of interposition. Coleman defeated its efforts, added Smith as a delegate, and kept Mississippi safe for moderation.[53]

Since Stevenson's nomination for president was a foregone conclusion, Smith concentrated his interest, as did the convention, on the nominee for vice president when Stevenson threw it to the convention for a decision. Smith's candidate from the beginning was John F. Kennedy. Kennedy had impressed Bob Jones, Smith's friend, and Jones probably influenced Smith, but Smith attributed his interest in Kennedy to his authorship of *Profiles in Courage*. Smith was especially impressed with a chapter dedicated to Mississippi hero L. Q. C. Lamar. Smith followed the convention's thinking that Kennedy could help the Democrats win the northern cities and give them a real shot at beating Eisenhower. Smith was still elated by the victory of overriding the president's veto of public works funding, and had hopes of a Democratic victory; also, he would have liked to see the party overcome its prejudice against nominating a Catholic. That a Mississippian might be able to lead the party in destroying a prejudice appealed to Smith's sense of irony. Coleman and Smith made a deal. Smith agreed to vote for Albert Gore on the first ballot, and Coleman promised to vote for Kennedy on the second. Smith toured the southern state delegations at the convention with Kennedy family members and worked the telephones to attract support. Kennedy did not get the nomination, but, as one of Kennedy's few southern supporters, Smith made an impression. For his part, Smith became convinced that Kennedy would be the nominee for president in four years.[54]

As he drove his family from Mississippi to Washington in August, Smith stopped off to attend a Stevenson strategy meeting in Knoxville. His primary contribution at the meeting was to prompt Stevenson to recognize former governor White as they entered the hall together. By fall he was back in Mississippi arguing forcefully for "calm," "unemotional," and "dignified" responses to integration. Through a "forceful, calm, and dignified" approach, he said, the South must win an "appeal to national public opinion." His own political power, Smith said, depended on achieving influence in Congress, and that could only be done by presenting "our viewpoint without hollering about racial issues."[55] In 1956, Smith devoted entire speeches to the "race issue" in his strongest appeal yet for his "moderate" policy. He played the most active role of any Mississippi Democrat supporting the national ticket, as he had in 1952, but in 1956, led by Governor Coleman, most of the congressional delegation joined him. An advertisement for the Democrats pictured Eastland, Stennis, Colmer, Whitten, Abernethy, Winstead, and Smith with the caption "Do You Believe These Men Would Betray Mississippi?"[56]

The voter was to believe that all of the men pictured were devoted to segregation and to trust Smith's argument that Mississippi would be better served by casting its lot with the national Democratic party. Obviously since 1952 the rest of the delegation had grown concerned that Eisenhower might carry the state. Smith told audiences that Adam Clayton Powell, the black congressman from Harlem, was voting for Eisenhower, and, while the national Democrats were not segregationists, they were better than the Republicans. In Smith's case the truth was that he did intend to betray segregation. To him that did not mean betraying his state, which he saw as ill served by the politicians who led its people to believe that segregation could be preserved. Perhaps the height of duplicity in his public speeches that fall came in a talk to librarians in Jackson. Smith had helped to pass an act providing federal support for local libraries and for that reason was invited to address a conference of Mississippi librarians. Stressing every person's need for literature and the training leaders received by reading—the usual arguments for public libraries—Smith concluded by stating that libraries would enable Mississippians to understand "our heritage," making segregation safe.[57] Given his own development and the fact that library reading had helped to destroy his faith in Mississippi's segregationist heritage, Smith's speech asserting that public libraries would serve the cause of segregation seems symbolic of the desperate battle he was waging. Using segregationist rhetoric to keep his people in the American mainstream, where he foresaw the end of segregation, was tortured political maneuvering.

Stevenson lost to Eisenhower in 1956, and in the fall of 1957 Eisenhower had to send the army to Little Rock to integrate the high school. As the Arkansas crisis played out on television screens, which were only beginning to appear in many southern homes, Smith spoke to the Mississippi County Sheriffs Association. He urged responsible behavior "in maintaining law and order and at the same time preventing the type of incidents that only serve as ammunition for those who seek to eliminate local control of our affairs." He called upon the sheriffs to defend "our" position to the country by "firm and equal justice which pours cold water on every incident that might flare into racial violence."[58] Trying to keep a lid on the violence threatening to erupt at any moment throughout the South, Smith also looked ahead to the 1960 presidential election.

Smith was convinced that Kennedy could win the nomination, and he hoped to have Mississippi support him. Kennedy did not conceal his acceptance of the *Brown* decision, but he courted white southern Democrats and black voters in northern cities at the same time. Smith hoped Kennedy would be the leader to begin the end of segregation. To assist in Kennedy's southern strategy, he engineered a Kennedy visit to Jackson to address Mississippi Democrats. Smith had just hired as a staff member Charles Deaton, a young Ole Miss law school student who had run out of GI bill support and needed a job. Deaton was involved in founding the Young Democrats in Mississippi with Gray Evans, another law student. Smith arranged for Kennedy to meet Deaton and discuss an invitation to address the first meeting of the new organization. Deaton recalled that Kennedy bought two Milky Ways, and they concluded the negotiations eating candy bars on the steps of the Capitol. Kennedy told him that he would have to secure consent from Eastland and Stennis before he could accept because of Senate protocol. Deaton tracked Smith down at a poker game in John Bell Williams's office to ask what to do, and Smith told him to see the senators. Eastland readily agreed, but Stennis delivered such a stinging lecture on Deaton's violation of Senate protocol that Deaton lost his temper and vowed to reconsider voting for Stennis's reelection. He left Stennis's office convinced he would be fired, but when he called Smith at his poker game, Smith laughed at his reaction and told him not to worry. Stennis was soothed and the invitation made.[59]

Although they had not planned it, Kennedy arrived just after the Little Rock confrontation in Arkansas, increasing the drama of the event. Reporters predicted that five hundred would attend and that Kennedy would evade the race issue. Two thousand came, including Kennedy's fellow senators, Stennis and Eastland. The other members of the congressional delegation chose to miss the event. Smith accompanied Kennedy from Memphis, acting as his host, and Coleman invited Kennedy to spend the night in the Governor's Mansion.[60]

In Jackson, Kennedy met with a variety of politicians in his hotel room and then decided to have a hot bath to help his aching back. Before he bathed, Kennedy ordered two beers. Deaton was shocked. Some Mississippi politicians drank heavily and often, but always in secret. Mississippi was a "dry" state. The Bostonian probably did not comprehend that having a beer was still a "sin" in Mississippi. Deaton was shocked by the idea that one could openly enjoy a beer without the stigma most Mississippians attached to it.[61]

In his speech, Kennedy confronted the race issue, directly stating that the *Brown* decision was the law of the land and that law and order had to be preserved. He quickly followed that with a challenge to the leader of the Mississippi Republican party to state just as clearly Eisenhower's position on integration. Kennedy got a standing ovation. The only miscue of the evening seems to have been when Kennedy tried to pour cream into Smith's coffee at dinner and got salad dressing instead. The *Jackson Daily News* described Kennedy's Beacon Hill accent as "strange in sound but warmly received in spirit."[62]

The daring visit was a triumph. At the Young Democrats meeting the next day, speakers stressed unity with the national party and declared there was no need for a third party in Mississippi. An impressive host came. Members of the legislature and dignitaries such as tax collector William Winter launched the new organization.[63]

The moderates and the hard-line segregationists battled for control of Mississippi in the late fifties. The legislature passed a law creating the

Sovereignty Commission to protect segregation, but the governor staffed it with moderates. When the federal government proposed to build an integrated veterans hospital in Jackson, the governor got Sovereignty Commission support for it, arguing that Mississippi would be "put in a bad light" if veterans were denied care. He said, "There's a great deal of difference between putting grown people together in a hospital and putting children together in a school." Segregationists called this type of reasoning "the little bit pregnant argument." To them accepting any integration would surrender the principle.[64]

The hard-liners appraising Smith's moderation began to promote another candidate for the next election. From Clarksdale, Smith's cousin warned, "I hear lots of local opposition saying you are not taking a stand on intergration [*sic*]....Sullivan is being mentioned."[65] Carr worried about Delta lawyer Charles Sullivan and farm bureau employee Buddy Bishop of Indianola. Sullivan toured the state touting the American Democratic Action's endorsement of Smith's voting record as proof that Smith was a liberal who had to be eliminated from Congress. Several members of the legislature encouraged him, but Eastland, having no desire to disturb the serenity of the congressional delegation, discouraged Sullivan from making the attempt to unseat Smith.[66]

Smith's hold on his seat grew more precarious after 1957. His record of accomplishments in Congress came to mean less and less to an electorate mobilized by the Citizens' Councils. The councils judged every candidate solely by his stand on segregation, and Smith's record was suspect. Perhaps his fellow classmates at Moorhead began to recall his youthful questioning of segregation. Some of his colleagues disliked his obvious liberal record in the House. The *Christian Science Monitor* identified him as a "moderate," and the ADA labeled his voting record as liberal.[67] Not many Citizens' Council members read those publications, but now the Citizens' Council leaders brought them to the voters' attention. Someone, probably with council connections, mailed those postcards about his assistant's bad reputation to Delta newspapers. There were rumors of all descriptions spreading through the Delta about Smith's ill-concealed liberalism.

In less stressful times, his private views would have gone unquestioned, but the late 1950s and the 1960s were far from normal times in Mississippi. Mississippians began to suspect their neighbors of disloyalty and in many cases to persecute those considered less than 100 percent loyal to segregation. Smith's appeals for calm and unemotional opposition to integration became red flags to the diehard segregationists who wanted emotion and hate to release the fear they felt as the federal government drew gradually closer to forcing integration upon them. From nearby Louisiana, Walker Percy described Mississippi as "insane." Using Faulkner to illustrate, he said that the "Gavin Stevenses" were gone and the "Snopeses" had won. The Stevenses "have shut up or been exiled or they are running the local White Citizens' Council."[68]

By being positive and active in the Congress and in the Democratic party, Smith labeled himself as a part of the federal government. Congressman John Bell Williams, by contrast, fought almost everything the government did and opposed his party in virtually every election.[69] The Mississippi public loved Williams and elected him governor when the Democrats finally stripped him of his congressional seniority. He was a successful politician because he continued to be elected. Smith's flaw as a politician was that he was not content with that. Smith understood that his people did not accept his ideas on race, but he knew they were eager for and needed federal assistance to work their way out of the worst poverty in the United States. He was not totally idealistic. He tried to appeal to Mississippians' interest in economic progress, thinking that if he could supply federal funds they would understand his value and keep him in Congress. But he was not content just to milk the federal cow for funds. He also intended to make Mississippians better human beings. He tried to lead them where he thought they should go because he was a liberal. He believed in the basic goodness of people, and, although he had witnessed horrible cruelty in Mississippi and during the war, he knew that human beings were capable of learning, changing, and becoming better. He tried to lead, to teach, and to improve in a time and a place where the majority of the people wanted to stand still, retain segregation, and look back to the moonlight and magnolias that had never existed.

Perhaps the real value of Smith's congressional career was best summed up by the little-noticed Library Services Act of 1956. This act broke new ground in that it committed the federal government to support and extend library services nationwide to populations previously unserved. The American Library Association had pushed the idea of federal support to extend library services to rural populations for a decade without success, until 1956, when Smith joined twenty-six other members introducing identical library bills in the House. Edith Green, reporting for her committee the bill bearing her name, said that it just as well could have been called the Frank Smith bill because Smith had supported the bill long before she adopted it. There was no political advantage to Smith in working for the Library Services Act. The ALA had no important lobby in the Delta, and certainly Smith would gain few votes by working for public libraries. Without Green's remark, Smith's efforts in the House might have gone completely unnoticed. He supported the enactment of the law because of his personal experience with a public library and because of his faith that others could and would educate themselves if books were made available to them. He believed that the federal government had to take a leadership role because he knew his state government would not. The act had a funding formula built in to assist poor rural states such as Mississippi, but it proved its worth to the nation as a whole. Librarians have agreed with Smith's prognosis. The act served as the springboard for other laws extending the federal role and leading states to develop far more comprehensive library systems in rural areas.[70]

His assistant, who knew Smith's work best, called Smith a "dogooder."[71] As a congressman, he tried to work for what he believed to be the best interests of all his people. A few whites in his district elected Smith, and he had to look after their interests to be reelected, but he remained conscious of all his constituents—black and white—and tried to serve faithfully their long-term interests in economic development, education, and social development. Serving the powerful planters who controlled economic and political life in the Delta while also straining to help the poor, oppressed majority made for a spotty record, but he was true to his long-term goals born in the depression-era Greenwood library. He wanted his people to accept integration and to use the federal government to improve the Delta's economy for the benefit of all. By the late fifties the question was how long he could continue to serve two masters—white and black, rich and poor—while being opposed by the raging segregationists determined to maintain the status quo.

CHAPTER TEN

Leaving Mississippi

It was obvious that Mississippi would lose another congressman after the 1960 census, because its population had not kept pace with the nation's increase. Smith would face a second redistricting fight, and Sillers still controlled the Mississippi House of Representatives. Smith knew he had lost Sillers with his voting record and moderate stand on civil rights. He hoped that his value as an advocate for flood control and supplier of funds to the district would convince Sillers and other leaders in the district to keep him in office, but he did not cultivate Sillers as he had his first two years in office. Alienated by the emotional defense of segregation at home, Smith grew more interested in the national and international scenes. As the Delta became obsessed with fanatical attachment to segregation and fear of "foreign influences" from places like Washington, Smith devoted himself to natural resource development and supported John F. Kennedy for president. Smith knew he risked political defeat, but he loathed the ugly segregationist mood dominating Mississippi and hoped he could win reelection based on the federal money and services that he was able to provide for the Delta.

"Charlie" Sullivan, a district attorney from Clarksdale, continued to explore the possibility of running against Smith, but in early 1958 he concluded that it would "take one hell of a fight" and went no further.[1] In the early spring, Smith dismissed Sullivan as a tool of the Jackson oil lobby and, instead of touring his district, stayed in Washington to play golf and to recuperate from a round of flu that had plagued him.[2] To prepare for the looming redistricting battle, he hired two new staff members from Mississippi. Gray Evans, a founder of the Young Democrats, whom Smith had met during the Kennedy visit to Jackson, replaced Charles Deaton, who returned to Ole Miss to finish law school in 1958.

Because his primary assistant, Audrey Warren, was an outsider and a liability in his reelection effort, Smith looked for ways to strengthen his staff for the impending political battle. To that end, the Public Works Committee created a new subcommittee for watersheds, providing Smith with a third assistant, Jack Warren. He was fresh from Ole Miss law school and served as the clerk of the new watershed subcommittee, housed in Smith's office.[3]

In Washington, Smith occupied himself with overturning the president's veto of public works funding and with passing his textile labeling act. Though busy, he did not neglect the district. He produced an unusually large number of news items about federal projects funded for the Delta. The Greenville harbor and industrial site stayed on the front pages, and Smith pushed for the establishment of a national weather service substation in the Delta to provide hourly reports to farmers. To increase his support in Greenwood, he called for dredging the Yazoo River and reopening barge traffic between the Mississippi River and Greenwood. The last steamboat to operate on the Yazoo had sunk in 1921, and there had been no commercial traffic since then, but Smith encouraged local promoters who dreamed of reopening the river.[4]

In May 1958, the Army Corps of Engineers provided a towboat, the *Fife*, and a barge to transport government officials. As they dined on box lunches and cookies provided by the corps, the barge glided at ten miles per hour from Greenwood to Yazoo City. The *Fife* radioed ahead for bridges to be turned so that their progress would not be slowed. The entire population of Belzoni turned out to see the sight, and at one stop the bridge tenders radioed back a message that they had urgent mail for Congressman Smith, the star of the performance. Smith vowed to seek $45 million for the navigation project, and the trip concluded in Vicksburg after a second day on the river. All in all, Smith orchestrated quite a demonstration of political power. He produced for his district. That was his strongest asset. He intended to make himself invaluable by delivering federal funds.[5]

The year 1958 was a wet one in the Delta. Local flooding and high water in the fields battered farmers and businessmen. Smith arranged with the Small Business Administration to establish a temporary field office in Greenwood so applicants for low-interest loans would not have to travel to Jackson. He announced that he would work with Stennis to fund the Yazoo Backwater Project, the last major corps flood control project left undone in the Delta. He and Stennis had funded fifty thousand dollars through their respective committees to begin planning the work. When the Delta needed enlarged cotton allotments, Smith worked for it. He clearly made his point: he was delivering services and funding for his district.[6]

In the fall Smith invited Sillers to accompany an Army Corps of Engineers group on an inspection tour of the Mississippi River, and Sillers accepted. Smith was reelected that fall as first vice president of the Mississippi Flood Control Association; his flood control leadership qualifications seemed solid. In 1958 he was reelected automatically to Congress.[7]

Yet things were out of joint. Both John Bell Williams and Whitten spoke in Smith's district "on the popular subject of segregation," while Smith attended his yearly NATO conference in Europe.[8] Speaking in another congressman's district was a breach of congressional etiquette, and their speeches obviously opened the redistricting battle. Smith received warning from Arkansas of what lay in store for him. Brooks Hays went down in defeat because he had been labeled a moderate on race. Smith consoled him: "I am afraid this is another of the burdens we are having to assume as a result of the tragic setback in all our affairs which [has] come since 1954."[9] Smith knew he had been lumped in the same category as Hays, and Hays's defeat worried him. Smith got bad news from the district, too. His field man, Woodley Carr, resigned after being elected sheriff of Sunflower County. Losing Carr deprived Smith of an effective district agent when he needed one badly. Smith had always found that Carr could talk both sides of any issue and listen well to others without saying too much. Smith never found another agent as capable as Carr.[10]

In January 1959, Smith tried to influence the state senate race in his district to provide him with an effective spokesman from Greenwood for the redistricting battle. Unfortunately, under the swap agreement between the two counties it was Tallahatchie County's turn to elect the senator, and Whitten was from Tallahatchie County. Smith naturally was interested in having his man, not Whitten's, in the legislature, and he telephoned former congressman Whittington about breaking the senate agreement between the two counties. Despite Smith's problem, Whittington opposed the idea of breaking the agreement, and Smith eventually had to abandon it.[11]

But he did not heed Whittington without a struggle. Smith's friends held a Democratic party meeting in Greenwood and voted to break the senate agreement so that Deaton could run for the senate. After some confused maneuvering, Deaton declined to run, citing his friendship with a Whitten relative and the "mistaken perception" that he would be Smith's candidate. The swap agreement stood. Spencer, Smith's stepbrother, warned him of growing suspicions that Smith was sponsoring Deaton to run for a house seat. Deaton, according to Spencer, was telling everyone that Smith and his cousin Gordon Smith were both behind him. Spencer warned that he and other Democratic leaders could not "turn their backs on" the older candidate for the house — a planter named Corbet Lee Patridge. Smith knew the man would not be an effective advocate for him, but it is not clear that he had prompted Deaton to seek the house seat, because Smith wrote to Evans asking if the rumor were true. Evans denied it, saying that he had "been extra careful not to even intimate any such connection."[12]

Politics in Smith's hometown seemed to be unusually contentious. An "outsider" from Yazoo City had moved recently to Greenwood for the purpose of entering politics. Harold Streibich had worked for a hardline conservative congressman from Georgia and was an ideologue dedicated to opposing Smith. After Streibich did some bragging about his war record at the VFW hall, Deaton wrote to Audrey Warren in Smith's office to ask for information on Streibich, warning her not to put it on Smith's letterhead. She sent army and congressional service records, which Deaton used to "smear" Streibich, in the words of Spencer. Deaton won election to the house and supported Smith, but the politics of the election left a bad taste in the mouths of some in Greenwood.[13]

Mississippi's volatile atmosphere became supercharged in 1959 when Charles Mack Parker, a black man accused of raping a pregnant white woman, was lynched in Pearl River County. Governor Coleman invited the FBI to find the lynchers, and the FBI employed such heavy-handed tactics that they enraged the local population. The community had not wanted the lynching, but they resented the FBI's treatment of witnesses and informants so much they would later elect the lynch mob's leader sheriff. State press coverage damned Coleman as "worse than a moderate" — a term used to describe a traitor in the war to preserve segregation. Contacted by a reporter for a comment on the situation, Smith said, "You're just trying to agitate something and make the situation worse" and hung up.[14]

The "moderates" were about to be routed in Mississippi. The Citizens' Council candidate, Ross Barnett, won the Democratic primary race for governor in the summer of 1959. Barnett called black people "niggers" in public speeches and played on white Mississippians' pent-up fear to extend control over the state. Smith took no part in the primary and remained in Washington. Barnett made the Citizens' Council practically an agency of state government, and many white Mississippians developed a hysterical fear of the world beyond their borders. The Sovereignty Commission began to spy on the "subversives" who favored integration. The college board hounded Smith's friend James Silver to leave the state. Any non-native Mississippian was suspected of being an outsider trying to destroy the "southern way of life."[15]

During the summer of 1960, while Mississippi Democrats were making their decision about whom to support for president at the national convention, Smith was in Europe with Helen. His legislative counsel, Gray Evans, reported to Smith that "things are pretty hot...." When he could not reach Smith or Stennis for advice, he called Eastland, who said that the two senators and Coleman would be making a statement on the nomination, but they would delay to give Evans time to reach Smith by telephone. Coleman told Evans that he, the senators, and Tom Hederman, owner of the *Clarion-Ledger,* had met and decided to wait for the convention to choose a candidate. But Governor Barnett and John Bell Williams ignored them and held a meeting of the Democratic Executive Committee. They voted to back "unpledged" electors rather than any Democratic candidate. Smith's stepbrother argued for forty-five minutes with Evans that Smith should not support the party in 1960 because it would mean the loss of the redistricting fight in two years.[16]

Smith attended the Democratic nominating convention as a delegate in 1960 only because the entire congressional delegation was invited to attend. The senators were supporting Lyndon Johnson, and Smith joined them, explaining to Kennedy that it was the only hope of defeating the unpledged slate committed to Barnett. Congressman John Bell Williams had already spread the rumor that the senators had to support Johnson for reasons of senatorial courtesy, but representatives were not bound to declare for the national ticket. Smith advised Kennedy not to talk to Barnett at the convention because the Mississippi governor "was hopeless." Mississippi nominated Barnett for president. For the first time since he had been elected to Congress, Smith did not campaign for the national party nominee in Mississippi.[17]

He spent the campaign working for John F. Kennedy in Washington, directing the Kennedy-Johnson Natural Resources Advisory Committee. The story of his work for the Natural Resources Advisory Committee is important for two reasons. First, it demonstrates Smith's attempt to escape the political situation at home. Second, the job began Smith's effort to make natural resource development an important part of the Democratic national agenda. Smith gladly escaped what he thought to be the growing turmoil of his state for work he firmly felt was good and productive. Believing the storm over segregation to be destructive, Smith needed desperately to find a positive outlet for his political energies. He believed passionately that the government should control and develop natural resources for the benefit of the entire population. He knew Kennedy did not share his passion for natural resources, but he was convinced Kennedy would make a great president. Smith joined his two unrelated passions by trying to use natural resource development as a means of promoting Kennedy. His hope was that after the election the new Democratic administration would adopt his ideas on natural resources.

Development of natural resources had been a major issue between Democrats and Republicans since 1948. Truman had campaigned on a platform dedicated to replicating the success of the Tennessee Valley Authority in other river valleys around the country. Those plans had not come to fruition, and the Republicans campaigned in 1952 on a promise to limit the government's control over resources and to favor private development. They called the Democrats' policies "socialist" and appointed Douglas McKay, a car dealership owner and former governor of Oregon, to clean the "socialists" out of the Interior Department. McKay's administration of the Interior Department cost the Republicans several elections in the Northwest, but despite the demonstrated value of the natural resources issue Stevenson ignored it in his 1956 campaign. Smith was distressed and wrote to Sam Rayburn identifying natural resources as the "sharpest" difference between the two parties. Pointing out the political lessons of recent elections, he urged Rayburn to strengthen the Democratic party's position on the issue.[18]

Between 1956 and 1960, Smith devoted much of his energies in Congress to natural resource development issues. His support for development projects outside his own district earned him respect from other congressmen. For example, a Texas representative wrote, thanking Smith for his support of a reclamation bill: "I am quite mindful of the fact that on an issue of this nature, which is necessarily local in that it directly affects a limited area, the easy thing is to vote against it. You can understand why that fact adds to my personal appreciation for your vote."[19] Another said, "A lot of folks from the West remember what you did in helping move the Forest Roads and Trails Program forward in those dry Eisenhower years."[20] Such support explains why Smith was able to lead the override of Eisenhower's public works funding veto. The override had been Smith's greatest leadership victory in Congress, and he was convinced that the coalition developed for that fight could prove a winner with the voters nationwide. The Republicans recognized their dedication to private development as a political liability and replaced McKay with a more astute politician at Interior. By 1960, it was apparent that the Republicans actually had changed natural resource policy little and that they had effectively obscured the issue, even though they reduced spending for natural resource development. But Smith still saw an opportunity to gain political advantage and to commit his party more strongly to government development of water and other natural resources.[21]

Bob Jones of Alabama, Smith's best friend in Congress, provided Kennedy with some help on "water" issues during his West Virginia primary and suggested that Smith run a committee during the presidential campaign. In his memo asking for the establishment of the committee, Jones argued that the ground had been plowed and planted. It remained only to harvest the fruit of the work already done by Democrats in Congress. He pointed out that the Izaac Walton League and the Wild Life Federation mattered more than farm organizations on these issues, because they influenced more voters. Therefore the committee needed to appeal to both the "birds and bees" and the "use groups." The idea would be (1) to stimulate letters from members of Congress and conservation leaders to support the campaign, (2) to develop brochures on conservation for the campaign, and (3) to name people to the committee for the publicity value.[22]

The press release from the Democratic National Committee announcing the establishment of the Kennedy-Johnson Natural Resources Advisory Committee emphasized how the Republicans had refused to finance new water projects, endangered the National Park Service, hurt mining, and worsened air and water pollution. Smith's initial appointments to the committee tended more toward industrialists than environmentalists, but he included representatives of both from all over the nation. By October, Smith had appointed over three hundred members and reported that he was adding more "every day." He and his contacts were careful to screen out Republicans, who might cause any "fuss." "Southern" congressmen declined the "honor of appointment," fearing it would hurt them at the polls, but Smith eventually appointed half the Democratic members of Congress and two thirds of the candidates for Congress. Each appointment was followed by press releases and publicity materials identifying the new member as a Kennedy-Johnson supporter. Smith sent speech ideas to Archibald Cox, a Kennedy assistant, and put out fires with water use organizations when they discovered that Kennedy had earlier taken positions hostile toward resource development.[23]

The committee worked out of Smith's congressional office; Warren was the number-one volunteer for the undertaking. Jones's assistant was number two, but he dropped out before the election. The National Democratic Committee furnished one secretary. Smith found other "volunteers," some of whom were loaned from congressional committees. It was a relatively inexpensive operation, costing less than four thousand dollars, and Smith absorbed almost 25 percent of the cost from contributions given by barge companies. Winding up the committee's work, Smith reported mailing one hundred thousand brochures, four hundred news releases, and an unspecified number of speeches for individuals assisting in the campaign.[24]

Smith asked committee members to send their ideas for transmission to the candidate, and many did. One woman concerned about the state of oyster beds transmitted three handwritten legal pages from her fishmonger. Most contributors, including congressmen, rode their favorite hobbyhorses or plugged their latest projects, although some members of Congress provided thoughtful analysis of where they thought national policy should go. Smith edited the submissions in order to prepare a report to be delivered at the inauguration. Some of the committee members had not understood the nature of the organization and asked for travel funds to attend the meeting. Smith had to inform them that they traveled at their own expense. Three hundred attended the inauguration, including thirty representatives and ten senators. Smith chaired the meeting, which was addressed by Stewart Udall, the new secretary of the interior, and Orville Freeman, the secretary of agriculture.[25]

Smith assured an assistant secretary at the Interior Department who had worked on the material for the platform that his committee was "primarily a campaign operation" and that its report would not differ from "Kennedy's commitments in this over-all field. . . ."[26] The Kennedy-Johnson Natural Resources Advisory Committee was purely an instrument to promote Kennedy's election. Kennedy had another natural resource advisory group within his campaign organization, and the Advisory Committee on Natural Resources of the Democratic Advisory Council had met in New Mexico in February to prepare the ideas that went into the Democratic platform. Smith did not actually work at developing policy. He used congressional personnel and tried to mobilize the issue to Kennedy's advantage during the campaign. It was a minor contribution to the campaign, but one Smith enjoyed and worked hard to make a success.[27]

The advisory committee's final report differed considerably from Smith's first draft and must have been reworked with the new Interior Department staff before the meeting. The result was a thirteen-page report heavy on development projects such as flood control and waterway construction and calling for a revival of the Civilian Conservation Corps (CCC) social programs to put "idle" young men to work on reforestation and soil conservation. The emphasis was on development, and it was even suggested that nuclear devices be used to construct waterway projects. On the fiscal side, the report called for the president to ignore budget office recommendations and to drop required local contributions so that the federal government took full financial responsibility for projects. It was a call for a highly active federal government to develop watersheds, atomic energy, and national parks.[28]

Udall paid no attention to the document, and Kennedy was not much interested in natural resources or conservation issues. Smith asked for, but never got, a meeting just after the election to discuss resource issues. He did send recommendations about appointments that Kennedy should be careful in making and a list of the hottest topics with important lobby groups. Perhaps Smith and his allies had an impact, because Kennedy made one speech in Billings, Montana, shortly after his election that incorporated all of their major points. But they did not turn Kennedy into an environmentalist or an active advocate for development. Kennedy seemed to understand resource development as most congressmen did—as "pork barrel." For example, when an assistant asked about the possibility of establishing a park in Kansas, Kennedy wanted to know why they should put one there. What had Kansas done for them? If other emergencies had not intervened, natural resources might have gotten attention, but the Cuban crisis and the civil rights movement overshadowed the issue. Smith's dreams of having the Democratic party deeply committed to natural resource development did not materialize, and his hopes were dashed by the all-pervasive race issue.[29]

Every time Smith saw Kennedy, the president's first question was always the same. What were Smith's chances for reelection? Kennedy was acutely aware that Smith's support for the national ticket had placed him in danger. To send a clear signal to Smith, Ross Barnett fired Smith's cousin, Gordon Smith, from a usually secure position as chief counsel to the state employment security commission. Newspapers reported that Gordon Smith was fired for two reasons: being Smith's cousin and supporting the national ticket in the presidential election.[30]

With the hard-line segregationist Mississippi political establishment growing openly hostile to him, Smith faced a challenge in Congress as well. The Democrats there were engaged in the biggest political fight since the revolt against Speaker Cannon in 1910. The leadership knew that Kennedy's legislation — minimum wages and federal aid to education, for example — would never pass the Rules Committee, chaired by "Judge" Howard W. Smith, as long as the coalition of conservative Democrats and Republicans remained in power. Rayburn first indicated he would strip "Bill" Colmer, Judge Smith's chief assistant from the Mississippi Gulf Coast, of his seniority and position, because Colmer had supported Barnett's unpledged presidential electors. But then the Speaker decided instead to pack the Rules Committee with enough liberal Democrats to out-vote Judge Smith. Frank Smith landed in the middle. He supported the administration, but it was the Mississippi delegation threatened with punishment by the leadership. The *Clarion-Ledger* carried the twists and turns in the House on the front pages so that Mississippians could watch the usually inscrutable events there unfold. It appeared that Rayburn might lose a showdown vote, and so the president got him to postpone it in order for the administration to bring all possible pressure to bear on Congress. Members were warned that the president had a long memory and that those who opposed him would suffer.[31]

Many southerners decided to go along with packing the Rules Committee. Smith's friend Bob Jones played a key role in rounding up the votes. Behind the scenes, Smith worked, too, and promised his vote if it were needed to carry the packing plan. He told his assistant that he would vote for the bill and then resign. Of course, he tried to keep it all secret because the word was out that packing the Rules Committee would lead to the passage of civil rights legislation. Kennedy had appointed black men to high office in his administration, and Mississippi already distrusted the "Kennedy boys."[32]

The day of the Rules Committee vote was one of high drama, because Rayburn went into the House unsure if he had the votes to win. Tensions grew as the roll call remained a close tie. Smith did not answer when his name was called, and only after the Speaker had won did he appear. A reporter described the scene: "The stout and perspiring Representative from Mississippi, Frank Smith, stepped out of the cloakroom and answered to his name. He had pledged his vote—one that could have killed him politically in his Delta district—to Sam Rayburn, if that vote was needed to win the Speaker's battle. Now, Frank Smith, sure of the outcome, was able to vote 'no,' making it two hundred and seventeen to two hundred and thirteen and no more names to call."[33]

Smith's Washington liberalism, which he concealed from Mississippians, caught up with him on that vote. Colmer, who had been a frequent golfing partner, was furious with Smith for his role. The *Clarion-Ledger* picked up a story that Smith and Bob Jones were rewarded for their support by the Speaker, who sent them to Australia for a meeting of the international roads organization. Smith had taken these trips for years, in part because he went along with the leadership and in part because he was on the roads subcommittee, but now his trip was portrayed as a payoff for his support on the packing vote. Smith denied the charges and claimed he had worked only to protect his colleagues, who had been threatened with the loss of their seniority, but there was no use denying it. The rumor of Smith's "treason" against segregation spread through the Delta. The story grew to the point that many voters believed that Smith had actually voted for packing the Rules Committee.[34]

That same year, another rumor made the rounds in Greenwood—that Smith was having an affair with his assistant. There was some upset in Smith's office. The assistant, Audrey Matthews, resigned, writing to Smith, "I don't think I can come back." With Smith's assistance, Jack Warren, the new watershed subcommittee assistant and presumably Audrey's lover, moved to a government agency. Smith asked Audrey back, and she returned to the office as Audrey Warren. She had married Jack.[35]

Despite his long-serving assistant's return, not much went well for Smith. Even a seemingly safe and innocuous history project proved troublesome. He had tried to establish a Civil War Centennial Commission years before at the urging of his former professor Bell I. Wiley, but a rival bill sponsored by the Washington Civil War Round Table and a friend of President Eisenhower passed instead. A retired colonel became the executive director and planned celebrations rather than scholarly work. Smith was not appointed to the commission until 1961, by which time it had degenerated into a divided, ineffective group. In the midst of Smith's redistricting and reelection campaigns, communities and historians clashed with one another and with the commission. Historians wanted substantive research that was unpalatable to those who wanted to celebrate, and Smith sided with the historians. The disagreements between the historians and the celebrators sparked controversies that sullied Smith's name with those hoping to preserve the "civic religion" of the defeated Confederacy. When the commission met in Charleston to commemorate the firing on Fort Sumter and the beginning of the war, a black member of the New Jersey delegation protested because he could not be accommodated in the hotel with other members. An uproar developed, and the South Carolina commission seceded from the ceremonies. President Kennedy intervened to suggest holding the banquet at the Charleston naval yard, which was integrated. The commission's executive director resigned after the debacle, and Smith had the pleasure of helping to install Allan Nevins, a distinguished historian, in his place. As a result, Smith became persona non grata with Civil War groups around the country, because they wanted celebrations, not solid research projects that did not feed their prejudices. The Civil War Centennial Commission became widely known and an object of jest. During the 1960 Cotton Carnival, the Memphis Press Club presented a skit in which Governor Barnett, dressed in a Confederate vest, presided over a council of Mississippi congressmen.

> **Governor:** We've got to make plans for the Civil War . . .
> **Smith:** War? You mean the Civil War Centennial, don't you?
> **Governor (bellowing):** Centennial! Hah! I'll make them think Centennial. We're using live ammunition and police dogs. . . .[36]

Unfortunately for Smith, all of this transpired as Mississippi considered how to redistrict and eliminate another congressman. Smith had tried to prepare. His chosen political image was "Mr. Flood Control" or "Mr. Water Development." The creation of his watershed subcommittee was not unconnected to his impending need to appear more important at home. He developed a new organization called the Mississippi Rivers and Harbors Conference, which provided him with an agent. His man could operate statewide to advertise Smith's importance to the state. In the spring of 1961, Smith toured the Delta with his watershed subcommittee, and in the fall he presided at the ceremonies opening the eleven-million-dollar Yazoo auxiliary channel. Beginning in late 1959, Smith ventured outside his district to speak throughout the state and enlarged the mailing list for his newsletter to include likely annexation targets.[37]

In January 1961, Smith mailed his ideas on redistricting to Sillers and to every member of the legislature who represented a portion of the third congressional district. His plan outlined the need to keep the third district intact by adding three or four counties from Whitten's or Williams's districts—all of which belonged to the Delta Council, he pointed out.[38] The legislature was not scheduled to meet until January 1962, and Barnett declined calls for a special session, saying he wanted to delay "until after there has been an opportunity to observe the new Kennedy administration and Mississippi's congressional delegation in the new administration."[39] Sillers made no response to Smith's suggestions on redistricting, but wrote to chastise Smith for his votes authorizing foreign aid. Smith's reply was terse: "We have to continue in order to maintain our military strength abroad and otherwise prevent the spread of Communist influence and military domination."[40] Smith did nothing to appease Sillers. In 1950–1952, he had courted Sillers shamelessly, but ten years later he was too proud and defiant. He hoped that Sillers's Delta patriotism would persuade him to keep the Delta together as a district, but Smith had little hope of it. He saw the realities of the situation and seemed to be depressed in the months leading to the redistricting vote.[41]

There was some talk of redrawing lines to pit Smith and Abernethy against one another because they had been the only two congressmen to support Kennedy in 1960, but Abernethy's support for Kennedy had not been enthusiastic, and Smith and Whitten lived in adjoining counties. Whitten's position on appropriations, which controlled millions of dollars in agricultural subsidies, made him a powerful figure. His district contained fewer people than Smith's, but far more white people and thus more voters. These factors made Whitten the favorite of those politicians wishing to rid the state of its liberal congressman.[42]

At the White House, Kennedy's men were well aware of the situation and did all they could to help Smith. Presidential assistant Henry Wilson told his boss, Lawrence O'Brien, that they could count on Smith to vote to provide development funds for depressed areas, but not much else. Smith needed a "conservative voting record," Wilson explained, because he was going to be redistricted in with Whitten. The White House thought it looked hopeless, but "if he wins, it will be the first fight the White Citizens [*sic*] Council will have lost since it got moving."[43] When Smith asked Kennedy to appoint one of his supporters to the Mississippi River Commission and an Arkansas senator wanted another man, Smith's candidate won. Smith also received the post office patronage in four districts, his own and those of the congressmen who had opposed Kennedy. The other congressmen went to Senators Eastland and Stennis, and Smith sometimes had to complain daily to the White House to keep from being outflanked by his colleagues and the bureaucrats who did not wish to anger powerful members of Congress. Area redevelopment projects were easier to handle, and Smith's district probably got more than its share.[44]

Smith worked hard to shore up his home base. In the fall of 1961, he apologized to Whittington for not visiting him while he was in Greenwood. It was, he said, the "most hectic fall I have had in Greenwood."[45] It was a one-man fight. Smith held only one meeting with supporters that year, and they fit comfortably into his stepbrother's office: Gray Evans, Charlie Deaton, Norman Brewer, Sonny Meredith, and "little" Hodding Carter, the son of Smith's old friend. All were young men with little power to influence the outcome in the legislature. The talk centered on using patronage to influence members of the legislature, but there was too little patronage to make much difference.[46] Delta leaders kept Smith away from public meetings held to discuss redistricting. Smith wrote stiffly to Sillers about one meeting that he had wanted to attend, but did not: "I am told that those who are sponsoring the dinner at Cleveland...believe that it would be best not to have any of the Members of Congress present so that there would be no question of personalities involved."[47] In response to Smith's inquiries, Whittington assured Smith that he did not want to see another member added to his district, but the former congressman did nothing to help.[48]

The outcome was a foregone conclusion. Newspaper writers and White House aides had spoken for a year of the coming Smith-Whitten contest. The legislature met early in January 1962, but got off to a slow start because of cold, ice, and snow. It did not take up redistricting until the third week of March. Everyone knew the plan. When a Delta patriot protested to Sillers that the Delta members of the legislature were more interested in seeing Whitten defeat Smith than they were in protecting the Delta's interests, Sillers refused to be "drawn out" and promised only to keep the "present counties" together in any new district. It was, he said, impossible to keep personalities and the political interests of the members of Congress out of the decision.[49] Bills simply to combine Whitten's and Smith's districts had overwhelming support in both houses of the Mississippi legislature. The "beauty" of this arrangement was that it made all the other congressmen and their supporters happy. It created a grotesquely large district, but it swamped the increasing number of blacks voting in the Delta with white voters from Whitten's hill district. The senate passed its bill first; the only opposition came from a handful of Delta senators who opposed it on grounds of Delta patriotism, not support of Smith. Senator W. J. Caraway produced some old-fashioned Mississippi-style rhetoric in opposition, describing the bill as "born out of wedlock and fathered by a many headed monster composed of power politics, unpledged electors, selfishness, and greed."[50] He predicted the electoral injustice of such a district would lead to court cases and federal control of voter-registration laws. The only humorous note came when a senator from Amory rose to change his support for the bill to opposition because his constituents had communicated to him that he would be hurting chances for the creation of the Tennessee-Tombigbee Waterway project by redistricting Smith with Whitten. He made it clear he did not like changing his position, but Smith's "Mr. Water Development" campaign must have had some impact.[51]

In a rare appearance, Sillers took to the floor of the house to speak in favor of an amendment to save the Delta district, but he could not carry it off. He said he would vote for Whitten. Then, while allegedly supporting the retention of Smith's district, he talked vaguely of the Delta's being most vulnerable to the "enemy within." Referring to Smith without saying so, he condemned the greedy politicians who would "tread under foot our most cherished traditions, lay waste to the culture of thousands of years of Anglo Saxon civilization in their bid for votes and political power."[52] Rambling and referring to a bill that had passed the U.S. Senate, Sillers said that he expected the "Kennedy boys" to remove poll taxes and literacy tests allowing "Negroes" to vote in "mass elections." Sillers made it clear that he saw Smith as a threat to segregation and the southern way of life. There would be no compromise this time.[53]

Smith still had support. The Greenwood *Commonwealth* denounced the new district. In Whitten's district the *Tupelo Daily Journal* decried the injustice of the legislature's depriving Mississippi of a fine representative while allowing Winstead to "warm a seat" from a small district. Kennedy offered to take Smith into his administration, but Smith wanted to make the fight. He refused to give up on his state. He had battled all his life against what he called the "know nothings" who wanted to detach Mississippi from the mainstream, and he wanted to try once again.[54]

On one hand the election was a battle to eliminate the "moderate" Smith from Congress; on the other, it was not so simple. Smith had done all he could to obscure his liberalism and his record. Despite all the rhetoric about states' rights and segregation, the election was also about which congressman was more valuable to the state in Washington. Whitten was as much a part of the federal system as Smith, but the Delta's flood control needs had largely been met. The subsidies Whitten provided would continue to be "needed" as long as there were crops. If the Delta had been in danger of flooding in 1962, the outcome might have been different, but the majority of the voters lived in the hills, safe from flooding. Both candidates made loud claims to be segregationists. Neither even hinted that he would compromise with integration. Smith supported Kennedy, and Whitten did not—that fact plus Smith's support of the United States's role in world affairs were the notable, public differences between the two men. To the average voter, all the other differences were symbolic, but the symbolic communication inherent in the segregated system since Reconstruction remained important. Segregation customs had never allowed for open discussion of race in campaigns, because segregationist rules held that all candidates had to be united in absolute support of the "southern way of life." The question was always below the surface: which candidate was the stronger protector of segregation? But the question could not be voiced or debated openly.

Despite Smith's early attempt to ignore race in deference to the all-important rule of protecting the "southern way of life," the primary election did not follow the usual pattern. For one thing it was too early. Primaries usually took place in July and August—months of almost unbearable heat in Mississippi—but the party scheduled this one in May and June, pleasant months by comparison. Second, Delta whites and hill whites rarely voted together. Their conflicts had shaped Mississippi's political history, but now they had to share a congressman. Third, there was a black candidate, Merrill W. Lindsey from Rust College in Holly Springs.[55]

In April, Whitten and Smith invaded one another's old territories while studiously ignoring the novelty of a black candidate. At first they found most people unaware that there was a campaign for Congress. Both candidates had ignored elections for years while the voters sent them back automatically. Whitten set a folksy tone, telling the story of old Charley, who, when he was asked to make a speech for his reelection to local office, said, "Folks, I want you to reelect me, but I ain't gonna do a bit better, for I been doing the best I can."[56] Whitten had not lost the common touch: drinking a Coke at a country store and passing the time of day, remembering all the men's names, and going into a shack to eat a piece of pie. At first, Smith ran against Barnett as the agent who had created this mess, instead of criticizing Whitten. Smith tried to be positive, stressing his congressional record. Early in the race a supporter asked Smith about his favorable rating by the "leftist" Americans for Democratic Action, and Smith responded characteristically: "The other members from Mississippi make considerable capital out of being against whoever is in power. I have never operated that way and I never will.... I believe that my record in Congress should be constructive both from a personal standpoint and in terms of service to my district."[57] Smith gave his campaign workers a telephone "talking list" that consisted of bills he had passed and program accomplishments such as the textile labeling act—not much to stir a voter's adrenaline.[58]

Yet despite the fact that the new district was stacked ten thousand votes against him, Smith had some hopes. Delta whites voted in higher numbers than hill whites. More Delta whites were middle class and thus were more likely to vote. Hill whites also saw their much smaller black population as less threatening and so were more often content to ignore politics. An examination of the votes cast in the 1960 presidential election broke down as follows: 22,165 for Kennedy, 22,330 for Barnett's "unpledged" electors, and 14,771 Republicans. If that pattern held steady, Smith might have eked out a victory. Kennedy was not unpopular in the South, with ratings of 65 percent compared to 68 nationally. Mississippi was unusual in its strong biases against Kennedy. Perhaps, Smith thought, Mississippi could be won for the moderates.[59]

Since the fall of 1960, the Mississippi Valley Flood Control Association had circulated copies of a letter from Kennedy praising Smith for his work on behalf of the Delta. At the same time, Smith appointed Drew Lundy, a member of the Citizens' Council from Humphreys County, as his campaign chairman. Lundy was not an experienced politician, but he was a respectable and energetic figure. Smith sent Evans back to Greenwood to work full-time while he polished up his ties with old allies such as the VFW, which held a Frank Smith appreciation night in the fall of 1961.[60]

The White House supported him with advice on the development of his campaign, patronage, and all the available "pork barrel" funds. Kennedy supplied only two thousand dollars in campaign money, but Smith squeezed the White House for all the federal grants available. When the budget office balked at funding a survey for a Yazoo River project, Henry Wilson, representing the White House, had to negotiate a deal among the budget office, Smith, and the Army Corps of Engineers. After "protracted negotiations," Wilson complained to his boss of being caught in the middle, but Smith would not concede. Finally, Wilson ignored the budget office and ordered the corps to work it out with Smith. Smith took big supporters and their business associates for meetings with the White House staff. When Whitten scooped Smith by announcing funding for a college housing loan at Ole Miss after Smith did all the work on it, Wilson ordered that in the future "we notify only Smith." Smith got the administration to promise to move ten north Mississippi counties from the Memphis FHA to Jackson. He asked for and got the power to tell hostile lawyers they were cut out of closing FHA loans and then replaced them with his supporters. In other words, the White House did all it could to help. The Justice Department held off filing a voting suit in Leflore County until after the election. Smith did not, as rumored, receive enormous sums of Kennedy money to finance his campaign. Most contributions came from within the district.[61]

Smith had a sample of how federal largess could turn on him when he announced that the area redevelopment program would pay almost half a million dollars to train twelve hundred tractor drivers in sixteen Delta counties. He knew that inexperienced drivers were a major headache for planters, and he felt everyone could benefit from training better, safer tractor operators. Whitten announced misgivings because the program might provide the wedge the federal government needed to begin the supervision of wages and hours for Mississippi's black agricultural workers, and Smith caught flak for endangering segregation. The program had to be dropped after planters began to worry that their laborers, trained with federal funds, might be organized into unions. Despite the lesson, Smith saw patronage and federal largess as his only hope and decided to use them for all they were worth.[62]

Whitten injected the race issue early, but Smith answered with the standard refrain: "Every responsible citizen knows that the less said about that the better. I will not discuss it any more, because maintaining our racial integrity is far more important than any man's political career including mine or Mr. Whitten's."[63] Smith resorted to the old tactic of maintaining silence about race, which some considered the truly "patriotic, southern" approach to campaigning. Smith countered with his heavy artillery, charging that Whitten had received favors from Billie Sol Estes, a protégé of Lyndon Johnson who had been indicted for bribery and fraud in big agricultural contracts with the federal government. Smith made headlines with the charges, put Whitten on the defensive, and cut Whitten's lead in the polls.[64]

Whitten responded by securing a letter from the Texas attorney general stating that there was no evidence linking Whitten to Estes other than a few social invitations. Smith contacted an old friend in Texas who had been forced to leave Mississippi as a result of his support of the Truman electors in 1948. The friend bribed a janitor at a newspaper owned by Estes to look for evidence linking Whitten to Estes. The janitor found evidence linking the two, but to use the information would have exposed him, which neither Smith nor his friend felt they could do. Smith revealed that Estes was printing campaign material for Whitten, but could use nothing more incriminating. It was not the bombshell he needed.[65]

Whitten toured with a band and singers who attacked Smith with the following lines:

> Sweet milk, buttermilk, clabber, and whey,
> Old Promising Frank's done had his day![66]

The press wisdom was that Whitten had begun with a big lead, but that Smith was closing the gap by mid-race. Yet Smith found it impossible to maintain his momentum. North Mississippi's biggest newspaper was killing Smith. The Memphis *Commercial Appeal* had altered its Mississippi edition to satisfy the segregationists, and the paper's slant hurt Smith badly. Hodding Carter wrote to Silver, "Call it a shaft or a yenching [*sic*] or whatever other vulgarity we might select, I'm afraid that's just what Frank is going to get and the damn Commercial Appeal [*sic*] is going to do the best it can to sink him."[67] Carter did all he could for Smith in the *Delta Democrat Times*. The Greenwood *Commonwealth* supported Smith, and some small papers, such as the *Deer Creek Pilot,* remained loyal, but their readership was tiny compared to the *Commercial Appeal*'s. The smaller Memphis *Press-Scimitar* was kinder to Smith but had limited impact in Mississippi.[68]

At the end of April, the *Press-Scimitar* provided a remarkable example of Smith's ability to move legislation through Congress. On March 27, according to the *Press Scimitar* story, it became obvious that spring flooding would prevent cotton planting on low-lying lands. By the next day, Smith had prepared a bill to swap cotton allotments in the flooded acres for land that had not been not allotted for cotton on higher ground. He introduced his bill into the House of Representatives on March 29, and on April 3 the Agriculture Committee approved it. Two days later the House passed the bill, and within days the Senate concurred. Concluding the laudatory piece praising Smith for his speed and know-how, the author noted that it was Smith's ninety-third enacted bill as authored or cosponsored.[69]

Aside from the *Commercial Appeal*'s reporting, Whitten's most potent weapon was a whispering campaign calling Smith a "liberal and secret integrationist." The campaign worked well, because it preserved the required "silence" on the race issue while still getting the message to the voters. Smith countered with "A Message from the Home Folks of Frank Smith" in which 120 people affixed their signatures to a statement asserting Smith's "integrity on race relations."[70]

Smith attacked Whitten for claiming to have served in the Pacific during World War II. Whitten was in Congress during the war and went on a fact-finding trip to the South Pacific, a trip he had transformed by careful wording into a stint of military service. Smith pointed to his own combat service in Europe and to his Bronze Star, but it had been too long since the war. The public was uninterested.[71]

The voting public was obsessed with race. Smith's success in keeping the issue quiet until mid-May amazed Lindsey, the black candidate, who observed in Greenville, "This is the first time two white men have run and didn't make the Negro their whipping boy."[72] Appearing with Whitten on a Citizens' Council platform in Grenada, Smith promised, "I shall never attempt to make political capital of this issue." Whitten's response was that integration was coming and that it would lead to "amalgamation," or race mixing. Smith had not been part of the fight to preserve segregation, Whitten charged, and by abandoning the South on the Rules Committee vote, he had proved he could not be trusted. The vote to pack the Rules Committee had received substantial press coverage, and many voters may have been aware of the rumors that Smith had supported the administration's efforts to destroy the conservative southern Democratic-Republican alliance that dominated Congress.[73]

In late May, Whitten's ads and rhetoric focused on the race issue, and the tide turned against Smith. In Durant, Whitten told a Rotary Club, "History proves that whenever you have integration, you have amalgamation. And whenever you have amalgamation of the races you're on your way downhill to ruin." Whitten ran ads demonstrating that Smith had voted for foreign aid and the Peace Corps, which, the ads noted, helped the emerging countries in Africa. Commenting on Smith's support for foreign aid, Whitten said, "We can't set our policy on the whim of every little old Congo tribe. You can't bring it down to a common denominator where we're all a chocolate brown."[74]

Whitten's most widely run ad damned Smith by association with Hodding Carter and Hazel Brannon Smith, both "moderate" newspaper editors who spoke out for the rights of black people. The ad consisted of a *Clarion-Ledger* column by Tom Ethridge that quoted Carter and Hazel Brannon Smith praising Frank Smith as an independent thinker. The ad concluded that Kennedy would appoint Smith to a federal job after Whitten won the election. The ad was effective. Editors of small papers quoted it and printed concerns about Smith's reputation as a free thinker. Some became vitriolic, portraying Smith as a friend of Kennedy surrounded by "the lowest scum of this nations [*sic*] socialist, fellow travelers, pinkos, and procommunists...." One editor called Smith "a blob of blubber." Carter protested for Smith, but his voice was suspect, too.[75]

Smith responded, "Representative Jamie Whitten has the kind of attitude which isolates Mississippi from the rest of the country."[76] That, of course, was exactly what the majority of the electorate wanted. Smith could not, or would not, connect with Mississippi voters. For example, in late May a reporter described Smith pitching washers at a hole in the ground beneath a tree at Chandler Donohoo's store in northeast Mississippi. As they pitched, Smith criticized Whitten for opposing the Lodge-Gosset bill, which would have reformed the electoral college. Smith said that such ignorant opposition on Whitten's part was the reason the NAACP was "trying to run the country." The little crowd under the tree must have been confused. Probably none of them had heard of the Lodge-Gossett bill. Most of them did not understand the electoral college. Either Smith was giving his audience credit for too much intelligence, or he was trying to bamboozle them with obfuscation. In either case it did not work.[77]

Whitten was more direct with his campaign song, adding verses as the election approached. One favorite ran:

Skunks in the stump holes,
Monkeys in the trees,
Franks [*sic*] crawled in bed
With the Kennedys.
And their money too.[78]

As the election date neared, Smith and Whitten made several television appearances, prompting this newspaper headline: "Old Fight Waged With New Style."[79] It was nicely symbolic of this election that Smith could go from tossing washers at a rural store to speaking on television from Greenwood. Television and modern communications would soon do much to revolutionize the racist society that had resisted reform for so long. Smith used his air time to assure farmers that agricultural subsidy appropriations were "automatic," and so they did not have to fear Whitten's departure from Congress. For his knockout punch, Smith put a picture of Whitten and Billie Sol Estes onscreen, charging, "I will myself reveal further details... unless he himself elects to come forward... and spare the people of Mississippi the embarrassment of having one of their elected representatives called before a congressional investigating committee...."[80] He had no more details to reveal, and Whitten did not offer any.

Smith tried to counter Whitten's effort to tie him to Africa through his votes for foreign aid and the Peace Corps by calling Whitten a communist sympathizer. Noting that Nikita Khrushchev had attacked the same programs, Smith asked whose "tool" Whitten was. Unfortunately for Smith, the Mississippi electorate found thinking of Whitten as a communist tool too farfetched.[81]

On the stump, Whitten had begun to tell audiences, "I believe what you believe." Smith must have seen that he was losing and decided he had to break his rule about ignoring the race issue. He had thought he was close to winning, but Whitten's labeling of him as a liberal and his warnings of "amalgamation" had taken their toll. Smith's ad attesting to his "strong and decided beliefs in our ideals of racial integrity" acquired a new headline, "Orphaned at Eight by Negro Assailant." Just days before the primary vote, Smith went on the offensive, issuing ads calling Whitten a closet integrationist. He attacked Whitten for sending his son and daughter to integrated schools. Smith said that, while he had moved to Virginia to avoid sending his children to integrated schools in Washington, Whitten had allowed his daughter to remain in a school from which Senator Eastland had removed his child. Whitten's son, Smith said, attended the University of Maryland, an integrated university. Smith's ad concluded, "You preach segregation, Mr. Whitten . . . Frank Smith *Practices* it!" Smith's mother and stepfather paid for signed newspaper ads saying that Smith "is devoted to the way of life of our people, . . . believes that protecting our racial integrity is more important than any man's political career [and is] . . . true to his principles as a man and as a Christian."[82]

Smith was working hard, and his whole family supported him. Near the end of the campaign Helen went door to door from 8:30 in the morning until after 11:30 at night. On one day, Smith was in Sardis announcing the approval of a new post office, shaking hands in other small communities, and attending the graduation of a friend's daughter in Clarksdale that evening. As Whitten tried to wind up with a major rally in Water Valley, Smith's workers placed circulars containing the charges about Whitten's children attending integrated schools on the car windows of those attending. Whitten called it the "rottenest kind of politics" and vowed he would never have any respect for Smith again.[83]

The campaign ended with a flurry of television appearances. Whitten had more money and had bought a half hour for the night before the election from every station in the district. Despite the rhetoric and Smith's efforts to match Whitten's racist appeal, their closing speeches still made the voters' choices fairly clear. Whitten spoke for "states' rights," the "southern way of life," and "local self-government." Smith said the election would determine "whether Mississippi sticks her head in the sand or moves toward the future determined to fight for her way of life and her economic progress as a part of the United States." Whitten's words and symbols asserted his adherence to segregation. Smith's hedged. Smith's phrase "progress as a part of the United States" told listeners well schooled in the language and symbolism of the time all they needed to know in order to reject Smith as a "moderate."[84]

The final days of the campaign did not go well for Smith. Whitten turned Smith's piling up of government grants and funding against him with ads consisting of sworn affidavits from four members of the Yalobusha County Board of Supervisors, who said Smith had offered them a four-million-dollar Area Redevelopment Administration grant if they would guarantee him 40 percent of the vote in the county. Whitten asked, Why vote for a man who would sell his influence and threaten his constituents? Then on June 4, Smith tried to conclude his campaign with a motorcade across the Delta as he had in 1950. The twenty-five-car caravan was to have visited twenty towns, but it rained so hard some cars pulled over when the drivers were unable to see. They became separated, and some turned back.[85]

Helen's father died in Alabama on primary election day, and a Greenville supporter sent a private plane to transport them to visit the family. They returned to Greenwood that night and learned that Smith had lost by eleven thousand votes. The black candidate received only thirteen hundred votes, suggesting that, perhaps, despite the last-minute appeals to racism, Smith may have gotten the majority of the black votes cast. He won his old district's vote, but the original White House estimate of a ten-thousand-vote margin was close to the final tally.[86]

The *Commercial Appeal* credited Whitten's victory to Smith's friendship with the Kennedys and the fact that Bobby Kennedy, the attorney general, had lawsuits all over the state, including a high-profile one to integrate Gulfport's beaches. The *Clarion-Ledger* cited the same reason and gloated over Smith's defeat. The paper crowed that Governor Barnett had spent the last day of the campaign at the White House meeting with Kennedy, thus indicating Smith was not needed to maintain relations with the White House. The *Clarion-Ledger* congratulated the voters for expressing "a preference for conservatism over Federal handouts and resulting Federal interference."[87] Having it both ways, the paper indicated that eliminating Smith would not end the "handouts." The *New York Times* called Whitten a "racial extremist" even by Mississippi standards and lamented the states' rights victory in purging Smith from office.[88]

Smith never had a chance of winning. The entire Mississippi political establishment was either against him or silenced by fear of the Citizens' Council's power to punish opponents. John Bell Williams had loaned his assistant to Whitten. The farm bureau provided Whitten manpower and support. Sillers and his followers had engineered the merger of Smith's and Whitten's districts and then thrown all their support to Whitten. Even in Greenwood, which remained mostly loyal, there were defections, which Smith's friends found shocking. The Citizens' Councils had never been Smith's friends, and they were at the peak of their power. Writing after the election, Smith's supporters tried to console him with the thought that it was the people of Mississippi who had lost the most. Smith did have a hard core of devoted followers. According to a newspaper editor in Tennessee, on the night of the primary a well-dressed young stranger who said he was a native Mississippian came into the office and asked about the election returns. Told Smith had lost, "[H]e dropped into a nearby chair and murmured, 'We've lost a great man' and cried."[89] Walker Percy summed up the election this way: "Smith was euchred out of his district by the legislature and defeated in 1962 by the usual coalition of peckerwoods, super-patriots and the Citizens' Councils."[90]

The loss devastated Smith, who felt he had made a simple deal with the voters. He would produce for them in Washington, and they would ignore his "peculiar" ideas and keep returning him to office as long as he was effective. He had been a successful congressman and delivered federal funds. He felt betrayed by the voters and was angry at them and at himself for the racist tactics he had employed at the end of the race.[91] By using the racist charges against Whitten, Smith had violated his own personal standards and debased himself as he had refused to do with Sillers in 1960. Living in Washington and enjoying the freedom and power conferred by his office, Smith had grown estranged from his state as it slid away from America and cut itself off from the rest of the world to preserve a racist society and government. Kennedy represented the hopes and the aspirations of the World War II veterans for a better world. Smith found he could not lead Mississippi into the American economic miracle, and his defeat destroyed the dreams he had cherished since high school. He bitterly vowed never to return as he drove toward Alabama the day after the election.

CHAPTER ELEVEN

Distant Battles

D riving to Washington after the primary election, Smith stopped in Scottsboro, Alabama, to see Bob Jones, his best friend in Congress, a fellow southern liberal, and a Public Works Committee colleague. Smith needed a job, and he wanted to talk to Jones about arranging one before returning to Washington with his family. The Tennessee Valley Authority had an opening on the board of directors. A White House aide had talked with Smith about the possibility of his going to TVA, and Smith found it the most tempting of the offers discussed informally before the election. Since he had been a young man, he had admired TVA as a model of federal assistance to the South. Jones welcomed his depressed friend, then called Robert Kennedy and Tennessee representative Ross Bass, who telephoned President Kennedy. Bass was more surprised and impressed to have Kennedy take the call on Smith's behalf at his lunch table than he was by Kennedy's enthusiasm for the idea. The White House quickly announced the appointment, with the story that Smith was being awarded the "plum job" to demonstrate the president's support for southern liberals.[1]

Departing Congress was difficult for Smith, because he loved the place. Kennedy asked him not to resign his seat immediately; neither Smith nor Kennedy wanted Ross Barnett calling a special election to fill Smith's seat. Smith stayed almost until the end of his term in hopes that he might be able to help the president, who had his hands full with the Bay of Pigs fiasco. Smith made one last trip to the NATO parliamentarians' conference, courtesy of Speaker Rayburn, who died just after appointing Smith to that delegation.[2]

As Smith lingered in his congressional seat, the civil rights movement washed over the state and turned it into a boiling cauldron of anger, fear, and depression. Freedom riders challenging segregation in transportation facilities had gone to prison. Protestors sat in at restaurants and libraries. Voter registration drives were directed toward blacks. The Citizens' Council had mounted campaigns to identify and punish those who registered, and, when economic intimidation failed to stop civil rights leaders, white night riders shot into their homes. By autumn of 1962, when the Ole Miss crisis broke, white Mississippians felt besieged.[3]

James Meredith, a black air force veteran who had the support of the NAACP, had overcome all the state's legal hurdles, and federal courts ordered his admission to the University of Mississippi. The state had resisted integration so long and so successfully because the Mississippi federal judges, supported by Eastland from his position on the Judiciary Committee, had not enforced the law in Mississippi as they had in other southern states; Eastland and the Citizens' Council had deluded Mississippians into believing integration would never come. Meredith's admission would be the first integration of a state institution. In a response typical of the Mississippi press and the public, the *Clarion-Ledger* called the Kennedys "power-drunk" and blamed them for the entire affair. In fact, Kennedy tried every option to avoid a confrontation. He did not want to force integration on the South. His views of Reconstruction were twenty-five years out of date, sounding as if they came from an old textbook. Because he still accepted the antiquated view that white southerners had overthrown corrupt black governments during Reconstruction, he sympathized with southern whites on the question of integration and had no desire for a second reconstruction in Mississippi. He had not endorsed the civil rights movement at the time of the Ole Miss crisis. He had appeared sympathetic to black aspirations, having appointed blacks to posts in his administration, ordered blacks included in the honor guards used in Washington, and made efforts to relieve discrimination against black diplomats in the United States. But despite his sensitivity, it was not clear that Kennedy was going to be a strong supporter of integration. At the same time, he was determined not to allow Barnett to flout the law and defy the United States government. Knowing the charged atmosphere at home and fearing a violent confrontation between Barnett and federal agents, Smith met privately with President Kennedy on the Friday before Meredith's scheduled arrival at the University of Mississippi. He brought a suggestion from a group of Mississippians who hoped to avoid violence. They proposed cutting off federal funds to the state until Barnett admitted Meredith.

The president pointed out to Smith that such a move was unconstitutional, and they both agreed that the plan was "neither practical nor probable."[4] Bobby Kennedy continued to negotiate with Barnett, who seemed to understand that he would have to surrender.

But Barnett was invited to speak briefly at an Ole Miss football game on that Saturday in Jackson. Knowing Meredith was scheduled to arrive in Oxford for registration, Barnett waved his arms at the emotional crowd and shouted, "I love Mississippi! I love her people! I love our customs!" "Inspired" students returned to campus and sparked a riot, attacking the federal marshals assigned to protect Meredith. As gunfire frightened many students back to their dormitories, armed outsiders poured onto the campus. Events forced Kennedy to order out the National Guard and to send twenty thousand troops to Oxford to restore order.[5]

Barnett's actions, appearing to defy the federal government, were wildly popular in Mississippi, and the entire political establishment supported him. A columnist expressed widespread sentiments when he wrote, "The skalawags [*sic*] and the moderates are going to crawl out of the walls now. [The state]...fought to the last. So watch the peace-lovers come to the fore, grab a nigger neck and start bellowing brotherly love. For us...we'll just go on being a bigot, a reactionary, a rebel and lick our wounds till the next fight starts.... We are licked not beaten."[6]

Smith stood at a crossroads. In the past he had been silent and even lied about his racial views to get elected and to preserve his political influence in Mississippi. He had done those things in hopes that he could lead his people away from their racism and into the mainstream of American democracy. It appeared in the fall of 1962 that he had failed. Mississippi seemed set to secede again in order to protect segregation.[7] Back in Greenwood, Evans feared that he knew what Smith would do, and he pleaded with Smith long distance to stay silent. Smith knew Evans spoke for his "home folks," but he ignored Evans's advice and issued a statement condemning Barnett's resistance to integration and the hardship it placed on his alma mater. Smith had been defeated for reelection and was only waiting to go to his director's post at the Tennessee Valley Authority. He had nothing to gain from his condemnation of Barnett and knew that he would hurt friends and family who had supported him, but Smith had lived with the burden of his secret too long. Before his defeat, he had been willing to sacrifice his career to pack the Rules Committee. Obviously, the Ole Miss crisis provided a dramatic turning point. The national government was using force to end segregation.

Smith had known since his teenage years where he stood. Speaking out provided a welcome catharsis. He was the only nationally elected Mississippi official who did not support the governor. When national television broadcast his statement, the reaction was intense. Segregationists flooded him with abusive telephone calls and letters, calling him Judas, quisling, and scalawag, the terms preceded by a torrent of profanity.[8]

With the exception of the group who would become known as the Mississippi underground, white Mississippi completely rejected Smith. The University of Mississippi refused the offer of his congressional papers for their archives. He sent the books from his congressional office to Mississippi Valley State College, a black school near Greenwood, and destroyed all of his routine files. He was told it would not be safe for him to walk the streets of Greenwood if he dared to return. His Mississippi colleagues did not sponsor the traditional congressional farewell session in the House that allowed congressmen to say nice things about the departing member.[9]

Smith took on a new role—confidante to Mississippians who disagreed with Barnett. They often feared to voice their thoughts at home, but they began writing to Smith to express admiration for his position and to describe their own anguish. A stranger wrote Smith, "Recent events are tragic both to the University and the state. And to natives such as myself, whose ancestors attended Ole Miss even before the Civil War, the situation is heart-breaking."[10] Some in scrawling handwriting maintained their dislike of integration but decried Barnett's idiocy. A representative example was a confused dissident who cried out to Smith, "If all the Southern States could not outdo the Federal Government in the Civil War, how can one State expect to win against it?"[11] Other correspondents seemed to ask for some explanation of the state. R. H. Mills, a retiree who had returned to Mississippi after a working life spent outside the state, wrote that he had come home "thinking I would find a vast difference from what I left in the early 1900s. I find in many ways it is even worse. I can't understand with so many good colleges and yet so much hate is taught. It seems they only teach hate and football."[12] These letters buoyed Smith by supporting his right to speak out, but others caused him pain.

A Grenada supporter who had been active in Smith's last campaign asked, "PLEASE tell me that you have some reason other than personal financial consideration in failing in any way to identify yourself with the people of your state during the present crisis."[13] Many of his critics were responding to hostile press coverage alleging that Smith had sold out his state for the TVA appointment. Smith could handle the overwhelming hostility because he expected it, but he worried about his mother. For reassurance, he turned to a sympathetic relative in Sidon. Telling Smith that she spoke with his mother every day, she reported that Sadie was "fine." But while trying to be supportive, she added, "Of course Mothers suffer untold agony when they feel that their children are hurt or betrayed but it is sort of an exquisite pain for it is medicated by the knowledge that the son is living by the never failing rule written by the hand of God." She closed with "you are right—time will prove it."[14] Smith needed family support: he intended to explain himself and admit the falsehoods he had told about his racial views as a step toward becoming an open leader for integration.

Back in Washington, Bob Jones of Alabama sponsored Smith's farewell House session. Several colleagues praised Smith as the best member in the House at welcoming freshmen and showing them the ropes. One claimed to have been inspired by Smith's philosophy of life, looking at the world as it "is today rather than as it was yesterday." Colmer seemed to absolve Smith of the charges of duplicity being made back in Mississippi. He cited Smith as a man of conviction willing to fight for a "different view." According to Colmer, Smith could leave Congress with a "clean conscience." Even Whitten spoke and wished Smith well.[15]

Whitten paid Smith and Warren a sort of tribute by asking Warren to join his staff. She commented, "There is no end at all to the gall, is there?"[16] To Smith, Warren wrote a touching farewell: "Nothing I could ever do or say would adequately convey to you my appreciation and affection for your kindness and your help. I suppose the highest compliment I could ever pay a man would be to feel that he is Clyde's [her first 'husband'] kind of gallant gentleman, and you are, indeed."[17]

Congressional leaders also expressed their appreciation in farewell notes. Hale Boggs thanked Smith for his work as assistant whip and his accurate information on votes. Boggs remembered that Smith's estimates were often within one, two, or three votes of the final result. The new Speaker, John McCormack, said, "It is very easy for one from northern states to vote for progressive legislation, but [it] takes one [from the South] with outstanding courage to do so, as you have consistently done, throughout the years."[18]

Both Mississippi senators sponsored Smith's nomination to be a TVA director, making confirmation a formality. The press praised Smith's appointment, and, by early November, Smith had moved into a new home in Knoxville. A local newspaper ran a photograph of the whole family there, surrounded by books and boxes. Smith was sworn in as a director at noon on November 23, 1962. In a "Dear Friends" letter, Smith praised the ideals of TVA employees and the lack of "ostentation and ceremony" he found there. After lunch he returned to his office and went to work. There were no receptions or celebrations—a procedure Smith appreciated and approved. He claimed TVA was "blissful relaxation" after the congressional rat race. He told Silver he could work as hard or as little as he wanted.[19]

Even as a "nonpolitical" TVA director, Smith's life was still linked to his home state and to the civil rights movement that was being played out there. He tried to turn the Mississippi post office patronage over to Gray Evans, who had returned to Greenwood to practice law, but Smith continued to take an interest in some appointments for years after he went to TVA.

Patronage became a "mess," according to the White House aide responsible for it. Mississippi post office appointments had a long, tortured history dating from the Trumanite scandals in the 1940s. Smith had taken on his district's appointments in 1951, only to lose them to Sillers when Eisenhower won the presidency. Smith regained control during his campaign against Whitten, not only in his district but in Whitten's, too. After his defeat Smith retained control, according to the White House, but Coleman and the senators were all involved. Robert Kennedy interfered for Eastland at times. In February, Evans complained to Smith that they had lost control over appointments, but Smith worked to fulfill his campaign commitments. He told a White House aide that Whitten was using the senators to block his men. "It will certainly be a pretty pass if the President cannot nominate a man to one of these jobs because he supports the President."[20]

By April, Louie Spencer, who had been working with Evans to handle patronage, had had enough of the "mess." He wrote Smith, "I think the time has come for us to ease out of this as gracefully as we can."[21] In his opinion the administration had "turned its back" on its supporters in Mississippi. The White House may have tried to escape from the morass of Mississippi post office appointments, but Smith's TVA files filled with correspondence about the appointments for years. In August, Smith suggested to the president's aide that the administration take advantage of the situation to begin appointing blacks to post office jobs. Blacks held fewer jobs in Mississippi than in any other state with such a large black population, he said, and the congressmen were not in a position to protest, since they had been stripped of the appointment privilege for disloyalty. There is no evidence the White House acted on Smith's suggestion to integrate the postal service in Mississippi. Coleman urged Smith to try to hang on to patronage for their "moderate" faction of the Democratic party, and Smith contacted the White House, explaining the symbolic significance. If patronage were restored to the congressman, he wrote, it would be taken as a signal not to "buck" the state leadership. It remained a "mess."[22]

From Knoxville, Smith tried to nourish the "moderate" wing of the Mississippi Democratic party. Moderate is the word they used to describe themselves, but in the Mississippi understanding of the term at that time, it meant liberal. The moderates were separated into "desegregationist" and "integrationist" factions. Desegregationists were realists who recognized that, even if they did not like integration, it was unavoidable. In the Mississippi political climate of the 1960s, integrationists and desegregationists were so outnumbered by the segregationists that they were forced to work together. Segregationists considered all "moderates" to be "radicals" or "communists." Coleman, a reluctant desegregationist, spent a weekend with Smith in September 1963, discussing what could be done to keep the moderate faction of the Mississippi Democratic party alive. From Knoxville, Smith encouraged his former assistant Charles Deaton to run against Sillers for speaker of the Mississippi House of Representatives. Smith visited with William Winter during football weekends in Knoxville, and they talked politics. Smith urged Winter to work quietly as state treasurer until 1965. By then, Smith said, he could begin to speak out for reconciliation with an eye on the governor's race and hopes of recapturing the office from the Citizens' Council, which had made Barnett their creature.[23]

The moderates knew there was no hope for victory, but they felt obligated to keep the moderate wing of the party alive. Smith praised Coleman for his efforts as a candidate for governor in the 1963 primary. Smith blamed Coleman's loss on the state of "misinformation" in Mississippi and the poor leadership outside politics, especially among the newspapers. He urged Coleman to continue his efforts, predicting, "So many changes are coming to the State in the next few years that nobody in office will be in a position to satisfactorily explain them to the people as a whole."[24] Their moderate faction, Smith implied, should be available to the state when integration had been accomplished and the people were ready to turn toward new leadership.

Smith encouraged opposition to the segregationists through every medium available. When twenty-eight young Methodist ministers issued a statement opposing racial discrimination, Smith wrote to the ministers expressing his support. When Jack Reed, a Tupelo businessman, made a statement calling for law and order, Smith sent him encouragement. Smith fed Hazel Brannon Smith, the crusading editor in Lexington, editorial ideas and sought financial assistance for her. He advised Mississippians who wanted to return and fight the segregationists, providing them with introductions and urging them to enter the fray. He answered long letters from Mississippi college students with equally long replies explaining how the future could be better. He tried to nurture links between the Mississippi moderates and the national Democratic party and to embarrass the Mississippi segregationists. His primary contact for this purpose in the House of Representatives was Richard Bolling, a leader of the Democratic Study Group, who had long wanted to discipline the southern Democratic conservatives by stripping them of their seniority. Bolling served with Colmer on the Rules Committee and became Smith's willing ally. Smith sent Bolling copies of editorials condemning Governor Barnett that had been published in Colmer's district, and, at Smith's suggestion, Bolling had the editorials printed in the *Congressional Record.* Communicating with friends in the administration, Smith identified lawyers who would be willing to help in emergencies to save civil rights workers in Mississippi communities. When Smith's old friends the Mullens suffered for running "moderate" editorials in their Madison County newspaper, Smith got the president to write Curtis Mullen a thank-you letter for a job well done.[25]

As Jim Silver, his former professor, did battle by speech and pen with the segregationists, Smith supported him by getting him help from the Southern Regional Council in Atlanta. Scheduled to make his presidential address to the Southern Historical Association in the fall of 1963 at Asheville, North Carolina, Silver planned with Smith to make it a denunciation of the state that would attract national attention. Silver worked on the address with SRC assistance, and the SRC alerted the press to cover the speech. Silver stayed overnight with Smith on his journey to the meeting, and they drove together from Knoxville to Asheville.

Their plan succeeded. Silver made headlines with the speech and returned to Ole Miss to write a book based on the materials that he had
gathered.[26]

Silver was a passionate participant in Mississippi events, eating with
Meredith in the cafeteria and then guarding his own home with guns,
while Smith enjoyed being the detached observer. Smith told Silver's
wife that he felt he had an advantage "having been away a year... the
reaction is not as acute as it might have been. I can look at it a little
more objectively...."[27] The state, he predicted, would need four more
years of "misdirection" before realizing it was part of the United States.
Distance and objectivity did not mean Smith was any less involved. The
role was similar to his experience in the artillery, when he sat in the fire
direction center taking the forward observers' reports and redirecting
the fire to wipe out the enemy. Smith certainly sympathized with those
who suffered for voicing moderate views. As repression grew in Mississippi and the Sovereignty Commission employed spies to still dissent,
Smith became the contact for those forced out of the state. When racial
moderates who spoke out against the segregationists had to leave, they
often turned to Smith seeking haven and jobs. The most famous of the
émigrés were the Heffners, who were forced to leave McComb after inviting civil rights workers to their home. Failing to find refuge in Jackson,
Heffner contacted Smith about employment possibilities. Smith could
not dispense patronage at TVA, but he used his contacts on behalf of
the refugees and sympathized with their plight.[28]

TVA provided Smith with the perfect base from which to play his chosen role as promoter of integration. A federal facility with enormous
power and local support, it provided Smith income, prestige, research
support, travel expenses, and insulation from the segregationists, who
would have destroyed him. The potential power of TVA in the civil rights
movement was demonstrated in 1963 at the agency's thirtieth anniversary celebration. At Smith's urging, President Kennedy came to speak
and took the opportunity to humble Alabama governor and segregationist spokesman George Wallace. Birmingham was then a major battle-
field of the civil rights movement, earning itself an enduring reputation
for segregationist violence because of police use of fire hoses and dogs
against demonstrators. Governor Wallace and some members of the Alabama congressional delegation met President Kennedy in Huntsville,
Alabama, to fly to Muscle Shoals for the president's speech. Before Wallace arrived, Kennedy asked Bob Jones if he should take up the excesses

of the Birmingham police with Wallace. Jones advised him against it because it would do no good. On the plane, Kennedy "ate Wallace's ass out." Kennedy told Wallace that he was not going to stand for the kind of behavior being broadcast to the world from Birmingham. Jones, the Alabama senators, and another congressman studiously surveyed the ground outside the small plane's windows, embarrassed and delighted to hear Wallace "chewed out" by the president. When they arrived at Muscle Shoals, Jones chortled to Kennedy, "Mr. President, I am glad you took my advice."[29]

Hundreds of southern federal employees cheered the president and applauded his speech in the heart of Dixie. As host, Smith had the "job of chaperoning Governor Wallace!"[30] He made it his business to stay between Wallace and the president so that photographers could not get a shot of the two men together. He was successful. The *Commercial Appeal* ran a photograph of Smith, Kennedy, and Wallace with the caption "Governor George Wallace of Alabama appeared to be a downcast man yesterday as he stood on the speaker's rostrum . . . with a smiling President Kennedy."[31] The *Washington Star* headlined its account "Lonely Wallace Wilts in Kennedy Spotlight." Wallace sat on the platform with his arms folded, looking, according to the *Star,* as if he were a teenager whose father had denied him the car for the night. Smith reported to a friend in Mississippi that it had been a hectic day playing host at an event complicated by Wallace's presence, "but I think it all worked out to the good."[32]

For Smith, the low point in Mississippi's behavior during 1963 came when many Mississippians rejoiced over John Kennedy's assassination. Smith heard the news of Kennedy's murder on his car radio while driving home from the Knoxville airport. He sat by the television watching the drama for four days. He made a quick flight to Washington and visited the bier at the White House to demonstrate his deep sense of loss. Writing to a CBS reporter, he said, "I have been living in a nightmare of agony since I last saw you." He felt, he said, that Kennedy was the victim of the "spirit of hate and violence that has grown up in our country . . . spawned" by the race issue.[33] In a letter to one of his Greenville supporters, Smith explained his appreciation of Kennedy's "obvious intelligence," his wit, his respect for others, and his "complete rejection of anything pompous." He said history would remember Kennedy for "the flexibility he brought to the cold war that offers for the first time some positive hope of resolving it without any surrender of our principles; and secondly, the full commitment that he made toward elimination of all racial injustice." He concluded, "[M]y greatest pride will always be that I was a Jack Kennedy man."[34] But Smith understood political realities and predicted, in another letter to a friend in Greenwood, that racial discrimination would become a "matter of federal law." People, he said, had no idea "what a powerful President Johnson will be."[35] He explained that Kennedy had no congressional majority but that no one knew how to work Congress better than Lyndon Johnson. Kennedy's murder made Smith more optimistic that change would come to Mississippi and more determined to help. William Winter expressed the emotions of their group in a letter to Smith, concluding, "I at least know that as far as I am concerned personally I am going to do more than I have been willing to do in the past to try to retain in this state a respect for the political heritage that was able to give us a man like John Kennedy."[36]

Smith's old district, the Delta, stood out as "a citadel of white supremacy and black subservience," and the toughest town in the Delta was Greenwood. Greenwood was one of the few cities in Mississippi able to marshal enough members of the Citizens' Council to work block to block organizing resistance to integration. In opposition to the segregationists, Smith joined the Atlanta-based Southern Regional Council and participated in efforts to encourage integration. Smith served on the SRC's Voter Education Project, and the VEP chose Greenwood as the target for a voter registration drive. Brave young men trained and financed by the VEP defied the local authorities and the Citizens' Council to organize a local movement. Law enforcement officers threatened and harassed demonstrators; the VEP organizer was denied a place to live because his landlords were intimidated; those arrested were tortured in jail. One young white man watching police set a dog on to protesters told a reporter, "We killed two-month-old Indian babies to take this country. And now they want us to give it away to the niggers."[37] Constant fear, confrontation, and violence threatened a major explosion. Both sides contacted Smith, who advised the Justice Department of individuals willing to help get the civil rights workers out of town alive. Smith tried to spur the Justice Department into action and, in one instance, requested FBI protection for the former editor of the *Commonwealth*, who was threatened and run out of town because he took his family to an integrated movie theater. The protection was denied in every case because the FBI left such tasks to local authorities, but Greenwood was the only place where the Justice Department threatened to use federal power to protect civil rights workers. Evans and others prevented a major bloodbath by working with the federal authorities. Without federal support, the VEP failed in the short term to accomplish its goals.[38]

Smith advocated that the federal government become more involved in prosecuting the violent segregationists and in protecting civil rights workers. After Byron De La Beckwith killed NAACP field secretary Medgar Evers, Smith contacted Robert Kennedy to describe Beckwith's visits to his office. One encounter, Smith said, ended with these words: "Let me know if I can kill a nigger for you." Smith assured Kennedy that the Citizens' Council "regularly used Beckwith as a promoter and agitator." Clearly Smith was saying to the attorney general, take these people seriously before they commit more murders. But none of Smith's urging produced much federal protection or direct support for those trying to fight segregation in Mississippi.[39]

Finally understanding during the spring of 1964 that the federal government would offer only limited support, Smith openly supported integration and encouraged communication between Mississippi and the rest of the world. In New York newspapers, Smith endorsed the passage of a civil rights bill. Spencer and Evans tried to keep the information out of the *Commonwealth* and were successful for a time, but copies of the statement were passed from hand to hand around Greenwood. Then the Memphis and Jackson television stations carried the story. Spencer reported "bitter resentment" against Smith, especially on the part of those who had made telephone calls as part of his campaign to assure voters that Smith was a segregationist. Silver's comment to Smith, when he saw the statement in the paper, was that Smith had cut his last ties to Mississippi.[40]

Smith had no such intention. He explained himself in great detail to a Mississippian attending Harvard law school, who wrote of his opposition to the civil rights bill. If Mississippi had been left to solve its own racial problem, Smith told the student, "Slavery would still be in effect...." To make any progress, Mississippi had to eliminate second-class citizenship, and the most important tool with which to accomplish that would be the enactment of the public accommodations provisions of the civil rights bill, so that every hotel and restaurant would have to eliminate discrimination. Equal accommodation of blacks in all public facilities would do the most, Smith said, to take away the "vast amount" of the feeling of discrimination. As for fears of "miscegenation," whites would simply have to outgrow those, Smith explained impatiently. Smith seemed to sense what Percy had identified as the need for public spaces that blacks and whites could share.[41]

Although Smith stated to everyone that he had simply decided to be honest about his opinions, former supporters did not believe him and attributed his new public views to betrayal. One blasted him, "How can you stoop so low as to try to sale [sic] your own state and other southern states down the drain for political powers [sic] and money?"[42] Some pleaded with him to get on the "correct road" and admonished him to think of others. "Surely you have thought about how friends, relatives and other connections in Holmes county and [the] entire state of Mississippi will be affected."[43] Smith did think of his family and friends. Answering his mother's distress, he said he was sorry to upset her, but it was impossible to be honest with himself and not disturb her. "Even when I was in Congress and trying to be especially careful. . . . I found that I could not take any course that did not offer them many problems. If there was anything I learned from you, it was never to hate anybody, for I don't believe that you ever spoke with hatred of anyone." He had tried, he said, for years to believe in gradual change, but in the last year he had become convinced that only the federal government could produce change in Mississippi. He told his mother that his book would be out in the fall and that its message was one of cooperation to end hate between the races in the South. "It may not do any good, but at least I will have done my duty to tell people the truth."[44]

She was not comforted, and she got little more sympathy from her daughter, who tried to convince her mother that Smith could be for the civil rights bill without necessarily being an integrationist. She reminded her mother of the violence loose in the state and condemned the situation in Greenwood that required people to side with the murderer Beckwith. Given the situation, she advised her mother to ignore people's comments and to be proud of her son. "You lost Fred Cecil [Smith's brother] in the war, my life has been a disappointment to you because I'm not a social leader or a bigwig church woman and do what I like instead of what other people consider proper, but your oldest son has made a mark in this world."[45] Be happy, she said, that he was not a politician such as Eastland or Stennis who supported segregation.

Other relatives got more blunt responses from Smith. He told his stepbrother, "The whole issue was decided for me . . . when I was given the Bible and American history books as a child."[46] He informed a cousin that the only way ever to have peace in the South again was to provide equal rights for "Negroes" and the means of doing that was to secure those rights by federal law. He said this was important to blacks, "but it is far more important to all of us as citizens who believe in American and Christian ideals."[47]

In June 1964, on the eve of Freedom Summer, Smith published an article in the New York *Herald Tribune* warning the freedom riders going to Mississippi that they were being portrayed as communists in the state's newspapers, that no political leaders were trying to quiet the fears inflamed by the press, and that the KKK was on the rise. Addressing Mississippians, he said there were two key questions: would the freedom riders be allowed to run freedom schools, and would the authorities protect them? Smith concluded with a direct appeal to Governor Paul Johnson to meet the test and to protect the students headed to Mississippi. Noting the white "unanimity" that seemed to exist in the state against integration, Smith contended, "The 'moderate underground' can emerge only with fear and trepidation, and it can do so only with the full support of the Federal government."[48]

His pleas were ignored. The students received little protection from either the federal government or state authorities. Churches housing them were burned across the state, and three young men were brutally murdered and buried in an earthen dam in Neshoba County. Hundreds were beaten and intimidated. Greenwood simmered on the point of explosion all summer. There Beckwith presided over Klansmen at the Crystal restaurant, which was one of those that had become a private club to maintain segregation. A relative in Sidon described the terror to Smith and said she was removed as a Sunday school teacher at the Methodist church because she refused to join the Citizens' Council. "It is quite hard," she concluded, "to converse with neighbors that we love, so we just stay home, run into Greenwood for groceries and back home. The tension mounts there daily and sooner or later someone will touch it off."[49] Another friend in Itta Bena reported the same problems, and closed by saying, "I feel sure if someone should get hold of this letter I'm writing you they would probably try to harm me."[50]

In the midst of the civil rights revolution, with family and friends fearing for their lives, Smith remained in his "fire direction center" at TVA. Although he cared passionately about events at home, Smith saw himself as an intellectual, and he always understood writing and other intellectual activities to be his role. He felt his major contribution would be to write his autobiography. Like his "teacher" Vincent Sheean, Smith did not see his role as that of a fighting revolutionary. As Sheean urged in his book, Smith tried to tell the truth and to make a revolution of the mind, hoping to nourish those in the state who agreed with him and to win over those who could be reached by honestly chronicling his story. As the civil rights workers invaded and his state neared explosion, Smith wrote his autobiography, confident in the long-term triumph of the goodness in his people.

He turned to his former congressional assistant, Audrey Warren, to serve as editor of his autobiography. She had edited his other book and articles when he was in Congress. She was not happy with his first draft this time, because she felt that he was compromising too much in order to reach white Mississippians. She accused him of "goofing this book" in his rush to get it published early, and she told Smith that he had no "philosophy." She maintained that he had not made his meaning clear, saying, "You obviously cannot write an acceptable book (admittedly, acceptable to me, but it was me you asked) and still be politically acceptable to your erstwhile constituents."[51] She urged Smith to take a stronger position and present a true picture of himself. She felt he was giving his readers a less than fully honest account of his life and ideas. In response he changed little; his desire was to reach his people, not please her. Nevertheless she completed her editing quickly, and Smith published *Congressman from Mississippi* in the midst of the civil rights battles raging in his Mississippi.[52]

He opened the book with the murder of his father by a black hitchhiker and concluded that both his father and the hitchhiker were victims of Mississippi's racist social customs. Explaining what he had tried to do with his career, Smith challenged other Mississippians to join him. "The surest way to shorten the suffering and eliminate the chasm between black and white is for all citizens to join in the effort to assure all Mississippians their rights as Americans."[53]

The reaction gratified Smith, who must have felt that he had accomplished his goal. A teacher from a freedom school thanked him. "I feel that *your* making these comments part of the public record is especially meaningful, because you are neither a part of the civil rights organization, nor are you an 'outside agitator.' " She predicted the book would help to "clarify" everyone's thinking.[54]

The segregationists detested Smith and the book. One wrote, "You are a coward. If Bilbo could answer you here on earth, you would cringe and whine like the dirty cur that you are."[55] Heber Ladner, the secretary of state, spoke for Bilbo: "It is a sad commentary that one who served for four years in the Mississippi Senate and twelve years in the Congress... would so stultify himself with his ghoulish journalism in which he attempts to invade graves and feast on the flesh of the dead. At least Theodore G. Bilbo was never so weak mentally or physically as to sell the birthright of the people of Mississippi and her traditions for a 'mess of porridge.'" Ladner predicted that "[w]hen the name of Frank Smith is buried in the dusty archives of the world, dedicated historians will still be acclaiming the life and accomplishments of Theodore G. Bilbo, the stormy petrel from Pearl River County."[56]

Others found it hard to believe what they read. They wrote Smith long history lessons reciting the horrors of Reconstruction and the lessons of the Civil War. They protested that they had never been unfair to blacks. Most of these "good people" felt betrayed and seemed to believe Smith could still be saved if they could set him straight about southern history, which justified segregation in their minds. Some of his attackers admitted they had not read the book, and Smith noted that he got less criticism "directly from the book" than he had expected, because, he said, "[V]ery few people who write those types of letters... get around to reading the book."[57]

His target audience, the moderates, loved the book. A correspondent unknown to Smith wrote from Greenwood that after the scathing review in the *Commonwealth* she was determined to read the book. "After I read it I felt we had a bond in common. I felt like I had a friend whom I have never met.... [T]he things you expressed in your book are the things I have felt and have never been able to put into words."[58] The novelist Walker Percy called the book an "authoritative indictment" and said, "One comes away, in fact with appreciation of the strengths and latent good qualities of the people—which makes the sense of tragedy even stronger of course."[59] Expatriates reported that the book made them feel guilty about leaving Mississippi, and some promised not to be silent when they returned home. William Winter wrote movingly, "I don't believe that I have ever read a book that has more meaning for me than this one. You have put in such clear perspective the cloudy thoughts that have moved back and forth through the minds of many of us that now I feel that at last I have a true picture of what I believe in and where I stand."[60]

Not all readers who saw the justice in the book promised to change. Gray Evans said there was "nothing but truth in the book," but, he continued, "I do know what is right but I guess I just don't have the strength to go against what most of my family and friends think and believe."[61] Another such correspondent praised the book but reported that he felt like a rat in a maze. He felt sure there was a way out but was unable to find it.[62]

Some Mississippi newspapers carried admiring reviews. John Emmerich wrote in his father's McComb paper that, while some might dispute Smith's contentions, "nobody can attack his Mississippi credentials."[63] That was what made Smith's book so important at the time. The segregationists claimed that no Mississippian could support integration, and Smith breached their basic defense by attacking the "sins" of his own people. Hostile papers simply accused him of lying for money and position.[64]

When potential readers sometimes had difficulty getting the book because stores refused to stock it, Smith filled orders out of his TVA office. Others, who did not want to spend the money to read the book, complained of long waiting lists at the public library. Outside of Mississippi, sales were not brisk. Smith blamed Silver, whose *Mississippi: The Closed Society* made the best-seller list at the same time. Smith urged, "Hurry up and get off the best seller list. I'm afraid it won't hold two from Mississippi at the same time."[65]

Smith reported his favorite review to his editor after he talked to a young planter from Coahoma County. The planter, who chaired a community-action program with Aaron Henry, president of the state NAACP, said "that he had read my book, and the suggestion I made that planters were the people in the white community who could do the most to break through toward interracial cooperation had been a challenge to him, and that was really the reason why he was active in the program. If nothing else, this, I think, makes the book worthwhile."[66]

Smith's enemies called him a Judas. His admirers thought him a hero for denouncing segregation. For the rest of his life, his enemies and others who suspected his "conversion" on the race issue would doubt that Smith told the truth at any point. The confusion about where he stood was a result of the lies that he had told to win political power and from the less-than-forceful way in which he described his views on race in his autobiography. In later years he offered no defense of his lies except to say that not having told them would have meant surrendering all the political power to the segregationists. He believed that a revolution in the minds of his people—southern white people—was possible. He sought a revolution that would free his people from their race prejudices. He had eliminated his prejudices against black people during his teenage years, but he would not abandon his people to their prejudice. He determined to do what he could to wean them of their racism, and he consistently strove toward a revolution in their minds similar to the one that he had experienced.

CHAPTER TWELVE

The Bands Don't Play

Smith played the role of an intellectual, but he remained a politician at heart. As a TVA director, he was supposed to be nonpartisan, but he never was. His constituency was small, because he was anathema to the segregationists and Mississippi moderates were few. Nevertheless, he persisted in supporting the moderates, believing in their eventual victory. Former governor Coleman called on Smith to help sort out the post office patronage mess, and Winter provided reports from the "closed society" as he called it in his letters. In June 1964, Winter despaired of continuing the battle with the Citizens' Council and segregationist forces. Asked to deliver the keynote speech to the Hinds County Democratic Executive Committee, he made an "innocuous" talk, only to watch those who had invited him get defeated for reelection to the committee. He said he continued to look for some way to keep party leadership in "moderate" hands, but "it may be that we are just going to have one tragedy after another until we exhaust ourselves. I think I know now how my Whig great-grandfather must have felt as he contemplated the impending Civil War."[1]

In response, Smith encouraged Winter to formulate a long-range plan to restore the "moderate" wing of the party. Telling Winter to "let it ride" for a year, he urged an effort to make moderation respectable in the state so that in a "number of years" it would be possible to return to power. In 1964, as he always did, Smith tried to mount a serious effort for the national Democratic ticket. Winter declined to lead it, because he saw no advantage in "getting cut up" when there was no hope of winning. As white Mississippians flocked to Barry Goldwater, who had opposed the Civil Rights Act of 1964, and black Mississippians tried to take control of the national Democratic party in the state, Winter worried that parties would develop along racial lines, which he thought would be disastrous. As Smith urged Winter's cooperation with the national Democratic party, Winter worried about the Mississippi Democratic party's becoming a "Black and Tan outfit" that would lose almost all white support. Returning from the state Democratic convention, he reported that "the leadership on our side is now almost non-existent." He could see no way to move into the vacuum without becoming completely isolated, but then, he told Smith, "[T]his is what your book is all about."[2]

Seeking to buoy Winter's spirits, Smith predicted that in the long run the development of a two-party system would have a good effect on state politics. He did not believe Mississippi could move from being a one-party Democratic state to being a one-party Republican state. "Somewhere along the line a cohesive group is going to take shape and will have to accept national realities.... They may not come to power for quite a while, but I believe that they will be there."[3] Smith promised Winter that he would try to sell President Johnson on the idea of supporting the Mississippi moderates after the election.

The most important political question before and just after the 1964 election was the appointment of a Mississippian to the fifth circuit court of appeals. "Mississippi's member" of the court, Ben F. Cameron, had died, and Smith warned his contact at the Justice Department that filling the place "is going to be considered something of a yardstick by what might be termed the moderate underground in Mississippi."[4] It was Senator Stennis's turn to make the appointment, and his candidate was Claude Clayton of Tupelo, but Clayton was unacceptable to the moderate faction, who did not want a judge hostile to the civil rights movement. Coleman, who had run for governor in the 1963 primary, had stated publicly that he did not want the appointment. As a result, when Smith contacted the Justice Department and the White House to suggest a list of candidates acceptable to the "underground," he did not include Coleman's name. Smith preferred Winter but felt the stronger strategy was to suggest a moderate without specifying a particular candidate. Pressed by Washington, he identified a list of men who would suit the moderates and at the same time be acceptable to the senators. He contacted Senator Philip Hart of Michigan, the ranking Democrat on Eastland's judiciary committee, to explain that, because Clayton had obstructed civil rights progress, the moderate group opposed him. Smith narrowed his list to Winter and visited Assistant Attorney General Burke Marshall at the Justice Department to lobby for him. Marshall called Attorney General Nicholas Katzenbach, who came to Marshall's office to join their discussion. He explained that the American Bar Association report weighed against Winter because he had too little courtroom experience. Smith argued that Winter's scholarship, public service, and character were more important. As a result, Katzenbach took Winter's name to Stennis, who asked if he were going to be forced to take a "liberal." Clayton campaigned for the job, but in the end Coleman took the appointment. Smith believed that the senators had used Coleman to block Winter, but, despite his disappointment, Smith supported Coleman as a man who could "grow into" the position. Believing a "desegregationist" moderate was the necessary compromise, Smith accepted Coleman's appointment as the best the moderate underground could do. On the eve of Coleman's confirmation, one senator tracked Smith to New Hampshire, asking on behalf of a Senate group for his advice. For the good of Mississippi moderates, Smith gave Coleman his endorsement.[5]

As they were outflanked on the left by the Freedom Democratic Party and on the right by the segregationists, the moderates suffered for the next several years. Some segregationists fled to the Republicans, but most stayed with the "regular" Democratic party and refused to accept integration. The Freedom Democratic Party had grown out of the civil rights movement and efforts to register black voters. Led by dynamic leaders such as Fannie Lou Hamer, the FDP began to challenge the regulars for control of the Democratic party in the state. Holding "elections" of their own in which disfranchised blacks "voted" for the FDP slate of candidates, the party demonstrated its support. Goldwater won the state in the 1964 presidential election, and, for the first time since Reconstruction, the Republicans emerged as a serious threat. Republican Prentiss Walker also won a congressional seat in 1964. During the presidential contest, the national Democratic party in Mississippi was represented by a moderate, Doug Wynn, who was not allied with Smith. Smith felt Wynn was too close to Eastland and kept his distance from him. Eastland already controlled most of the campaign money in the state, and Smith feared his influence. After the election Smith seemed to see no other choice and urged Wynn to keep some organization together to handle patronage.[6]

Any effort to found a faction truly loyal to the policies of the national party seemed impossible. Most of the regular Mississippi Democrats walked out of the 1964 convention when the national party offered a compromise to the biracial FDP. Three regular Democratic delegates, including Wynn, refused to leave and suffered ostracism when they returned home. One of the three turned to Smith's book during his ordeal. After reading it, he called Smith for sympathy, reporting that he had been harassed, had lost most of his law clients, and had to get the police to escort his children to school each morning. In the face of such solid opposition to the national party in Mississippi, it appeared that little could be done.[7]

Returning moderates to power seemed to be a very long-range project. Smith told a writer who speculated on the possibility of Smith's running again, "Actually, since leaving Congress I have had no serious thoughts about going back into politics in Mississippi; but I don't want to quarrel with that part of your story since it gives a little drama, and we all do daydream."[8] Having accepted the end of an active career in Mississippi politics, he exchanged condolences with racial moderates Brooks Hays of Arkansas and Carl Elliot of Alabama, who had been eliminated by the segregationists in their states. Hays called Mississippi and Alabama "sick" and just hoped they would live to see the development of a few islands of progress. Smith was not embittered. He consoled Elliot for his loss, writing, "From a purely personal viewpoint, however, I think you will find there will be more compensations to being out of Congress to having stayed. The sense of freedom that you will acquire will be very refreshing."[9] He added that in some ways Elliot would be able to make a greater contribution.

From Mississippi, Winter reported some good news about the acceptance of integration, which had been forced on the state by the Civil Rights Act of 1964. "I was eating lunch at the Heidelburg coffee shop one day last week, when three Negroes came in. They were promptly served by a white waitress, and so far as I could tell none of the other patrons seemed concerned. Ross Barnett's man, Martin Fraley, was seated at an adjacent table, and I observed that he did not leave until the leisurely completion of his meal."[10] Desiring to promote economic development, Governor Johnson had in fact quietly surrendered to federal authority. Although he provided little public leadership for moderation on race issues, behind the scenes he tried to keep order while a quiet revolution ensued, destroying some of the most blatant practices of segregation.[11]

In the fall of 1964, Smith ventured to Millsaps College in Jackson to address the student body. In his speech, Smith called on Mississippians to condemn violence and to stop blaming "outsiders" for all the state's problems. Reminding the students that the South had lost the Civil War, he called on state leaders to recognize the supremacy of the federal government. He later told a correspondent, "I don't think Mississippi has ever had as frank a speech about what the situation is there...."[12]

A man in Crystal Springs heard about the speech and wrote Smith a long, admiring letter. Referring to his war experiences, which had weaned him from his racism, he told Smith that it was supposed to take guts to climb into a landing craft and assault a beach. But he had done that, he said, and "it does not require half the guts and backbone it takes to stand against the status quo in Mississippi." When he came home from war, he said, the bands played and the people cheered, but "[a]ny time a white man bucks the situation in Mississippi the bands don't play and the people don't cheer."[13]

Smith expected no cheers. He simply went on with what he believed would be a long campaign. While doing some historical research, Smith came across George Washington Cable's Ole Miss commencement speech for 1882 centering on the "Negro question." Smith asked Silver, "Do you suppose we can get a return engagement on the same subject by 1982?"[14]

Odd as it may seem, the complete break between Smith and the hard core of his former supporters did not come until 1965, when he spoke to the Mississippi Council on Human Relations. The council was a religious-affiliated organization founded thirty years before the civil rights movement to promote better race relations. The Catholic bishop, Joseph Brunini, was the secretary-treasurer, and Ernst Borinski, head of the sociology department at Tougaloo College, was a member. The council received some funds from the Southern Regional Council, and, in the charged atmosphere of the times, both organizations were condemned as communist fronts. As a part of the overall effort for integration, Jesse Brent, a Greenville businessman and Smith supporter, invited him to address the council, which was actively promoting integration. In 1965, the council represented the heart of integrationist forces in Mississippi, and by speaking to them Smith labeled himself an integrationist, too. That ended any possible pretense that Smith had simply trimmed his political sails in a new position. Smith's sister had not been alone in rationalizing Smith's support of the civil rights bill. Many family members and supporters still had not grasped that Smith supported integration. Even many of those who had read his book felt that he had stopped short of declaring himself an integrationist. Evans, again on behalf of Greenwood, asked Smith to remain silent. Evans contacted Smith's mother, who made it clear that she would not ask Smith to cancel the trip to Jackson. Evans then appealed to Smith's sense of loyalty, asking if he realized the effect his civil rights views had on his friends. "[T]he reaction operates against your family and close friends also. My business has been affected and my wife has been hurt by your past statements...." Your friends are suffering, he said, and "you owe them something."[15] Pressure was brought to bear on Smith's mother, and at one point he telegraphed the council: "Intolerable pressure has been placed on my mother since the announcement of my scheduled speech...which I was invited to make by some of the finest citizens of Mississippi. I am, consequently, regretfully canceling the speech."[16] Later, after talking to his mother again, Smith responded to Evans that she had given her permission. He regretted hurting his friends, he said, and appreciated his mother's agony, but it had to be done. "I believe that the various services I rendered for the town and county were enough, on a quid pro [quo] basis, to balance the books on the general support I received." He offered Evans assistance in looking for another position if necessary. Referring to his book and other efforts, Smith said, "I realize this is a drop in the bucket, but somebody has to make the first twist of the faucet."[17] Evans replied that he did not have the strength to go against friends and family, but "I respect you for having the strength and being in the position to do so."[18]

Jackson's hotels refused to host the integrationist event, and the speech was moved to Tougaloo College, center of civil rights activities in the state. Smith's speech to the council was really aimed at the political leadership in Mississippi, asking them "simply" to condemn murder as a tool of preserving segregation. He urged council members to combat racism, which had prevented Mississippi's development for two hundred years. Endorsing integration, he concluded, "[W]e have the opportunity to relieve ourselves of the burden of conscience which white Mississippians have been carrying for years; now we do have the opportunity, within the Judaic-Christian heritage we claim as our own, to acknowledge the Fatherhood of God and the brotherhood of man."[19] Blaming segregation for stunting Mississippi's economic development for two hundred years, Smith left no doubt that the state should embrace integration.

Reporting to his mother later, Smith tried to calm her fears about his consorting with integrationists. He described the audience as more white than black, neat and well dressed, and containing lay leaders of the Methodist conference, along with four priests. She was a Methodist, and he probably felt she would find the description reassuring.[20]

The newspapers played up Smith's comment that the Civil Rights Act of 1964 gave politicians a shield with which to protect themselves from the racists. Understanding the need for political cover in a state determined to preserve segregation, he advised Mississippi leaders to accept integration and to use the act as a means of shifting blame to the federal government so that they could work to improve the state's economy. Moderates felt it was unsafe to comment, but less literate critics sent hate mail. "Hully Gulley" wrote, "If you have to keep opening your big fat mouth. . . . I suggest you do it elsewhere than Mississippi. Why not try Harlem? P. S. You don't smell very good in Mississippi."[21]

Although he remained a strong integrationist, Smith disliked the direction the civil rights movement was taking. He was concerned not only about the white segregationists, but also about the FDP and more radical black activists, who he believed would make integration impossible. Dedicated to integration, he redoubled his efforts to create an integrated Mississippi Democratic party linked to the national Democrats. He moved closer to Wynn and connected him to others who wanted to help establish a national party in the state. In Washington, he talked with a black congressman to explain the need for a black-white coalition capable of winning white votes in the state. He allied with Claude Ramsay, the head of the Mississippi AFL-CIO, to enlist organized labor in the effort. Ramsay had decided that the FDP was becoming a dangerous, radical group, because it was advising young black men to refuse military service. He and Smith both knew that an overwhelming majority of Mississippians would call refusing military service treason. Ramsay arranged for Smith to speak to a group on the Mississippi Gulf Coast and reported later that the group "learned a lot." The result was an agreement to create a loyalist, integrated party.[22]

Smith's open endorsement of integration and the publication of his book hurt him among the desegregationists in the moderate camp and narrowed his influence in Mississippi. Smith continued to count on Winter as the champion of the moderates. By the summer of 1965, he was providing Winter with contacts in the Delta for their planned speaking campaign on behalf of moderation. Winter reported a good reception in Greenwood and sensed "a new breeze blowing" in the state. He felt he was reaching the civic club audiences but doubted any penetration of the "lower income groups." He concluded that, although he was having his say, "I don't know whether this is any way to try to get elected governor."[23] Following the speaking campaign, Smith scouted Mississippi labor leaders for Winter and advised him to wait until 1971 to make his bid for governor.[24]

Meanwhile, Smith followed up on a national initiative to get a "branch of the national Democratic party established in Mississippi." Smith had kept in touch with the Democratic Study Group in Congress because it was most interested in enforcing Democratic party discipline and eliminating southern conservatives. Frank Thompson, a New Jersey Democrat who belonged to the Democratic Study Group, spoke to a lawyer who contacted Smith, and Smith flew to Washington for a meeting. The result was the formation of the Mississippi Democratic Conference, made up of white moderates and such black leaders as Aaron Henry and Charles Evers. Independently, Henry had reached the same conclusion as Smith—that the FDP and the growing black power movement would destroy the opportunity for integration. Smith reported to his Washington contact that this was "a significant break from the support of the Freedom Party [FDP]."[25] A staff member of the Democratic National Committee attended the MDC's organizational meeting in Jackson but refused any commitment from the national Democratic party. The political fact was that the president needed Stennis's support for his Vietnam policy and Eastland's for his judicial appointments. The moderates, who, Smith said, were "pretty radical for Mississippi," wanted to prevent the development of an all-black party controlled by the FDP, or, on the other hand, the reassertion of the regulars as the official party. A conference delegation including Ramsay, Henry, and Evers went to Washington looking for commitments in the fall of 1965, but found none.[26]

To further complicate the picture, Billy Silver, Jim Silver's son, returned from Harvard with Smith's encouragement to establish the Young Democratic Club of Mississippi in December 1965. The new organization's letter of introduction to "Fellow Democrats" claimed that, since the club was chartered by the Young Democratic Clubs of America and since there was no "senior party" in the state, the Young Democratic Club was the Democratic party in Mississippi. Smith got them in touch with the Democratic Study Group in the House. The study group provided speakers, but no money. From Jackson, Billy reported to Smith that a speech followed by an integrated party had led to a garbage-strewn lawn, a cross burning, and a fistfight. After making further Washington contacts, Smith informed Billy that he did not know of a "chance in the world" of any money for the club. After these maneuverings grew byzantine, Smith joked to the elder Silver that the "Freedom Party" should nominate one of his racist colleagues in the history department for governor "to broaden their base of support."[27]

As Mississippians tore themselves apart over integration, Lyndon Johnson passed his civil rights act, the voting rights act, and his Great Society legislation intended to end poverty in America. Simultaneously, he committed the United States to a major land war in Vietnam and created an increasingly radical protest movement more obsessed by the war than by civil rights. Mississippians, of course, remained untouched by war protests; however, with people distracted by the coverage of the war and protests on television, changes in race relations developed quickly. Federal funds flowed into the state; easing poverty and creating a larger black middle class, this money paved the road toward progress. In 1965, one of Smith's journalist friends commented, "I think love of money is going to succeed where love of fellow man failed in Mississippi."[28] He observed that Mississippians liked the "feel" of money from the "mortal enemy" and were beginning to see segregation as too costly to continue.

By 1965 Smith's influence in Mississippi had begun to wane. He did not have the same close relationship with the Johnson advisors that he had enjoyed with Kennedy's. As others like Doug Wynn established direct contacts with Washington, Smith's role began to be less significant. Portions of his book had offended some of the desegregationists among the moderates. Mississippi politicians, as a rule, did not read Smith's book, but they passed copies of portions of it from hand to hand. Coleman disliked Smith's observations about the state and never forgave him for them. While splitting from the desegregationists, Smith refused to cooperate with "black radicals," who, he believed, were making integration impossible.[29]

Although he continued to dabble in Mississippi affairs, Smith's role in the state became a marginal one. He tried again to assist a candidate in opposing Sillers as Speaker, but had no effect. Most of his activities by this time were less directly political. He nominated Duncan Gray, Jr., an Episcopal priest, for the Medal of Freedom for his leadership against violence during the Ole Miss riots. He looked for a grant that would fund the distribution of paperback copies of Silver's book *Mississippi: The Closed Society* to libraries throughout the state. He had little influence in post office appointments by this time, even though they remained a "mess." Lawrence O'Brien, who was appointed postmaster general in 1965, joked to Smith that "the thought of running 35,000 post offices is a bit awesome. Almost as bad as the thought of handling postmaster appointments in Mississippi."[30] Eastland controlled appointments by 1966.[31]

As his power diminished, Smith did not stop trying to influence Mississippi's development. For example, he advised his friends in Congress and supplied them with information needed to strip John Bell Williams of his seniority. This was a serious step, because a congressman's power depends on his committee positions, which are assigned by seniority. Williams, who had supported Goldwater for president, had allied himself with the most vociferous racists since his election to Congress, and Smith knew Williams would probably run for governor. Smith also knew that stripping Williams of his congressional seniority would make him a martyr. He did not believe Williams could be defeated in 1967, and he considered enforcing party discipline an important precedent. Williams lost his congressional seniority and ran for governor. Winter ignored Smith's advice to wait and also ran for governor in 1967. As Smith had predicted to a Winter supporter, the Coleman group went for Williams as the best possibility for defeating Barnett, who was trying to return to office. The "martyred" Williams defeated Winter in the runoff.[32]

Williams pledged not to accept federal aid for the state, but he broke that promise quickly and established a new bureaucracy to handle the influx of Great Society funds. Despite Williams's racist views, enormous change occurred during his administration. Leaders began to accept the changed political landscape created by thousands of new black voters enfranchised by the voting rights act. In 1967, the first crop of black elected officials attended a Voter Education Project training program in Jackson, and Smith was their first speaker. Despite Smith's activist role in promoting black voting, or perhaps because of it, Whitten made his peace with Smith at a Washington party they both attended for Larry O'Brien. Blaming campaign excesses on staff he had been unable to control, Whitten let it be known "to one and all" at the party that he and Smith were friends again. Coleman had gone to the appeals court and, like Smith, was removed from the action, but Winter's good showing in the 1967 gubernatorial race gave heart to moderates.[33]

After engaging a group of Alabama politicians in informal discussions on race and politics, Smith reported being amazed by Alabamians' openness. "Despite Wallace, the differences between Alabama and Mississippi are great," Smith noted. "No politician from any part of Mississippi would talk like that [so openly about race] to someone unless he had ten or fifteen years of association to know that the talk would not be repeated," he concluded.[34] Perhaps Mississippians' fears about speaking openly on race accounted for the fact that so little progress seemed to be taking place in Mississippi.

After 1966, Smith's contacts with Mississippi became less frequent. He and others like him seemed to be permanently excluded from power, and Smith began to discover wider interests throughout the South. But in 1967, while reading about a black Mississippian who had won the Medal of Honor, Smith had an idea for another book to help develop better race relations in Mississippi. He proposed to publish the stories of an equal number of black Mississippians and white Mississippians who had won the medal, in hopes of creating heroes both races could admire. He sold the idea to Jack Reed, the Tupelo businessman, who promised to help gain support from the Mississippi Economic Council and the state department of education. Smith convinced the Southern Regional Council to pay Audrey Warren, his former congressional assistant, to help him write *Mississippians All*. When he contacted Hodding Carter, who had started a press in Louisiana, about publishing the book, Carter groaned in jest. "People are beginning to think that William Winter is going to be elected. Then you come home."[35] Published in 1968 by Pelican Publishing House, the book was a series of war-hero biographies intended for a junior high school audience; it had no chance of attracting an adult lay readership. The state department of education did not adopt the book for the schools as Smith had hoped, and it was never widely distributed. Smith must have sympathized with a correspondent, who wrote to compliment *Mississippians All*, saying of the struggle to win acceptance for integration, "I want you to know that you would be right proud of the nucleus that are daily fighting to get us in the twentieth century before it passes. We've got the ball and we are running with it, but so far we haven't made a real dent in the line."[36]

There had been more progress than he realized. In 1968, Smith attended a conference for elected officials at Ole Miss and was delighted and amazed at the change in race relations. The meeting symbolized to him the accomplishment of what he had worked for in the state. Writing to his old friend Phil Mullen while "still in a state of relative euphoria," Smith described Vice President Hubert Humphrey's visit to Ole Miss (Humphrey was the keynote speaker for the meeting): "Perhaps

the highlight of the night before [Humphrey's speech] was the Sunflower County hospitality room, presided over by two members of the
Board of Supervisors (one a former president of the Indianola Citizens'
Council), the Chancery Clerk, and including among the officials present the Circuit Judge whose home is Indianola. Among their cordially
received guests in the normal convention fashion were Charles Evers
and Aaron Henry, plus every other Negro who could be found among
the overnighters at the Alumni House. (More showed up from Sunflower County the next day, and sat together in good mixed fashion at
the breakfast.)"

The next morning Smith enjoyed the comments of blacks savoring
their first visit to the University of Mississippi. It gave him a thrill to report that "[o]n the way over to the cafeteria... one of the Negro guests...
commented on the Grove (at its loveliest greenery) that he had always
heard about how pretty his state university was, and now he was glad to
see it for the first time."

Smith was amazed to see the mixture of political leaders and civil
rights veterans and enjoyed the camaraderie of the group:

> The breakfast had more than three hundred people, at least 35 percent
> black. I spent a bit of preliminary time shaking hands with previous sup-
> porters, a lot of Negro former constituents that I had never met before,
> and meeting a lot of Negroes whose names I knew from the poverty pro-
> gram and from civil rights activities. From the podium with Reverend R.
> L. T. Smith [a black civil rights activist and Jackson businessman] giving
> the invocation was Lt. Governor Charles Sullivan (William Winter in the
> audience), serving to emphasize the absence of the Governor [John Bell
> Williams] also was a telegram of welcome from the two senators.
>
> I sat with the all-white Leflore County group (if there were any Ne-
> groes present from Greenwood I did not meet them or learn of them.)
> But I was pleasantly surprised to see even the white representation. When
> they stood up and waved to me from across the hall, it was nice to join
> them.

"Nice" was an understatement. The Leflore delegation's request for
Smith to join them was recognition of his victory. He had been right,
and they were glad to accept him again. He did not believe they had
changed their hearts, but he saw hope that it could happen. Although
Smith had never been a fan of the vice president, he felt Humphrey
was the ideal choice for this occasion. "[His speech] was a lot from his

ever renewed fountain of homilies about the dignity of man and the verities of brotherhood, which fitted exactly the audience and was what could help make a lesson out of it." Smith was not overwhelmed with enthusiasm for the conference, reporting finally, "[N]one of this means that a millennium has come, and I am sure some of the people on hand were still stout resisters. But for Mississippi, they have reached a stage that is a vast change. Politically, it also means that there will be a determined campaign for the Democratic nominee this fall. The odds are still strongly with Wallace, but he will be fought."[37]

The conference presented a scene that Smith had never believed he would witness. In 1962 when he went to TVA, it would have been impossible for a racially mixed audience to eat together anywhere in the state. In 1968, the state's integrated leadership were sharing a meal at Ole Miss, the symbol of resistance to integration. Some of the whites present might have been "secret resisters," as Smith said, but they obviously had come to accept the new political realities.

On the other hand, Wallace won 60 percent of the Delta vote in November. Smith was right about a new political landscape in Mississippi, but the moderates could not translate the changes into political power. Some white Democrats had accepted a coalition with blacks because black leaders demonstrated a "new political sophistication" and played down civil rights issues in order to elect compromise candidates, but the Mississippi underground did not emerge victorious for several years. Smith had urged that 1971 be the target year for moderates to win the governorship with a black-white coalition behind a liberal white candidate. But his candidate, William Winter, settled for the lieutenant governor's office in 1971. William Waller, Byron De La Beckwith's prosecutor, allied openly with Eastland and secretly with blacks to win the title of first New South governor in Mississippi without ties to Smith's faction. Charles Evers, brother of the slain civil rights leader, repudiated the coalition and split the black vote by running as an independent. Smith congratulated Waller on his accomplishment, but the two never became close.[38]

If Smith had lost influence in Mississippi, he had gained it as a spokesman for white southern liberals. He made such a name for himself as a spokesman for integration that Barry Goldwater targeted Smith for criticism in Arizona. At a hundred-dollar-a-plate dinner, he told a Republican fund-raising audience, "I don't believe we have to destroy the

Constitution of the United States to placate Martin Luther King, Frank Smith or anybody else."[39]

As a TVA director, Smith used his position to hammer home the idea of accepting integration. His standard speech in 1965, delivered across the South to audiences in cities such as Huntsville, Birmingham, and Oak Ridge, called on the South to face its "racial responsibilities." His appeals for integration were personal and not TVA policy. The TVA news releases covering Smith's speeches eliminated his pleas for integration and ignored events such as his book signings for *Congressman from Mississippi*. The official TVA news releases mentioned only Smith's remarks on topics such as "natural resources" and eliminated all calls for integration. Smith never let the hostility of the TVA bureaucracy toward his mission to encourage integration stop him.[40]

He not only spoke but also wrote extensively. He published an article on the development of isolationism among southern congressmen in the *South Atlantic Quarterly* and a new, more honest assessment of the South in the *Virginia Quarterly*. When he was in Congress, his article for the *Virginia Quarterly* had avoided the issue of integration; from TVA he endorsed it. He quickly incorporated both articles and earlier works into a book that LSU Press published as *Look Away from Dixie*. Warren tried to talk him out of publishing the book because it would not add to his "stature as a writer." She urged Smith to "shoot for" national prominence, but he ignored her advice and fired his agent later in the year because she refused to help an old congressional colleague with a book. Apparently, his interest lay more in crusading for change in the South than in developing his career as a writer. He wrote invited articles for newspapers and worked on a book entitled "100 Acres and a Tractor," in which he argued for the development of family farms to halt the migration of the poor into city slums. He never sold "100 Acres," and he tired of another project, a history of the Mississippi River Valley. Telling the publisher he enjoyed not having a book hanging over his head, he offered to pay back an advance to be let out of the project. He seemed to be motivated to write only if the writing served some immediate purpose. He switched to writing about the environment as that subject became the center of debate for him and TVA, but he never abandoned his goal of integrating southern society.[41]

Soon after arriving at TVA, Smith set out to establish himself as a spokesman for white southern integrationists. He joined the Southern

Regional Council headquartered in Atlanta and the ACLU. Smith spent half of his weekends for six or seven years flying to Atlanta for meetings. The seemingly interminable meetings were often held in airport motels, and Smith became weary of the grind. But he persisted in his determination to further integration. Because of his "nonpolitical" position at TVA, he had to be circumspect. For example, he declined to become chairman of the Voter Education Project and nominated a black educator, Dr. Samuel Cook, instead. He took other low-key tasks, serving as chairman of the nominations committee, for example, when the Southern Regional Council had to separate from VEP in order to maintain the SRC's tax-exempt status. In a host of small ways he demonstrated his support for integration. He convinced President Kennedy to write a letter to the mayor of Knoxville praising him for carrying out the peaceful integration of the city. Smith thanked NAACP executive secretary Roy Wilkins for appealing to southern members of Congress to support the civil rights movement. He assured Wilkins that there were southern members of Congress who would like to support the movement and would as soon as they felt it would not mean immediate defeat. He spoke to the Tennessee Human Relations Council, advocating a federal drive to integrate juries in southern courts. He became a lay speaker for the United Methodist Church, which supported civil rights activities. He reported to a friend, "I am thoroughly enjoying it all."[42]

Despite his commitment to integration, Smith was disturbed by the direction of the civil rights movement as early as 1966 and distanced himself from the black power advocates. Although he privately agreed with critics of the Vietnam War, he never spoke out publicly on that issue because he feared being identified as a left-wing radical. Smith's first priority was integration. He refused to accept advocates of black power because he believed they would reverse the progress toward integration and interracial cooperation. In a 1966 letter, Smith condemned black power advocate Stokely Carmichael for practicing the "same racial demagoguery" that white segregationists were known for. But he reserved his greatest scorn for the "liberal and intellectual circles" creating the "Carmichael cult." He believed that liberal intellectuals were enabling the "fringe" of the civil rights movement to identify the themes for the whole movement and that "black power" would alienate the movement from the majority of voters. Smith's goal was to win the minds of southern whites for integration at a time when, he thought, the excesses of black power advocates were driving white southerners away.[43]

Historian David Donald, who knew Smith from their junior college days in Mississippi, gave Smith a forum in which to develop his ideas. He invited Smith to address a joint meeting of the Organization of American Historians and the Southern Historical Association. Donald suggested as the title for Smith's paper "Problems of Liberals in the Present Day South." Smith used the speech as an opportunity to suggest a program for southern liberals. After paying respect to the black heroes of the civil rights movement, Smith claimed that the "tolerance" of the southern white community was just as important in bringing about integration as the black civil rights workers had been. In an appeal for recognition of the role southern whites had played in the civil rights movement, he estimated that thousands of whites had been turned out of their homes and jobs because they ignored the customs of segregation. He contended that more white families had split over their views of the civil rights movement than had been divided over the Civil War. He called on southern liberals to declare themselves and to work openly to move the South into the American mainstream despite the hardships of publicly supporting integration.

Smith laid claim to the term "liberal" to describe southerners who supported integration, but he denounced the "romanticization" of the "Negro" in the 1960s. He compared it to the idolization of the "working man" by communists and socialists in the 1930s. He said southern liberals should not be expected to accept "promises without performance and protests without purpose" from blacks. But Smith called on southern liberals to work for job opportunities, education, and state laws to guarantee full citizenship to blacks as long as blacks worked hard toward the same goals. Above all, he declared, southern liberals had to work toward voting rights for blacks. Progress, he implied, would have to await the complete acceptance of black voters, because "until the South is rid of the curse of racist politics, the Southern liberal is going to have to make his choice on the basis of the racial attitudes, both public and private, of the candidate and the parties."[44] Only after the race issue was settled, Smith thought, could the South move on to confront other problems with full vigor. In the tumult of the 1960s, Smith's appeal to a history conference received little attention. The nation was listening to louder, more strident, voices.

Faced with the growing strength of George Wallace and the threat to civil rights gains Wallace represented, Smith joined with Brooks Hays, Carl Elliot, Ralph McGill (editor of the *Atlanta Constitution*), and Vernon

Jordan, chief administrator for VEP, to organize the Southern Committee on Political Ethics in 1967. Chartered in Washington as a nonprofit
organization, SCOPE was to have its headquarters in Atlanta; its primary goal was to ensure blacks their full civil rights in the South. The
new organization quickly evolved into an anti-Wallace crusade. Its leaders were fearful that Wallace might be able to throw the 1968 presidential election into the House of Representatives, as he threatened; therefore SCOPE abandoned other activities to mount an effective opposition
to Wallace. The organization employed a public relations firm to produce a booklet on Wallace portraying him as a fascist without actually
using the word, and sold 425,000 copies of "Wallace Labor Record" to
labor unions for distribution to their members, as well as sending one
to every editor of a daily newspaper in the country. Smith worked behind the scenes in all these efforts. Not surprisingly, the IRS denied
SCOPE tax-exempt status. The group tried to spin off another organization to reapply for tax exemption, but SCOPE died a lingering death.[45]

As the ineffectiveness of SCOPE became apparent, Smith helped
found a new organization promoted by Thomas H. Naylor, an economics professor at Duke University who had grown up in Mississippi and
attended Millsaps College. Naylor and his friend Jim Leutze, a former
aide to Hubert Humphrey, wanted to create an organization "to help
legitimatize liberalism in the South." They proposed to use "snob appeal" to attract "moderates and some conservatives" into an integrated
organization that would provide speakers "all over the South" to beat
the conservatives "at their own game." They defined their target as the
"white middle class in the South." Claiming to have good connections
with the "younger political liberals in the South," Naylor asked for Smith's
assistance drawing in older liberals.[46] Noting that SCOPE and other organizations had suffered from "personality problems" and that, as a
"Federal official with a nonpolitical agency" he had to limit his involvement with such organizations, Smith expressed interest. Smith visited
Naylor in North Carolina and put him in touch with SRC staff. Naylor
in turn visited the Smiths in Knoxville, and, by April 1969, he and Smith
were discussing a name for the budding organization.[47]

After reading Smith's portrait of Lamar in *Mississippians All,* Naylor
suggested that the organization be named the L. Q. C. Lamar Society.
Smith demurred, thinking Lamar too conservative. He told a noted
southern liberal, Virginia Durr, that "Lamar was certainly not a perfect
model for a present-day young Southern idealist."[48] Despite Smith's

reservations, the name stuck. Naylor photocopied Smith's chapter to distribute to members at the first meeting, and the name L. Q. C. Lamar was adopted.[49] The organization had two wings from the beginning. One faction was impatient with temporizing and wanted an activist, ideological, political association. The other wing, the majority, wanted a nonideological organization, including all party affiliations, working for practical solutions for the South's problems.[50]

Incapable of nonpartisanship, Smith favored the first wing but played only a secondary role in assisting Naylor. Smith's main role was to assure worried friends that he had helped Naylor to manage the overlapping membership with SCOPE and other organizations to avoid conflicts. Smith said that he had the highest hopes for the Lamar Society because of the "ability and interest of the two chief promoters." But as the society developed, so did Smith's reservations, because the new organization seemed to ignore blacks. When Naylor sent a draft of a book to be published by the society, Smith protested that black authors were not represented and suggested two to be contacted.[51]

Smith sponsored an east Tennessee organizational cocktail party for the society. Similar efforts across the South resulted in a membership of five hundred by 1971. The membership rule requiring participants to live in the South was stretched to include such southerners as Willie Morris, editor of *Harper's*. The society prospered until Naylor grew tired of doing all the work. It never raised any money or employed any staff. Naylor left, and the organization withered without him. But before its demise, one of its meetings brought together Terry Sanford of North Carolina and four of the "new southern governors" to give birth to the Southern Growth Policies Board. It was Sanford's idea, but Smith endorsed and encouraged its establishment.[52] Critics said the Lamar Society had been "more reflective of a mood than equipped with a viable program...." It withered as the "mood" passed.[53]

As a TVA director, Smith proved exceptionally active outside the agency, straining the definition of "nonpolitical" by working constantly for integration and for the Democratic party. Aside from participating behind the scenes in Mississippi politics, he also secretly played a small role in Tennessee's. For example, he wrote letters under a pen name for the senatorial campaign of Congressman Ross Bass and advised him occasionally.[54]

During the turbulent sixties, his politics appeared to become more conservative. In 1971, speaking to Millsaps students, he outlined the changes in Mississippi since 1954 and praised integration. But he ended on a note of caution, warning that "real sophistication" would come to Mississippi politics only when black voters understood that "black demagogues [can be] just as self-seeking and just as race-minded as the worst white ones...."[55] He was not alone in this trend. Hodding Carter, who had left Mississippi to become writer-in-residence at Tulane, reacted much more angrily to the black power movement. He reverted to racist views, calling Stokely Carmichael "a little black Power Sambo." He said, "To be truthful, I am getting pretty damned well fed up with what I once called jigs and I am about to call them again."[56] Smith's rejection of black power did not lessen his support for integration. The year before Smith made his Millsaps speech, his church, Concord United Methodist, cut its pledge to the annual budget of the United Methodist Church because it supported the National Council of Churches, which encouraged integration. Smith protested and reduced his pledge to the church in order to contribute to "other religious purposes."[57] He believed that black radicals hurt integration as much as white segregationists, and he opposed them both.

The most impressive fact about Smith's career was its consistency. He lied to get elected and to keep his seat in Congress. But freed from the restraints of office, Smith reverted openly to the beliefs he had developed as a teenager; he spent the remainder of his career working to integrate the South and to bring economic development to all southerners. David Lilienthal, one of the founders of TVA, praised Smith's work at TVA as carrying on the New Deal tradition. Lilienthal had been Smith's hero—he treasured Lilienthal's praise above that of all others. He even sent Lilienthal's letter to his mother.[58] Smith was a New Deal Democrat: he believed the government existed to improve the lives of its citizens. He worked hard throughout his career to continue the work begun by liberals in the 1930s and added racial equality to his own New Deal agenda. As TVA director, he wrote, spoke, and organized for over a decade trying to integrate the South, especially Mississippi.

CHAPTER THIRTEEN

TVA and the Death of New Deal Liberalism

S mith had idolized the Tennessee Valley Authority since the depression. For him it represented a noble experiment in which the federal government worked with the people of the Tennessee Valley to eliminate poverty. Growing up in Greenwood reading his *New Republic* with intensity, fighting Roosevelt's war against fascism, battling racism secretly and then openly, Smith became a devout New Deal liberal. He was certain that if the country and the world would adopt liberal, New Deal policies, a good and just life would be attainable for all. He had been right about race. He had helped to make a revolution in the South in the 1960s. He had witnessed scenes of racial acceptance and cooperation he never believed would occur in his lifetime. Since his teens, Smith had considered himself to be on the left of the political spectrum and in a position of moral superiority. Favoring integration made him a radical in Mississippi, and the isolation and secret conspiracy of his crusade nourished his sense of superiority; in the late 1960s, however, he found himself outflanked on the left.

At TVA, Smith expected to carry on the revolution he had helped to foster in southern society. He knew that maintaining the gains made toward racial integration would require further economic growth. TVA power, he believed, would fuel the needed industry in a vast area of the South. But environmentalists told Smith that TVA's power production was destroying the land and polluting the air and water. Smith considered himself a conservationist, but increasingly he found himself labeled a reactionary by the environmentalists—people who often also opposed the war in Vietnam and sometimes admired black power advocates. They claimed the high moral ground and the left wing of the Democratic party, but Smith would concede neither to them. Instead he did battle for his

New Deal version of liberalism, which he believed would complete the Americanization of Dixie through economic development.

Smith's experience at TVA was not a happy one. During his tenure, the TVA bureaucracy attained complete control under the chairmanship of Red Wagner. Perceiving Smith to be an outsider and a threat to their close-knit family, the bureaucrats banished him from "family" affairs. But Smith's clash with TVA was not simply a struggle between a politician and the bureaucrats; it was a struggle between the idealism that had given birth to TVA and the increasingly conservative establishment that the New Deal had created. Smith's clashes with the new left wing of the Democratic party, the environmentalists, and the TVA leadership illustrate the death throes of New Deal liberalism so well that it makes a compelling story.

Since high school, Smith had lived for ideas. His intellectual journey in Greenwood had taken him far from his native racist environment. During his journey, Smith had absorbed a large dose of Western man's Enlightenment-born faith in progress. Like the French philosophes, he believed in science and in man's competence to rebuild Eden. His reading was reinforced by a lifetime of personal experiences, which proved to him the "rightness" of his social, political, and environmental philosophy. As a child he had been flooded out of his home, had taken refuge in the courthouse, and afterwards had watched the levee built across the street to keep the Yazoo in its banks. Living among some of the poorest people in America in the 1930s, he had seen the white middle class gain some economic security from the New Deal and by the late sixties was seeing blacks moving to join them. He had seen atomic energy harnessed, made into artillery shells, and transformed into electricity. With most Americans, he adopted complete faith in science to solve any problem. His life confirmed his intellectual belief in progress and liberalism. Therefore the environmentalists threatened his entire worldview. For them, progress was not limitless; they contended that the earth's resources were finite and that growth must be restricted to protect the land. They implied, if they did not say outright, that humans are not rational. They cannot be trusted to manage the earth's resources. Smith's differences with the environmentalists and with his TVA colleagues made his role in the agency a battle from the start.

The Tennessee Valley Authority had been founded by Franklin D. Roosevelt to rescue one of the poorest regions of the United States. The land was eroded; the Tennessee River frequently flooded and was not navigable for much of its course. The population suffered from a variety of diseases, including malaria. TVA took on the task of physical and social reform by damming the river, providing fertilizer, and educating the population. The agency had attracted some of the best and brightest minds and did excellent work, but, despite its reputation, the TVA Smith joined in 1962 was not a crusading or reforming New Deal agency. Eisenhower and the Republicans had wanted to destroy TVA when they came to power in 1953 because it symbolized to them a drift toward socialism. Instead of destroying the agency, Eisenhower compromised, sending an Army Corps of Engineers general to oversee it and to make certain that it did not conduct dangerous, socialistic experiments. TVA bureaucrats converted the general, Herbert Vogel, into a TVA true believer, but along the way TVA lost its enthusiasm for social improvement and began to concentrate single-mindedly on producing cheap electric power. TVA's friends in Congress inadvertently contributed to the trend when they passed the self-financing act, allowing TVA to sell bonds to raise money for expansion and operation. Smith had cooperated with Alabama congressman Bob Jones and other allies to pass the bill in order to provide TVA the necessary funds to continue expanding its power production during the lean Republican years. TVA prospered under the system but had to make a "profit" to pay off the bonds. This self-financing scheme ended most congressional oversight and left the bureaucracy on automatic pilot. Financial independence and lack of congressional oversight also contributed to the perception of the agency as a regional rather than a national entity. Bureaucracies do not by nature initiate bold projects, and TVA languished as a social reform agency even while it grew as a power company. President Kennedy and others had noted the change in mission and publicly criticized TVA for becoming merely "another power company."[1]

Vogel, Eisenhower's appointee, resigned as chairman because he understood the Democratic administration wanted to make some changes. Smith took Vogel's seat on the board but did not become chairman. Bob Jones had asked that Vogel's resignation be kept secret until after Smith's primary against Whitten, but Vogel ignored the request and leaked the news to demonstrate his independence from partisan politics. The myth was that TVA did not participate in politics. Vogel's leak and events leading to Smith's nomination brought the myth into question and caused confusion about the appointment, which cast a cloud over Smith's arrival at TVA.[2]

TVA's powerful Washington lobbyist Marguerite Owen wanted Red Wagner, the general manager, to be appointed chairman of the board. Wagner, a lifetime employee who had worked his way through the ranks, was credited with saving the agency by converting Vogel into a TVA man. Owen had a close working relationship with Alabama's Senator Lister Hill, as well as with Mississippi's Stennis and Whitten, and she wanted Wagner appointed chairman to emphasize the president's support for the TVA professionals. Wagner's promotion, she thought, would reward long, loyal service and build morale within the agency. Wagner had joined the board when Brooks Hays, another defeated southern liberal who had been sent to TVA by Eisenhower, resigned to return to Washington and a place in the Kennedy administration. At that point, in response to Owen's pleas, Kennedy had offered to appoint Wagner chairman, but Wagner had demurred because he thought replacing Vogel damaged the perception of TVA as being isolated from political influence. Not knowing Kennedy's promise to Owen and Wagner, Smith believed he was to be made chairman when he was appointed to Vogel's place on the board. Hearing from a reporter that Wagner was being appointed chairman, he thought Robert Wagner, mayor of New York, had been named to the post because he had never heard of Red Wagner. Smith mounted a campaign among some of his friends in Congress to keep the chairmanship for himself, but he had no chance of succeeding. Owen had too much influence with key senators, and Kennedy, before appointing Smith, had given his word to make Wagner chairman.[3]

Smith arrived at TVA to find a worried new chairman—a man who had spent his life among TVA employees. Wagner wrongly assumed Smith to be in close touch with Kennedy and hurriedly assured Smith he would support the president. He offered Smith the position of vice chairman of the board, which was then occupied by A. R. Jones, who had urged the creation of the title and then filled it. Jones was a Republican accountant whom Wagner described as unenthusiastic about everything. Smith declined the vice chairmanship offered by Wagner and suggested that they operate on a seniority system. Wagner need not have worried; Smith had no instructions from the president. Kennedy's only advice to Smith about TVA was "don't give it away."[4]

Three board members appointed by the president for nine-year terms governed TVA, acting more as a management committee than a conventional board of directors. Each board member had one vote, and the directors usually voted in response to staff initiatives. Questions from the staff framed in a "yes or no" format were designed to ward off directors' involvement in developing policy. Neither Smith nor the other two directors who served during Smith's tenure had much impact on TVA policy. Wagner had the loyalty of the TVA staff, who effectively shut out the other board members by dealing with the chairman. Smith had one secretary at his command and one vote out of three on the board of directors. He could interview employees, but they were all responsible to the new general manager, who was Wagner's friend. Wagner and the general manager owned adjoining vacation homes at Watts Barr, where they probably settled major issues in long evening talks. Wagner did not dominate the board by weight of force or superior intellect but as a father figure to the TVA staff, and he enjoyed their loyalty. Wagner's method of operation was to reach a consensus and avoid conflicts; he consulted Smith and tried to get agreement ahead of meetings to prevent confrontations, but Smith was frozen out of real power from the beginning at TVA. He described the situation as an impenetrable triangle, with the TVA family hostile toward outsiders. TVA failed, Smith thought, to recognize its friends or to accept friendly criticism. Wagner saw Smith as a political animal who would do damage to TVA, and his view inevitably spread to the staff.[5]

Each director operated his own office. Most of the official mail went to the chairman; he referred letters to the staff members, who drafted responses. All top administrators had their secretaries listen to telephone conversations and take notes. Secretaries also usually screened all calls and visitors. Smith ignored TVA administrative customs. He asked his secretary, Mary Knurr, never to listen to his telephone conversations. Smith often ignored the staff referral policy and drafted his own letters. He followed the policy of sending copies to the other board members when he sent out an official letter, but he kept up a massive personal correspondence, too. He took all calls and saw anyone who asked for an appointment, allowing no screening. He worked with an open door while on the telephone or conducting meetings. His secretary found his unpretentious style refreshing and had no difficulty making the transition after working for Vogel, but she also recognized that Smith was excluded from the TVA family. He even played golf alone.[6]

Despite Smith's exclusion from full TVA family membership, he demonstrated his human concern for the staff. Not long after he arrived at TVA, staff members were shocked when he visited the home of a secretary whose husband had died. Smith never conformed to the behavior expected of a director by the staff. He lost his temper frequently and alienated some.[7]

Smith remained politically active, in a violation of the spirit if not the letter of the law governing his position on the board. Wagner was just the opposite. Relying on his engineer's mind, he expected to give anyone the facts and let the facts determine every decision. In public, Smith and Wagner maintained a friendly facade, but in private board meetings, they fought like cats and dogs. Smith did not take these differences personally, he said, but he believed that Wagner was incapable of separating disagreements over policy from personal animosity. Smith agreed with most of Wagner's basic ideas, but Smith wanted a more environmentally friendly TVA with a more aggressive social development policy.[8]

Smith's model was David Lilienthal, who had created the historic TVA myth. In his books and speeches articulating the democratic ideal of TVA as an organization, Lilienthal invented the idea that TVA was dedicated to transforming the valley into an Eden by mobilizing its resources and its people. Wagner wanted the same results, but thought they could be achieved scientifically by good engineering. Smith agreed with Lilienthal that the goals could be obtained only by motivating people in the valley and in Congress to work with the agency. Smith, a political creature, understood that the political process was the only way to achieve results in a democracy. Wagner, having spent his life as a bureaucrat, feared and distrusted politicians. He had absorbed the TVA attitude that politicians were the enemy because they ignored merit, awarding jobs by patronage, and argued for popular placement of dams, disregarding all engineering advice.[9]

Smith's formal duties consisted of attending two official board meetings each month and ten or twelve informal meetings—where the real work was done. Connected to those required tasks were the ceremonial duties. He delivered hundreds of speeches to diverse audiences each year and greeted thousands of visitors, showing the more important ones TVA's dams and installations. Since his army days Smith had hated any pomp and circumstance; to balance the unsatisfying ceremonial activities, Smith made it his role to build a relationship with newspaper editors throughout the valley and to keep up his relations with Congress. The latter activity presented a challenge to the bureaucracy—specifically to Marguerite Owen, who had been accustomed to telling directors whom to see in Washington and even what to say. By hard work, dedication, and self-effacing behavior, Owen had become the unchallengable voice of TVA in Washington.[10]

Smith's and Owen's relationship got off to a bad start when Smith remained in Congress after his appointment to TVA. Urgent job seekers inundated Smith with requests. Smith knew that politicians could not influence hiring at TVA, but some of the requests seemed to have merit. Smith sent the meritorious ones to Owen, who forwarded them to the personnel office in Knoxville without acknowledging Smith's letters. After Smith moved to Knoxville and assumed his duties, the other board members must have told him that he was expected to see Owen if he went to Washington. On his first visit as TVA director, Smith went by her office as requested, and she lectured him for two hours. He did not go back. Instead, he visited Washington approximately twice each month on his own, a habit that must have driven Owen and the rest of the bureaucracy mad with anxiety.[11]

Working in such isolation, Smith naturally developed problems with the TVA staff. Charles McCarthy, the TVA lawyer, said, "Frank Smith was a very difficult person, he was kind of a loose cannon. You didn't know what he was going to do or what he was going to say or when he was going to blow up right through the roof. He would not blow his top every time he met somebody, but every once in a while he would. He would be in a meeting some place and he'd slam the book down and go roaring out of the room. He just had a short fuse."[12]

Smith's perspective was that his talents were not being used. He agreed with most of Wagner's policies and plans but believed Wagner failed to sell them to Congress and the public. Wagner, he thought, reacted rather than "moving out on issues." Smith thought TVA lacked visionary leadership that could define an "overarching vision" and sell it to the public. Smith wanted to take on such a role, but the chairman did not want to deal with the world outside TVA unless forced to do so. Agreeing on the New Deal mission of TVA, Smith and Wagner could work together, but disagreeing on how to achieve their ends, they never got along comfortably.[13]

Smith arrived in November 1962, to find TVA under attack for buying strip-mined coal. Harry Caudill, a lawyer in rural eastern Kentucky, had published an article in *Atlantic Monthly* accusing TVA of destroying the Kentucky mountains by buying coal from strip miners who churned the mountains into piles of wasteland. Condemning TVA as a development-minded institution, he claimed it had become unresponsive and insensitive to the public. Instinctively Smith sided with Caudill. He made looking into TVA's strip-mining policy his first order of business. The staff reacted defensively and presented the board with a plan for TVA to encourage the states to pass reclamation laws and urge education activities. The power people behind the plan wanted as little done as possible because reclamation would cost money—money that sooner or later would be passed on to customers in the form of higher rates. Disappointed by the staff suggestions, Smith went to Kentucky to see the mines for himself and talked to field workers who disputed the rosy picture of strip mining painted for him back in Knoxville. Feeling somewhat misled by the staff, Smith proposed as a solution a federal law to require reclamation, but the other members of the board supported the power division and refused to accept Smith's recommendation. Smith's fall-back position was to have TVA's coal suppliers sign contracts containing reclamation clauses. The board delayed that suggestion and took the position that state laws should be enforced where they existed and passed where they were lacking.[14]

To address the strip mining problem, Smith assumed two roles. He tried to defend TVA to the outside world while stimulating the agency internally to take more responsibility. He wrote to the editor of *Atlantic Monthly* and indicated his support for reclamation. The dubious editor asked for an article. Smith drafted a piece and sent it to the magazine without first distributing it for approval. Only when the editor rejected the article did Smith draw the staff into the effort to defend the agency's policies. The publicity director told Smith the real point was missing from the first draft: "We can have our cake and eat it too" by restoring the land surface.[15] Accepting his advice on the article, Smith revised it to open with a scene at a reclamation site and included his favored solution—a federal law requiring reclamation—in his conclusion. The editor called the article "a reasonable defense" but offered only to edit it down to a five-hundred-word letter. Smith declined, deploring the *Atlantic*'s refusal to "publish some accurate version."[16]

Meanwhile, Smith courted Caudill. He wrote cordially to Caudill in 1963 outlining TVA's efforts to establish a reclamation demonstration site and assured Caudill that TVA was studying the problem. He felt that the TVA effort offered a "practical method of reducing the undesirable effects of strip mining...."[17] When Caudill wrote a book, *Night Comes to the Cumberlands,* expanding the attack made in the *Atlantic* article, Smith asked to review it in the *Nashville Tennessean.* Giving the book a good review, Smith again wrote Caudill, expressing his support for federal action "to check the present inexcusable waste of natural and human resources."[18] None of his attempts to initiate dialogue had any effect.

Smith had considered strip mining an evil for twenty years, since reading an exposé. Indeed, he considered himself "a strong believer in conservation principles." But he accepted strip mining as a "necessary evil" in an "efficient economy."[19] He wanted to do the right thing and disliked the position created by TVA's intransigence; however, just as he had tried to work from within the racist political system, he tried to prod TVA toward his view while defending it to the public, hoping to make his position inside the agency stronger.

Smith never deviated from his insistence on reclamation. After two years of negotiations, he forced the other two board members to accept reclamation clauses in TVA contracts by threatening to go public with his reservations about TVA policy if they did not. Wagner was furious with Smith and considered him a traitor for siding with the environmentalists. Smith, having achieved his reclamation contracts, did his best to defend TVA from its critics while continuing to push for a stronger federal law.[20]

Wagner made a date to visit eastern Kentucky and to dine with Caudill and his wife in hopes that a personal appeal would silence TVA's chief critic. Not knowing of Wagner's visit, Smith wrote to Caudill seeking reconciliation; Caudill told Smith of Wagner's impending visit and invited Smith to accompany Wagner for dinner at his home. Smith did not formally decline, but the chairman went alone. In the end, Wagner only made matters worse with Caudill by denying TVA responsibility for the land destroyed by strip miners.[21]

Reclamation did not satisfy the critics of strip mining, and Smith's energetic defense of TVA eventually enraged them. At TVA, with the power people considering Smith a traitor for dealing with the environmentalists, the animosity grew. It got so strong that his secretary knew never to ask anyone from the power division to meet Smith's plane when he traveled to inspect TVA installations.[22]

Attitudes about the environment changed dramatically between 1960 and 1962. Smith's natural resources committee, used as a tool to elect Kennedy, assumed that resources would be developed to the maximum to ensure economic growth. The main question was how to manage resources in the public's best interest. No one protested the committee report issued after the inaugural meeting in 1960. Two years later, Rachel

Carson published *Silent Spring*, describing the impact chemicals had on the Earth and its inhabitants. Lawrence Rockefeller's commission on outdoor recreation reported vanishing natural spaces, and Kennedy held his promised White House conference on natural resources. What Smith and his friends in Congress had called the "birds and bees" conservationists were transforming themselves into environmentalists, and lobbying groups multiplied. The new environmentalists did not compromise. As the political culture grew more violent with black power and antiwar protests, compromise went out of style, and no group was less compromising than environmentalists. The earth became sacred for them, and despoiling it, even in a good cause, became evil. Secretary of the Interior Stewart Udall supported the movement, even adopting its language in official department publications. Smith could never comprehend their view of the earth or what he thought to be their unreasonableness.[23]

Yet among the TVA directors, it was Smith who took the most interest in the environment. He pleased the TVA forestry staff by taking a major interest in Arbor Day, and he worked to improve controls on water pollution. Two weeks after his arrival, Smith heard of a plan for a park TVA might build on land located between two TVA lakes in the Tennessee and Cumberland rivers on the borders of Tennessee and Kentucky. Robert Howes, the head of recreation in the reservoir properties division, had conceived the idea and taken it through the various administrators to the general manager. The board approved the idea and initiated negotiations to give TVA authority to establish the park. Smith adopted the idea as his special project and urged an ecological theme for the park to give TVA something "to be proud of." When Wagner and staff members met with secretary Udall to claim TVA control of the project, Smith went along to make sure there were no compromises relaxing TVA ownership. Throughout his service with TVA, Smith took a paternal interest in the development and growth of the land between the lakes.[24]

The other project Smith especially favored was the Tributary Area Development Program. Wagner had developed the program in response to criticism that TVA had lost its New Deal fervor for developing the full human, as well as the natural, resources of the valley. The idea was to plant the seeds to grow mini-TVAs in the tributary valleys feeding the Tennessee River. In other words, TVA had worked for the Tennessee Valley in the 1930s, so state and local governments could do the same things in the Elk River Valley, the Duck River Valley, and all the others. It was not a new vision, but it was the TVA plan for the 1960s. TVA helped to establish citizen boards for the valleys, but the boards began to go directly to Washington to seek funding that TVA did not provide. Frightened as always of political entanglements, TVA refused to cooperate with them in lobbying Congress. As a politician, Smith did not share TVA's phobia. In a panel discussion the day after President Kennedy visited Muscle Shoals to celebrate TVA's thirtieth anniversary, Wagner and Smith engaged in a rare public dispute when a televised panel criticized the directors for concentrating on production of cheap power to the detriment of development on the tributaries. Smith agreed with the panel that TVA needed to shift its priorities toward the tributaries, but Wagner defended TVA's focus on its cheap power mission. The tributary area development might have accomplished more had it been pursued aggressively and supported by TVA, but Wagner's political timidity thwarted Smith's enthusiasm for the program.[25]

Smith rebelled constantly against what he considered a narrow vision of TVA's roles and accomplishments. He wanted TVA to serve as a role model for the world, not just the country. Soon after he arrived, he arranged for an old friend from Mississippi, James C. Baird, Jr., who had worked for USAID in agriculture projects abroad, to write a report entitled "Expanding the Use of TVA's Knowledge and Experience in the USAID Programs Overseas." The basic idea was to use TVA expertise in fertilizer development to increase agricultural yields. By September 1963, Smith gleefully reported that requests had been received from Morocco, Korea, and Brazil.[26]

He rebelled also against the nonpartisan, nonpolitical stance adopted by the chairman. When Barry Goldwater ran for president in 1964 and suggested the idea of selling TVA, Wagner apparently let it be known that he was not concerned. Edmund Orgill, an old hand in Tennessee politics, reported to Smith that he had heard the same story in Knoxville, Chattanooga, and Memphis. Smith's response was quick and strong. He called the report "stupid or deceitful" and said this type of rumor needed to be "squashed" at once. Goldwater, he assured the man, was more likely to destroy TVA than he was to repeal the civil rights law. Therefore, Smith assured the man, Wagner could not possibly have said that Goldwater did not threaten TVA. Smith closed with a warning that he would be around for eight more years, and for the sake of peace and harmony he hoped never to hear of any TVA employees wearing

Goldwater buttons. Smith collected editorials and sent anti-Goldwater materials to the White House. He supplied Tennessee senator Ross Bass, whom he had secretly helped to elect, a copy of a speech entitled "Keep TVA Out of Politics" in a plain envelope marked "personal." He alerted the White House that Goldwater's vice presidential nominee, William E. Miller, had tried to arrange a bribe for Smith when they were in Congress together. Smith found nonpartisan behavior impossible and considered it stupid not to attack Goldwater when he had promised to destroy TVA.[27]

With Johnson elected president, TVA could proceed safely with its new projects. One of the most ambitious was Tellico Dam. Tellico became the center of TVA's new thrust and the object of protests and controversy. Wagner, who had unleashed a building boom after Vogel's departure, wanted this dam, but the cost-benefit analysis did not justify construction. A TVA study yielded unfavorable results, but the analysis was not shared with the board. The general manager told Wagner about the figures, but the other board members did not know that the study had been done, and the staff saw no reason to burden them with its results. Jones opposed the dam based on the information available, but Smith sided with Wagner and approved the project. To justify the cost, Wagner and Smith endorsed a plan to buy up the land surrounding the new lake and to build a planned community on its banks. Smith was enthusiastic about the "new town concept" and the recreation opportunities it would offer. He wrote a friend in the Bureau of Land Management: "Tellico . . . is the most imaginative TVA reservoir project in many years."[28]

When *Nation's Business* ran an article entitled "Now Uncle Sam's A Real Estate Speculator," Smith was incensed and called from Washington to arrange an interview with a friendly Tennessee journalist to refute the charges. In a forceful interview, Smith defended Tellico as good planning to protect the public interest. Tellico opponents struck again with a "choreographed" visit by the Supreme Court justice William O. Douglas designed to attract national attention. Douglas's widely reported assertion that the dam would destroy a free-flowing trout stream triggered scorn from Smith, who wrote Douglas that the Little Tennessee was controlled by another TVA dam upstream and that it was stocked with trout, which did not reproduce naturally there. To fight the developing opposition, Smith talked to all the Democratic members of the public works appropriations subcommittee and contacted Tennessee senator Albert Gore to be a spokesman for the project.[29]

His efforts were not enough. Congress defeated the funds for Tellico in 1965, and TVA brought Vogel back to provide his blessing for the dam. Smith made "TVA: Democracy in Action" the theme of his public speeches for the year to combat the image of TVA's forcing the dam on Tennessee; however, the Tennessee Game and Fish Commission opposed the dam. Smith tried personally to negotiate a settlement with the commission, but discovered that nothing short of eliminating the project would satisfy the commission. The public uproar grew, and TVA circled its wagons to protect the project. When the spokesman for the Knoxville chamber of commerce began to campaign against the dam, both Jones and Smith tried to have the chamber spokesman silenced by business leaders in the community. Neither political pressure nor protests from the board had much impact on the public opposition. Testifying before a congressional committee, Smith tangled with John Dingell, powerful head of the Energy and Commerce Committee, who was trying to legislate TVA cooperation with state agencies because of Tellico. Dingell pressed Smith on TVA's lack of cooperation with the Tennessee Game and Fish Commission until Smith exploded and admitted that nothing short of stopping construction would satisfy them and therefore he had broken off negotiations. Smith retorted that TVA could not be made subservient to every state agency in its territory. Nothing would ever get done. The debate was cut off by a roll-call vote, and Smith was left frustrated by the congressional encounter.[30]

Smith conceded to a friend that wildlife groups were in the forefront of opposition to the dam, but privately he charged that the opposition was financed by two or three large industries in the area "that do not want any higher wage industries in their vicinity."[31]

The controversy dragged on for years beyond Smith's tenure on the board. Douglas returned in 1969 and published an emotional appeal in *True*, "This Valley Waits to Die," including references to fish, islands, Native Americans, and settlers reluctant to move. Smith responded again by correcting errors of fact and lobbying Congress. The dam would be built in the end, but Smith's shining hope for a model community to serve as an example for future development never materialized. TVA's attempt at new leadership produced opposition and controversy instead of a following.[32]

In the midst of these battles with environmentalists, Smith published *The Politics of Conservation,* a plea for his brand of conservation. Smith had wanted to call the book *Pork Barrel Politics,* but his editors found his title too "negative." The book provided a history of American conservation efforts and an argument for conservation as an important element of liberal political ideology. Smith called on environmentalists to recognize the political realities he had encountered in Congress: "[M]ost of us rapidly learned that to achieve anything, we would have to master the multiple art that is pork barrel politics—the ever-shifting coalitions, the compromises, the trades, the inter-agency lobbies, the special interest alliances—the lesser evil from which has come the greater good." In the introduction of the book, Smith warned readers that "this book is written with a decided bias in favor of viewing conservation as an essential element of the democratic faith that created and sustains the development of the American system of government and the American economy."[33] For the American system to continue, Smith said, resources had to be developed, and the government had to play a major role in protecting citizens from monopolies—and that sometimes would mean government direction of development.

Smith found conservationist heroes throughout American history—men of action unafraid to expose their minds to "some of the scholars and scientists of the day." John Wesley Powell, Theodore Roosevelt, and Gifford Pinchot were role models identified by Smith. He included a critique of the environmentalists, whom he condemned as "sentimentalists." He found their calls for preserving the status quo ridiculous and their romantic notions of Native Americans absurd. "[T]hey have ennobled not only his environment but his every action except his failure to enforce a restrictive immigration policy."[34] By contrast, Smith summarized with his own philosophy— "total acceptance of the [idea] that all resource use and development is for the purpose of improving the environment and the life of the human resource." In addition he made a plea for the public to realize that "pork barrel politics is an inescapable element of the American political structure."[35] Smith asked his readers to accept the healthy, American, democratic, political process based on compromise and negotiations and not to insist on an unattainable goal that would limit economic growth.

The *New York Times* said, "Smith may be described as an idealist and a political realist."[36] Even the journal of the Audubon Society found the book to be a fair treatment of pork barrel politics, but, after admiring the strength of his writing, most reviewers noted his patronizing treatment of environmentalists. Secretary of the Interior Udall attacked the book in a *Virginia Quarterly* review and launched a defense of his department, which Smith had criticized in the book. But the only violent attack came from Smith's long-time enemy Justice Douglas in the *New York University Law Review*. Douglas began by admitting he should not review the book. Then he launched into a spirited condemnation of Smith and the book. He compared Smith to Ronald Reagan and said the book was "one of the most obvious propaganda publications I have seen. . . ."[37] Douglas accused Smith of having no feeling for nature, of seeing only lumber in forests and only hydroelectric power in water. Smith prepared an equally spirited rebuttal, but the TVA legal staff asked him to withdraw his response, because Douglas would be hearing a strip-mining case against TVA during the next session of the Supreme Court. Reluctantly, Smith agreed to remain silent. A leading academic historian who admired Smith's book called Douglas a "low form of life" for using the book review to "put forward his own thesis." Despite earning generally good reviews and the respect of experts, the book did not sell well.[38]

Smith was swimming against the tide. Environmentalism had emotional appeal, and the public was questioning liberalism, which had given them the Vietnam War, social security, and TVA. Beyond his battle with environmentalists, Smith also struggled to deal with other challenges to liberalism in the late 1960s. When Daniel P. Moynihan called for liberals to abandon federal programs as the means of dealing with urban problems in the aftermath of riots, Smith wrote to him, "As one who has seen most of the changes for the better come through federal initiatives and pressures, I do not want to lose this most effective tool."[39] Smith began to research and think about "urban ghetto problems," and his study led him to "rural small town migration patterns." He developed the idea of cutting off migration to the ghetto by providing the poor a better living in the country. His ideas grew into a book outline. His first working title was "Town and Country USA." It evolved into "Bootstraps and Elbow Grease" and then "100 Acres and a Tractor," in which he proposed creating small family farms. According to his plan, farmers would survive on the land through the adoption of specialty cash crops such as tomatoes and chickens. He reasoned that rural migrants lacked the skills to cope with urban life and work, so they would be better off on the land, where they could earn a subsistence living rather than drawing welfare in the city. His idea was a reworking of the New Deal resettlement program. Thus, Smith's response to the crisis in liberal government was to return to its New Deal roots. He told a correspondent he preferred the work programs of the depression era to the welfare provided in the 1960s. Few shared interest in his idea, however, and, despite extended efforts on the manuscript, Smith never found a market for his book.[40]

Smith thought that the Vietnam War was wrong, but took no public position. In private, he supported Senator Albert Gore's efforts toward a negotiated settlement in 1968 and tried to encourage Stennis to have "a more independent reaction to the situation."[41] But he refused efforts to become involved in a large-scale lobbying effort aimed at Stennis, because he felt it would be ineffective. His solution for Vietnam as touted in *Politics of Conservation* was to create a TVA-like development of the Mekong Delta that would provide economic progress and win the people away from communism.[42]

His faith in New Deal-type economic development survived the challenges of the war and of environmentalists. A strong supporter of the TVA fertilizer program, Smith undertook a new initiative to spread TVA technology around the world in 1968. He contacted Robert McNamara at the World Bank and asked to discuss how TVA could help the bank improve the world's food supply. Subsequent negotiations with staff and McNamara produced an agreement for TVA to supply staff on contract to India, where they assisted with the green revolution.[43]

Yet even with his continuing commitment to New Deal liberalism, Smith seemed to have doubts about TVA. By the mid-1960s, he had begun to express reservations about the agency. He found the people there uninterested in books and, by extension, in ideas. He admitted to an academic expert that TVA was closed-minded and made decisions without proper responsiveness to the public. He recognized that the emphasis on saving power production from Republican cuts in the 1950s had limited TVA's role as a promoter of general economic development. Smith also saw that the Tributary Area Development programs were not going to bring about much change because they were dominated by state agencies. In 1966, President Johnson appointed Don McBride, an Oklahoma congressional aide, to replace the retiring Jones, but the new face on the board did not bring about much change. In *Politics of Conservation,* Smith took some public shots at his own agency. He noted, for example, that TVA could have done more to promote integration in the valley. He criticized TVA's failure to accept responsibility for the destruction caused by strip mining. He chastised the area's congressmen for taking TVA for granted and thinking the agency had "little political sex appeal remaining."[44] Doubtfully but loyally he soldiered on with declining enthusiasm. In 1969, Wagner was reappointed as chairman, and Smith told Howard Baker, a friendly Tennessee congressman, that he did not think he would want to be named again when his term ended.[45]

TVA began to raise rates to cover increasing energy costs, spurring charges that the agency was becoming inefficient. As a response, TVA entered into nuclear energy production. Everyone, including the environmentalists, welcomed the switch to nuclear fuel because it would reduce the use of coal and limit strip mining. Smith agreed but urged Wagner to go slow and not put all of his eggs in one nuclear energy basket. Despite Smith's reservations, TVA launched a massive nuclear program. The problems associated with nuclear production of electrical power were not yet apparent. Nuclear energy was hailed as the wave of the future by almost everyone. Smith's uneasiness was an unscientific, political instinct to keep options open, but he was right.[46]

Smith began 1970 by acting the statesman. Speaking to the Academy of Sciences in New York City on the theme of TVA's role in the new decade, he called for TVA to demonstrate ways to improve the quality of the total environment. He said this would mean reconciling protection from pollution and economic development. He wanted TVA to coordinate state, local, and private efforts and use TVA "specialists" to demonstrate how to achieve growth without pollution.[47]

During the year, Smith engaged in a three-way correspondence with Leslie Dunbar, the former Southern Regional Council executive director, and Harry Caudill. In their letters they tried to settle on some common policies for the future. Smith assured Dunbar, a liberal grants warrior of the 1960s who was then at the Field Foundation, that he felt himself to be a good conservationist, but he also considered himself a realist. Power, he said, was going to be produced "by capitalism, Marxism, or Third Force."[48] He listed some TVA reclamation efforts and wondered what else Caudill could want. Dunbar remained skeptical of Smith's arguments and responded that energy would be produced only as long as the earth was capable of producing it. Speaking in the mode of the environmental movement, he contended that it was not rational to stimulate consumption of beer cans and ABM missiles because, he warned Smith, mountains cannot be reclaimed. Dunbar, who was visiting and talking with Caudill, sent Smith an advance copy of a chapter from a new book Caudill was writing. Smith responded to Dunbar, who shared the letter with Caudill. Smith claimed that Caudill was mistaken in his criticism of TVA because he did not understand that TVA was required by law to buy its coal from the lowest bidders, "who it just happened" were the strip miners. TVA did not encourage strip mining by choice, he argued; economics mandated it. Water quality, contrary to Caudill's claims, was getting better, not worse, and Caudill was wrong in asserting that English reclamation operations were better than TVA's. Smith said he had seen them both and TVA's equaled those in England. Smith reminded Dunbar that he had been advocating a federal law for reclamation for eight years. He closed by suggesting that Caudill needed to consult a psychiatrist.[49]

Despite Smith's suggestion not to pass the letter on, Dunbar sent it to Caudill. Caudill responded to Dunbar that "the attitudes of the people who run the Tennessee Valley Authority are monstrously irresponsible. . . ." He explained how TVA had forced down the price of coal in the 1950s, thereby compelling companies to switch to strip mining. He accused Smith of "hypocrisy" for saying that he favored a federal law. He closed, "I hope you will keep after Mr. Smith. If there is anybody connected with TVA who might develop some concern for the environment, it is he."[50]

Smith then responded to Caudill directly. "You are drowning in your own irresponsible rhetoric . . . ," which was a pity,[51] Smith said, because he thought Caudill said much worthwhile. He concluded with a challenge to Caudill's claim in the correspondence that Wagner had said TVA was not responsible for the land destroyed by strip mining and various other arguments against TVA. He bet Caudill a thousand dollars against a six-cent stamp that he could not support his charge against Wagner. Caudill shot back that Wagner had said it at his dinner table during a visit and claimed the bet. He told Smith to send it to a group fighting strip mining. He did not counter some of the other points, and Smith declined to pay, saying he saw no point in continuing unless Caudill could continue the exchange on a "rational basis" without resorting to "deliberate falsehoods."[52]

Rational dialogue broke down. The next year an even more radical young man involved in the fight against strip mining accused Smith of "insensitivity and racism" because of his testimony to Congress on strip mining. "Smith and TVA have got to go the way of the Bull Connor's [*sic*] and Ross Barnett's [*sic*], and the other racists and profit-mongers who stalk this land,"[53] he said in a newsletter. The *New York Times* printed the charges, prompting Walker Percy to write, telling Smith how ignorant and unfair the young man had been. But, Percy wrote, "I keep wanting to ask you: do you really approve strip-mining? [W]hy shouldn't TVA be on the side of the angels. . . ."[54] Smith provided the novelist with a very candid answer. "I do not approve strip mining without rigid reclamation requirements." He went on to argue that reclaimed land was better than mountains because it could be used for pasture. It supported more game. Underground mining was harder on people because of black lung disease, and going back to underground mining would cost each consumer an average of $150 each year. If he had his way, he said, he would do away with both coal and cotton because they were both bad for the land and for the people who worked them, "but we are stuck with coal as an energy source . . . [and] I think we have to use it the best we can."[55]

Smith felt trapped with a policy he did not like and attacked by those who should have been his friends. Caudill recognized his sympathy for them, and for that reason Smith received more than his share of criticism. Smith, the one director who had doubts about strip mining, became a special target for environmentalists. Yet despite his sympathies with environmentalists, Smith could not understand Caudill's argument about the aesthetic damage done to the mountains. Caudill grieved for the beauty destroyed when the mountains were turned into hills of processed earth. Smith saw the processed hills as potentially more valuable to people who could then produce more from them. He saw no need to preserve nature; he wanted to use it for people.

To counter the charges against his agency, Smith tried to seize the initiative by asking that TVA be given regulatory power over water pollution along the Tennessee River. But his efforts for enlarged TVA regulatory powers produced no action, and critics continued their attacks.[56]

Stung by environmentalists, Smith began to strike out at his critics, whom he increasingly saw as evil as well as misguided. When Dunbar asked him a question in a public meeting, Smith "jumped down" his throat, according to Dunbar. Smith later apologized, "If I jumped, I didn't realize it. [I was] angry primarily at the attacks that Harry Caudill and others have made about 'TVA's callous disregard for human values,' 'destroying a people,' 'economic destruction,' etc."[57] He had tried to explain to Dunbar: "[I]t is very discouraging to be involved in attempting to improve conditions in this sort of situation to have to run up against utter irrationality on all sides. The land is important, but doing something for the people is far more important."[58]

When Smith drafted a letter to another critic of strip mining suggesting reclaimed lands were better than useless mountain land, Wagner persuaded him not to send it. A Kentucky newspaper published two articles critical of TVA projects, and Smith counterattacked with a strong letter to the editor. Wagner wrote, without telling Smith, to say he was distressed by Smith's letter and "to assure you that Mr. Smith was speaking only for himself."[59] What Wagner may not have understood was that Smith knew the editor from the Lamar Society and probably felt able to speak openly with him. Smith's secretary learned of the letter, and Wagner had to come to Smith's office and deliver a copy of the offending letter along with a confession. The editor asked Smith for fifteen hundred words for the editorial page, and Smith delivered a blistering attack on environmentalists. "Throughout recorded history the major obstacles to man's improvement have been ignorance and apathy on the one hand and organized resistance to change on the part of those who have feared the loss of their own special privileges through any change.... [T]he entire environmental movement is today threatened with subversion by the same reactionary forces which have always impeded man's progress because they fear it will bring the economic and social changes which they abhor.... [E]nvironmentalists overlook the evil of the worst human environment—poverty. If we accept the idea that economic growth and environment are incompatible, we are succumbing to the delusion of ignorance...."[60]

Smith had been called a racist because of his economic policies, and he eventually retorted by calling his tormentors reactionaries. Convinced of the evil they were doing, Smith became increasingly blunt in his criticism of environmentalists and provoked more reactions in return. Contacted by a friend at the *Charlotte Observer*, Smith agreed to consider an article outlining "some of the ominous signs of the way some of the extremists in the current ecology movement are joining up in a natural alliance with the most radical economic foes to oppose any type of change in the South."[61] In the resulting article, Smith argued for economic progress to end poverty and defended Tellico Dam. He cited the archaeological work done by TVA on Cherokee villages before the resulting lake would cover them as sensitive, fruitful work resulting from good government planning for development. His effort produced more opposition. The Cherokee nation announced its intention to stop construction of Tellico before it covered their ancient village sites.[62] In the autumn 1971 issue of the *South Atlantic Quarterly,* Smith answered his critics; while the environment should be protected, he said, "[L]et us not forget that a lot of our environment needs its quality vastly improved before it is worth protecting." Humans need natural resource development too, he wrote, but environmentalists had lost historical perspective. There had been more pollution in a Cherokee or a Choctaw wigwam, he claimed, than existed today in Knoxville or Los Angeles. Their villages were "befouled" with waste and water pollution. He warned that well-intentioned people who adopted environmentalist ideas ran the risk of maintaining black people "in the bleakest of environments in the name of protecting the quality of our environment."[63]

His reasoning turned the racist argument on the environmentalists. By the 1970s, Smith had ceased to attempt any dialogue or compromise with environmentalists and began to treat them as political enemies to be beaten for the public's good. He told a correspondent early in 1972 that people who wanted to limit the use of resources really wanted to go back to the old days when "darkies were happy strumming the banjo in the quarters ... [and white folks were] ... at Scarlet's [*sic*] cotillion ball."[64] Unless the economy expanded, economic justice would have to be abandoned, he thought, and those who opposed expansion did so because they feared social change—not because of their concern for the environment. Writing to a sympathetic journalist who was retiring, Smith mused, "I have always thought of myself as a conservationist from the word go with a lot of preservationist instincts, but I am afraid that too many of the people on the present bandwagon are nothing more than faddist, or else they are attempting to subvert the movement of economic development either for the traditional reactionary reasons or revisionist ideas about collapsing the whole economy."[65]

Smith's 1960 feelings of sympathy for environmentalists had turned to scorn. For example, when the curator of a North Carolina museum published an attack on dams for killing ecological systems, Smith wrote, "Dr. S ... should realize that unless a few mollusks are eliminated that civilization cannot afford either Ph.D.s or state museums."[66] Smith could usually identify an ulterior motive for most individuals who made environmental attacks on his agency. For example, he wrote privately to Congressman John Dingell in response to charges that TVA had become the worst air polluter in Alabama. He told Dingell that he suspected the charges emanated from the Alabama assistant attorney general, whose wife owned land that TVA wanted to buy for a nuclear power plant. In addition, she was running for Congress against Bob Jones.[67]

Smith told the vice president of the National Waterways Conference that the conference should organize a campaign to refute "environmental organizations" and sell the case for economic opportunity.[68] Smith had mounted some successful counterstrikes of his own. One was against TVA's most effective critic, Harry Caudill. Caudill had gone to work with the Natural Resources Defense Council and issued a strongly worded letter on the council's stationery accusing TVA of destroying a beautiful region and ruining the lives of "thousands of men, women, and children."[69] The NRDC had filed a lawsuit against TVA for failing to file separate environmental impact statements for each coal mining contract it signed, and, as a result, the TVA lawyers had warned board members to avoid "off-the-cuff remarks." After identifying Gifford Pinchot as an NRDC board member, Smith sent him a copy of *Politics of Conservation*; Pinchot was the son of Theodore Roosevelt's conservationist, and Smith pointed out that he had modeled his conservationist ideas on Pinchot's father's. Correspondence led Smith to invite Pinchot and others associated with the NRDC to visit TVA in order to see a strip mine reclamation site. Smith offered a journalist friend an opportunity to cover the "story," which he did—favorably. The upshot was that NRDC withdrew its support of Caudill, forcing him to cancel a fund-raising letter.[70] In another instance, a California academician writing in *Harper's* made the statement that the American Power Company had been more ecology minded than TVA, and Smith countered with a request for evidence. When the professor supplied it, Smith responded point by point until the professor recognized TVA's superior attention to the environment. "I am convinced, and I apologize,"[71] he wrote.

In these same years Smith had undertaken a major academic job of his own, editing a documentary history of conservation in the United States. It was a five-volume work covering the entire history of the United States from 1492 to 1970. Smith edited two volumes on land and water himself and employed academicians to edit the other three. The history received favorable reviews in 1971, but the publisher, Chelsea, went bankrupt just before publication and did not do the necessary promotion to sell the volumes.[72]

At the same time, Smith published *Land Between the Lakes*, which described TVA's establishment of the park by that name. In the introduction, Smith wrote, "It is my hope this book will increase the impact of the Land Between the Lakes demonstration in creating an awareness of the demands and importance of the new conservation."[73] In the book, Smith provided a history of the park and an argument for this type of conservation—an education facility deliberately created without a master plan to allow it to evolve as a resource for the community. By 1971 the number of visitors to the park had already reached one and three quarters of a million annually, providing proof that Smith's faith in the park had been justified. As Smith had hoped, the park was a source of pride to TVA, but appreciation for it was lost amidst the continuing uproar over rate increases and strip mining.[74]

In response to rate increases, Smith became convinced that oil companies were inflating energy costs by monopolizing coal supplies. He urged friendly editors to assign reporters to sniff out the story and eventually called for government investigation and legislation to protect consumers.[75]

His crusade against the monopolistic oil companies never caught fire because by the 1970s Smith lacked a constituency. He had alienated the environmentalists, including his former allies in the civil rights movement, and he certainly did not endear himself to big business, especially the energy industries. Furthermore, despite his energetic defense of the agency, he was not fully appreciated at TVA. The general manager had successfully initiated McBride into the agency. Jones, in retirement, reported that Wagner had successfully isolated Smith, keeping him powerless. Smith and Wagner disagreed before Congress over strip mining in February 1972: Smith argued for banning mining on land difficult to reclaim and for a federal law to require reclamation, while Wagner argued for mining in more mountainous areas and for leaving regulation to the states. The same month Smith publicly broke with Wagner over strip mining; he shot off a memorandum to the general manager criticizing a staff report on the potential for a rural development institute in the TVA area. "I regret," he said, "that the TVA staff has no more imagination or initiative than displayed in this report."[76] The pressures must have been intense. An article covering Smith's relations with Wagner in the *Tennessean* angered Smith so much that he wrote the editor, calling one statement a "bare-faced, premeditated lie" and declaring that he did not take orders from the chairman, Congress, or anyone else.[77]

Smith heard that Caudill said, "Frank Smith has betrayed every liberal instinct he may once have had." Smith's liberal friend Dunbar came to his defense, saying, "[H]e's the only one of the directors who gives a damn. But he has defended the indefensible — and not very well."[78]

None of the criticism deterred Smith from working for projects he believed would help the South to develop its economy. In this same period, Smith became a major supporter of the Tennessee-Tombigbee Waterway. Objecting to a *Newsweek* article saying that the Army Corps of Engineers cost/benefit analysis was unrealistic, Smith wrote the editor, "The same forces of reaction which have sought to obstruct human progress in this country throughout its history are today seeking to subvert the environmental movement to use it as a force to obstruct the economic and social change which they fear. If they succeed, they will visit upon us the pollution of stagnation . . . [the] blight of poverty."[79] He delightedly mailed out copies of an Alabama black judge's comments condemning Tenn-Tom opponents as a screen for political forces hostile to the poor. In a letter to the judge, Smith endorsed his remarks and repeated his charge that the whole environmental movement was "knowingly or unknowingly" being used to prevent needed social change in the South.[80]

In secret, Smith helped Fred Stinson, a friend who had gone to work for the Tenn-Tom development agency, to organize an "environmental conference" at Mississippi University for Women to promote the project while heading off environmentalists. He prompted Tennessee governor Winfield Dunn to counteract environmental criticism of the Tenn-Tom and instructed Stinson at the Tenn-Tom organization to lobby Whitten on the point. At TVA, Smith laid the groundwork for Tenn-Tom by having the TVA staff help with the development of Yellow Creek port near the termination point of the Tenn-Tom on the Tennessee River. Smith then supported the construction of a nuclear power plant at the site. In all these activities he either opposed the environmental movement or ignored its protests. His intention was to defeat it whenever possible.[81]

Smith's outspokenness in 1972 may in part be explained by his decision to leave TVA. He had been offered an academic post during his tenure but had turned it down. Nearing the end of his time at TVA, he began to contact all of his academic friends seeking employment. He told Silver he did not want an administrative post but preferred teaching, writing, and a bit of travel if possible. Smith had chosen the wrong time to seek an academic career. An old friend explained the situation to him bluntly. Without a Ph. D., which was the equivalent of a union card, the chances of finding academic employment were slim. New Ph. D.s were getting jobs only at "fourth rate" schools, and the market was not expected to improve for ten years. When hundreds of inquiries produced nothing, Smith decided he had better stay at TVA. Reluctantly he began to campaign for another term.[82]

President Nixon had promised Stennis any appointment he wanted in return for support on a new draft bill. Based on Nixon's promise, Stennis assured Smith he could handle the president. Smith approached Howard Baker about supporting him and flew to Washington to plan strategy with him. Baker warned Smith that he and Stennis were too optimistic; Baker did not believe it was possible even though he was friendly toward Smith. Senator William Brock had defeated Smith's friend, Albert Gore, Sr., in 1970 and was determined to see TVA rid of Smith. His candidate was a Republican former speaker of the Tennessee House of Representatives, who had resigned to run for governor. Analyzing the situation, Smith said, "It is a matter of making way for a Republican appointment, plus the fact that I have been a little too aggressive in pushing for conservation measures here (without at the same time fawning to some of the crypto-ecologists) and in seeking administration activity to break up the growing fuel monopoly."[83] Newspaper accounts generally supported his analysis. The *Tennessean* additionally pointed out, "Smith has been attacked both by the political right and left for his support of TVA programs and his defense of the agency's policies in the fields of public power and conservation."[84]

When it became certain that he would not be reappointed, Smith wrote to everyone he knew asking about work. He was only fifty-four and had two children in college. By this time, he knew academia was not an option. Bolling gave him the bad news from Washington. "It's pretty rough ... unless you are a card-carrying Republican."[85] Smith was just the opposite, and TVA was not a place to further a director's career. Because directors are excluded from influencing appointments in the TVA bureaucracy, Smith was twelve years removed from most patronage. A Mississippi state appointment was out of the question because his faction of the Democratic party was still out of office; then, suddenly, Abernethy announced his intention not to run for reelection in a new congressional district that included part of Smith's old district. Smith jumped at an opportunity to run again for Congress.

Leaving TVA was much easier for Smith than his departure from Congress had been. He had found most of his satisfaction as TVA director

outside the agency, establishing himself as a regional statesman, further-
ing the civil rights revolution, and promoting economic development.
Assessing his own performance at the time of his departure, Smith cited
three accomplishments. "I forced a complete overhaul in TVA personnel operations in relation to minority employment,"[86] a feat, he recalled,
that required several years of insistence. Second, he noted introducing
strip mining regulation. Finally, he claimed a "fair share of credit" for
expanding TVA's wildlife program. A few years later, speaking to a TVA
historian during an oral history interview, Smith said, "I think I helped
preserve the overall basic TVA idealistic concept that it was for the integrated development of the resources of the valley for the overall benefit of all the people."[87] He remembered his greatest disappointment as
the failure to have TVA adopt higher water standards to protect water
quality throughout the system.

Historians' assessments of TVA during the 1960s have not been kind.
TVA has been criticized as a worn-out New Deal project that failed to
respond to the new challenges of the era. It made all the wrong decisions, which have now been abandoned and overturned as TVA has rejected nuclear power and stopped building new power plants in favor
of conservation promotion. Historians have saddled Wagner with most
of the blame because he resisted new ideas and kept trying to repeat
old programs. Most recent analysts have ignored Smith's role in TVA
because his objections were ignored at the time. They have questioned
TVA's contribution to economic development in the valley, and many
have concluded that TVA made little difference. Under President Jimmy
Carter, the environmentalists triumphed, with TVA adopting the philosophy of energy conservation and constrained growth.[88]

Oral histories reveal TVA personnel who had lost the crusading spirit
in the 1960s. Going home at five o'clock for the first time in their lives,
TVA employees reported dissatisfaction and self-doubt, which was a new
experience for those who remembered the depression. Had Smith been
chairman he would have supported many of the same policies Wagner
approved, but he also would have engaged in a spirited debate over all
the questions about the agency's policies with the bureaucrats at TVA
and with the world at large. He would have invited outside criticism and
destroyed the cozy, comfortable TVA society that excluded him. Smith
retained the fire of New Deal liberalism because he had been energized
by the civil rights movement. Perhaps he would have been overwhelmed

by the tides of environmentalism and defeat born from the Vietnam War, but he was ready to do battle for his creed. He would not have surrendered quietly. In retrospect, Wagner recognized Smith's value to TVA and somewhat wistfully conceded that Smith was "not so bad."[89]

Land Between the Lakes may be the best monument to Smith's ideas about TVA. It was the last new initiative undertaken by the agency. It was controversial at the time because its development required the use of eminent domain to remove some stubborn people who wished to keep their homes. The land lacked any dramatic natural beauty that would draw tourists, and the park was not intended to preserve natural treasures. But the park is used. Portions are set aside for all-terrain vehicles. Permits are issued to the public for hunting and for cutting Christmas trees. Buffalo, red wolves, and eagles have been restored. In 1991, LBL was designated a "Biosphere Reserve," meaning that the park will focus on environmental education and cooperative research in the future. It is, as Smith wanted, a park surrounded by lakes created by TVA dams, filled with TVA campgrounds and man-made fishing lakes, and managed for the use of the public, but TVA has at the same time restored the animals earlier hunted to extinction.[90] The park is a fitting monument to Smith's view of TVA. It would not please the preservationist, because it did not save a natural area. It is a man-made park. One critic said it took TVA back to its roots, which meant designing an ideal environment and building a dream world as a model.

At TVA, Smith acted on his basic liberal philosophy. He believed humans to be good creatures capable of controlling their environment and improving it to create better lives for themselves. While much of the country came to doubt those human abilities in the 1960s, Smith refused to surrender the idea that people acting through government can solve their problems and create a better world. He was unable to stem the tide running against New Deal liberalism. TVA bureaucrats did not share his wider vision, and he could not see the world ecosystem understood by environmentalists. The bureaucrats and war protestors played a significant role in destroying New Deal liberalism, but it was the environmentalists who did the most damage by questioning the very heart of liberalism — that humans are good, rational creatures. Smith had nourished his belief in the goodness of people and their ability to learn and to change through the darkness of racism. He would not surrender to the idea that people were incapable of controlling their environments.

To Smith, it was essential that people continue to use natural resources in order to create more wealth, especially in the South, which had not shared fully in American prosperity. Smith left TVA battered by the revolutions of the 1960s and clinging to New Deal liberalism, which most of the country viewed as an anachronism.

CHAPTER FOURTEEN

Exile and Return

Coming home in 1972 to run for Congress was a strange experience for Frank Smith. Mississippi was in a holding pattern. It had not absorbed the changes pressed upon it after the Ole Miss riot of 1962. Americanization had not taken root. Oxford, home of the university, did not have a national fast-food franchise. Beer in Oxford was illegal, because the county had not approved sales in a referendum since 1934, but the town's one bar served liquor, which had been approved in a referendum under the 1966 law ending statewide prohibition. The public schools had just been integrated, but private academies were packed with fleeing white children. Mississippi had become an industrial state since Smith left, but most of the factories were garment-manufacturing plants, sawmills, or other wood-related industries. Many Mississippians were in transition, with the wife working in a garment plant and the husband spending forty hours at a job in town, while they both commuted from the old family farm where they raised a vegetable garden and cattle. Tenancy was no more. The total black population had declined to only about 35 percent. Landless blacks had moved to the cities, while white landowners stayed in the country. In politics everyone was a "moderate." The meaning of the term had changed, however; in 1972, it was used for the whites who had not accepted integration but did not intend to fight it anymore. Blacks had the vote, but they had not yet learned to use it effectively. William Waller, the prosecutor who had earnestly tried to convict Byron De La Beckwith for the murder of Medgar Evers, had just been elected governor over Charles Evers, Medgar's brother. Forty-four percent of the blacks who voted for Evers did not vote for local black candidates. Aaron Henry, head of the state NAACP, and Fannie Lou Hamer, famed civil rights leader, were among those defeated in that election as a result. William Winter had won the office of lieutenant governor; Eastland and Stennis were still in the Senate; Whitten was still in the House. Mississippi's delegation had the greatest seniority of any in Congress, but the state remained the nation's poorest. Eastland owned 5,400 acres in Sunflower County and collected $150,000 in federal farm subsidies, while 72 percent of the county's blacks and 17 percent of whites lived below the poverty level. The much-heralded War on Poverty injected $3 million in federal funds to fight poverty in Sunflower County, while the Department of Agriculture sent Sunflower County planters $12 million in direct payments. Much had changed, but much remained the same.[1]

In 1971, Smith kept uncharacteristically quiet at TVA, speaking mostly to service clubs in Mississippi. His favorite topic in those speeches was the plan for Yellow Creek development—the Tennessee River port and nuclear plant near Iuka. He had searched for academic employment without success, and he had to plan for the end of his term at TVA. Perhaps he "daydreamed" more often about returning to Mississippi politics as the end of his TVA term neared.[2]

The 1970 census had mandated another redistricting of Mississippi's congressional seats and created a new political map. David Bowen, former governor Williams's director of federal programs, spent the year dropping hints he might run against Abernethy. Bowen maneuvered to keep Bolivar County, his home, in the new second district to facilitate his run for Congress. When faced with new district lines, Abernethy, Colmer, and Griffin announced their retirement. Smith began to receive calls from Mississippi suggesting that he consider running for Congress in the new second district, which stretched from Columbus to Greenville and encompassed hill and Delta counties in one incongruous entity. Smith had represented a portion of the district and had friends along the Tombigbee in the eastern end. Because he had lived out of the state for ten years, Smith worried that residency requirements might bar his running, but he found that they did not.[3]

By March 15, 1972, Smith needed only "assurance about the necessary money for TV and radio" to convince him to run. When he felt he had commitments for enough money, Smith took leave from his TVA post. His mother had moved to McCarley with her second husband. Smith took up temporary residence with her, and opened his campaign headquarters in an empty gas station building in nearby Carrollton.[4]

Some of his old supporters from Greenwood offered assistance. Members of the council for the Tennessee-Tombigbee Waterway pledged support. Some leaders of organized labor promised to work for him. Smith recruited assistance from the young members of a Millsaps College seminar on politics that he had addressed. The Tupelo paper, although not in the district, called on Smith to run, citing his seniority and friendship with congressional leaders as an invaluable asset.[5]

Smith had not been foolish. When Claude Ramsay, head of the Mississippi AFL-CIO, had urged him to run against Eastland in 1972, Smith had refused, knowing that it would be impossible to win. But the second district looked promising; without an incumbent, the race was wide open. Blacks made up over 40 percent of the population and about a third of the voters. Given his early and strong support of civil rights legislation, Smith seemed likely to capture the black vote.[6]

Smith left Knoxville hurriedly to open the campaign. Helen manned the office, and Smith employed the Miles public relations agency in Tupelo to advise him. Paul Neville, a young lawyer from Meridian who had met Smith at Millsaps, worked long weekends with Smith and took on responsibility for federal reports as well as some fund-raising efforts.[7]

Funding quickly became and remained the most important problem of Smith's campaign. His friends sent a few hundred dollars each. Winter gave two hundred dollars, Percy five hundred. Lilienthal sent a hundred dollars. Civil rights leader R. L. T. Smith made a contribution, and several historians anted up small amounts. Eric Goldman, resident intellectual in the Johnson administration, sent twenty-five dollars and a comment: "It's a token of how much we hope you win so we can have your civilized voice in the national Congress."[8] Smith appreciated the sentiment, but it did not pay the bills. Jim Wright explained the money situation in Washington when Smith inquired about assistance: "The hordes of Presidential candidates have moved through like a plague of locusts and just about stripped everything bare."[9] He and Tip O'Neill sent small sums in cash to demonstrate moral support. Liberals out of state did not help much. One replied that all the money she knew about was devoted to antiwar and prisoners' rights campaigns. The Committee for an Effective Congress, which had promised "several thousand," came through with only five hundred dollars. As a result, Smith ran a shoestring operation — only two secretaries and one field worker were paid. He never received any large donations from outside the district.[10]

Smith summarized the race with a quip: the white voters remembered him, but the black ones had forgotten him. White opposition was well represented by one man who responded to an appeal for funds as "quite ludicrous. Surely you can not have forgotten Frank's past history and his extremely close affiliation with the late Kennedys." He had known Smith in the army, he said, and Smith had always been a liberal. To support him would be to support a "changing Deep South," he thought. Asked who was running against Smith, the correspondent wrote, "I will promptly remit to the opponent a nice campaign contribution."[11]

Smith worked his Atlanta connections and recruited the support of black leaders, but, with few funds, he could offer none of the black "bosses" the customary "transportation" money required to turn out black votes. He did not realize, either, that in keeping with the custom of the day he should have promised secretly to hire a black congressional assistant. Smith had not participated directly in an election in a decade, and the rules had changed.[12]

The field against him in the primary grew to eight men scattered across the district in an electoral free-for-all. His old enemy Corbet Patridge, a planter in Leflore County, ran, in Smith's view, not to win but for the specific purpose of hurting Smith's campaign. Pat Dunne, mayor of Greenville, and a local attorney, Harrison Miller, dominated Washington County—one of the important population centers. Congressman Abernethy backed Tom Cook, a former sheriff of Oktibbeha County who had moved to the Delta to be superintendent of the penitentiary at Parchman. The hills produced several candidates, including two from Kosciusko—Hugh Potts and Clant Seat, an assistant secretary of state. Wallace Dabbs, a press aide to former governor John Bell Williams, probably had some media muscle. But the most formidable candidate proved to be David Bowen of Cleveland. He had spent four years distributing millions of Great Society dollars to sheriffs and supervisors in the district. Looking toward the possibility of a race, he had manipulated press releases and speaking engagements to win friends and influence voters in the district. He developed personal relationships with Head Start administrators and school officials throughout the area. He believed that weak newspaper reporting allowed him to tell each group what it wanted to hear without his remarks being reported to the community as a whole.[13]

Smith got no more press than the other candidates. Usually each man got a few lines in balanced newspaper coverage. The Carter paper in Greenville, left in the care of a nonfamily editor, even tried to destroy Smith's main campaign theme by questioning his claim that he would regain his seniority in Congress. Smith had run as a campaign advertisement an editorial from the *Tupelo Daily Journal* that asked him to reclaim his seniority in Congress. The *Democrat Times* produced an article demonstrating that Smith would be unable to reclaim his seniority because his tenure had been interrupted. In an interview for the *Democrat* article, Smith said their story was true. He simply had not corrected or elaborated on the Tupelo editorial. Smith's point was that he knew congressional leaders and that, because of his relationships with them, he would be more effective than a freshman. But the *Democrat Times* article probably hurt his campaign.[14]

Smith distributed a campaign "newspaper" throughout the district containing no photographs of black people. He opposed school busing to achieve racial balance but otherwise dismissed the race issue. In an attempt to link himself to the Republican president, Smith noted his attendance at a NATO conference with Richard Nixon when they were serving together in Congress. He concentrated on the federal funds he expected to secure for the Tennessee-Tombigbee canal, for education, and for highways while promising to limit taxes on the "working class." In other words, he tried to appeal to all of the white voters without an open plea for black votes because he still considered that goal to be politically impossible.[15]

He contacted local officials as every candidate did, adding as a special target the members of governing boards of TVA power districts. No doubt worried about Smith's activities, TVA warned its employees to stay out of the campaign and posted new notices reminding employees of the rules forbidding political activity. Smith got no help from that quarter.[16]

The outcome was in doubt to the end. Winter told Smith the betting was on Smith to be in the second primary against Cook, but David Bowen edged Smith out of the runoff by fifteen hundred votes. Each home base voted for its local candidate. The Greenville candidates took Washington County. Bowen got two thousand votes in Bolivar County. Smith won his new home in Carroll County, but the sparsely populated county gave him only about four hundred votes. Turnout was down everywhere, with only 15 to 20 percent of the electorate participating.[17]

No burning issues surfaced in the campaign to generate enthusiasm. Neither candidates nor electorate had much passion for the contest. A young commentator in the Greenwood *Commonwealth* dismissed one candidate's characterization of Smith as a Kennedy supporter because, he said, the Kennedys were dead and buried. Corbet Patridge, who had supported the Citizens' Council, won the black vote in Leflore County. In the black town of Mound Bayou, Smith came in a close second behind the Greenville mayor. Smith estimated he won only 15 percent of the black vote in the district. If he had controlled a larger home base, he might have edged Bowen out of the second primary and defeated Cook, but he was doomed by a small home base, a lack of funds, and apathy in the black community. Coleman blamed Smith's defeat on his book *Congressman from Mississippi,* believing that whites could not forgive his criticism of the state. Bowen found voters worried by Smith's physical appearance. He was overweight, as always, and the physical strain of campaigning showed in his face to the extent that voters questioned his stamina for the Washington rat race.[18]

Smith's heart never really seemed to be in the contest as it had been in his earlier elections. He worked hard, but he was no longer on a crusade. There was no fire in his quest for Congress this time. Young liberals like Ray Mabus worked for him. A few university professors campaigned enthusiastically for him. Some of his old supporters stuck by him, but blacks voted for Bowen, who had been more help to them recently, or followed the white pattern of voting for the local candidate. Smith's children, Kathy and Fred, joined the campaign after their school semesters ended, and he enjoyed their participation. His mother stood with him again, housing and feeding the family and a few campaign workers, but Smith did not enjoy this contest as he had his earlier ones. The times were different. A Republican, Gil Carmichael, was promising to give Eastland a strong fight in November. George Wallace was shot and paralyzed in Maryland a few days before the primary vote. George McGovern was leading the Democratic party into a disaster in the race against Nixon. Smith's tactic of talking conservative while acting liberal had been mastered by Bowen, who knew the new political geography better than Smith did. Smith had been isolated at TVA for too long. He had lost the ability to tell each group what it wanted to hear. Confronted by environmentalists in a college crowd at Mississippi State University, Smith bluntly rejected their criticism and condemned their ecologists' position, thereby insulting some of his chief supporters.[19]

After the primary, Smith tried to remain in Mississippi. He applied for the position of director at the Yellow Creek port that he had helped to create on the Tennessee River near Iuka. Failing to get the appointment, Smith moved back to Knoxville. His retirement from TVA had become final during the campaign, and he was eligible for a civil service pension. But in his mid-fifties Smith had no wish to retire completely. Teaching had been his first choice for what he called his "ancient years," but the academic depression made that impossible. He tried newspaper writing as a second choice but found no market for his columns. With funding from the SRC, he began work on a lower Mississippi Valley study designed to discover the causes of poverty among the area's citizens and to suggest how better use of the valley's natural resources could remedy the situation. But the SRC would not fund a major study. Then Smith established an energy resources consulting company as a means of cashing in on the demand for ideas and studies growing out of the energy crisis brought on by OPEC and the Arab oil embargo.[20]

Early in 1973 he joined the consulting firm of his young friend Naylor as a vice president, but none of his efforts produced much income or satisfaction. He admitted being depressed by unemployment and relative inactivity. His most ardent desire was to return to Mississippi, and he raised the possibility with William Winter that he might become the director of the department of archives and history. During the summer of 1973, Smith pursued the appointment through Coleman, who, as a member of the archives board, had promised to support Smith's application. Smith had been told the board would not necessarily promote from within and that they might seek a director outside the agency, but Coleman found that Smith had too much opposition. John R. Junkin, the speaker of the Mississippi House of Representatives, was asked about the possibility of Smith's appointment and expressed his displeasure. In the end, Coleman reported, Smith was seen as "political," and he could not be separated from the controversies that had always surrounded him. Smith saw the decision as a matter of his old opponents in the legislature coming forward to veto him. A candidate was appointed from within the archives department.[21]

Shortly after that rejection, Smith joined with columnist Bill Minor to fulfill one of his oldest dreams — to edit a newspaper in Mississippi. At great expense he moved to Jackson to launch a new paper that he hoped would become a statewide weekly. Unfortunately, he had not understood the nature of his role. Thinking he would be in charge of the project, he resigned quickly when it appeared to him that he was being asked to be "window dressing" for the paper.[22]

With both his children at Millsaps and having recently purchased a house, Smith had no desire to leave the state again. He offered his services as a professor to the state's universities at nominal expense but was rejected by the schools and by every state agency that he approached. His experiences mirrored those of former congressman Carl Elliot in Alabama. State establishments were not ready to embrace those who had led integration. There was too much resentment against them among whites, and, as Smith said, blacks did not remember them. Smith had to look elsewhere for employment.[23] Answering an ad in the *Chronicle of Higher Education*, Smith went to Illinois to head a study of environmental and energy educational programs for the board of higher education. He was given a list of impressive titles—associate director of the board and visiting professor of public affairs at Sangamon State University—but his sole duty was the study. He used his Washington contacts to enlist the assistance of the Environmental Protection Agency and at first found the project interesting. He told a friend at TVA, "The great challenge of this job is that nobody has done it before. The only master plans I've found are nothing but collections of clichés and generalities. Of course there is also some advantage to me as I operate in the land of the blind."[24] Smith enjoyed his first brush with academic politics, but after a month "at the console of higher education" he wrote to Silver that "my long held [negative] ideas about academics are correct...."[25] In his second year, Smith complained that nothing could be done with his study. The state would not commit support to the schools for new programs, and the state required that all new programs originate with individual schools. Stymied by education bureaucracy, Smith nonetheless finished with a flourish by throwing a banquet and having Congressman Edward Boland speak as he presented his report to the board. It was used to develop the board's master plan for education in Illinois and as a guide to approving new programs proposed by the system's institutions.[26]

Helen had remained in Jackson for most of the time that Smith had "camped out" in Illinois. He returned to Mississippi when the grant money for his position ended. He had revived his plans to write a history of the Mississippi River, but during his second year in Illinois he informed his editor, "I have discovered that I am too old and lazy to do much work on the Mississippi in my spare time here...."[27] He thought he might return to it if he decided to devote full time to writing.

His mother died in the fall of 1973 as Smith prepared to depart for Illinois. He and his sister established an award in her honor for the best articles published in the *Advocate,* the Methodist publication she had always read and admired. In an *Advocate* article announcing the prize in his mother's name, Smith recalled with some bitterness the attacks by "benighted bigots" on his mother during his efforts at "racial reconciliation." The remark was one of the few bitter comments Smith ever made about his home state. No doubt he felt his state's rejection deeply.[28]

Mississippi was still not prepared to welcome Smith home. His alma mater rejected giving him a position even at nominal "remuneration." In 1977, Smith conducted an extensive campaign for reappointment to the TVA board and was disappointed when Red Wagner and Marguerite Owen responded with leaks from TVA alleging that he had been disruptive during his first years of service. Smith's campaign failed because President Jimmy Carter had decided to change TVA's basic direction, and he had no intention of reappointing anyone who might be contaminated with old ideas about the agency. In 1978, Delta State University got approval to establish a center to study the Mississippi River Valley, which was to be funded by the Army Corps of Engineers. Smith would have headed it, but the funding never materialized, and Smith had to withdraw.[29]

Unhappy with full-time writing, he turned to the *Chronicle of Higher Education* for another temporary academic post. Virginia Polytechnic Institute hired Smith for its political science department, and he conducted a seminar surveying the South. Later, Smith published the twenty-two papers presented in the series of seminars under the title *I'll Still Take My Stand.* In the introduction, he wrote that the original *I'll Take My Stand* had been a mistaken effort to preserve too much of the Old South. Smith argued that the South should join America and cease romantic efforts at "preservation." Age had not mellowed his views on the South and the direction that it should take.[30]

In 1979, Smith's friend William Winter finally won election as governor, and he invited Smith to join his administration as special assistant—an "idea man." Smith was delighted. Winter revealed his concept of what he wanted to accomplish as governor in an interview with the *Atlanta Constitution.* Establishing realistic goals, he said, "It is what the people of Mississippi are willing to do for themselves. It involves individual effort." But he indicated a desire for major changes in Mississippians' attitudes. "If I can inspire people to appreciate what they can contribute on a day to day basis to help make the state a better place to live, I think that will be a very significant contribution." Gently, Winter alluded to what he believed to be the mistaken, wrong-headed leadership since World War II: "And I think this has been what has been lacking in the political leadership of this state."[31] He, like Smith, wanted a revolution of the mind. When the reporter quoted Smith's autobiography on voting against his conscience to gain office in the 1950s, Winter responded, "Yeah, Frank said it a little early and there weren't too many people listening then."[32] Winter and Smith discussed inaugural activities and decided a symposium would replace the usual ball. Smith planned a symposium replete with symbolism. Mississippi writers Eudora Welty and Margaret Walker Alexander were joined by Catholic bishop Bernard Law and others who had opposed the segregationists in the 1960s to look at the past and speculate about the future. Former governor Cliff Finch, a populist, had reunited the Democratic party in 1976, but Winter's administration announced the victory of the "moderate underground" in Mississippi.[33]

Margaret Walker Alexander, a hard-to-impress independent thinker, told Smith later in Winter's administration, "I believe Governor Winter has truly fulfilled his promise as Governor. Naturally we [black Mississippians] regard him as the finest Governor Mississippi has had in our life time."[34] When the president of Dillard University, who had worked with Smith on the Voter Education Project, got a letter from Smith with his title on it, he wrote back, "[T]here is a redemptive dimension in human history. [And] [p]oetic justice!" He said Smith deserved the position "because you contributed so much, sacrificially, to the emergence of the New South. I am simply overjoyed."[35] Smith felt the same. He told George McLean, owner of the Tupelo newspaper, "Working with William offers the opportunity for a very satisfactory climax to my public service activities, and it makes worthwhile some of the frustrations since 1972."[36]

Smith had never been short of ideas, and he produced a stream of memos to Governor Winter. Some were small things—for example, in filling out the form for state employment, Smith found he had to check "White" or "Colored," and he suggested an executive order to change the form. He urged a study of state water resources. He commented on the coalition of black Democrats and white Democrats Winter was "cementing" as a winning formula. His frustration with the role was that "sometimes it is difficult to keep up on following through with the ideas, but even with the overstretching, I thoroughly enjoy it."[37]

Smith's enjoyment was cut short by a triple bypass heart operation, which forced him to curtail his activities during most of the administration. His efforts were not universally appreciated by the young men with whom Winter staffed his administration. Winter had not adequately explained Smith's role as "idea man" to the "boys of spring," as the young men were called, and they resented the fact that Smith did not appear in his office until midmorning and left before five. Smith's gruff temperament and his long-standing friendship with the governor irritated them and isolated Smith from much of the staff. The governor did most of his work in the mansion, and Smith's office was in the Sillers Building, so they did not meet regularly.[38]

For employment purposes, Smith's title was "planning specialist," and he undertook responsibility for overseeing several gubernatorial activities. For example, he planned the Governor's Colloquium on Science, Engineering and Technology, which brought Nobel Prize winner Arno A. Penzias to address Mississippi's best students. He organized the governor's office's contribution to the tricentennial of the La Salle expedition and a banquet celebrating the hundredth anniversary of Franklin D. Roosevelt's birth. Smith played a major role in the establishment of the "Dinner at the Mansion" series that Winter used to showcase the new Mississippi. The series featured distinguished visitors, who came for dinner and a night in the Governor's Mansion. After dinner the guests were invited to speak informally and to answer questions from selected small audiences. At breakfast the next morning, a new set of guests was given an opportunity to talk with the visitor. At midmorning, a press conference ended the visit. Guests included statesman Dean Rusk, ambassadors, writers Willie Morris and his friend William Styron, and performers such as Leontyne Price. The dinners made headlines of the sort Winter desired for the state, but, more important, they provided the type of leadership he believed would make a long-term impact on the collective mind of the state. To a friend, Smith described the dinner with the Chinese ambassador as illustrative of the new Mississippi. The usual people interested in cotton exports were present, he reported, including B. F. Smith of the Delta Council, but the star of the evening, who received the most attention from the ambassador, was Unita Blackwell, the black mayor of Mayersville, a small Delta town. Blackwell had visited China frequently on exchange programs, and the ambassador focused on this "old friend" rediscovered in Mississippi.[39]

The dinners were also used to reward old friends. Winter invited Jim Silver, who had taught him history, for a night at the mansion. Smith wrote playfully to his old friend, "The Governor informs me that he has invited you to the Mansion on the condition that you sleep in the Bilbo Room. I know that a man of your high principles will refuse to lend yourself to the scheme to add your prestige to such an infamous person, and that you will accordingly decline the invitation."[40] He did come, of course, and the "Red Professor," who had been hounded out of the state by the Sovereignty Commission and the board of the Institutions of Higher Learning, was honored by the governor at the mansion. The morning after the dinner, Silver sat in Smith's office, marveling at the changes in the state. What had impressed him more than anything else was the sight of a young, professional black woman in Smith's son's bookstore the previous day paying a hundred dollars for used books. He and Smith shook their heads in amazement that Mississippi had come so far in their lifetimes.[41]

Elise Winter, with Smith's assistance, produced a book to chronicle the dinners at the mansion. In it she noted her that husband was a fiscal conservative but one who believed in economic and social progress to remove "the last vestiges of the long-time burden of racial discrimination and divisiveness."[42] It was for that reason that Smith had supported Winter throughout his career. They agreed that a revolution in the collective mind of the state would be necessary to produce any lasting changes in any other area—political, economic, or social. This revolution of the mind had been Smith's lifelong goal. His was a more amorphous challenge than most politicians adopt, but an argument can be made for the idea that changing minds is in the end the most revolutionary activity possible.

Smith also participated in more concrete activities. His biggest personal project was the Tennessee-Tombigbee Project Area Committee — a four-state committee funded with Army Corps of Engineers money to ensure that the poor and disadvantaged would benefit from the Tennessee-Tombigbee Waterway then under construction. Smith was elected chairman and served throughout the Winter administration. The committee took over the responsibility of assuring nondiscrimination in employment among contractors who worked on the project. Smith also tried to ensure that small landowners would benefit from the canal and the resulting economic activity.[43]

Smith served the governor in a variety of other ways. For example, he was the governor's alternate on the Southern Growth Policies Board and successfully promoted Winter as chairman of the organization. He invited journalist friends from around the country to visit with Winter and told them how Winter was transforming the state. He coordinated Winter's lobbying effort for Tennessee Tombigbee-Waterway funding. He became the confidant of Jamie Whitten, who called regularly to talk politics and funding for various projects.[44]

When Winter began his historic drive to reform education, Smith mounted a private initiative with the governor's approval, writing letters to everyone who might be influenced by his advice and asking their support for the reform package. Smith also talked to his old friend Billy Skelton, who oversaw the editorial section of the *Clarion-Ledger,* and urged Winter to enlist the active support of the paper in the drive for education reform. When the package passed, Smith wrote Winter, "I believe you have just about accomplished the greatest legislative victory of a Governor since Mike Conner passed the sales tax."[45]

By 1982, Smith was ready to retire. He wrote, "I haven't been to Washington for about a year, and don't try to come unless I have to. I do talk to Jamie Whitten every month or two. I've enjoyed my present work (the Governor is a friend from college days and early political beginnings) but I will not be looking further after it is finished."[46] Remembering his war service, Smith invited the 243rd to a reunion in Hattiesburg. His friend Skelton published two articles outlining Smith's career and announcing his intention to retire to the bookstore Smith had been helping his son to establish.[47]

He told Silver the next year that "there is a great deal of satisfaction in working with my son." He was pleased with Fred's "absorption" in the challenge of getting the store, Choctaw Books, stocked and running. Kathy joined them later, but it was not a worry-free retirement. He said, "The children may eventually decide that we have blown their inheritance, but it wouldn't have been much in the first place...."[48] Smith delighted in being free of politics. When Bill Minor asked Smith to attend Jim Eastland's funeral with him in 1986, Smith enjoyed refusing. Being free of politics, he felt no obligation to go.[49]

Smith wrote a series for the *Clarion-Ledger* in which he told the stories of Mississippi writers. He worked short days in the store with Fred. He continued his voracious reading and gladly visited with reporters who dropped in to chat and buy books when they wanted to write about Mississippi. He once remarked that he would not have traded continued service in Congress for the years he was enjoying with his family among the growing stacks of rare and used books. He was gruff with callers who had trouble comprehending his directions to the store — patience was never Smith's virtue; he wanted a revolution and helped to make one. Gradually he was accepted again by Mississippians. For example, in 1986, he was elected president of the Mississippi Historical Society.

Explaining the rise of massive resistance to integration, Numan Bartley says that the South in the 1950s had few independents, men he defines as having "an emancipated intellect and a tendency to visualize problems in long term perspective...."[50] He named four — Senators J. William Fulbright and Albert Gore, Sr., and Representatives Brooks Hayes and Frank E. Smith. The South, Bartley explained, lacked the institutional foundation to produce liberal thinkers. It lacked labor unions to support economic liberals concerned for the working classes. It lacked a liberal voting population to provide the base for electoral victory. Despite those handicaps, Smith developed a liberal mind in isolation and lived a life dedicated to changing his society. His efforts were not popular. A few years ago, on a day trip to the Delta, Smith and I dropped in at the Leflore County Courthouse to see Gray Evans. He was presiding over a trial, and so we turned to leave. As we did, we encountered a woman in the hallway. When Smith started to introduce himself, the woman interrupted disdainfully, saying, "I know who you are." Then she walked away without another word. I doubt that she really knew. She still believed Smith to be a traitor to the white race.

Smith died in 1997. It was a slow death; he was incapacitated by strokes but was cared for at home by Helen and two black nurses hired by the family. Those two nurses were the only black people to attend his funeral, a small affair with few political leaders present. Several staff members of the department of archives and history were there, along with representatives of the University Press of Mississippi and old friends from the press like Bill Minor. Governor Winter and I spoke. I ended with almost the same words that Smith had used to sum up his friend Willie Ruth's life at her funeral: "The world is a better place because he was here."

In an editorial on Smith's death, the *Clarion-Ledger* concluded,

It is a tribute to him that his 'Delta District' would some 20 years later be reconstituted to elect the first black representative in modern times. He was a visionary and great man. Mississippi owes a debt of gratitude and a tremendous amount of respect to this man: Frank Smith.

He served his state and his nation well.[51]

NOTES

CHAPTER ONE

1. *Clarksdale Register,* 9 July 1926; *Greenwood Commonwealth,* 28 August 1926; Frank E. Smith, *Congressman from Mississippi* (New York: Pantheon, 1964), 5.

2. *Greenwood Commonwealth,* 7 July 1926.

3. *Greenwood Commonwealth,* 8 July 1926; Smith, *Congressman,* 6.

4. There had been a burning nearby just a few months before Frank E. Smith's murder (*Greenwood Commonwealth,* 12 July 1926). After a particularly brutal lynching in 1929, the *Commonwealth* editorialized that the jury should have found that the victim committed suicide because that was what he did when he killed a white man (*Greenwood Commonwealth,* 1 January 1929, 2 January 1929).

5. *Greenwood Commonwealth,* 10 July 1926, 12 July 1926, 16 July 1926, 20 July 1926.

6. *Greenwood Commonwealth,* 27 July 1926, 23 August 1926, 27 August 1926.

7. Smith, *Congressman,* 7; Frank E. Smith, interview by author, 27 July 1982.

8. John Egerton, *Speak Now Against the Day: The Generation Before the Civil Rights Movement in the South* (New York: Knopf, 1994), 19. See also James C. Cobb, *The Most Southern Place on Earth: The Mississippi Delta and the Roots of Regional Identity* (New York: Oxford University Press, 1992).

9. See Albert D. Kirwan, *Revolt of the Rednecks, 1876–1925* (Lexington: University of Kentucky Press, 1951) for an account of the conflict.

10. David L. Cohn, *Where I Was Born and Raised* (Boston: Houghton Mifflin, 1948), 206.

11. William Alexander Percy, *Lanterns on the Levee: Recollections of a Planter's Son* (New York: Knopf, 1941), 3–7; Cobb, *Southern Place,* 98–124.

12. For an account of the Chinese in the Delta, see Robert Seto Quan, *Lotus Among the Magnolias: The Mississippi Chinese* (Jackson: University Press of Mississippi, 1982); Robert L. Brandfon, *Cotton Kingdom of the New South* (Cambridge: Harvard University Press, 1967), 164–65.

13. Percy, *Lanterns,* 20; Brandfon, *Cotton,* 113; Cobb, *Southern Place,* 109–12; Pete Daniel, *The Shadow of Slavery: Peonage in the South 1901–1969* (Urbana: University of Illinois Press, 1972), 174–75.

14. For an account of segregation in the Delta, see John Dollard, *Caste and Class in a Southern Town* (1937; reprint, New York: Doubleday, 1957); Hortense Powdermaker, *After Freedom: A Cultural Study in the Deep South* (1939; reprint, New York: Russell & Russell, 1968).

15. Dollard, *Caste,* 137–41; Cohn, *Where I was Born,* 61–66.

16. W. Fitzhugh Brundage, *Lynching in the New South* (Urbana: University of Illinois Press, 1993), 13; Walter White, *Rope and Faggot: A Biography of Judge Lynch* (1929; reprint, New York: Arno Press, 1969), 256; Jessie Daniel Ames, *The Changing Character of Lynching*

(Atlanta: Commission on Interracial Cooperation, Inc., 1942), 42–45; Percy, *Lanterns*, 225–41, 278; Cobb, *Southern Place*, 149.

17. Dollard, *Caste*, 282–85.

18. Percy, *Lanterns*, 230.

19. Ibid., 20.

20. Brandfon, *Cotton*, 135; "Century Mark," newspaper clipping, Frank E. Smith Papers loaned to the author at Jackson State University and now in the possession of the family at Choctaw Books in Jackson. Hereinafter cited as Smith Papers. This article is an interview with "Uncle Charley" on his one hundredth birthday. It is dated May 27, 1957, but the name of the newspaper is not on the clipping. Smith's mother's family seems to have arrived in Carroll County in an ox wagon about 1834. The family spent the night at Columbiana Church and buried their daughter, who died there, in the church cemetery before moving on to settle. WPA County History, Carroll County, microfilm 2856.

21. C. M. Smith, interview by Frank E. Smith, 10 October 1957, Smith Papers. Smith notes that this is the "best account" of his "great-grandfather's murder of McCarty."

22. Frank E. Smith, interviews by Orley B. Caudill, "The Mississippi Oral History Program of the University of Southern Mississippi," vol. 154, 1980, 1–3; Frank E. Smith, interview by author, 27 July 1982.

23. Dunbar Rowland, *Mississippi: Comprising Sketches of Counties, Towns, Events, Institutions, and Persons*, vol. 2 (Atlanta: Southern Historical Publication Association, 1907), 664; Frank E. Smith, interview by author, 27 July 1982.

24. Frank E. Smith, interview by author, 27 July 1982; Frank E. Smith, *Congressman*, 9–18. The author received the best picture of the family history during a visit to the Delta with Frank E. Smith. Visiting the sites of Smith's childhood elicited stories and reflections not provided in years of recorded interviews. The conversations of that day will be noted as an interview on 15 August 1988, but in fact it was a day-long remembering prompted by the places visited.

25. Powdermaker, *After Freedom*, 19.

26. Frank E. Smith, interview by author, 15 August 1988; Smith, *Congressman*, 11.

27. WPA Federal Writers' Project, *Mississippi: A Guide to the Magnolia State* (New York: Viking, 1938), 190; Frank E. Smith, interview by author, 15 August 1988.

28. *Magnolia State*, 189–93; Mildred Spurrier Topp, *Smile Please* (Boston: Houghton Mifflin, 1948); Mildred Spurrier Topp, *In the Pink* (Boston: Houghton Mifflin, 1950); Cobb, *Southern Place*, 237.

29. Frank E. Smith, interview by author, 15 August 1988.

30. Frank E. Smith, interview by author, 27 July 1982.

31. Smith, *Congressman*, 28; Frank E. Smith, interview by author, 27 July 1982; Sadie Thorn, interview by author, 11 August 1988.

32. Sadie Thorn, interview by author, 11 August 1988; Frank E. Smith, interview by author, 15 August 1988; Smith, *Congressman*, 3–4.

33. Frank E. Smith, interview by author, 15 August 1988; Smith, *Congressman*, 27; *Greenwood Commonwealth*, 17 July 1988, 26 July 1926.

34. Frank E. Smith, interview by author, 15 August 1988; Sadie Thorn, interview by author, 11 August 1988.

35. Sadie Thorn, interview by author, 11 August 1988; Smith, *Congressman*, 17; Gordon Smith, interview by author, 15 August 1988. Smith describes one of these Sunday visits in an unpublished short story called "Old Riptare," Smith Papers.

36. Frank E. Smith, interview by author, 15 August 1988; Frank E. Smith to Barret Shelton, 20 May 1974, Smith Papers.

Chapter Two

1. Frank E. Smith to Helen McPhaul, 12 April 1946, Smith Papers. This story of Smith's intellectual development is based on letters he wrote to his future wife while he was serving in Europe during the Second World War. He told her what he had read to shape his thinking and suggested she read the same books so that they could be compatible on the "all important" question of race. He had decided against becoming more involved with other women because of their ideas on the "South." These ideas were extremely important to Smith. I read the books Smith read and recognized some of the thoughts from his letters. Smith provided some help through interviews, but, of course, he had never tried to reconstruct the development of his ideas in a chronological fashion. He was most pleased with this portion of the biography and said that it accurately reflected his development as he could recall it. I based this account on his papers, not on interviews, because, understandably, Smith could not provide many details or much analysis of his intellectual development. The one reservation he had about my interpretation was that he did not believe he was ever as much of a socialist as I believe his writings indicate he was.

2. Cohn, *Where I Was Born*, 40–41.

3. Ibid., 16.

4. Topp, *In the Pink*.

5. Sanders Smith was not a relation. Bethel Fite to Frank E. Smith, 29 November 1964, Smith Papers; WPA Source Material for Mississippi History, Leflore County, microfilm A764; Smith, *Congressman*, 30; Frank E. Smith, interview by author, 27 July 1982.

6. Edwin R. Embree, *Brown Americans: The Story of a Tenth of the Nation* (1931; reprint, New York: Viking Press, 1946), 35. In 1974, Smith wrote to Morton Sosna that the book "was a major influence on my thinking in the formative years" (Frank E. Smith to Morton Sosna, 18 October 1974, Smith Papers).

7. Embree, *Brown Americans*, 59.

8. Frank E. Smith to Helen McPhaul, 15 December 1944, Smith Papers.

9. James Weldon Johnson, *Along This Way: The Autobiography of James Weldon Johnson* (1933; reprint, New York: Viking Press, 1973), 57.

10. Ibid., 411–14; Smith, *Congressman*, 49.

11. WPA, Leflore County, microfilm A764; Quan, *Lotus*, 45.

12. Smith, *Congressman*, 7; Frank E. Smith, interview by Orley B. Caudill, "Oral History," 27–28; Tom Sancton to Frank E. Smith, 26 January 1943, Smith Papers.

13. Frank E. Smith to Helen McPhaul, July 15, 1944, Smith Papers.

14. Lincoln Steffens, *The Autobiography of Lincoln Steffens* (New York: The Literary Guild, 1931), 591; Frank E. Smith to Helen McPhaul, 11 August 1945, Smith Papers; Willie Ruth Cowan, interview by author, 21 March 1985.

15. Steffens, *Autobiography*, 873.

16. Vincent Sheean, *Personal History* (1934; reprint, New York: Doubleday, 1940), 159, 225, 324, 370. In 1975 Smith wrote to Eric Sevareid to thank him for a tribute to Sheean. "I read 'Personal History' as a boy of fifteen when it was first published, and it certainly had a major influence on me" (Frank E. Smith to Eric Sevareid, 27 March 1975, Smith Papers).

17. Sheean, *History*, 428.

18. Frank E. Smith, interview by author, 27 July 1982; Smith, *Congressman*, 30–31.

19. *Bulldog Broadcast* in *Greenwood Commonwealth*, 16 October 1933, 18 December 1933, 6 February 1934, 13 February 1934; Gordon Smith, interview by author, 15 August 1988.

20. Frank E. Smith, interview by author, 15 August 1988; Cobb, *Southern Place*, 188–89.

21. *Bulldog Broadcast,* 23 October 1933, 11 December 1933, 18 December 1933.

22. Cobb, *Southern Place,* 194; Sadie Thorn, interview by author, 11 August 1988.

23. Ibid.

24. Frank E. Smith, interview by author, 15 August 1988; *CBS Reports* interview with Frank E. Smith, 24 November 1963, Smith Papers.

25. An enlarged account of Smith's reading and his reaction to southern writers can be found in Dennis J. Mitchell, "Frank Ellis Smith: An Intellectual Journey," *Journal of Mississippi History* 52 (February 1990).

CHAPTER THREE

1. James B. Young and James M. Ewing, *Mississippi Junior Colleges* (Jackson: Mississippi Junior College Association, 1978), 130–33; *Indianola Enterprise,* 30 August 1934, 31 January 1935; Frank E. Smith, "Life with Papa," Smith Papers.

2. Gordon Smith, interview by author, 15 August 1988.

3. Willie Ruth Cowan, interview by author, 21 March 1985.

4. *Sunflower Petals,* 22 October 1934, 5 November 1934, 26 November 1934.

5. Willie Ruth Cowan, interview by author, 21 March 1985.

6. Ibid.; Frank E. Smith, interview by author, 13 September 1990.

7. *Sunflower Petals,* 17 December 1934, 20 December 1934, 28 January 1935, 18 February 1935, 6 May 1935.

8. Frank E. Smith, interview by author, 13 September 1990; Smith, *Congressman,* 47; *Sunflower Petals,* 6 May 1935.

9. Frank E. Smith to Helen McPhaul 15 July 1944, Smith Papers; *Sunflower Petals,* 25 October 1935, 28 November 1935, 23 January 1936, 10 April 1936, 8 May 1936.

10. Willie Ruth Cowan, interview by author, 21 March 1985.

11. Ibid.

12. Fred Sullens to Frank E. Smith [May 1936], Smith Papers.

13. Frank E. Smith, interview by author, 27 July 1982.

14. Ibid.; Smith, *Congressman,* 49–50; Willie Ruth Cowan, interview by author, 21 March 1985; unpublished manuscripts; Helene Richards to Frank E. Smith, 14 September 1937, Smith Papers.

15. *Common Sense,* 21 April 1937, 21–22.

16. *Plain Talk,* 19 September 1937, 8–11.

17. *The Fight Against War and Fascism* (pamphlet), July 1937.

18. David Holloman to Frank E. Smith, 6 June 1937, Smith Papers; Willie Ruth Cowan, interview by author, 21 March 1985.

19. Dale Mullen to Frank E. Smith [1938]; Lawrence Hutton to Frank E. Smith, 4 May 1938; Arnold Gingrich to Frank E. Smith, Smith Papers; *The Crisis* 41 (January 1936), 7.

20. Frank E. Smith to Helen McPhaul, 5 June 1945; Dale Mullen to Frank E. Smith [1942], Smith Papers.

21. Dale Mullen to Frank E. Smith [29 June 1938], Smith Papers.

22. Dale Mullen to Frank E. Smith [July 1938], Booth File, Smith Papers.

23. Paula Snelling to Frank E. Smith, 15 May 1937, Smith Papers.

24. Smith, *Congressman,* 52.

25. Frank E. Smith to Helen McPhaul, 10 March 1945; Fred Cecil Smith to Frank E. Smith [February 1940]; Ann Elmo to Frank E. Smith, 20 September 1939, Smith Papers.

26. Lillian Smith to Frank E. Smith, 20 April 1940, Smith Papers; Mississippi Series of the Southern Politics Collection, Jean and Alexander Heard Library, Vanderbilt University (hereinafter cited as the Heard interviews).

27. Smith, *Congressman,* 53–54; James W. Silver, interview by author, 9 November 1982.

28. Dale Mullen to Frank E. Smith [1942]; Sam H. Franklin, Jr., to Frank E. Smith, 14 March 1940; Dorothy H. Franklin to Frank E. Smith, 21 January 1940, Smith Papers.

CHAPTER FOUR

1. James W. Silver, interview by author, 9 November 1982; Willie Ruth Cowan, interview by author, 21 March 1985.

2. Dale Mullen to Frank E. Smith, 25 February 1942, Smith Papers.

3. Frank E. Smith to Helen McPhaul, 9 February 1945, 27 September 1944, Smith Papers.

4. Sadie Smith to Frank E. Smith, 20 April 1942, Smith Papers.

5. Frank E. Smith to Willie Ruth Cowan, 7 June 1942, Cowan Papers, in the possession of Kathy Smith.

6. Smith, *Congressman,* 58–59.

7. Frank E. Smith to Willie Ruth Cowan, 7 June 1942, Cowan Papers.

8. Frank E. Smith to Willie Ruth Cowan, 16 September 1942, Cowan Papers.

9. Frank E. Smith to Sadie Smith [1943], Smith Papers; "Battle Diary" notes, Smith Papers.

10. Frank E. Smith to Helen McPhaul, 2 September 1944, Smith Papers.

11. Frank E. Smith to Willie Ruth Cowan, 16 January 1943, Cowan Papers; Sadie Smith to Frank E. Smith, 28 December 1943, Smith Papers; Mother Ellis to Frank Ellis Smith, 16 January 1943, Smith Papers.

12. "Battle Diary" notes; "Battalion Diary" draft 1–2, Smith Papers.

13. Frank E. Smith to Helen McPhaul, 2 July 1944, 4 July 1944, 9 July 1944, 20 May 1945, Smith Papers.

14. "Battle Diary" notes; Frank E. Smith to Helen McPhaul, 7 February 1945, Smith Papers.

15. "Battalion Diary" draft, 23; Frank E. Smith to Helen McPhaul, 20 August 1944, Smith Papers.

16. "Battalion Diary" draft, 34; Frank E. Smith to Helen McPhaul, 8 October 1944, Smith Papers.

17. Frank E. Smith to Helen McPhaul, 29 August 1944, 13 February 1945, Smith Papers.

18. Frank E. Smith to Helen McPhaul, 6 December 1944, Smith Papers.

19. Frank E. Smith to Helen McPhaul, 29 November 1944; "Battalion Diary" draft 20, Smith Papers.

20. Frank E. Smith to Helen McPhaul, 16 August 1944, Smith Papers.

21. Bud Harrison, interview by author, 14 November 1985; Frank E. Smith to Helen McPhaul, 22 November 1944.

22. Frank E. Smith to Helen McPhaul, 29 August 1944, Smith Papers.

23. "Battalion Diary" draft 47, Smith Papers.

24. Ibid., 45.

25. Frank E. Smith to Helen McPhaul, 13 July 1944, Smith Papers.

26. Frank E. Smith to Willie Ruth Cowan, 2 March 1944, Cowan Papers.

27. Frank E. Smith to Willie Ruth Cowan, 16 April 1944, Cowan Papers.

28. Frank E. Smith to Helen McPhaul, 25 June 1944, Smith Papers.

29. Frank E. Smith to Helen McPhaul, 15 July 1944, 24 August 1944, 28 August 1944, 6 September 1944, 19 September 1944, Smith Papers. The *North Georgia Review* changed its name to *South Today.*

30. Frank E. Smith to Helen McPhaul, 10 January 1945, Smith Papers.

31. Ibid., 18 February 1945, Smith Papers.

32. Ibid., 7 December 1944, Smith Papers.

33. Ibid., 4 February 1945, Smith Papers.

34. Frank E. Smith to Willie Ruth Cowan, 5 January 1945, Cowan Papers.

35. Ibid.; 8 September 1944; Willie Ruth Cowan to Frank E. Smith, 19 December 1944, Smith Papers.

36. Frank E. Smith to Helen McPhaul, 21 October 1944, Smith Papers. A copy of the outline is in Smith Papers.

37. Ibid., 29 January 1945, 6 January 1944, 25 July 1944, 12 September 1944,13 April 1945, Smith Papers.

38. Ibid., 13 April 1945, Smith Papers.

39. Ibid., 2 December 1944, 3 August 1945, Smith Papers.

40. Ibid., 4 February 1945, Smith Papers.

41. Ibid., 11 December 1944, Smith Papers.

42. Ibid., 22 October 1944, Smith Papers.

43. Ibid., 25 July 1944, Smith Papers.

44. Ibid., 11 August 1945, Smith Papers.

45. Ibid., 15 July 1944, Smith Papers.

46. Ibid., 3 May 1945, 27 May 1945; "Battalion Diary" draft, Smith Papers.

47. Frank E. Smith to Helen McPhaul, 1 August 1945, 12 January 1945, 24 May 1945, 12 June 1945, 20 July 1945, Smith Papers; Frank E. Smith to Willie Ruth Cowan, 25 August [1945], Cowan Papers.

48. Frank E. Smith to Helen McPhaul, 8 September 1944, 13 September 1944; Tom Sancton to Frank E. Smith, 10 February 1943, Smith Papers.

CHAPTER FIVE

1. Egerton, *Speak Now*, 337–38.

2. Ray Skates, *Mississippi: A Bicentennial History* (New York: Norton, 1979), 149–56.

3. Frank E. Smith, conversation with author; Kenneth H. Williams, "Mississippi and Civil Rights, 1945–1954" (Ph.D. diss., Mississippi State University, 1985), 47–48.

4. Williams, "Mississippi and Civil Rights," 47–48; Egerton, *Speak Now*, 327; Frank E. Smith, conversation with author, 15 August 1988.

5. William Russell, *A Wind Is Rising* (New York: Knopf, 1950); Greenwood *Morning Star*, 20 August 1946, 21 August 1946; *Jackson Daily News*, 6 August 1947, 16 February 1948, 17 February 1948.

6. Egerton, *Speak Now*, 221.

7. Williams, "Mississippi and Civil Rights," 58; Brundage, *Lynching*, 252; "Killed While Resisting Arrest," unsold article, Smith Papers.

8. Egerton, *Speak Now*, 432–48.

9. Calvin Cox to Frank E. Smith, 22 February 1945, Smith Papers.

10. Ann Waldron, *Hodding Carter: The Reconstruction of a Racist* (Chapel Hill: Algonquin Books, 1993), 150–52, 160–61; Egerton, *Speak Now*, 461.

11. Hodding Carter to Frank E. Smith, 15 May 1946, Smith Papers; Smith, *Congressman*, 65.

12. Memphis *Commercial Appeal* (n.d.), Smith Papers; Frank E. Smith, interview by author, 6 December 1990.

13. Hodding Carter to Frank E. Smith, 30 May 1946, Smith Papers; Frank E. Smith, interview by H. T. Holmes, Mississippi Department of Archives and History, 6 January 1977.

14. Notice, Greenwood *Morning Star,* 8 July 1946.
15. Jim Alsop to Frank E. Smith (series of letters and notes with no dates), Smith Papers.
16. Ibid.
17. Ibid.
18. Greenwood *Morning Star* (n.d.), Smith Papers.
19. Greenwood *Morning Star,* 9 May 1947, 13 June 1947; Dean Acheson, *Present at the Creation* (New York: Norton, 1969), 219–22.
20. Greenwood *Morning Star,* 13 July 1946, 25 July 1946, 30 July 1946, 9 August 1946, 12 June 1947.
21. Greenwood *Morning Star,* 9 May 1946.
22. Ibid., 14 April 1947.
23. Frank E. Smith to Jim Alsop (n.d.), Smith Papers.
24. Greenwood *Morning Star,* 10 June 1947, 30 June 1947.
25. Ibid., 7 June 1947, 6 August 1947, 7 August 1947; Frank E. Smith, interview by author, 14 January 1985.
26. Jim Alsop to Frank E. Smith (n.d.), Smith Papers; Frank E. Smith, interview by author, 10 December 1990.
27. Frank E. Smith, interview by H. T. Holmes, 6 January 1977; Greenwood *Morning Star,* 8 August 1947.
28. Frank E. Smith to Dudley Fraiser, 20 May 1953, Smith Papers.
29. *Jackson Daily News,* 14 September 1947; Smith, *Congressman,* 70–72; Frank E. Smith, interview by author, 28 January 1991.
30. Jackson *Clarion-Ledger,* 6 November 1947.
31. Williams, "Mississippi and Civil Rights," 126.
32. *Jackson Daily News,* 12 October 1947, 18 October 1947, 23 October 1947; Frank E. Smith to Hodding Carter, 3 December 1947, Smith Papers; see, for example, *Delta Democrat Times,* 26 October 1947, 28 October 1947, 30 October 1947, and Memphis *Commercial Appeal,* 7 October 1947, 9 October 1947, 11 October 1947, 15 October 1947, 16 October 1947, 18 October 1947; Williams, "Mississippi and Civil Rights," 128.
33. Frank E. Smith, interview by H. T. Holmes, 6 January 1977.
34. Walter Sillers to Frank E. Smith (copy), 15 October 1951, Walter Sillers Papers, Delta State University Archives.
35. *Journal of the Senate of the State of Mississippi,* January 6–April 14, 1948; Frank E. Smith, interview by H. T. Holmes, 6 January 1977; Memphis *Commercial Appeal,* 7 January 1948. For a discussion of political factions in Mississippi, see V. O. Key, Jr., *Southern Politics in State and Nation* (New York: Knopf, 1949), 304–7.
36. *Journal of the Senate,* 899, 914, 1008.
37. Frank E. Smith to Philip Mullen, 23 March 1949, Smith Papers; Frank E. Smith, interview by H. T. Holmes, 6 January 1977.
38. *Jackson Daily News,* 20 February 1948; Memphis *Commercial Appeal,* 4 February 1948; 5 February 1948.
39. Memphis *Commercial Appeal,* 31 January 1948. Jones received more space in the article.
40. Ibid., 14 April 1948; H. M. Ray to Frank E. Smith, 1 February 1965.
41. *Jackson Daily News,* 23 January 1948.
42. Ibid., 29 January 1948, 6 February 1948.
43. Ibid., 30 January 1948, 12 February 1948, 19 March 1948; Frank E. Smith, interview by author, 10 December 1990; Heard interviews.
44. Philip Mullen to Frank E. Smith, 15 July 1948; James W. Silver to Frank E. Smith, 22 November [1948], Smith Papers.

45. Philip Mullen to Frank E. Smith, 5 December 1948; James W. Silver to Frank E. Smith, 22 November [1948], Smith Papers.

46. James W. Silver to Frank E. Smith, 22 November [1948]; Philip Mullen to Frank E. Smith [1948], Smith Papers.

47. Frank E. Smith to Hodding Carter, 20 November [1948], Carter Papers; Alexander Heard, *A Two-Party South?* (Chapel Hill: University of North Carolina Press, 1952), 23, 24; Egerton, *Speak Now*, 499, 506.

48. Dale Mullen to Frank E. Smith, 4 September 1948, Smith Papers.

49. Silver was pushing during this period to get Stennis to hire William Winter, a student member of the legislature who had impressed Silver with his promise and desire to serve. James W. Silver to Hodding Carter, 27 July 1949, Carter Papers, Mississippi State University Archives; James W. Silver to Frank E. Smith, 10 July [1949], Smith Papers.

50. Williams, "Mississippi and Civil Rights," 221.

51. Frank E. Smith to Hodding Carter, 26 August [1949], Carter Papers; Philip Mullen to Frank E. Smith, 31 January 1952, Smith Papers.

52. *Jackson Daily News*, 16 November 1949, 23 November 1949, 28 November 1949, 6 December 1949.

53. John Stennis to Hodding Carter [1950], Carter Papers; *Jackson Daily News*, 2 January 1950.

54. Newspaper clippings (n.d.), Smith Papers.

55. *Journal of the Senate of the State of Mississippi*, 1950, 1387, 1399; *Jackson Daily News*, 24 January 1950.

56. *Journal of the Senate*, 1390, 1399, 1409; *Jackson Daily News*, 12 January 1950, 8 February 1950.

57. Greenwood *Morning Star*, 5 January 1950, 15 January 1950, 22 January 1950, 29 January 1950.

58. Memphis *Commercial Appeal*, 15 March 1950; *Jackson Daily News*, 14 March 1950.

59. Memphis *Commercial Appeal*, 1 January 1950, 3 January 1950.

CHAPTER SIX

1. Heard, *Two-Party*, 274–75; Heard interviews; Williams, "Mississippi and Civil Rights," 73.

2. Willie Ruth Cowan, interview by author, 21 March 1985; Frank E. Smith, interview by author, 27 July 1982; Hodding Carter, *Where Main Street Meets the River* (New York: Rinehart, 1953), 219–22.

3. Philip Mullen, column in *Osceola Times*, 7 October 1965, Smith Papers; Carter, *Main Street*, 219–20.

4. James W. Silver to Frank E. Smith, 25 April 1950, Smith Papers.

5. Stephen K. Bailey, *Congress at Work* (New York: Holt, 1952), 50, 54, 56.

6. Scrapbook of newspaper clippings regarding the 1950 election, Smith Papers; Frank E. Smith to Willie Ruth Cowan (n.d.), Cowan Papers.

7. Scrapbook regarding 1950 election, Smith Papers; Earl Black and Merle Black, *Politics and Society in the South* (Cambridge: Harvard University Press, 1987), 7.

8. Greenwood *Morning Star*, 3 June 1950; Frank E. Smith, interview by author, 14 January 1985.

9. Frank E. Smith to Willie Ruth Cowan, 24 May 1950, Cowan Papers.

10. Ibid.

11. Smith, *Congressman*, 80; Frank E. Smith, interview by author, 31 January 1991.

12. Scrapbook regarding 1950 election, Smith Papers; Bailey, *Congress,* 58–59; Frank E. Smith, interview by author, 31 January 1991.

13. Scrapbook regarding 1950 election, Smith Papers.

14. Handwritten draft of campaign platform, Sillers Papers; scrapbook regarding 1950 election, Smith Papers.

15. Campaign file, 1950; Louie C. Spencer, Jr., to Frank E. Smith, 27 July 1949; John C. Stennis to Boswell Stevens, 21 September 1950, Smith Papers; Letters Mailed to Alumni, Cowan Papers.

16. Scrapbook regarding 1950 election, Smith Papers.

17. Greenwood *Morning Star,* 6 June 1950; scrapbook regarding 1950 election, Smith Papers.

18. *Delta Democrat Times,* 18 August 1950; scrapbook regarding 1950 election, Smith Papers.

19. Walter Sillers to J. B. Boyles, 6 September 1950, Sillers Papers; Greenwood *Morning Star,* 12 September 1950.

20. Scrapbook regarding 1950 election, Smith Papers.

21. Ibid.; Greenwood *Morning Star,* 25 August 1950, 31 August 1950.

22. *Delta Democrat Times,* 3 September 1950; Greenwood *Morning Star,* 7 September 1950.

23. *Greenwood Commonwealth,* 11 September 1950; Frank E. Smith, interview by author, 14 January 1985.

24. Greenwood *Morning Star,* 9 September 1950; *Greenwood Commonwealth,* 8 September 1950; *Delta Democrat Times,* 11 September 1950; scrapbook regarding 1950 election, Smith Papers.

25. Walter Sillers to Hraddock Goins, 25 September 1950, Sillers Papers.

26. Carter, *Main Street,* 220–21.

27. Precinct vote breakdown; campaign flyers in scrapbook regarding 1950 election, Smith Papers; Frank E. Smith, interview by author, 27 July 1982.

28. *Delta Democrat Times,* 11 September 1950, 13 September 1950.

29. John C. Stennis to Boswell Stevens, 21 September 1950, scrapbook regarding 1950 election, Smith Papers; Frank E. Smith, interview by author, 31 January 1991.

30. Scrapbook regarding 1950 election, Smith Papers.

31. David Williams, interview by author, 1 March 1991.

32. *Greenwood Commonwealth,* 21 August 1950.

CHAPTER SEVEN

1. Quoted in Warren Weaver, Jr., *Both Your Houses: The Truth About Congress* (New York: Praeger, 1972), 98.

2. For an account of the U.S. House of Representatives during this period, see Richard Bolling, *House Out of Order* (New York: Dutton, 1964) and *Power in the House* (New York: Capricorn Books, 1968); George Goodwin, Jr., *The Little Legislatures: Committees of Congress* (Amherst: University of Massachusetts Press, 1970), 168.

3. Smith's former assistant described one of the preachers in Holmes County. David Williams to Frank E. Smith, 8 July 1953, Smith Papers; Bolling, *Power,* 185; *Jackson Daily News,* 12 January 1950; Numan V. Bartley, *The Rise of Massive Resistance: Race and Politics in the South During the 1950's* (Baton Rouge: Louisiana State University Press, 1969), 340–41.

4. See Bruce J. Diernfield, *Keeper of the Rules: Congressman Howard W. Smith of Virginia* (Charlottesville: University Press of Virginia, 1987).

5. Bolling, *Power,* 181. This is the theme of both of Bolling's books.

6. Carl Elliot, Sr., and Michael D'Orso, *The Cost of Courage* (New York: Anchor Books, 1992), 109; newspaper clippings, 1951, Smith Papers; Robert E. Jones, interview by author, 20 June 1994; Arthur Winstead, interview by author, 21 September 1994; Sandra Vance, "The Congressional Career of John Bell Williams, 1947–1967" (Ph.D. diss., Mississippi State University, 1976); Thomas Abernethy, interview by author, 8 June 1993; William Winter, interview by author, 16 June 1994; R. William French, "The Change in Southern Congressional Voting Patterns 1954–1968" (unpublished thesis), Smith Papers.

7. Frank E. Smith to Hodding Carter, 17 January 1951, Carter Papers.

8. Reapportionment Subject File, Mississippi Department of Archives and History.

9. Clarence Pierce to Frank E. Smith, 3 February 1952; Walter Sillers to Frank E. Smith, 26 December 1950, Smith Papers.

10. Will M. Whittington to Frank E. Smith, 13 September 1950, Smith Papers; George B. Galloway, *History of the House of Representatives* (New York: Crowell, 1976) 60–61.

11. Frank E. Smith to Louie Spencer, Jr., 12 December 1950, 10 December 1951, Smith Papers.

12. Newspaper clippings, 1950–1951, Smith Papers.

13. Stephen K. Bailey and Howard D. Samuel, *Congress at Work* (New York; Holt, 1952) 126–27; David Williams, interview by author, 6 March 1991.

14. Bailey and Samuel, *Congress at Work,* 127. The Smith congressional files are still in those envelopes, mixed with TVA files that are stored in file folders.

15. David Williams, interview by author, 1 March 1991; Bailey and Samuel, *Congress at Work,* 127, 131; Meg Cosby, telephone interview by author, 29 August 1994; Frank E. Smith to William A. Brokwell (n.d.), Smith Papers; Walter Sillers to Frank E. Smith, 15 October 1951, Sillers Papers.

16. Audrey Warren to Frank E. Smith, 21 October 1955, Smith Papers.

17. Hodding Carter to Frank E. Smith, 2 June 1951, Carter Papers.

18. Frank E. Smith to Hodding Carter, 7 June 1951, Carter Papers.

19. Bailey and Samuel, *Congress at Work,* 129–30; newspaper clippings, 1951, Smith Papers.

20. Gary B. Mills, *Of Men and Rivers: The Story of the Vicksburg District* (Vicksburg: Corps of Engineers, 1978) 148, 157; Arthur Maas, *Muddy Waters: The Army Engineers and the Nation's Rivers* (Cambridge: Harvard University Press, 1951), 151, 207; newspaper clippings, 1950–1952, Smith Papers; Walter Sillers to Frank E. Smith, 11 April 1951, Sillers Papers.

21. Newspaper clippings, 1950–1951, Smith Papers.

22. Smith inserted articles from the *Progressive Farmer* into the *Congressional Record* frequently. Henry C. Dethloff, *A History of the American Rice Industry 1685–1985* (College Station: Texas A&M University Press, 1988) 169, 176; newspaper clippings, 1950–1951, Smith Papers.

23. *Congressional Record,* index, 1951; newspaper clippings, 1950–1951, Smith Papers.

24. *New York Times,* 24 May 1952; *Wall Street Journal,* 21 September 1951, Smith Papers. Gerald Horne, *Communist Front?: The Civil Rights Congress* (Rutherford, N.J.: Fairleigh Dickinson University Press, 1988), 13–25, 74–98.

25. "Report from Washington," Frank E. Smith Newsletter; Walter Sillers to Frank E. Smith, 11 May 1951; Frank E. Smith to Walter Sillers, 14 May 1951, Sillers Papers; John Dittmer, *Local People: The Struggle for Civil Rights in Mississippi* (Urbana: University of Illinois Press,1994), 21–22; Horne, *Communist Front,* 74–98.

26. Newspaper clippings, 1950–1951, Smith Papers; Frank E. Smith to O. J. Scott, 18 July 1951, Sillers Papers; "Report from Washington," 2 April 1951; "The Negro Soldiers in Europe," unsold article, Smith Papers.

27. Frank E. Smith to Forrest Cooper, 26 September 1951; Curtis Saxton to Frank E. Smith, 27 February 1951; Frank E. Smith to Curtis Saxton, 16 March 1951, Smith Papers.

28. Meg Cosby, telephone interview by author, 29 August 1994; Smith, *Congressman,* 104–105.

29. Frank E. Smith to Hodding Carter, 17 January 1951.

30. Frank E. Smith to James W. Silver [1948], Silver Papers; Bailey and Samuel, *Congress at Work,* 134; Greenwood *Morning Star,* 18 September 1952; newspaper clippings, 1951–1952, Smith Papers; Alfred O. Hero, Jr., *The Southerner and World Affairs* (Baton Rouge: Louisiana State University Press, 1965), 382; "Report from Washington," 23 April 1951, Smith Papers.

31. Newspaper clippings, 1951, Smith Papers; *Congressional Record,* 1951, 3888.

32. Frank E. Smith to Curtis Saxton, 16 April 1951; Woodley Carr to Frank E. Smith, 18 April 1951, Smith Papers.

33. Ibid.

34. *Congressional Record,* 1951, 2661–2662; Frank E. Smith to Curtis Saxton, 16 April 1951, Smith Papers.

35. Frank E. Smith to Gordon Smith, 13 January 1951, Smith Papers.

36. Philip Mullen to Frank E. Smith, 4 February 1951; Frank E. Smith to Curtis Saxton, 16 March 1951, Smith Papers.

37. Woodley Carr to Frank E. Smith, 26 July 1951, Smith Papers; Frank E. Smith, interview by author, 28 February 1991.

38. Woodley Carr to David Williams, 13 December 1951; Frank E. Smith to Gordon Smith, 15 February, Smith Papers.

39. Curtis Saxton to Frank E. Smith, 22 January 1951, Smith Papers; Heard interviews.

40. Walter Sillers to Frank E. Smith, 23 January 1951; Frank E. Smith to Walter Sillers, 20 January 1951, Sillers Papers.

41. Curtis Saxton to Frank E. Smith, 9 November 1950; Frank E. Smith to Curtis Saxton, 14 November 1950; Frank E. Smith to Curtis Saxton, 15 February 1951; Woodley Carr to Frank E. Smith, 10 April 1951, Smith Papers; Walter Sillers to E. O. Spencer, 24 June 1953, Sillers Papers.

42. Frank E. Smith to Louie Spencer, Jr., 12 February 1951; Frank E. Smith to Louie Spencer, Jr., 4 April 1951; Willie Ruth Cowan to Frank E. Smith, 13 February 1951; J. W. Smith to Frank E. Smith, 19 February 1951, Smith Papers.

43. Frank E. Smith to Louie Spencer, Jr., 4 April 1951, Smith Papers.

44. Frank E. Smith, interview by author, 14 January 1985; Frank E. Smith to Woodley Carr, 2 May 1951, Smith Papers.

45. Frank E. Smith to J. W. Smith, 22 February 1951; Walter Sillers to Frank E. Smith, 25 October 1951, Smith Papers.

46. Reapportionment Subject File, Mississippi Department of Archives and History.

47. Interview with J. P. Coleman, Southern Oral History Program, no. 4007, A102, Wilson Library, University of North Carolina.

48. Frank E. Smith to Clarence Pierce, 16 March 1951; Clarence Pierce to Frank E. Smith, 3 February 1952; Woodley Carr to David Williams, 13 December 1951, Smith Papers.

49. Walter Sillers to Frank E. Smith, 10 March 1952, Smith Papers.

50. Clarence Pierce to Frank E. Smith [1952], Smith Papers.

51. Woodley Carr to Frank E. Smith, 7 February 1952; Will M. Whittington to Frank E. Smith, 13 March 1952, Smith Papers.

52. Frank E. Smith to Gordon Smith, 10 April 1952, Smith Papers.

53. Woodley Carr to Frank E. Smith, 5 April 1952, Smith Papers.

54. Curtis Saxton to Frank E. Smith, 2 June 1952; Hodding Carter to Frank E. Smith, 12 May 1952; Hodding Carter to Frank E. Smith, 14 April 1952; Frank E. Smith to J. W. Smith, 21 May 1952, Smith Papers; Walter Sillers to Frank E. Smith, 9 June 1952, Sillers Papers.

55. Walter Sillers to Frank E. Smith, 16 May 1952, Sillers Papers.

56. Woodley Carr to Frank E. Smith, 19 June 1952, 12 June 1952, Smith Papers.

57. Woodley Carr to Frank E. Smith, 19 June 1952, Smith Papers; Walter Sillers to Frank E. Smith, 20 June 1952, 16 May 1952, Sillers Papers.

58. Woodley Carr to Frank E. Smith, 1 July 1952, Smith Papers.

59. Frank E. Smith to James W. Silver, 5 August 1952, Smith Papers; *Newsweek*, 4 August 1952; Greenwood *Morning Star*, 28 July 1952, 29 July 1952; newspaper clippings, 1952, Smith Papers.

60. Frank E. Smith to Willie Ruth Cowan, 6 August 1952, Smith Papers.

61. Newspaper clippings, 1952, Smith Papers; John C. Stennis to Frank E. Smith, 6 September 1952; David Williams to Frank E. Smith, 11 October 1952, Smith Papers; Meg Cosby, telephone interview by author, 29 August 1994.

62. Woodley Carr to Frank E. Smith, 2 October 1952; Frank E. Smith to Woodley Carr, 9 August 1952, Smith Papers; Frank E. Smith, interview by author, 7 March 1991.

63. Philip Mullen to Frank E. Smith, 27 July 1952; James W. Silver to Frank E. Smith, 5 March 1951, Smith Papers.

64. Joseph G. Rucks to Frank E. Smith, 7 August 1952, Smith Papers.

65. George Carbone to Frank E. Smith, 5 August 1951; Hodding Carter to Frank E. Smith, 24 January 1951, Smith Papers.

66. George Carbone to James W. Silver, 24 January 1952, Smith Papers.

67. Meg Cosby, telephone interview by author, 29 August 1994.

Chapter Eight

1. Personnel folders, various correspondence, Smith Papers; Frank E. Smith, conversations with the author over lunch for a period of thirteen years. Smith and I ate lunch at the Mayflower once a week for over a decade. We discussed his life and the research for this book at many of those lunches, and Smith revealed information not captured on tape. In cases where documentation exists, I have cited it, but some revelations are not on tape or in any other source. In a few instances, it was necessary to cite these conversations. Meg Cosby, telephone interview by author, 29 August 1994; Gray Evans, interview by author, 17 October 1994.

2. Personnel folders, Smith Papers.

3. Ibid.; Gray Evans, interview by author, 17 October 1994; Charles Deaton, interview by author, 17 October 1994.

4. Frank E. Smith to James W. Silver, 29 April 1953, Smith Papers.

5. David Williams to Frank E. Smith, 11 October 1952, Smith Papers.

6. *Congressional Record*, 1953, 3176.

7. *Delta Democrat Times*, 16 August 1953; Woodley Carr to Frank E. Smith, 12 February 1953, 18 January 1953, Smith Papers.

8. Newspaper clippings, 1953, Smith Papers; *Congressional Record*, 1953, 487.

9. Newspaper clippings [1954], Smith Papers.

10. Frank E. Smith to William Winter, 24 June 1958; newspaper clippings, 1958, Smith Papers.

11. Charles W. Crawford, "An Oral History of the Tennessee Valley Authority," Memphis State University, 3 August 1973, 10.

12. Carl Carmer to Frank E. Smith, 20 May 1953, Smith Papers.

13. *Christian Science Monitor* [1954], *Chicago Tribune*, 16 May 1954, Smith Papers.

14. Frank E. Smith, "The Changing South," *Virginia Quarterly Review* 31 (1955). The book manuscript is in the Smith Papers. Smith probably began writing it as early as 1954 and made some efforts to publish it as late as 1963 or 1964. Frank E. Smith to Jean Crawford, 27 July 1954; Frank E. Smith to Audrey Warren (n.d.), Smith Papers.

15. Frank E. Smith to James W. Silver, 5 November 1953; Frank E. Smith to William Winter, 31 December 1953; newspaper clippings, 1954, Smith Papers.

16. Frank E. Smith to Sadie Smith, 24 March 1953, Smith Papers.

17. Smith loved mysteries. There are no lists of his reading during these years, but, after he went to TVA, his former assistant supplied several each week from the Library of Congress. Audrey Warren file, Smith Papers. Meg Cosby, telephone interview by author, 29 August 1994; Gray Evans, interview by author, 17 October 1994; Charles Deaton, interview by author, 17 October 1994.

18. Newspaper clippings and *Congressional Quarterly* clippings, 1952–1956; Hubert Humphrey to Frank E. Smith, 1 July 1955, Smith Papers.

19. *Clarion-Ledger*, 16 June 1955, 12 July 1955, Smith Papers.

20. Frank E. Smith, conversation with author, September 1994.

21. Frank E. Smith to Jere Cooper, 8 January 1955; Frank E. Smith to Sam Rayburn, 17 November 1954; Omar Burleson to Frank E. Smith, 1 February 1955; *Congressional Record*, 1955, 1075; newspaper clippings, 1955, Smith Papers; see Goodwin, *Little Legislatures*.

22. Robert E. Jones, interview by author, 20 July 1994; newspaper clippings, 1956, Smith Papers.

23. Frank E. Smith to L. C. Spencer, Jr., 17 April 1959, Smith Papers; *Congressional Record*, 1958, 3793; newspaper clippings, 1955, Smith Papers.

24. Memphis *Commercial Appeal*, 4 June 1957, 24 April 1958, 14 May [1958], Smith Papers; *New York Times*, 11 September 1959.

25. Memphis *Commercial Appeal*, 27 February [1958], 12 March 1958, 13 March 1958, Smith Papers.

26. Smith, *Congressman*, 197, 198; *New York Times*, 11 September 1959.

27. United States Federal Highway Administration, *America's Highways, 1776–1976: A History of the Federal-Aid Program* (Washington, D.C.: GPO 1976), 165–71; newspaper clippings, 1954, 1955, 1956, Smith Papers; *Congressional Record*, 1954, 2844; *Congressional Record*, 1955, 11538; Frank E. Smith to Will Whittington, 27 April 1956, Smith Papers.

28. *America's Highways*, 172, 173; newspaper clippings, 1956, Smith Papers.

29. *Congressional Record*, 1960, 18818, 18819; newspaper clippings, 1959, 1960, Smith Papers; *Nation*, 8 April 1961, 300.

CHAPTER NINE

1. Walter Sillers to Frank E. Smith, 8 May 1953, Sillers Papers; newspaper clippings, 1955, 1956, Smith Papers.

2. Frank E. Smith to Florence Sillers Ogden, 13 July 1955; newspaper clippings, 1955; F. Eugene Ackerman to Frank E. Smith, 20 October 1956, Smith Papers.

3. W. Gordon McKelvey to Frank E. Smith, 18 January 1956, Smith Papers.

4. Frank E. Smith to Lister Hill, 12 January 1956; Frank E. Smith to Howard D. Samuel, 26 April 1956, Smith Papers.

5. Frank E. Smith to Boswell Stevens, 18 May 1956; Frank E. Smith to David Denton, 31 July 1956, Smith Papers.

6. Frank E. Smith to Banks Young, 17 September 1956; Albert R. Russell to Robert L. Stovall, 28 September 1956; Frank E. Smith to Christine Sadler, 17 October 1956; Sam G. Spal to Arthur G. Klien, 11 October 1956; Frank E. Smith to Sam G. Spal, 31 October 1956; Banks Young to Frank E. Smith, 9 November 1956; memorandum for Mr. Spal, 26 November 1956, Smith Papers.

7. "Statement by Representative Frank E. Smith on H.R. 469, 85th Congress, Textile Fiber Products Identification Act Before the Subcommittee on Commerce and Finance, House Committee on Interstate and Foreign Commerce," 29 April 1957; Frank E. Smith to Robert Hall, 1 July 1957; newspaper clippings, 1957; Frank E. Smith to George M. Rhodes, 31 January 1957; Frank E. Smith to F. Eugene Ackerman, 6 April 1957, Smith Papers.

8. *Congressional Record*, 1957, 13450; newspaper clippings, 1957, Smith Papers.

9. B. F. Smith to Frank E. Smith, 18 February 1958; Calendar No. 1689, 85th Congress 2nd Session, Senate Report No. 1658, 6 June 1958; Frank E. Smith to George A. Smathers, 10 March 1958, Smith Papers.

10. Frank E. Smith to James A. Eggar, 3 June 1958, Smith Papers.

11. Frank E. Smith to Dexter W. Masters, 29 July 1963; Memphis *Commercial Appeal*, 23 August [1958]; John Sparkman to Frank E. Smith, 11 June 1958, Smith Papers.

12. "Statement by Frank E. Smith before the FTC 469 Rule Hearings, March 10, 1959"; newspaper clippings, 1960; Paul A. Twachtman to Frank E. Smith, 4 June 1960, Smith Papers; *Good Housekeeping*, July 1962, 129–31; *Consumer Reports*, March 1960, 148–51; Susan Wagner, *The Federal Trade Commission* (New York, 1971), 165–66.

13. Frank E. Smith to Walter Sillers, 9 June 1953, Sillers Papers; newspaper clippings, 1953, Smith Papers.

14. Frank E. Smith to Tom Karsell, 10 August 1953; newspaper clippings, 1955, 1956; Dwight Eisenhower to Frank E. Smith, 9 July 1960; Bryce Harlow to Frank E. Smith, 17 May 1960, Smith Papers.

15. New Orleans *Times-Picayune*, 19 July [1957], various clippings, 1953, 1955, 1956, 1957, 1958, Smith Papers; *Congressional Record*, 1956, 9900–9904.

16. Newspaper clippings, 1955; NATO Parliamentarian Conference files; Audrey Warren to Mama and Papa and Martha Sue, 10 November 1957, 13 November 1957, 17 November 1957, 22 November 1957, Smith Papers.

17. Newspaper clippings, 1954, 1955, 1956, 1957, Smith Papers; *Congressional Record*, 1956, 12935–12937, 12939; *Congressional Record*, 1957, 8643–8644, 8649, 9214; *Congressional Record*, 1960, 5465; William M. Colmer to Frank E. Smith, 9 December 1958; Frank E. Smith to William Colmer, 13 December 1958, Smith Papers.

18. Walker Percy, *Signposts in a Strange Land* (New York: Farrar, Straus, and Giroux, 1991), 48–49; Elliot and D'Orso, *Courage*, 114–15; Albert Gore, *Let the Glory Out: My South and Its Politics* (New York: Viking Press, 1972), 101; Egerton, *Speak Now*, 487; Bartley, *Rise*, 343.

19. Smith, *Congressman*, 105; Frank E. Smith, interview by author, 14 January 1985; David Williams to Frank E. Smith, 14 January 1954; see Stephen J. Whitfield, *A Death in the Delta: The Story of Emmett Till* (New York: Free Press, 1988).

20. Frank E. Smith to Felix Underwood, 18 March 1953, Smith Papers.

21. Frank E. Smith to J. O. Emmerich, 2 March 1953, 16 February 1956, Smith Papers.

22. Hodding Carter to Frank E. Smith, 11 September 1952, Smith Papers.

23. Frank E. Smith to Hodding Carter, 8 May 1953, Smith Papers.

24. Woodley Carr to Frank E. Smith, 5 February 1953, Smith Papers.

25. Frank E. Smith, interview by author, 14 January 1985.

26. Newspaper clippings, 1953, Smith Papers.

27. James W. Silver to Frank E. Smith, 21 January 1953; minutes, Mississippi Historical Society meeting, 4 October, 1952, Smith Papers.

28. Daniel Kelly to Frank E. Smith, 14 March 1953; James W. Silver to Frank E. Smith, 21 January 1953, Smith Papers.

29. Program, Mississippi Historical Society, 1953, Smith Papers.

30. Newspaper clippings, 1954; Woodley Carr to Audrey Matthews, 18 October 1955, Smith Papers.

31. Hodding Carter III, *The South Strikes Back* (New York: Doubleday, 1959), 45; Egerton, *Speak Now,* 609.

32. Francis M. Wilhot, *The Politics of Massive Resistance* (New York: G. Braziller, 1973) 51–55.

33. Jackson *State Times,* 30 September 1955, Smith Papers; see Will Campbell, *Providence* (Atlanta: Longstreet Press, 1992).

34. James W. Silver to Frank E. Smith, 19 January 1954, Smith Papers.

35. Hodding Carter to Frank E. Smith, 23 January 1953, Smith Papers; James W. Silver to Hodding Carter, 27 February 1955, Carter Papers; James W. Silver to Frank E. Smith, 23 March 1960, Smith Papers.

36. Bartley, *Rise,* 85; Frank E. Smith, interview by H. T. Holmes; Frank E. Smith, interview by author, 14 January 1985.

37. Newspaper clippings, 1954; Frank E. Smith to David Williams, 4 December 1953; David Williams to Frank E. Smith, 2 May 1953; Woodley Carr to Frank E. Smith, 15 February 1954, Smith Papers.

38. Philip Mullen to Frank E. Smith, 17 August 1954; newspaper clippings, 1954, Smith Papers.

39. William Winter to Frank E. Smith, 22 May 1954, Smith Papers.

40. J. P. Coleman to Frank E. Smith, 20 September 1954, Smith Papers; Frank E. Smith, interview by author, 14 January 1985.

41. See Whitfield, *Death in the Delta;* Frank E. Smith, conversation with author.

42. Jackson *State Times,* 12 June 1955; various clippings, 1955, Smith Papers.

43. Frank E. Smith to J. P. Coleman, 20 January 1956, Smith Papers.

44. Frank E. Smith to J. P. Coleman, 31 August 1955, Smith Papers; Robert Sherrill, *Gothic Politics in the Deep South* (New York: Grossman Publishers, 1969), 192, 193; James W. Silver to Frank E. Smith, 23 December 1955, Smith Papers.

45. William Winter to Frank E. Smith, 27 January 1956, Smith Papers.

46. Carter, *South Strikes Back,* 58–59; Bartley, *Rise,* 136.

47. Jack Bass and Walter DeVries, *The Transformation of Southern Politics: Social and Political Consequences Since 1945* (New York: Basic Books, 1976), 195.

48. Letter to the editor, *Clarksdale Press Register,* 3 February 1956, Smith Papers.

49. Woodley Carr to Frank E. Smith, 14 April 1956; Frank E. Smith to David Williams, 23 August 1956, Smith papers.

50. Woodley Carr to Frank E. Smith, 12 January 1956, Smith Papers.

51. Ibid., 24 May 1956, Smith Papers.

52. Frank E. Smith to Woodley Carr, 29 May 1956, Smith Papers.

53. Frank E. Smith to Robert Timms, 20 July 1956, Smith Papers; Bartley, *Rise,* 158–59.

54. Interview with Frank E. Smith from *Delta Democrat Times* [August 1956]; Clarence Pierce to Frank E. Smith [1956], Smith Papers; interview with J. P. Coleman, The Mississippi Oral History Program of the University of Southern Mississippi, vol. 203, 1982, 214.

55. Newspaper clippings, 1956, Smith Papers; Frank E. Smith, conversation with author.

56. Ibid.

57. Ibid.

58. Newspaper clipping, Memphis *Commercial Appeal,* 1 October 1957, Smith Papers.

59. Charles Deaton, interview by author, 21 October 1994.

60. Newspaper clippings, 1957, Smith Papers.

61. Charles Deaton, interview by author, 21 October 1994.

62. *Jackson Daily News,* 18 October 1957, Smith Papers.

63. Jackson *State Times,* 18 October 1957, Smith Papers; Neal R. Pierce, *The Deep South States of America* (New York: Norton, 1974), 172.

64. Carter, *South Strikes Back,* 77; Bartley, *Rise,* 181.

65. J. W. Smith to Frank E. Smith, 27 November 1957, Smith Papers.

66. Woodley Carr to Frank E. Smith, 27 November 1957, Smith Papers.

67. *Christian Science Monitor,* 22 October 1955, Smith Papers.

68. Percy, *Signposts,* 40.

69. See general correspondence in John Bell Williams Papers, Mississippi Department of Archives and History.

70. *Congressional Record,* 1956, 7690; Hawthorne Daniel, *Public Libraries for Everyone* (New York: Doubleday, 1961), 44, 45, 180, 181.

71. Audrey Warren to Frank E. Smith (n.d.), Smith Papers.

CHAPTER TEN

1. Woodley Carr to Frank E. Smith, 10 February 1958; Frank E. Smith to Charles Deaton, 20 January 1958, Smith Papers.

2. Frank E. Smith to Charles Deaton, 31 March 1958; Charles Deaton to Frank E. Smith, 27 March 1958, Smith Papers.

3. Personnel folder, Smith Papers; Gray Evans, interview by author, 17 October 1994.

4. Newspaper clippings, 1958, Smith Papers.

5. Ibid., 1957, 1958.

6. Ibid., 1958, 1959.

7. Frank E. Smith to Walter Sillers, 11 September 1958, Sillers Papers; newspaper clippings, 1959, Smith Papers.

8. Woodley Carr to Frank E. Smith, 20 November 1958, Smith Papers.

9. Frank E. Smith to Brooks Hays, 7 November 1958, Smith Papers.

10. Frank E. Smith to Woodley Carr [telegram 1958], Smith Papers; Frank E. Smith, conversation with author.

11. Will Whittington to Frank E. Smith, 28 January 1959, Whittington Papers.

12. Gray Evans to Frank E. Smith, 27 May 1959; Louie Spencer to Frank E. Smith, 14 May 1959, 26 May 1959, 19 June 1959, Smith Papers.

13. Louie Spencer to Frank E. Smith, 14 May 1959; Charles Deaton to Audrey Matthews [1959], Smith Papers; Charles Deaton, interview by author, 17 October 1959.

14. See Howard Smead, *Blood Justice: The Lynching of Mack Charles Parker* (New York: Oxford University Press, 1986); newspaper clippings, 1959, Smith Papers.

15. See Neal McMillen, *The Citizens' Council: Organized Resistance to the Second Reconstruction, 1954–64* (Urbana: University of Illinois Press, 1971); Erle Johnston, *I Rolled with Ross* (Forest, Miss.: Moran 1980); James Silver, *Running Scared* (Jackson: University Press of Mississippi, 1984).

16. Gray Evans to Frank E. Smith, 1 August [1960], Smith Papers.

17. Ibid.; Smith, *Congressman,* 209–11.

18. Elmo Richardson, *Dams, Parks and Politics: Resource Development and Preservation in*

the Truman-Eisenhower Era (Lexington, Ky.: University Press of Kentucky, 1973), 98, 101, 102, 106, 110; Frank E. Smith to Sam Rayburn, 13 November 1956, Smith Papers.

19. O. C. Fisher to Frank E. Smith, 5 August 1957, Smith Papers.

20. Robert E. Wolf to Frank E. Smith, 8 February 1966, Smith Papers.

21. Richardson, *Dams*, 196–99, 201; newspaper clippings, 1955, 1956, 1957, 1960, Smith Papers.

22. Oral History Interview with Robert E. Jones by John A. Stewart, 21 May 1968, 13, Kennedy Papers housed in the Kennedy Library, Boston; Robert Jones, memorandum to John F. Kennedy (n.d.), Kennedy Papers.

23. News release from publicity division of the Democratic National Committee, 20 September [1960]; Frank E. Smith to Robert Johnson, 16 June 1961; Memorandum: Members of the Advisory Committee on Natural Resources, June 1960; Frank E. Smith to John F. Kennedy, 6 October 1960; Porter Hardy, Jr., to Frank E. Smith, 14 October 1960; Advisory Council: Kennedy Natural Resources Advisory Committee (list and staff instructions); Carol Richmond to Frank E. Smith, 14 September [1960]; Charles H. Stoddard to Frank E. Smith, 16 September 1960; Frank E. Smith to Captain Donald Wright, 20 October 1960; Frank E. Smith to Sam Rayburn, 1 November 1960; Frank E. Smith to Archibald Cox, 12 September 1960, Kennedy Papers.

24. "Expenses Paid by Frank E. Smith"; Frank E. Smith to John F. Kennedy, 7 November 1960, Kennedy Papers.

25. Marie S. Ball to Frank E. Smith, 10 January 1961; statement of the Warrior-Tombigbee Development Association, 17 June 1961; John F. Kennedy to Ed Edmondson, 18 October 1960; Frank E. Smith to committee members, 1 November 1960; Jim Wright to Frank E. Smith, 2 January 1961; Jim Trimble to Frank E. Smith, 6 December 1960; David Gardner to David King, 23 January 1961; Frank E. Smith to Jesse Tuttle, 28 December 1960; Newell George to Frank E. Smith, 13 December 1960; Lester Johnson to Frank E. Smith, 14 December 1960; J. W. Penfold to Charles H. Stoddard, 20 December 1960; Clyde Ellis to Frank E. Smith, 6 January 1961; minutes of the January 17 meeting, Kennedy Papers.

26. Frank E. Smith to Girard Davidson, 14 November 1960, Kennedy Papers.

27. Girard Davidson to Frank E. Smith, 13 September 1960, Kennedy Papers; Oral History Interview with Robert E. Jones by John A. Stewart, 21 May 1968, 6–7, Kennedy Papers.

28. Draft for final N.R.A.C. report; Resources for the People–Confidential Draft, Kennedy Papers; *Wall Street Journal*, 18 January 1961, Smith Papers.

29. Frank E. Smith to John F. Kennedy, 9 November 1960; Frank E. Smith to John F. Kennedy, 14 November 1960; newspaper clippings, 1960; Oral History Interview with Stewart Udall by W.W. Moss, 16 February 1970, 34–38; Oral History Interview with Clyde T. Ellis by Ronald J. Grele, 5 April 1965, Kennedy Papers.

30. Smith, *Congressman*, 217; newspaper clippings, 1960, Smith Papers.

31. Jackson *Clarion-Ledger*, 3 January 1961, 4 January 1961, 12 January 1961, 30 January 1961; Tom Wicker, *JFK and LBJ: The Influence of Personality Upon Politics* (New York: Morrow, 1968), 32.

32. Wicker, *JFK and LBJ*, 64, 65, 78; Gray Evans, interview by author, 17 October 1994.

33. Wicker, *JFK and LBJ*, 81.

34. Editorial, Jackson *Clarion-Ledger*, 28 February 1961; interview with Frank E. Smith, Memphis *Commercial Appeal*, 30 January 1961; J. D. Lundy to Frank E. Smith, 3 July 1961, Smith Papers.

35. Gray Evans, interview by author, 17 October 1994; Audrey Matthews to Frank E. Smith (n.d.), Smith Papers.

36. Frank E. Smith to Norman Lederer, 7 November 1969; newspaper clippings, 1957, 1960, Smith Papers; *Newsweek*, 24 April 1961, 40.

37. Newspaper clippings, 1960, 1961, Smith Papers; Frank E. Smith, interview by author, 18 January 1983; Frank E. Smith to Hugh Middleton, 10 August 1961, Smith Papers.

38. Frank E. Smith to Walter Sillers, 4 January 1961, Sillers Papers.

39. Jackson *Clarion-Ledger*, 2 January 1961.

40. Frank E. Smith to Walter Sillers, 29 March 1961, Sillers Papers.

41. Frank E. Smith, interview by author, 18 January 1983.

42. Newspaper clippings, 1960, 1961, Smith Papers.

43. Henry H. Wilson, Jr., to Lawrence O'Brien, 7 March 1961, White House Staff File, Kennedy Papers.

44. Richard K. Donahue to Larry O'Brien, 3 June 1961; Larry O'Brien to Henry Wilson, 22 April 1961; Henry Wilson to Lawrence O'Brien, 4 December 1961; Henry H. Wilson, Jr., to Claude Desaultels, 15 March 1962; Larry O'Brien to Henry Wilson, 22 September 1961, White House Staff File, Kennedy Papers.

45. Frank E. Smith to Will Whittington, 8 November 1961, Whittington Papers.

46. Frank E. Smith, interview by author, 14 January 1985, 18 January 1983.

47. Frank E. Smith to Walter Sillers, 17 January 1962, Sillers Papers.

48. Will Whittington to Frank E. Smith, 9 January 1961, Whittington Papers.

49. William H. Morgan to Walter Sillers, 19 February 1962; Walter Sillers to William H. Morgan, 20 February 1962, Sillers Papers; newspaper clippings, 1961, 1962, Smith Papers; Henry H. Wilson to Lawrence O'Brien, 7 March 1961, Kennedy Papers.

50. Jackson *Clarion-Ledger*, 5 March 1962, 20 March 1962, 21 March 1962, 22 March 1962.

51. Memphis *Commercial Appeal*, 22 March 1962.

52. Jackson *Clarion-Ledger*, 29 March 1962.

53. Ibid.

54. Newspaper clippings, 1962, Smith Papers.

55. Ibid.

56. *Birmingham News*, 22 April 1962, Smith Papers.

57. Frank E. Smith to Pat Holcomb, 22 February 1962, Smith Papers; Pierce, *Deep South States*, 201.

58. Campaign Workers Telephone Instructions, Smith Papers.

59. Henry H. Wilson to Lawrence O'Brien, 7 March 1961, Kennedy Papers; Memphis *Commercial Appeal*, 28 May 1962, Smith Papers.

60. John F. Kennedy to Frank E. Smith, 21 October 1960; Bruce Tucker to Frank E. Smith, 26 October 1960, Kennedy Papers; Frank E. Smith, interview by author, 18 January 1983; newspaper clippings, 1962, Smith Papers; Carl M. Brauer, *John F. Kennedy and the Second Reconstruction* (New York: Columbia University Press, 1977), 139–40.

61. Frank E. Smith to Henry H. Wilson, 4 May 1961; Henry H. Wilson to Lawrence O'Brien [1961]; Henry H. Wilson to Lawrence O'Brien, 24 May 1961, Kennedy Papers; Frank E. Smith, interview by author, 18 January 1983.

62. Newspaper clippings, 1962, Smith Papers; Smith, *Congressman*, 283.

63. Memphis *Commercial Appeal*, 11 May 1962, Smith Papers.

64. Newspaper clippings, 1962, Smith Papers.

65. Ibid.; Frank E. Smith, conversation with author, 23 August 1994; Frank E. Smith to Julius Duscha, 17 June 1964.

66. *Delta Democrat Times*, 3 June 1962, Smith Papers.

67. Hodding Carter to James W. Silver, 4 April 1962, Carter Papers.

68. Newspaper clippings, 1962, Smith Papers.

69. Memphis *Press-Scimitar,* 27 April 1962.

70. Editorial, *Greenwood Commonwealth,* 7 May 1962; campaign ad, 10 April 1962, Smith Papers.

71. Newspaper clippings, 1962, Smith Papers.

72. *Delta Democrat Times,* 18 May 1962, Smith Papers.

73. Ibid.

74. Memphis *Commercial Appeal,* 26 May 1962, Smith Papers.

75. Newspaper clippings, 1962; source of quotations *Quitman County Democrat,* 31 May 1962, 24 May 1962, Smith Papers.

76. *Clarksdale Press Register,* 30 May 1962, Smith Papers.

77. Memphis *Commercial Appeal,* 26 May 1962, Smith Papers.

78. Newspaper clipping, Whitten campaign ad, Smith Papers.

79. Memphis *Commercial Appeal,* 4 June 1962, Smith Papers.

80. *Sunflower County News,* 31 May 1962, Smith Papers.

81. *Delta Democrat Times,* 1 June 1962, Smith Papers.

82. Newspaper clippings, 1962; quotation from Smith campaign ad, *Winona Times,* 31 May 1962, Smith Papers.

83. Jackson *Clarion-Ledger,* 3 June 1962, Smith Papers.

84. Ibid., 5 June 1962, Smith Papers.

85. Newspaper clippings, 1962, Smith Papers.

86. Official Vote Tabulation, Representative, 2nd Congressional District, Mississippi Primary Election, 5 June 1962, Smith Papers; Frank E. Smith, conversation with author.

87. Newspaper clippings, 1962; quotation from Jackson *Clarion-Ledger,* 6 June 1962, Smith Papers.

88. *New York Times,* 6 June 1962.

89. Frank E. Smith, interview by author, 14 January 1985; Horace L. Merideth to Frank E. Smith, 7 June 1962; Louis Post, Jr., to Frank E. Smith, 27 June 1962; Aubrey Seay to Frank E. Smith, 17 June 1962; G. T. Alexander to Frank E. Smith, 13 July 1962; newspaper clippings, 1962; quotation from *Chattanooga Times,* 7 February 1965, Smith Papers.

90. Percy, *Signposts,* 46.

91. Louis Post, Jr., to Frank E. Smith, 27 June 1962, Smith Papers; Gray Evans, interview by author, 17 October 1994; Willie Ruth Cowan, interview by author, 21 March 1985.

CHAPTER ELEVEN

1. Crawford, "Oral History"; Frank E. Smith, interview by author, 2 August 1983; H. M. Ray to Frank E. Smith, 1 February 1965; Frank E. Smith to H. M. Ray, 9 February 1965, Smith Papers; *New York Times,* 25 June 1962.

2. Frank E. Smith to Sara Blackburn, 16 September 1994; newspaper clippings, 1962, Smith Papers.

3. Dittmer, *Local People,* 91–138.

4. Jackson *Clarion-Ledger,* 4 October 1962; Frank E. Smith to Walter Lord, 15 January 1965, Smith Papers; Brauer, *John F. Kennedy,* 67–68.

5. Dittmer, *Local People,* 104, 141.

6. Jackson *Clarion-Ledger,* 2 October 1962; Bass and DeVries, *Transformation,* 199; Bartley, *Rise,* 118.

7. See Russell H. Barrett, *Integration at Ole Miss* (Chicago: Quadrangle Books, 1965).

8. Gray Evans, interview by author, 17 October 1994; Betty Stone to Frank E. Smith, 4 October 1962, Smith Papers; Robert B. Patterson to Bill Colmer, William Colmer Papers in University of Southern Mississippi Archives.

9. Frank E. Smith to Jerome Mileur, 3 December 1964, Smith Papers.

10. William T. Hicks to Frank E. Smith, 8 October 1962, Smith Papers.

11. R. E. Meek to Frank E. Smith, 4 October 1962, Smith Papers.

12. R. H. Mills to Frank E. Smith, 15 October 1962, Smith Papers.

13. Dorothy M. Crane to Frank E. Smith, 4 October 1962, Smith Papers.

14. Emma Dell Warren to Frank E. Smith, 20 October 1962; newspaper clippings, 1962, Smith Papers.

15. *Congressional Record,* 1962, 22804–22809; Washington *Evening Star,* 9 October 1962, Smith Papers.

16. Audrey Warren to Frank E. Smith, 15 December 1962, Smith Papers.

17. Ibid., (n.d.), Smith Papers.

18. John W. McCormack to Frank E. Smith, 9 October 1962; Hale Boggs to Frank E. Smith, 6 October 1962, Smith Papers.

19. John Stennis and Jim Eastland to John F. Kennedy, 22 June 1962, Smith Papers; TVA News Index, 1962; Schedule of Pending Engagements, TVA files, newspaper clippings, 1962; Frank E. Smith to Dear Friends, Smith Papers; Frank E. Smith to James W. Silver, 10 September 1962.

20. Frank E. Smith to Henry H. Wilson, Jr., 30 September 1961, Smith Papers; Oral History Interview with Michael Monroney by John Stewart, 27 October 1967, Kennedy Papers; Frank E. Smith to Lawrence O'Brien, 27 November 1962; Henry H. Wilson to Lawrence O'Brien, 30 November 1962, Kennedy Papers; Gray Evans to Frank E. Smith, 21 February 1963, Smith Papers.

21. Louis Spencer, Jr., to Frank E. Smith, 30 April 1963, Smith Papers.

22. Frank E. Smith to William Winter, 29 August 1963; William Winter to Frank E. Smith, 3 September 1963; Frank E. Smith to J. P. Coleman, 29 August 1963; Frank E. Smith to Lee C. White, 16 August 1963; Lee C. White to Frank E. Smith, 2 August 1963; Frank E. Smith to Walter Jenkins, 11 March 1964, Smith Papers.

23. Charles Deaton to Frank E. Smith, 11 February 1963; Frank E. Smith to Charles Deaton, 13 February 1963; Frank E. Smith to Mrs. W. V. Tarver, 6 September 1963, Smith Papers.

24. Frank E. Smith to J. P. Coleman, 29 August 1963, Smith Papers.

25. Tupelo *Daily Journal,* 3 January 1963; Frank E. Smith to Jack Reed, 7 February 1963; Frank E. Smith to Philip Stern, 15 February 1963; Frank E. Smith to Hazel Brannon Smith, 20 February 1964; Frank E. Smith to Hazel Brannon Smith, 16 March 1964; Frank E. Smith to Hazel Brannon Smith, 10 February 1965; Frank E. Smith to Travis H. Clark, Jr. [1963]; Frank E. Smith to Burke Marshall, 31 October 1963; Frank E. Smith to Richard A. Bolling, 25 March 1963; Theodore Smith to Frank E. Smith, 2 May 1963; Frank E. Smith to Theodore Smith, 9 April 1965, Smith Papers; Frank E. Smith, interview by author, 14 January 1985.

26. Frank E. Smith to Dwight E. Sargent, 26 November 1963; Frank E. Smith to Leslie W. Dunbar [1963]; newspaper clippings, 1963, Smith Papers.

27. Frank E. Smith to Dutch Silver, 30 August 1963, Smith Papers.

28. Chester Molpus to Frank E. Smith, 22 October 1962, 8 July 1963, 10 July 1963; Frank E. Smith to Brooks Hays, 10 July 1963; Albert W. Heffner, Jr., to Frank E. Smith, 14 August 1964, Smith Papers; Erle Johnston, Jr., to Tom Tubb, 2 December 1963, Paul Johnson, Jr., Papers in University of Southern Mississippi Archives.

29. Robert E. Jones, interview by author, 20 June 1994; newspaper clippings, 1963, Smith Papers.

30. Frank E. Smith to P. L. Coleman, 22 May 1963, Smith Papers.

31. Memphis *Commercial Appeal,* 19 May 1963, Smith Papers.

32. *Washington Star,* 19 May 1963; Frank E. Smith to Billy Skelton, 22 May 1963, Smith Papers.

33. Frank E. Smith to William Peters, 26 November 1963; Frank E. Smith to Rose Kelly, 5 December 1963, Smith Papers; Frank E. Smith to Edward Morgan, 27 November 1963, Cowan Papers.

34. Frank E. Smith to Wade W. Hollowell, 5 December 1963, Smith Papers.

35. Frank E. Smith to Daniel Kelly, 6 December 1963, Smith Papers.

36. William Winter to Frank E. Smith, 10 December 1963, Smith Papers.

37. Cobb, *Southern Place,* 237; see Charles Payne, *I've Got the Light of Freedom: The Organizing Tradition and the Mississippi Freedom Struggle* (Berkeley: University of California Press, 1995); Bartley, *Rise,* 197.

38. Dittmer, *Local People,* 93–95.

39. Frank E. Smith to Robert F. Kennedy, 26 June 1963; Frank E. Smith to James W. Silver, 21 July 1964, Smith Papers.

40. Louie Spencer, Jr., to Frank E. Smith, 10 April 1964; James W. Silver to Frank E. Smith [6 April 1964], Smith Papers. Silver told Smith: "Of course Mississippi will mourn you in the year 2065 as a young man who...exhibited a profile of courage."

41. Frank E. Smith to James L. Robertson, 24 April 1964, Smith Papers.

42. Mrs. Clint Herring to Frank E. Smith, 9 April 1964, Smith Papers.

43. Mrs. Julia Frances Algood to Frank E. Smith, 22 April 1964, Smith Papers.

44. Frank E. Smith to Sadie Spencer, 20 April [1964], Spencer Papers.

45. Sadie Thorn to Sadie Spencer, 24 April 1964, Spencer Papers.

46. Frank E. Smith to Louie Spencer, Jr., 13 April 1964, Smith Papers.

47. Frank E. Smith to W. W. Ellis, 7 April 1964, Smith Papers.

48. *New York Herald Tribune,* 28 June 1964, Smith Papers.

49. Mrs. Hugh Warren, Sr., to Frank E. Smith, 17 August 1964; John Herbers to Frank E. Smith, 14 October 1964, Smith Papers; Dittmer, *Local People,* 242–71.

50. Mrs. A. R. Peebles to Frank E. Smith, 30 September 1964, Smith Papers.

51. Audrey Warren to Frank E. Smith, 10 October 1964, Smith Papers.

52. Ibid., 20 January 1964; drafts of *Congressman from Mississippi,* Smith Papers.

53. Smith, *Congressman,* 331–32.

54. Madeleine F. McHugh, 4 October 1964, Smith Papers.

55. D. M. Russell to Frank E. Smith [22 September 1964], Smith Papers.

56. Memphis *Commercial Appeal,* 19 September 1964, Smith Papers.

57. Frank E. Smith to P. Bourgin, 12 February 1965; Mrs. G. C. Hudson, Sr., to Frank E. Smith [9 September 1964], Smith Papers.

58. Bobby Jean Nutt to Frank E. Smith, 1 June 1965, Smith Papers.

59. Walker Percy to Frank E. Smith, 24 August 1964, Smith Papers.

60. William Winter to Frank E. Smith, 9 September 1964; John S. Poohter to Frank E. Smith, 16 April 1965; Read P. Dunn, Jr., to Frank E. Smith, 10 November 1964; Sue S. McCann to Frank E. Smith, 1 January 1965, Smith Papers.

61. Gray Evans to Frank E. Smith, 6 March 1965, Smith Papers.

62. John O. Bronson, Jr., to Frank E. Smith, 21 February 1965, Spencer Papers.

63. McComb *Enterprise-Journal,* 15 October 1964; John Emmerich to Frank E. Smith, 23 October 1964; *Clarksdale Press Register,* 21 September 1964, Smith Papers.

64. Newspaper clippings, 1964, Smith Papers.

65. Frank E. Smith to James W. Silver, 18 August 1964; Seth Wheatley, Sr., to Frank E. Smith, 23 November 1964; Nolan Fortenberry to Frank E. Smith, 12 October 1964, Smith

Papers. Many refused to read it. Hugh Clegg, criticized by Smith for his part in the Ole Miss crisis, said he had never read the book. Oral History Interview with Hugh H. Clegg, Mississippi Oral History Program of the University of Southern Mississippi (1977), 226.

66. There was an outpouring of letters from "moderates"; they are collected in a scrapbook in the Smith Papers. Frank E. Smith to Sara Blackburn, 8 November 1965, Smith Papers.

CHAPTER TWELVE

1. William Winter to Frank E. Smith, 25 June 1964; J. P. Coleman to Frank E. Smith, 2 March 1964, Smith Papers.

2. William Winter to Frank E. Smith, 9 September 1964, 11 September 1964; Frank E. Smith to William Winter, 30 June 1964; William Winter to Frank E. Smith, 4 August 1964; William Winter to Frank E. Smith, 20 August 1964, Smith Papers.

3. Frank E. Smith to William Winter, 11 September 1964, Smith Papers.

4. Frank E. Smith to Burke Marshall, 7 April 1964, Smith Papers.

5. Frank E. Smith to James L. Robertson, 24 April 1964; Frank E. Smith to Robert L. Netterville, 4 November 1964; Leslie Dunbar to Frank E. Smith, 11 December 1964; Frank E. Smith to Philip Hart, 5 January 1965; *Tupelo Daily Journal* [1964]; Frank E. Smith to Louis Lusky, 6 August 1965; Frank E. Smith to J. P. Coleman, 2 August 1965, Smith Papers; typewritten manuscript by Smith detailing his involvement in the appointment, Smith Papers. These letters are in a box of papers from the period when Smith was special assistant to Governor Winter. The papers were loaned to the author but returned to Smith. Helen Smith retains possession.

6. Regarding the FDP, see Payne, *Light*; Frank E. Smith to Douglas C. Wynn, 12 November 1964, Smith Papers.

7. Frank E. Smith to Milton Viorst, 28 October 1964; Frank E. Smith to Theodore Smith, 16 November 1964, Smith Papers.

8. Frank E. Smith to Milton Viorst, 5 November 1964, Smith Papers.

9. Frank E. Smith to Carl Elliot, 9 June 1964; Brooks Hays to Frank E. Smith, 22 December [1964], Smith Papers.

10. William Winter to Frank E. Smith, 4 August 1964, Smith Papers.

11. Reid S. Derr, "Our Share of Tomorrow," *Journal of Mississippi History* 59 (1997), 323. "He remained a staunch enemy of the civil rights movement throughout his tenure yet he acquiesced...to the legal and social changes wrought by the civil rights acts of 1949 and 1965."

12. Frank E. Smith to Meg Katrishen, 20 November 1964; newspaper clippings, 1964, Smith Papers.

13. Allen Crozier to Frank E. Smith, 14 December 1964, Smith Papers.

14. Frank E. Smith to James W. Silver, 31 March 1964, Smith Papers.

15. Gray Evans to Frank E. Smith, 22 January 1965, Smith Papers; subject file, Mississippi Council on Human Relations, Mississippi Department of Archives and History.

16. Frank E. Smith to Rev. Donald Thompson, 19 January 1965, Smith Papers.

17. Frank E. Smith to Gray Evans, 25 January 1965, Smith Papers.

18. Gray Evans to Frank E. Smith, 6 March 1965, Smith Papers.

19. *Lexington Advertiser,* 4 February 1965; Duncan M. Gray to Frank E. Smith, 3 January 1965; Frank E. Smith to Duncan M. Gray, 5 January 1965, Smith Papers.

20. Frank Ellis to Sadie Spencer, 6 February [1965], Spencer Papers.

21. Newspaper clippings, 1965; "Hulley Gulley" to Frank E. Smith [1965], Smith Papers.

22. Frank E. Smith to Claude Ramsay, 23 November 1964; Frank E. Smith to Lelia Wynn, 28 August 1964; Frank E. Smith to Doug Wynn, 28 August 1964; Claude Ramsay to Frank E. Smith, 4 March 1965; Frank E. Smith to Claude Ramsay, 8 March 1965; Claude Ramsay to Frank E. Smith, 5 April 1965; Claude Ramsay to Frank E. Smith, 2 August 1965; Claude Ramsay to Frank E. Smith, 4 March 1968, Smith Papers.

23. William Winter to Frank E. Smith, 22 July 1965; William Winter to Frank E. Smith, 23 September 1965; Frank E. Smith to William Winter, 10 June 1965; George W. Rogers to Frank E. Smith, 9 June 1965, Smith Papers; William Winter, interview by author, 16 September 1994.

24. Frank E. Smith to William Winter, 19 August 1966, Smith Papers.

25. Smith sent materials from Mississippi newspapers documenting the disloyalty of Mississippi congressmen. Blatnik responded that the DSG hoped to "vindicate" Smith's position and to make the party safe from "defection and duplicity." Frank E. Smith to James Rowe [1965]; John A. Blatnik to Frank E. Smith, 18 November 1964; Frank E. Smith to John A. Blatnik, 20 November 1964, Smith Papers; interview with Aaron Henry, Lyndon Baines Johnson Library History Collection, by T. H. Baker, 12 September 1970 (copy in Mississippi Department of Archives and History).

26. Newspaper clippings, 1965; Frank E. Smith to James Rowe, 8 February 1965; secretary's note to file, 9 March 1965; Frank E. Smith to Eugene Patterson, 26 August 1965; Frank E. Smith to W. Don Ellinger, 10 October 1965; Robert Oswald to Frank E. Smith, 30 September 1965, Smith Papers.

27. Bill Silver to Fellow Democrats, 5 December 1965; Frank E. Smith to Bill Silver, 17 January 1966; Jackson *Clarion-Ledger,* 30 April 1966; Bill Silver to Frank E. Smith, 6 May 1966; Frank E. Smith to Bill Silver, 9 May 1966; Frank E. Smith to James W. Silver, 10 September 1966, Smith Papers.

28. Billy Skelton to Frank E. Smith, 3 February, 1965, Smith Papers.

29. William Winter, interview by author, 16 September 1994; interview with J. P. Coleman, Mississippi Oral History Program, University of Southern Mississippi, 239 (commenting on Smith's book, Coleman said, "I think he wrote a lot of things that, for his own good, he could have left off....[O]rdinarily you do not reform people by telling them that they have clay feet"); Frank E. Smith to James C. Baird, Jr., 15 June 1964, Smith Papers.

30. Lawrence O'Brien to Frank E. Smith, 30 November 1965; Frank E. Smith to Robert E. Wolf, 2 March 1966; Frank E. Smith to Jack Brooks, 25 June 1965; Frank E. Smith to Ney Gore, Jr., 17 June 1965, Smith Papers.

31. Frank E. Smith to Y. T. Eggleton, 24 February 1966, Smith Papers.

32. Frank E. Smith to John A. Blatnik, 27 October 1964; John A. Blatnik to Frank E. Smith, 1 December 1964; Frank E. Smith to Dick Sanders; newspaper clippings, 1967; Frank E. Smith to Robert E. Baker, 15 November 1963, Smith Papers. Smith believed the Kennedy administration's big mistake was in not stripping the seniority from the disloyal congressmen in 1961.

33. Newspaper clippings, 1968; *Delta Democrat Times,* 16 December 1967; Frank E. Smith to Gray Evans, 21 October 1965, Spencer Papers.

34. Frank E. Smith to Audrey Warren, 15 February [1965], Smith Papers.

35. Hodding Carter to Frank E. Smith, 9 May 1967; Frank E. Smith, interview in New Orleans *Times-Picayune,* 8 November 1968; Frank E. Smith to Jack Reed, 20 January 1967; Jack Reed to Frank E. Smith, 24 January 1967, Smith Papers.

36. Smith tried to award first authorship to Audrey Warren and refused to publish the effusive introduction Carter wrote for the book. Oscar C. Carr, Jr., to Frank E. Smith, 31 January 1967; Frank E. Smith to Garvin Johnston, 6 December 1968; Garvin Johnston to Frank E. Smith, 16 December 1968; Paul Anthony to Kenneth Dean, 20 January 1969;

Betty Carter to Frank E. Smith, 9 January 1970; draft introduction to *Mississippians All;* Frank E. Smith to Lucy R. Core, 22 July 1968, Smith Papers.

37. Frank E. Smith to Phil Mullen, 26 April 1968, Smith Papers.

38. J. Wesley Watkins III to Frank E. Smith, 17 November 1968; Frank E. Smith to Mrs. Tom Ragland, 14 June 1971; Frank E. Smith to William Waller, 24 November 1971, Smith Papers.

39. (Tucson) *Arizona Daily Star,* 20 April 1965, Smith Papers.

40. TVA News Index, 1965; TVA news release, 4 February 1965; *Huntsville Times,* 5 February 1965, Smith Papers.

41. Frank E. Smith to Paula McGuire, 31 January 1969, Smith Papers; Frank E. Smith, *Look Away from Dixie* (Baton Rouge: Louisiana State University Press, 1965); introduction and outline, "100 Acres and a Tractor" (unpublished manuscript); Audrey Warren to Frank E. Smith, 12 February 1965, Smith Papers.

42. Frank E. Smith to James C. Baird, 7 July 1966; Frank E. Smith to Walter H. Bishop, 15 March 1965; Frank E. Smith to Mitchell Sviridoff, 27 May 1974; Frank E. Smith to Robert F. Kennedy, 22 May 1963; Frank E. Smith to Roy Wilkins, 29 August 1963; Memphis *Commercial Appeal,* 5 November 1965, Smith papers; TVA News Index, 1967.

43. Frank E. Smith to James A. Wechsler, 29 November 1966; Frank E. Smith to Dr. Samuel D. Cook, 23 September 1966, Smith Papers.

44. Frank E. Smith, "Liberal Leadership in the Present-Day South" (paper presented at joint session of the Organization of American Historians and the Southern Historical Association, Chicago, Ill., 28 April 1967), 3, 4, 6, 18; David Donald to Frank E. Smith, 4 August 1966, Smith Papers.

45. Conflict between Hays and the one staff person ended with the "staff" leaving to join Robert Kennedy's presidential campaign, reducing the organization's effectiveness. *Atlanta Constitution,* 10 November 1967; Frank E. Smith to Carl Elliot, 24 June 1968; Carl Elliot to Frank E. Smith, 15 July 1968; Brooks Hays, memorandum (confidential) to SCOPE Members [1965]; secretary's note to Frank E. Smith, 4 November; SCOPE minutes of meeting, 17 July 1968; *Washington Post and Times Herald,* 25 August 1968; Brooks Hays, memorandum to SCOPE members, 31 December 1968; SCOPE minutes of meeting, 24 January 1969; Frank E. Smith to James G. O'Hara, 4 October 1968; Frank Thompson to Frank E. Smith, 11 October 1968, Smith Papers.

46. Thomas H. Naylor to Frank E. Smith, 30 December 1968, Smith Papers.

47. Frank E. Smith to Thomas H. Naylor, 3 January 1969, 25 February 1969; Thomas H. Naylor to Frank E. Smith, 3 March 1969, Smith Papers.

48. Frank E. Smith to Virginia Durr, 24 November 1969, Smith Papers.

49. Thomas H. Naylor to Frank E. Smith, 14 April 1969, 26 May 1969, Smith Papers.

50. H. Brandt Ayers and Thomas H. Naylor, *You Can't Eat Magnolias* (New York: McGraw-Hill, 1972), 368.

51. Frank E. Smith to Mrs. Tom Ragland, 4 June 1669; Frank E. Smith to Thomas H. Naylor, 2 February 1970, Smith Papers.

52. Frank E. Smith to Ruth S. Golden, 6 January 1971; Thomas H. Naylor, memorandum to board of directors, 5 April 1971; Thomas H. Naylor to Brandt Ayers, 23 February 1972; *Atlanta Constitution,* 1 May 1971; Frank E. Smith to Terry Sanford, 4 May 1971; Thomas H. Naylor, memorandum to directors, 18 June 1971, Smith Papers.

53. Wilhot, *Politics of Massive Resistance,* 223.

54. Verities to editor, *Chattanooga Times* [1 September 1964]; Ross Bass to Frank E. Smith, 20 November 1964, Smith Papers.

55. Frank E. Smith, "Mississippi in the Seventies" (speech delivered at Millsaps College, 18 February 1971), Smith Papers.

56. Waldron, *Carter,* 313.

57. Frank E. Smith to Finance Commission, Concord United Methodist Church, 10 August 1970, Smith Papers.

58. David E. Lilienthal to Frank E. Smith, 18 January 1965, Spencer Papers.

CHAPTER THIRTEEN

1. New Deal Network, http://newdeal.feri.org; Erwin C. Hargrove, *Prisoners of the Myth: Leadership of the Tennessee Valley Authority, 1933–1990* (Princeton: Princeton University Press, 1994), 162, 163, 193, 194; *Washington Post and Times Herald,* 6 January 1963, from TVA News Index, 10 January 1963.

2. Hargrove, *Prisoners,* 160; Robert E. Jones, interview by author, 20 June 1994.

3. A. R. Jones said Owen opposed his appointment, too, and he never trusted her. He made a point of the fact that he never invited her to his home. Crawford, "Oral History," interview with A. R. Jones, part 2, 24 (hereinafter cited as Crawford Series); Hargrove, *Prisoners,* 160; TVA Employee Series, Oral History Collection, Frank E. Smith, 8; Frank E. Smith to Lt. Col. Fred Stinson, 14 June 1962; Frank Thompson, Jr., to President Kennedy, 7 June 1962; Chet Holifield to President Kennedy, 21 June 1962, Smith Papers.

4. TVA Employee Series, Smith, 11, 12, 13; Aubrey Wagner, 3.

5. William Chandler, *The Myth of TVA* (Cambridge: Harvard University Press, 1984), 7; TVA Employee Series, Smith, 49; Crawford Series, A. R. Jones, 38.

6. Mary Knurr, interview by author, 28 December 1994.

7. Ibid.; Paul Evans, telephone interview by author, 15 February 1995.

8. TVA Employee Series, Smith, 43–45; Erwin C. Hargrove, "The Task of Leadership: The Board Chairman" in *TVA: Fifty Years of Grass-Roots Bureaucracy,* ed. Erwin Edwin and Paul K. Conkin (Urbana: University of Illinois Press, 1983), 99.

9. See David E. Lilienthal, *TVA — Democracy on the March* (New York: Harper and Brothers, 1944); Hargrove, "Task," 98–101.

10. Frank E. Smith to Billy Skeleton, 22 May 1963; *Chattanooga News-Free Press,* 10 February 1964; TVA Employee Series, Smith, 49.

11. B. M. Haskins to Frank E. Smith, 9 October 1962, Smith Papers; TVA Employee Series, Smith, 16, 18; Paul Evans, telephone interview by author, 5 February 1995.

12. TVA Employee Series, Charles McCarthy, 9.

13. TVA Employee Series, Smith, 13; Paul Evans, telephone interview by author, 5 February 1995.

14. Harry M. Caudill, "The Rape of the Appalachians," *The Atlantic* (April 1962), 37–42; TVA Employee Series, Smith, 23–27; Walter L. Creese, *TVA's Public Planning: The Vision, The Reality* (Knoxville: University of Tennessee Press, 1990), 125.

15. "Facts of Life on Strip Mining" (manuscript; secretary's note sent to *Atlantic* 25 September 1963); Edward Weeks to Frank E. Smith, 8 January 1963; Paul Evans, memorandum to Frank E. Smith, 27 March 1963, Smith Papers.

16. "Facts of Life on Strip Mining" (revised manuscript); Edward Weeks to Frank E. Smith, 8 April 1964; Frank E. Smith to Edward Weeks, 13 April 1964. Other magazines were uninterested. Morris H. Rubine to Frank E. Smith, 20 May 1963; Lester Markel to Frank E. Smith, 23 April 1963, Smith Papers.

17. Frank E. Smith to Harry M. Caudill, 15 February 1963, Smith Papers.

18. Frank E. Smith, review of *Night Comes to the Cumberlands,* by Harry Caudill, *Nashville Tennessean,* 7 July 1963, Smith Papers.

19. Frank E. Smith to Audrey Warren (n.d.); draft, "Facts of Life on Strip Mining," 15 March 1963, Smith Papers.

20. Kenneth J. Siegworth, memorandum to Dr. O. M. Derryberry, 8 November 1962; Report of Interdivisional Strip Mining Team, TVA, November 1962, Smith Papers; Paul Evans, telephone interview by author, 5 February 1995; Frank E. Smith to Audrey Warren, 24 November 1965, Smith Papers.

21. Harry M. Caudill to Frank E. Smith, 10 March 1964; Frank E. Smith to Harry M. Caudill, 11 March 1964; Harry M. Caudill to Frank E. Smith, 14 October 1970, Smith Papers.

22. Mary Knurr, interview by author, 28 December 1994.

23. *New York Times,* 18 January 1961; Richard A. Cooley and Geoffrey Wanderforde-Smith, eds., *Congress and the Environment* (Seattle: University of Washington Press, 1970), xiii; Frank Graham, Jr., *Since Silent Spring* (Boston: Houghton-Mifflin, 1970), xiv, 50, 176–81; Frank Graham, Jr., *Man's Dominion* (New York: M. Evans, 1971), xi, 313, 315; Robert C. Paehlke, *Environmentalism and the Future of Progressive Politics* (New Haven, Conn.: Yale University Press, 1989), 28, 29; J. J. McCoy, *Shadows Over the Land* (New York: Seabury Press, 1970), 113.

24. Mary Knurr, interview by author, 28 December 1994; Frank E. Smith to Audrey Warren, 30 January 1963, Smith Papers; TVA Employee Series, Robert Howes, 16–20.

25. Hargrove, *Prisoners,* 160; TVA Employee Series, Smith, 55, 56; newspaper clipping, 1963; Frank E. Smith to Audrey Warren, 24 November 1965, Smith Papers.

26. Frank E. Smith to James C. Baird, Jr., 6 September 1963, Smith Papers.

27. Edmund Orgill to Frank E. Smith, 30 August 1964; Frank E. Smith to Edmund Orgill, 1 September 1964; Frank E. Smith to Lee C. White, 14 November 1963; Frank E. Smith to Ross Bass, 22 January 1963, Smith Papers; Smith, *Congressman,* 137–39.

28. Frank E. Smith to Robert E. Wolf, 23 September 1966, Smith Papers; William Bruce Wheeler and Michael J. McDonald, *TVA and the Tellico Dam 1936–1979* (Knoxville: University of Tennessee Press, 1986), 39, 44.

29. *Nation's Business,* November 1965; Mary Knurr, memorandum for the files, 10 November 1965; *Nashville Tennessean,* 14 November 1965; Frank E. Smith to Paul R. Coppock, 8 November 1965; Frank E. Smith to William O. Douglas, 23 November 1965; Frank E. Smith to Albert Gore, 11 November 1965, Smith Papers.

30. TVA News Index, September 1965; *Knoxville News Sentinel,* 12 May 1966, Smith Papers; Wheeler and McDonald, *Tellico,* 65, 81, 83, 85, 109, 110.

31. Frank E. Smith to Robert E. Wolfe, 23 September 1966; 3 October 1966, Smith Papers.

32. *True,* May 1969; Frank E. Smith to Philip A. Hart, 21 May 1969, Smith Papers (an editor who checked the facts for Douglas's article wrote to tell Smith, "In my two years of checking articles, I have not seen a job of reporting quite as sloppy and irresponsible as his was"); Anfrea Potash to Frank E. Smith, 21 August 1969, Smith Papers; Wheeler and McDonald, *Tellico,* 183, 189.

33. Frank E. Smith, *The Politics of Conservation* (New York: Pantheon Books, 1966), ix, xi; Frank E. Smith to Michael Frome, 6 March 1967, Smith Papers.

34. Smith, *Politics of Conservation,* 58, 296, 297.

35. Ibid., 310.

36. *New York Times,* 26 February 1967.

37. *New York University Law Review* (April 1967), 386–87; *Atlantic Naturalist* (April–June 1967); *Virginia Quarterly Review* (spring 1967), Smith Papers.

38. Frank E. Smith, memorandum to the files, 18 August 1967; Frank E. Smith to Paula McGuire, 9 June 1967; Frank E. Smith to Peter D. McKenna, 15 August 1967; Elmo Richardson to Frank E. Smith, 11 August 1967; Frank E. Smith to Robert E. Wolfe, 2 March 1966, Smith Papers.

39. Frank E. Smith to Daniel P. Moynihan, 3 October 1967, Smith Papers.

40. Frank E. Smith to Paula McGuire, 18 December 1967; manuscripts, "100 Acres and a Tractor," "Bootstraps and Elbow Grease"; Frank E. Smith to Ralph McGill, 30 January 1969; Frank E. Smith to Leslie W. Dunbar, 8 August 1967, Smith Papers.

41. Frank E. Smith to Albert Gore, 4 September 1968; Albert Gore to Frank E. Smith, 14 April 1970; Frank E. Smith to Tristram Coffin, 1 March 1968, Smith Papers.

42. Tristram Coffin to Frank E. Smith, 27 May 1969; Frank E. Smith to Tristram Coffin, 4 June 1969, Smith Papers; Smith, *Politics of Conservation*, xii.

43. Frank E. Smith to Robert S. McNamara, 14 October 1968; Robert S. McNamara to Frank E. Smith, 30 October 1968; Frank E. Smith to Rainer B. Steckham, 12 March 1969; Frank E. Smith, memorandum to A. J. Wagner, 21 March 1969, Smith Papers.

44. Smith, *Politics of Conservation*, 227, 238, 239; Frank E. Smith to Emma Llewellyn, 18 March 1968, Smith Papers; Crawford Series, Louis Van Mol, 39.

45. Frank E. Smith to Howard Baker, Jr., 27 July 1971, Smith Papers.

46. Frank E. Smith to Leslie Dunbar, 11 September 1970, Smith Papers; Mary Knurr, interview by author, 28 December 1994; Hargrove, *Prisoners,* 78, 79.

47. TVA Newsrelease, 13 January 1970, Smith Papers.

48. Frank E. Smith to Leslie Dunbar, 11 September 1970, Smith Papers.

49. Ibid.; Leslie Dunbar to Frank E. Smith, 14 September 1970; Frank E. Smith to Leslie Dunbar, 6 October 1970, Smith Papers.

50. Harry M. Caudill to Leslie Dunbar, 30 September 1970, Smith Papers.

51. Frank E. Smith to Harry M. Caudill, 10 October 1970, Smith Papers.

52. Harry M. Caudill to Frank E. Smith, 14 October 1970; Frank E. Smith to Harry M. Caudill, 16 October 1970, Smith Papers.

53. Jim Branscome to Dear Friends, 27 September 1971, Smith Papers.

54. *New York Times,* 2 April 1972; Walker Percy to Frank E. Smith, 21 December 1971, Smith Papers.

55. Frank E. Smith to Walker Percy, 5 January 1972, Smith Papers.

56. Frank E. Smith, lecture delivered at Coventry Cathedral, Coventry, England, 12 October 1971; TVA Newsrelease, 12 October 1971, Smith Papers.

57. Leslie Dunbar to Frank E. Smith, 14 July 1971; Frank E. Smith to Leslie Dunbar, 4 August 1971, Smith Papers.

58. Frank E. Smith to Leslie Dunbar, 1 July 1971, Smith Papers.

59. Frank E. Smith to Ken Hechler, 3 August 1971; Aubrey J. Wagner to Barry Bingham, Jr., 15 September 1971; Mary Knurr, note to the files, 20 October 1971, Smith Papers.

60. *Louisville Courier-Journal,* 27 November 1971; Cyrus MacKinnon to Frank E. Smith, 24 September 1971; Mary Knurr to Frank E. Smith, 27 September 1971; Mary Knurr, note to files, 20 October 1971, Smith Papers.

61. Frank E. Smith to Reese Cleghorn, 2 September 1971, Smith Papers.

62. *Charlotte Observer,* 20 December 1971; *Knoxville Journal,* 2 February 1972, Smith Papers.

63. Frank E. Smith, "Improving the Southern Environment," *South Atlantic Quarterly* 70 (autumn 1971), 507, 517.

64. Frank E. Smith to Ed Yoder, 7 February 1972, Smith Papers.

65. Frank E. Smith to Paul R. Coppock, 6 March 1972, Smith Papers.

66. *Charlotte Observer,* 24 January 1972; Frank E. Smith to Reese Cleghorn, 27 January 1972, Smith Papers.

67. Frank E. Smith to John Dingle, 28 February 1972, Smith Papers.

68. Frank E. Smith to Harry N. Cook, 2 February 1972, Smith Papers.

69. Harry M. Caudill to Dear Friend, 8 June 1971, Smith Papers.

70. Robert H. Marquis, memorandum to Lynn Seeber, 10 March 1971; Frank E. Smith to Thomas Seessel, 10 March 1971; Frank E. Smith to Gifford B. Pinchot, 10 November 1971; G. M. Woodwell to Frank E. Smith, 15 July 1971; Gifford B. Pinchot to Frank E. Smith, 29 November 1971; Frank E. Smith to Nat Caldwell, 17 September 1971; Mary Knurr, memorandum to Frank E. Smith, 26 October 1971; *Nashville Tennessean,* 21 November 1971, Smith Papers.

71. Peter F. Drucker, "Saving the Crusade," *Harper's,* January, 1972, 71; Frank E. Smith to Peter F. Drucker, 1 February 1972; Peter F. Drucker to Frank E. Smith, 10 February 1972, Smith Papers.

72. Review, *Forest History* (April 1972), 30; Frank E. Smith to Philip O. Foss, 27 July 1970, Smith Papers; Frank E. Smith, ed., *Land and Water,* volume of *Conservation in the United States: A Documentary History* (New York: Chelsea, 1971).

73. Frank E. Smith, *Land Between the Lakes* (Lexington: University Press of Kentucky, 1971).

74. Ibid., 58; Clipping, *Library Journal,* August 1971, 2505, Smith Papers.

75. Frank E. Smith to Willie Morris, 28 July 1970, Smith Papers.

76. Crawford Series, A. R. Jones, part 2, 37 (Jones said, "Smith would be a good director if he had a chance, but Red's [Wagner] running a one-man board, so he can't"); *Knoxville News-Sentinel,* 26 February 1972; Frank E. Smith, memorandum to Lynn Seeber, 10 February 1972, Smith Papers.

77. Frank E. Smith, letter to editor, *Nashville Tennessean,* 5 March 1972, Smith Papers.

78. *New York Times,* 2 April 1972.

79. *Newsweek,* 13 September 1971, 5; Frank E. Smith to editor, *Newsweek,* 17 September 1971, Smith Papers.

80. *Nashville Tennessean,* 23 December 1971; mailing list for clipping; Frank E. Smith to William McKinley Branch, 29 December 1971, Smith Papers.

81. John Stennis to Frank E. Smith, 9 October 1970 (on Yellow Creek, Stennis commented, "I want you to know that I am well aware of the key role you have played in the project since the time of its conception"); Fred Stinson to Frank E. Smith, 16 July 1971; Charles Hogarth to Frank E. Smith, 11 May 1970; Frank E. Smith to Winfield Dunn, 29 January 1971; Frank E. Smith to Fred Stinson, 21 August 1970, Smith Papers.

82. Frank E. Smith to James W. Silver (n.d.); Tom Hammond to Frank E. Smith, 20 November 1971, Smith Papers.

83. Mary Knurr, interview by author, 28 December 1994; Frank E. Smith to Morris K. Udall, 9 March 1972; newspaper clippings, 1972; Frank E. Smith to George McLean, 8 March 1972, Smith Papers.

84. *Chattanooga Times,* 11 March 1972; *Huntsville Times,* 27 March 1972; *Nashville Tennessean,* 9 March 1972, Smith Papers.

85. Richard Bolling to Frank E. Smith, 14 March 1972; Frank E. Smith to John A. Blatnik, 9 March 1972, Smith Papers.

86. Frank E. Smith to John Seigenthaler, 9 March 1972, Smith Papers.

87. TVA Employee Series, Smith Papers, 64, 65.

88. See William C. Havard, Jr., "Images of TVA: The Clash over Values," in Edwin and Conkin, eds., *TVA,* 297–316; Hargrove, *Prisoners,* 160.

89. Wagner said, "Frank E. Smith was a politician....[H]e would always try to figure out the political consequences of an action before he would take it. That was my only fault with him. In retrospect, he looks pretty good though." TVA Employee Series, Aubrey Wagner, part 2, 4.

90. See Linda Hopkins, ed. and comp., *Land Between the Lakes: Handbook* (March 1993), published by TVA.

Chapter Fourteen

1. See Skates, *Mississippi*; Pierce, *Deep South*, 188–89, 198; interview with Hodding Carter III, Southern Oral History Program, no. 4007, A100, Wilson Library, University of North Carolina.

2. TVA News Index, March–May, 1971.

3. David Bowen, telephone interview by author, 18 December 1994; *Tupelo Daily Journal*, 21 March 1972; Frank E. Smith to Joan Bowman, 15 March 1972; Joan Bowman to Frank E. Smith, 20 March 1972; Frank E. Smith to John Seignthaler, 9 March 1972, Smith Papers.

4. Frank E. Smith to Joan Bowman, 15 March 1972; Mary Knurr to Meg Cosby, 6 April 1972, Smith Papers.

5. Dan Kelly to Frank E. Smith [1972]; William J. Holayter to Wylie Chaffin, 13 July 1971; W. R. Lewis to Frank E. Smith, 28 April 1972, Smith Papers; *Tupelo Daily Journal*, 21 March 1972; Paul Neville, interview by author, 3 February 1995.

6. Paul Neville, interview by author, 3 February 1995.

7. Campaign file, 1972, Smith Papers; Paul Neville, interview by author, 3 February 1995.

8. Eric F. Goldman to Frank E. Smith, 15 April 1972; list of contributors, 1972, Smith Papers.

9. Jim Wright to Frank E. Smith, 29 March 1972; Thomas P. O'Neill, Jr., to Frank E. Smith, 4 April 1972, Smith Papers.

10. Sara Blackburn to Frank E. Smith, 16 April 1972; Frank E. Smith to Harry Huge, 22 May 1972, Smith Papers.

11. W. Howard Pritchartt, Jr., to Robert Netterville, 4 April 1972, Smith Papers.

12. Frank E. Smith, interview by author, 27 July 1982; Paul Neville, interview by author, 3 February 1995.

13. Newspaper clippings, 1972 (the best article on the opening of the primary is in the Memphis *Commercial Appeal*, 4 May 1972); Frank E. Smith to James W. Silver, 30 June 1972, Smith Papers; Paul Neville, interview by author, 3 February 1995; David Bowen, telephone interview by author, 18 December 1994.

14. *Delta Democrat Times*, 16 April 1972; *Starkville Daily News*, 5 May 1972; 3 June 1972; *Delta Democrat Times*, 30 May 1972; *Commercial Dispatch*, 5 June 1972.

15. Campaign newspaper, 1972, Smith Papers.

16. Mailing lists in campaign file, 1972; Wylie E. Chaffin to Frank E. Smith, 19 May 1972; TVA Announcement: Political Activities, 10 May 1972, Smith Papers (Red Wagner refused even to wish Smith good luck in private); Paul Evans, telephone interview by author, 5 February 1995.

17. A Lamar Society friend from Alabama reported that Governor Bill Waller spoke "glowingly" of Smith and his election prospects. Joseph R. Sasser to Frank E. Smith, 25 April 1972; William Winter to Frank E. Smith [1972], Smith Papers; *Greenwood Commonwealth*, 6 June 1972, 7 June 1972; *Delta Democrat Times*, 7 June 1972; *Commercial Dispatch*, 7 June 1972.

18. *Greenwood Commonwealth*, 27 May 1972; *Delta Democrat Times*, 7 June 1972; Frank E. Smith, interview by author, 14 January 1985; Frank E. Smith to Wylie E. Chaffin, 11 April 1972, Smith Papers; interview with J. P. Coleman, Mississippi Oral History Program, University of Southern Mississippi, 239; David Bowen, telephone interview by author, 18 December 1994.

19. Frank E. Smith to Bell Wiley, 6 June 1972; Raymond Mabus to Frank E. Smith, 8 June 1972, Smith Papers; Paul Neville, interview by author, 3 February 1995.

20. Frank E. Smith to Billy Tidwell, 7 June 1972; Frank E. Smith to Leslie Dunbar, 7 March 1972; Frank E. Smith to James W. Silver, 11 February 1972; Harrison E. Salisbury to Frank E. Smith, 10 August 1972; George H. Esser, Jr., to Frank E. Smith, 5 October 1972; Hodding Carter III to Frank E. Smith, 8 October 1973; LeRoy Percy to Frank E. Smith, 13 October [1972], Smith Papers.

21. Thomas H. Naylor to Frank E. Smith, 29 January 1973; Meg Cosby to Frank E. Smith, 14 March 1973; William Winter to Frank E. Smith, 16 December 1971, 21 February 1972; J. P. Coleman to Frank E. Smith, 6 August 1973, Smith Papers.

22. Frank E. Smith to J. C. Baird, 6 February 1975, Smith Papers; Bill Minor, interview by author, 28 August 1994.

23. William L. Giles to Frank E. Smith, 21 March 1973; Porter L. Fortune to Frank E. Smith, 7 March 1973, Smith Papers; see Elliot, *Courage.*

24. Frank E. Smith to Paul Evans, 21 March 1974; Steven B. Sample to Larry Korte, 1 February 1974, Smith Papers.

25. Frank E. Smith to Bell Wiley, 29 October 1974; Frank E. Smith to Mr. and Mrs. James W. Silver, 3 April 1974; Frank E. Smith to Jim Silver, 11 July 1974, Smith Papers.

26. Frank E. Smith to A. R. Jones, 12 February 1975; Frank E. Smith to Edward P. Boland, 5 March 1975; newspaper clipping, 7 May 1975, Smith Papers; Carolyn Lorton, Associate Director, Board of Higher Education, State of Illinois, to author, 6 December 1994.

27. Frank E. Smith to Paula Maguire, 10 January 1975, Smith Papers.

28. "Announcing the Sadie Smith Spencer Award," *Advocate,* 5 June 1974.

29. Frank E. Smith to Arthur DeRosier, Jr., 26 February 1975; Arthur DeRosier, Jr., to Frank E. Smith, 21 March 1975, Smith Papers; TVA Employee Series, Smith, 41, 42; Paul Evans, telephone interview by author, 5 February 1995; collection of letters of recommendation to President Carter, Smith Papers; for Carter's attitude toward TVA, see the last chapters of Hargrove, *Prisoners.*

30. Frank E. Smith, *I'll Still Take My Stand* (Vicksburg: Yazoo Press, 1980), 6–8.

31. *Atlanta Constitution,* 14 April 1980. Smith Papers, in possession of Helen Smith. Hereinafter cited as Smith Papers/s.

32. Ibid.

33. Frank E. Smith to William Winter, 20 November 1979, Smith Papers/s.

34. Margaret Walker Alexander to Frank E. Smith, Winter Papers, Mississippi Department of Archives and History.

35. Samuel DuBois Cook to Frank E. Smith, 14 May 1980, Smith Papers/s.

36. Frank E. Smith to George McLean, 6 May 1980, Winter Papers.

37. Frank E. Smith to Phil Mullen, 25 November 1980, Winter Papers (even while out of state in academic work, Smith sent Lieutenant Governor Winter a string of suggestions); Frank E. Smith to William Winter, 15 May 1974, 14 June 1974, Smith Papers; Frank E. Smith to William Winter, 11 February 1981, Smith Papers/s; Frank E. Smith, memoranda to Governor Winter, 2 September 1980, 5 November 1980, Winter Papers.

38. Randy Patterson, interview by author, 7 October 1994; William Winter, interview by author, 16 September 1994.

39. Folders on each topic, Winter Papers; Frank E. Smith to Mr. and Mrs. James C. Baird, Jr., 27 January 1981, Winter Papers; see Elise Winter, *Dinner at the Mansion* (Oxford: Yoknapatawpha Press, 1982).

40. Frank E. Smith to James W. Silver, 15 September 1982, Silver Papers.

41. James W. Silver, interview by author, 9 November 1982.

42. Winter, *Dinner,* 8.

43. Jackson *Clarion-Ledger,* 3 November 1980; Frank E. Smith, memorandum to Governor Winter, 16 September 1981, Smith Papers/s.

44. Frank E. Smith to Charles Barlett, 2 September 1980; Frank E. Smith to Brady Deaton, 2 March 1981; Frank E. Smith to Ben Stone, 19 February 1981; Frank E. Smith to Beverly Smith Olds, 30 September 1982; Frank E. Smith to Neil Pierce, 22 December 1982, Winter Papers.

45. Frank E. Smith to Governor Winter, 17 December 1982, Smith papers/s; Frank E. Smith to Governor Winter, 10 November 1981; 25 January 1982, Winter Papers.

46. Frank E. Smith to Jack Seum, 4 June 1982, Winter Papers.

47. Frank E. Smith to 243rd Field Artillery Battalion, 9 July 1982, Smith Papers/s; Jackson *Clarion-Ledger,* 31 January 1982, Winter Papers.

48. Frank E. Smith to James W. Silver, 8 February 1983, Silver Papers

49. Ibid., 18 February [1986].

50. Bartley, *Rise,* 25.

51. Jackson *Clarion-Ledger,* 5 August 1997.

INDEX

Higgenbotham, Ellwood, lynching of, 36
Highway Trust Fund, 118
Hill, Lister, 69, 105, 207; and textile
labeling, 121
Historical markers commission, 64–65
Hitler, Adolf, 33, 39, 51
Holloman, David, 30, 36
Holmes County, 12, 81
House Un-American Activities Committee,
131
Howes, Robert, 214
"Hulley Gulley," 192
Humphrey, Hubert, 114, 202; at
University of Mississippi, 196–97
Humphreys County, 76
Hutton, Lawrence, 36

I'll Still Take My Stand seminars, 241
I'll Take My Stand, 241
Indianola, Miss.: Citizens' Council of, 131,
197; and racial violence, 99
Institutions of Higher Learning, Board of,
244
Integration, 140–41; and armed forces,
95; and F. Wright, 66; and Methodists,
175; and *Mississippians All,* 196; and
1950 congressional election, 82; of
schools, 165, 233; and Truman, 62;
and TVA, 220; of University of
Mississippi, 169–71, 196
Interior, U.S. Department of, 93, 148,
149, 151
Internationalism, 59, 88
Interracial marriage, 10
Interstate highway system, 117, 118
Isolationism, 50, 59, 88, 97, 111, 124,
199
Italians, in the Delta, 8, 15
Iuka Normal School, 29
Izaac Walton League, 149

Jackson Daily News, 34, 101; on Kennedy
visit, 139; on Stennis, 70; and Sullen,
30; and white supremacy, 130
Jackson, Mitchell, 4
Jackson, Stonewall, 20
Japan, 111, 121
Jefferson Davis School, 16, 18
Jesus, teachings of, 21
Joe, Ray, 23

Johnson, Governor Paul, 87, 133; and
freedom riders, 181
Johnson, James Weldon, 21, 22
Johnson, Lyndon B.: and civil rights act,
194; and Gore, 123; as Mississippi
moderates supporter, 187; and 1960
presidential race, 147; and TVA, 216,
220
Johnson, William, 130
Johnston, Erle, 77, 81; and F. Wright
campaign, 61
Jones, A. R., 208
Jones, Bob, 115, 116, 120, 136, 150, 152,
168, 176, 226; on farewell House
session, 172; and J. Kennedy, 149; and
Tellico Dam, 217; and TVA, 207
Jones, Fred, and prohibition, 65
Jordan, Vernon, 201–02
Judaic-Christian heritage, 191
Junkin, John R., 239

Katzenbach, Attorney General Nicholas,
188
Kefauver, Estes, 69
Ken, 37, 38
Kennedy, John F., 194, 213; assassination
of, 177; and *Brown* decision, 138–39;
and Deaton, 138; as integration sup-
porter, 200; in Jackson, 138–39; and
Mississippi River Commission, 156; in
Muscle Shoals, 176–77, 215; and
natural resources, 147–51, 214; and
1960 presidential race, 147; on
reconstruction, 169; and South
Carolina Commission, 154; and TVA,
168, 207, 208
Kennedy, Robert: and De La Beckwith, 179;
and Eastland, 173; and 1962 congres-
sional race, 166; and TVA, 168; and
University of Mississippi crisis, 169–70
Kennedy-Johnson Natural Resources
Advisory Committee, 147–51
King, Martin Luther, Jr., 199
Knurr, Mary, 209
Korean War, 24, 79, 81, 86, 117
Kosciusko, Miss., 13
Ku Klux Klan, 10, 131, 133, 181

La Salle Tricentennial, 243
Labour Party, 50

Smith, Frank Ellis *(continued):* Silver Jim,
support of, 40, 75; on Southern
Regional Council, 200; and Spencer,
90; state's rights, as campaign theme,
80; and Stennis, support for, 62, 106;
on strip-mining, 221; and Sullen, 36;
teaching career of, 239, 240, 241;
temperamental nature of, 211; on
Tenn-Tom Project Area Committee,
244; Tenn-Tom Waterway, support for,
228; on third-party politics, 35, 36, 50;
Tributary Area Development Program,
support of, 214, 220; Truman, as hero,
85; on TVA, 26, 36, 79, 83, 86, 168,
170, 172, 186–232, 234, 239, 241;
undergoes heart surgery, 243; and
Underwood, 128; United Methodist
Church, as lay speaker for, 200, 204; in
the U.S. House of Representatives,
86–157, 172; Voter Education Project
(VEP), role in, 195; and W. Percy, 167;
on W. Winter gubernatorial staff,
241–42; W. Winter, support of, 133,
235; and Wagner, 210–11, 213, 215,
241; Wallace, opposition to, 201, 202;
water resources, study of, 242; World
War I, 32; World War II, military service
in, 40–54, 81
Smith, Fred, 238, 245; adoption of, 113
Smith, Fred Cecil (brother), 13, 16, 17,
38, 43, 180
Smith, Gordon, 17, 98, 134, 146, 152
Smith, Harry, 12, 17
Smith, Hazel Brannon, and integration,
175
Smith, Helen McPhaul, 43–45, 47–49, 51,
57, 58, 79, 125, 147, 165, 240; father,
death of, 166; and Frank Smith, death
of, 246; and 1972 congressional race,
235
Smith, Howard W., 87
Smith, J. W., 79
Smith, "Judge" Howard W., 88, 152
Smith, Kathy, 238, 245; adoption of, 113
Smith, Lillian, 37
Smith, Ocie, 12
Smith, Reverend R. L. T., 197, 235
Smith, Sadie (mother), 6, 12, 17, 28, 75,
83, 113, 172, 180, 191, 204, 234; death
of, 241; and 1972 campaign, 238

Smith, Sadie (sister), 13, 26, 42, 190
Smith, Sanders, 20
Snelling, Paula, 37
Social security, 219
Soil conservation, 94
South Today, The, 48
Southern Committee on Political Ethics
(SCOPE), 202, 203
Southern Growth Policies Board, 203, 245
Southern Historical Association, 175, 201
Southern Manifesto, 131
Southern Regional Council, 53, 175,
190–91, 196, 221, 239; and Voter
Education Project, 178
Southern Review, 37
Southerner Discovers the South, A (Daniels),
48
Sovereignty Commission, 176, 244;
founding of, 140, 147
Sparkman, John, 97, 105
Speak Now Against the Day (Egerton), 53
Spencer, L. C., 79
Spencer, L. C., Jr., 79
Spencer, Louie, 101, 103, 146, 179; and
civil rights bill, 179; and patronage,
173
St. Lawrence Seaway, 93
Stalin, 49
State's rights, 66, 74, 83, 98, 99, 158; and
Democratic Party, 107; and 1962
congressional race, 166; and prohibi-
tion, 65; and Sillers, 104; and Stennis,
62; and Wright, 67
Steffens, Lincoln, 24, 25, 47
Stennis, John, 32, 68, 79, 109, 156, 187,
208, 233; and judicial appointment,
188; and Kennedy, 137, 138; and 1947
special election, 61; and Nixon, 229;
and poll tax, 66; and proposed abolition of public schools, 131; and racism,
70, 180; and Vietnam War, 193, 220
Stevens, Boswell, 84
Stevenson, Adlai, 105–07, 129, 134,
136–38; and natural resources, 148
Stinson, Fred, 228
Streibich, Harold, 146
Strip-mining, 219, 221–24, 226, 227, 230
Sullen, Fred, 30, 34; and Dixiecrats, 67;
and poker games, 101; and white
supremacy, 130